IT'S NOT
YOUR FAULT!

IT'S NOT
YOUR FAULT!
BECAUSE YOU'RE NOT CHOOSING!

Do you know that
you **are not choosing, most of what you think,**
feel and do each day? . . .
Only read this book if you are interested in finding out
what **is choosing . . .**

ELIZABETH HELEN IVORY

authorHOUSE®

AuthorHouse™
1663 Liberty Drive
Bloomington, IN 47403
www.authorhouse.com
Phone: 1-800-839-8640

Published by AuthorHouse   10/22/2012

ISBN: 978-1-4772-2726-8 (sc)
ISBN: 978-1-4772-2727-5 (e)

Contents

*All creation starts with imagination . . . and yet we say
imagination is not real . . . Richard Wilkins*

FOREWORD

This isn't a book! There are millions of great books, and this isn't one of them.

This is the key to your heart. There is only one goal—to feel good. Feeling good drives all we do. Feelings are free, so what's stopping us. What's amazing about this book is that it will show you what stands between you and the feelings you want.

Elizabeth and I are partners in love, in business, in fact in every sense of the word. Even though a close friend had given Elizabeth one of my books, we didn't meet until years later when I gave a talk in Glasgow, Scotland. Elizabeth says "Richard talked for an hour, and I cried for an hour". Elizabeth is more of an intellectual; I'm more of an 'outer-llectual'; that combination works brilliantly. We had both looked in the field of personal development, and we both found the field empty. All the personal development was well intentioned, always identifying the issue, but never giving either of us the 'HOW'. A quote we wrote sums it up . . .

'Our greatest confusion isn't that we don't know what to do. In actual fact it's knowing precisely what to do . . . but still not doing it.'

Like everyone else, more than anything, Elizabeth and I simply wanted to feel good. Those feelings can only come from us, so what was stopping us from feeling them? Personal Development said 'you choose to be happy and you choose to be sad.' If that's true, then why the hell did we keep choosing the negative, even after doing course after course and reading book after book?

Something was missing! "It's Not Your Fault" will not only show you how and why you're not choosing, it will show you what is!

The key this book will give you is the same key that's allowed Elizabeth and I to unlock the feelings that we all long for (and deserve). It has also given many, many other people the same key, people who had been searching for as long as we had.

So it is then that I say with an unlocked heart:, "I love Elizabeth Ivory, I love this book". Without its key I, like so many, would not have found, the 'How' and my heart would have remained locked with all the feelings I longed for trapped inside, complete but inaccessible. As I said, this is so much more than a book.

I congratulate you on your find.

Richard Wilkins . . . UK Minister of Inspiration & Co-founder of BC

There are two worlds, what people do and what people would choose to do . . . Elizabeth Ivory

ACKNOWLEDGMENTS . . .

Firstly I would like to say a huge *Thank You* to all my lovely Family and Friends (you know who you are) for continuing to love me and believe in me, particularly when I didn't love or believe in myself, and also for encouraging me to write this book.

Especially my partner Richard Wilkins without whom this book would not have been possible. The last four years have been the best years of my life, for at last you have helped me to discover and feel good about "who I really am". There are no words that could ever express my gratitude to you for this gift.

I would also like to thank my beautiful daughter Siobhan. You have been my driving force throughout all these years of searching to find a way to live at peace with myself. It's thanks to your unconditional love for me and my unconditional love for you that I have learnt how to truly love myself.

Also I would like to say a special thank you to Charlotte Robinson for daring to go beyond the Script and create the fabulous illustrations that are in this book. I know that this is just the beginning of your exciting, creative journey Charlotte.

And lastly I would like to thank all the amazing people who have done our Broadband Consciousness Course and to all my fantastic clients over the years. You are our absolute certainty that BC not only works and lasts but is unlike many other processes, for it actually gets stronger not weaker with time.

I love you all . . .

Elizabeth

If you were the only you in the world you would be the best at everything . . . the great news is you are the only you in the world . . .
Elizabeth Ivory

Dedication . . .

This book is dedicated to **You!!!**

And to every single person that makes up this wonderful world that we have the joy of being part of.

My wish for you is that through reading this book, you gain the same freedom and contentment that I have from discovering "who you really are"

Until the day that we meet in person, . . . ("I am enjoying that already!")

I am sending you a big virtual hug . . .

Elizabeth

You don't need to be fixed . . . you need to be found . . .
Elizabeth Ivory

CHAPTER ONE

The 3 Main Aims Of This Book

This book isn't like most other books out there. Often they give you a list of things to go and do. Although this can be useful it's not really where the solution lies.

You don't need to be given more information about what to do because you know what you should be doing . . . the confusion, and where this book will help you, is to understand why you don't do what you know you should.

It will explain what it is that's holding you back, how you can get beyond this, take control of your life and be free at last to do the things that you choose.

The three main aims of this book are:

Firstly to introduce you to the concept we call the Script . . .

Secondly to prove to you that you are not the Script . . .

Thirdly to assist you in separating the Real You from the Script . . . and start living the life that you choose. There is a massive difference between choices we are conscious of and choices made consciously.

Once you've separated from the Script it will be impossible for you to retain the same identity as before.

Then your behaviour will naturally and organically follow this new identity.

And this will change everything easily and effortlessly.

Isn't that what you really want?

Why take responsibility for choices, that if you were actually given the choice, you wouldn't choose? . . . Elizabeth Ivory

CHAPTER TWO

Introduction To The Script

Do you know that 99% of people aren't choosing most of the things they feel, think, say and do throughout their whole life.

So if that is true, and having worked in the field of human development for over 20 years, I promise you it is, then the majority of people, which is likely to include you, are not really running their own life. So who or what is?

Let me explain . . .

What you are doing, metaphorically, is reading from a Script.

A Script that was given to you by your parents, peers, teachers and society at large . . . A Script that's been around for hundreds of years and is based mainly on folklore, superstition and control . . .

This means that most of the time, The Script is choosing almost everything you feel, think and do . . . and you don't even know it. It's like you are on automatic pilot but no one has told you.

> Real change is when you see the same old things differently . . .
> Richard Wilkins

Just ask yourself: Doesn't the idea that there is a Script, that is choosing most of the things you do, seem to make more logical sense than the alternative which is that you are choosing to:

Criticise and beat yourself up daily

Never believe that you're enough

Never feel like you are complete

Spend your most valuable commodity which is your time, doing a job you dislike

Eat/drink/smoke yourself to an early grave

Feel bad when you could feel good

Focus on what you don't want instead of what you do want

To always be striving instead of feeling content

Focus on what you don't have instead of being grateful for what you do have

And that you are choosing to think, feel and act in ways that are detrimental to your well being . . . do you still believe that? . . . because we don't.

Through this book we want you to realise that it really "isn't your fault "because the Script is the one who has been making the majority of the decisions in your life. What you've had is the illusion of choice which really means no choice at all.

*Dare to be wrong about who you **Think** you are . . .*
Elizabeth Ivory

CHAPTER THREE

My Story . . . How The Script Nearly Killed Me . . .

Writing this book was never in my plan, neither was running courses or being a Coach. This was mainly because of the extremely poor relationship that I've had with myself. For most of my life I have never ever felt that I was good enough, so there is no way that I would even try to do something like this. I thought "what could I possibly have to say that anyone would be in the slightest bit interested in hearing?" Therefore you can imagine the Civil War that's been raging in my ears between the "real me" and "the script" as I write these words.

Just to explain to you what the Script is, it's the negative voice that's in all of our heads, I call mine Sid because at times he can be quite vicious but I also call him "Sid the Kid" because I now choose to see him just like a little frightened child. Even now as I write this he's shouting at me "who do you think you are to write this" but the truth is who am I not to? You see the information that I am going to share with you in this book not only saved my life but gave me a level of personal contentment that I could never have imagined. For this I am more grateful than I could ever express so I genuinely feel in my heart that I have a responsibility to pass this gift on to others.

It's like I have somehow found a pathway that cuts right through the mine field of life but I can still see people who are trapped on the other side and can't seem to find their own way through. I don't want you to think for one moment that this is the only way through or that people must follow what I have done. I just know, a bit like Rodger Bannister, that once people are aware that something is possible because someone has actually done it, it becomes much easier for them to believe that it may also be possible for them to do it. That's my main intention in writing this book.

Broadband Consciousness, which is the 5 day Program that my partner Richard Wilkins and I run together, is where the content for this book has come from. It's a combination of both Richard and I and also all the pearls of wisdom that we have gained from all of the people who have done our course—who we now consider to be part of our ever growing extended family.

Even before Richard and I met he was teaching courses and so was I . . . he was and still is an International Author & Speaker. In fact that's how we met—at one of Richard's speaking events.

I was already working as a Life Coach and I was also teaching Fire Walking but if I was being honest, I was still searching. I still felt that there was something missing, there was something I still didn't have. I went to the talk because I was running a Firewalk that evening and needed some inspiration because I felt a bit low. Part of this was due to the voice in my head saying to me: "how come after doing so many courses and even becoming a teacher you still feel bad more of the time than you would ever admit to anyone". So you can imagine the pressure and discomfort this created inside of me because in some ways I felt like a bit of a fraud waiting to be found out. I was teaching these things, that yes had helped me in some ways, but hadn't created the lasting change that I was desperate for. I now realise that I wasn't really sure of the question, let alone the answer! I just knew that I had to be better than the way I was, therefore I was always striving.

When I listened to Richard, who hadn't done any courses but had learned from his personal life experiences, he talked about being "There". He said he was "There" and asked if we were "There" or were we "Nearly There"? This blew me away because it summed up exactly how I felt. That "there" was always just ever so slightly out of reach. That I had to achieve something else and that there was always something to accomplish before I could truly say that I was "There". How about you, are you "There"? If you're not now, when will you be? What has to happen before you can honestly say that you are "There"? Is this what you would choose?

Richard and I spoke briefly at the end of the event and I said that I really thought he could help a lot of people with his message. You see he had been a Multi-Millionaire with all the trappings and yet still he never felt that he was "There". He'd had to lose all of it in the recession before he discovered where "There" was. Through this he discovered that the only reason we ever do anything is to feel good and that those feelings we long for are already inside each and every one of us right now. What he still struggled to understand was, with all these good feelings inside us, what was stopping us from accessing them easily and why did we still choose to feel bad? It took us another 4 years to be able to answer those questions.

After that day we didn't see each other again for about 7 months, but when we did we instantly felt that we were supposed to be together. It was quite weird because right up until I saw Richard again I couldn't really remember what he looked like. Yet the minute he was standing there in front of me it somehow felt right. This was obviously a heart thing, not a head thing.

For the next 4 years we worked together running workshops. It was during this time that we created the concept of The Script. We had developed this one day course called "Beyond Words". It was all about telling your story. We had hundreds of people do this process and yet every time it was exactly the same; the person telling their story would somehow be unable to see how amazing they really were. Everyone else in the room would see them better than they saw themselves. It was this consistent incongruence, that we continuously observed, that lead us to realising that there are two people in all of us the "real us" and the "us that we had been taught to be": this character that we've been moulded into, that somehow we've forgotten is a role, and therefore we defend it and cling to it even though it limits us drastically. It was through this discovery that we created the concept of The Script and at long last we were able to answer the question that had eluded us "why do we choose to feel bad?" The answer is because we don't choose, the Script does. Stick with me. I promise this will all make more sense as we go on.

As I said earlier Richard and I now run a 5 day program together. Part of this course is when everyone tells their life story. Not so much what they have done, but more, how they have felt, what it's been like to be them. This is without a doubt the most powerful process I have ever experienced for all concerned. It is so much more than just an exercise. It's more like an exorcism as it helps people to release themselves from their mistaken identification with the Script. You would be amazed how terrified people are of sharing their story" One guy said "I would rather fight a saber tooth tiger than tell my story", and yet when he did it, he said that the feeling of freedom and relief was greater than he had ever felt. You see it takes a lot of energy to keep our story hidden, you would not believe the things that people have dared to share with Richard and I. Things that they have never told another human being, not even their family or friends. Things they have been terrified of others finding out, because of what they believed they would think of them.

The reason that they share these innermost secrets with us is because Richard and I dare to show our vulnerability and share our story with them first. We lead by example.

I always pre-frame my story by saying that "I still can't believe I am going to voluntarily tell you things about myself that I have spent most of my life being ashamed of and trying to hide and that I've spent thousands, and I do mean thousands, of pounds in Personal Development trying to change". I also often say "I have done more courses than Red Rum. You name it, I have done it." I am qualified in so many different things I honestly can't even remember half of them.

Things like Reiki, NLP, Hypnosis, Life Coaching. As I said I even used to run my own Fire Walking events. However, if I am being totally honest, although I had some absolutely extraordinary experiences none of these actually lasted and neither did they change how I felt inside about myself, my identity. In fact in some ways they just reinforced my already hugely negative self image, by making me think "there must be really something wrong with me". How come I had done all these courses and yet I still felt like there was something missing, still felt there was something not quite right. It's like what my friend Dr David Hamilton wrote about me in his book "Destiny Versus Free Will". He said that "Liz almost became a victim of Personal Development" which was so true.

The reason I called this book "It's Not Your Fault" is because most of my life I've been told and believed that it was my fault, that everything I went through was somehow my fault. Also, Personal Development taught me that I had to take responsibility for things in my life in order for me to change them but although this sounds like a brilliant theory it didn't actually help. Let me explain why. If your best friend did things or things happened to them while they were sleep walking, would you say it was their fault? I doubt it. Well that's what we are all doing the majority of the time" *"Just because our eyes are open doesn't mean we are awake."* So much of our behaviour is totally unconscious. Which means that you and I are not choosing most of what we think, feel and do in our average day. You'll find out by reading this book that what is making these choices is the Script. Also why would you take responsibility for choices that, if you were really given the choice, you wouldn't make? If and when you do take responsibility for these choices, you in turn take responsibility for that identity, and as we always live up to who we know ourselves to be, all this taking responsibility does is just reinforce and solidify even more this identity that doesn't serve us.

Let me share with you how my Script was formed. My very first memory is that I can almost remember being born. Not the birth canal experience, thankfully it was before that.

Through hypnosis I found out that while in the womb at around about eight and a half months old, I felt excitement, anticipation and I just couldn't wait to get here.

I thought it was going to be like an amazing holiday and that we were all going to be one big, happy family where we took care of and really loved one another. Unfortunately, for me, I quickly found that the reality was something completely different.

You see I was born a very sensitive child but I was born in Scotland and the commonality between Scotland and sensitivity starts and ends at the "S". I also lived in Glasgow which is even less known for its sensitivity and then I grew up in what I call the "best parts" of Glasgow which are the housing schemes where any hint of sensitivity is seen as a weakness, therefore it's ridiculed and used against you.

I really felt like I had been abandoned, dropped off in a planet of giant aliens. I wanted to go back home. I didn't feel I belonged here. It felt as though I were in the movie Star Trek, where they go to an alien planet but then they sense that they are in danger, and then Captain Kirk shouts "beam me up Scottie" to get them out of danger. That is exactly how I felt as a child. My older brother Bobby was my hero. He seemed to be the only one that I felt was the same as me but then when he went to school I noticed him beginning to change too. I now know that this was the start of him being handed the Script. There's an analogy that says they don't put frogs into boiling water because they would jump out. What they do is put them in cold water and turn the heat up gradually so they don't notice that they are being cooked. That's the best example that I've found so far to describe how the Script is passed down through generations. I wondered when this would happen to me. "When would I forget who I really was and how life was supposed to be?" I used to be scared to go to sleep at night for fear of this. It did happen and I don't really know when exactly. It was more of a gradual process of me becoming unconscious, but what I do remember is that I felt more aware at 3 years of age than I did at 23. By the age of 23 the Script had come to form my identity "who I knew myself as". Therefore the voice that I listened to the most, and let determine what to feel about myself, was the negative one. It got to the stage that I didn't even try to do the things that I really wanted to do, because my Script paralysed me with the fear of failure.

The thought of failing was more painful than words can truly describe because the meaning that I attached to this was that it proved that I was a failure, a useless pathetic failure who didn't deserve to succeed, someone who didn't deserve to feel good about themselves because the truth was, I was a nobody and

I couldn't do anything right. I soon figured out that if I did as little as possible then at least I could hide this fact and no one would know what I was really like. So began my pattern of hiding and avoiding things.

My father was often drunk and he was a very violent man towards all of us. He was also abusive in every sense of the word. My mum would try to protect us but he was crueler to her than any of us. Nothing that you did was ever good enough for him, he would criticise everything that you said and did. I tried so hard to please him because I loved him and all I really wanted was to be good enough so that he would love me too. I longed for us to be a happy family just like the perfect family I used to watch on the television show "Little House On The Prairie". My dad was also an extreme perfectionist so even when I achieved 97% in my exams instead of him being proud of me he told me I was lazy and that if I was able to get 97% then I should have been able to get 100%. Unfortunately, I believed him. This became part of the Script that was passed on to me, however I amplified it and I became even tougher and more critical of myself than he ever was. For the next 30 years or so I couldn't do anything no matter how good, which would be enough for me to feel proud of myself. I constantly felt like I could do better, so even when I was winning it still felt like I was losing. It was like going to the well of life with a bucket with a hole in the bottom, so I always came back empty. It was the equivalent of sleeping with the enemy. If people could have seen how cruel I was to myself they would have been horrified. It was as if I was constantly punching myself in the face. I was emotionally black and blue but because these bruises were all internal and I was also such a great actress, nobody knew how I felt. I had a permanent smile on my face and was always so kind and helpful to other people. My strategy for life then was to never let people know how I really felt but to pretend to be whatever they wanted me to be. It was as if I were on the program "Stars in Your Eyes" where the contestants turn up and pretend to be someone else who they hope the audience will like.

My dad left my life at age 13 after a very damaging court case during which I had a nervous breakdown. It was then I think that my dislike of myself ramped up to self loathing. I even seriously contemplated taking my own life and it was only because of a couple of great friends that I didn't. They were the only people who remotely knew how I felt.

They helped me to feel a bit better because they made me feel that they really cared about me and liked me for who I was, even if I didn't. I have a lot to thank them for because I really don't know if I would have made it through that period without them. I was in so much emotional pain that I eventually turned to food to help me cope. I used food as a drug to medicate my feelings but because I was so terrified of being fat and ugly I started doing what I now know as bulimia.

At the time I felt so alone because I thought I was the only person who had ever done this and that no one else had felt the way I did. I was very embarrassed and ashamed of my behaviour. I felt weak and so angry at myself because even when I didn't want to do it anymore, I soon realised that I couldn't stop. None of my family were aware of this because I did everything I could to hide it. It was a very secret world which although it continued for years no one ever knew about. The first person to rumble me on this was my dentist as the acid was eroding my teeth. This is something that now seems like such an obvious side effect but which at the time I didn't even consider. Sometime later my younger sister also found out and she made me go to the doctor who sent me to see a specialist but she had never had an eating disorder so I didn't really think that she understood how I felt. So this didn't really help. The strange thing was I always felt I was fat even when I was thin. Years later I became a fitness instructor with 15% body fat which is really low for a female and yet I still felt I was fat! What I now know is "I was fat on the inside" so when I looked in the mirror that was what I would see and felt was my identity. This meant that, even though I would do every diet known to man, I was, in my mind's eye, a fat person who was constantly trying to become thin. This strategy could never work long-term because it was like having an elastic band secured firmly to the fat me that I knew I really was. Although I would lose weight, as soon as my will power waned a little I would ping right back to being the overweight person that I really hated being, but that somehow felt like the real me. It was like a constant battle, a tug of war. No wonder they call it Yo-Yo Dieting. I eventually overcame bulimia by myself but it took me a very long time, it was almost 26 years, until we created the concept of the Script.

After recognising that I wasn't the negative voice in my head, I then knew that it wasn't me who was choosing to binge and make myself sick, it was the Script that was choosing. I also discovered that bulimia wasn't who I was, it was something that I did. I had been told by well meaning professionals that "I was bulimic" and so this became my identity. This meant that even during the periods of my life when I wasn't actually making myself sick, I still felt controlled by it.

It was as if it was always there on my shoulder just waiting to pounce on me and I was constantly fearful of it. It's the same as someone who identifies with being an alcoholic. They are often terrified because they feel it will only take one lapse and they will end up drinking again because that is who they know themselves to be. If you see yourself as an alcoholic then the behaviour you will naturally revert to is drinking.

The great thing with drink is at least you can totally abstain from it. With an eating disorder it's a bit trickier because you have to eat to live, and food plays such a big part in our everyday lives. During this time I tried to get help from various sources but I constantly met people who were either still in the midst of doing bulimia, or they were in recovery which meant they weren't completely cured therefore it could come back anytime. I wanted something better than that. I knew that this was just a crutch that I had needed to allow me to cope. I also remembered that there was a time when I hadn't felt the need to do this. I was determined to become that person again. During all my years of searching I only ever met one lady who said to me that she was "way beyond just recovering" and that she had a healthy attitude towards food. I listened to the tone of her voice and looked into her eyes and I absolutely knew that she was telling me the truth. After that there was no way I would settle for anything less because she had convinced me of what was possible. Once I understood that the voice that was telling me to make myself sick wasn't my voice and I therefore didn't have to believe it and do what it said, the war at last was over. That voice of the Script doesn't have to stop talking, you just have to stop listening to it. Eating disorders are rife at the moment especially amongst females. Statistics state that 95% of all women don't like their bodies and it doesn't seem to make much difference whether they are fat or thin, they are never good enough. There is so much work to be done in this area because the Script we are handing to our children is not one that we would choose, this may well be the topic of my next book.

When I was 19 years old I had my daughter Siobhan and my greatest fear for her was that she would end up like me. At some level I knew that I hadn't always been like this. It was as if feeling bad had been passed on to me like a virus but what I didn't know was how to prevent myself from passing it on to her. I thought that if I really loved her and told her all the time how beautiful and special she was that this would stop it but I know now that children don't really listen to a lot of what adults say.

They tend more to copy what we do and what I taught her to do, by my own behaviour towards myself, was how to be cruel to herself. Ask yourself: "Is there anyone on the planet who treats you as badly as you treat yourself?" I bet there isn't. Would you choose to do this? I bet that, given the choice, you wouldn't.

One day when I was looking in the mirror and hating everything about myself which was a daily habit. I was saying really horrible things internally to myself. I knew not to say them out loud, as I didn't want to upset Siobhan but right out of the blue she said: "Mummy you're not fat." She would have been about 4 years old. I was speechless. I didn't understand how she could know that was how I felt. I tried to make light of it and reassured her that I hadn't said anything but she just looked straight at me and said "I feel it mummy". It was as if my worst nightmare was coming true. Later that night I sat down with a large piece of paper and logically tried to work out how I could prevent Siobhan from being like me. Through a process of elimination I eventually concluded that the only way to do this was to make sure that I wasn't around to infect her. However there was no way that I could have left her and lived without her, and I had tried everything else, so after much deliberation I accepted that the only solution left was for me to take my own life. I now know that The Script actually convinced me that if I really loved my daughter that I should do this for her. It used my love for Siobhan and turned it against me. It told me that she would be better off without me. I thought it all through and reassured myself that she would forget all about me because she was still so young and that her dad would meet someone and then she would have a chance of a normal life with them. This is how powerful the Script can be. It can convince you that the best thing that you can do, if you really love your daughter is to not be around. I know this doesn't make logical sense but we are not logically driven, we are emotionally driven, and I can tell from the suicide rates that I am not the only person who has felt like this. In fact, statistics show that here in the United Kingdom suicide is the number one killer for young males under 35years old and that three times as many men commit suicide as women. There isn't a country in the world where this is any different. No matter what the ratio there are always more men than women who commit suicide. So why do you think that is? Aren't women known for being more emotional than men? Therefore wouldn't you think that it would be more of a women thing? I think the reason there are more men is because in general they suppress their feelings more than women. The Script that's passed on to them is "big boys don't cry", so they don't. Many of them take their lives instead, just like I had planned to take mine.

I had it all figured out. I was already on anti-depressants, so I saved up all the tablets prescribed by the doctor. My sister Gina and I were living together, but I knew she would be away and that Siobhan would be staying with family. To cut a very long story short, the reason that I am here today is because my daughter cried so much for a toy that my family came to my flat and found me unconscious. They took me to hospital where they waited to see if I regained consciousness. I can remember waking up. It was the middle of the night and it was pitch black and I was terrified because one of the other reasons that I probably hadn't tried to take my life before that was the fact that my friend Annemarie, who was a Catholic, had told me that if you committed suicide you went straight to HELL!!! I can remember saying to her "you mean there is a worse place than here?" and she said "Oh yes much worse" and I believed her because I thought that because she was a Catholic she knew everything about God and his rules. So when I woke up in total darkness I was terrified because it seemed like she might be right but then suddenly out of the corner of my eye I noticed this light coming towards me. It was all white and I felt quite a relief. I hoped that maybe, by some fluke, I was in heaven after all. So I turned to it and said "are you an angel" to which the vision replied "no I'm a nurse and you are in the psychiatric unit". I could tell from the look on her face, as she came closer, that she thought "I've got a right fruit cake here".

The next day, before they let you go home, you have to see a shrink. I knew this would be part of the routine as I had seen quite a few of them over the years, none of which had helped as I found them quite scary in their white coats. I was clever enough to know that, if I told them how I really felt, they would probably lock me up, so I never did. I just told them what I thought they wanted to hear. I knew this game well, they may have studied it for a few years but I had lived this game all my life, so it was quite easy to know what to say. I had already prepared my story. I would say it was an accident that I had been working too hard, was drinking alcohol and took more tablets than I had intended by mistake. That should pacify them, or so I thought.

However this guy was different. As soon as I walked into the room he said: "Alright Elizabeth, you can relax and put your feet up because I am going to tell you my story". I remember being quite shocked and thinking, they never do this, they never tell you anything about themselves.

He said: "why should you trust me enough to tell me about you, if I don't trust you enough to tell you about me" and he proceeded, for the next 40 minutes, to tell me what his life had been like. He told me that he had tried to kill himself at one point and lots of other things but the most important thing for me was he made me feel like I wasn't alone and that it was alright to feel the way I did. This really felt like the deepest and most meaningful conversation I had ever had in my entire life. He was the first person that I felt safe enough with to tell how I really felt, it was so liberating. He told me that I was the sanest person he had ever met and that I was normal. It was the others who were emotionally de-sensitised who really had a problem. Ironically this ended up being one of the best days of my life. I couldn't thank him enough. I had planned to keep seeing him, but being the NHS they moved him and sent me an appointment for another doctor, just as if anyone else could take his place. I made a decision that day. I decided that I would spend the rest of my life searching for the answer to how to live a fulfilling and contented life. And also to find my true self and, if and when I did this, I promised that I would help others to do the same. I had always tried to help others but I had to learn that I had to put my own oxygen mask on first because you can only give what you've got. How could I really help anyone else to feel good about being themselves until I could honestly say that I felt good about being me? Only then could I tell them with absolute certainty that it was possible, because I had actually done it.

That was over 20 years ago now. As I said earlier, I had travelled all over and studied with all of the top teachers in Personal Development. Yet, even though I had had wonderful adventures such as 10 day silent retreats, various out of body experiences, had taken part in sweat lodges and even walked over 50 foot long hot coals, it wasn't until just over 4 years ago, when Richard and I created the concept of the Script, that I really "got a life" because with this awareness I was able to change at the identity level which is the highest level of personal change. It was only then that I discovered "who I really am". I did this by discovering "who I am not". I realised that there was nothing wrong with me and there never had been, even though I had been totally convinced that there was for all of those years. I now knew that I didn't need to be fixed, I just needed to be found.

All that was ever wrong with me was I was handed a really crap script and therefore I delivered a crap performance and I felt crap about being me. I now recognise that this is natural.

Anyone reading from the same Script as I was, would feel and act exactly the same way I did. It's just like being an actor, they are only as good as the Script they are given. They don't write the Script but they must read and act like it tells them to. I spent all of those years trying to figure out and fix what was wrong with me, instead of discovering and embracing all that was right with me. I was looking in the wrong department. You can't focus on what's wrong and expect to find what's right. All of us deep down know that the answer is to love more but it's hard to love yourself until you know yourself. Now I know who I really am and I love who I am and although this may sound a bit clichéd it genuinely is the greatest gift of all because nothing can, nothing ever will exceed the relationship that you have with yourself.

In my opinion, if you don't change someone's self image you change nothing. All you really do is just move things around. I go into this in more depth later in the book. I feel that I've come full circle to being the person that I always hoped I was. The Script stole many precious years and many opportunities from me and I hope that by writing this book that maybe, as Richard says "you can learn from my mistakes instead of insisting on making your own". The best part of this for me is that Siobhan has also done BC and I feel so relieved and delighted that I was able to pass this knowledge on to her. I know it's the most important thing I have ever given her because now at the tender age of 25 she knows who she is. This is a priceless treasure and we have the most amazing relationship that any mother and daughter could ever have. I have no regrets regarding my life because it is the good, the bad and the ugly that has made me who I am today. I would never give up what I have now because it is of such immense value that I want everyone to have it. So that's the very short version of my very long life story. Please remember, never underestimate the power of telling someone your story. It may not seem to mean a lot to you but it could mean the world to someone else, but of course you will never know this unless you dare to share . . .

The reason I am happy is because I don't like the alternative . . .
Richard Wilkins

CHAPTER FOUR

Who Is Running Your Life?

My objective here is to let you see what's really running your life . . .

So let me ask you some questions so that you can realise this for yourself.

Aren't most of the following how you feel right now . . .

You feel scared that you are going to be rumbled, found out don't you?

Your greatest confusion, isn't not knowing what to do, it's knowing exactly what to do and yet still not doing it. That is what frustrates you isn't it?

You've probably read many Personal Development books but fundamentally nothing has really changed has it?

You still feel like there is another person inside of you trying to get out, don't you?

You're still chasing the stuff yet you know that's not where it's really at, don't you?

You know that the only thing that you really want is to feel good, but there's still something that keeps stopping you from accessing those feelings isn't there?

You have never had so much and yet you have never felt so unfulfilled. You still feel that there is something missing, don't you?

You really want to cut to the chase, because you know all this intellectually but what you want is the HOW, isn't it?

You'll be pleased to know this book is the HOW that you've been waiting for . . . !!!

The only thing that can ever hurt you is the Script . . .
Elizabeth Ivory

CHAPTER FIVE

Will The Real You Please Stand Up

Let me ask you another few questions: Who are you? How do you know? Where do you go for the answer? If you are anything like most people you will go to the past, to who you have been taught to be . . . that's like looking at the wake of the ship to find out the possibilities of where it may go next. It's like your name, did you choose your name, probably not, it's been given to you, well that's the same for most of the beliefs you hold to be true about yourself. Just like your name you were told these things often enough until one day they became your identity, who you knew yourself to be. Yet how can that be true? You could change your name tomorrow but you would still be you, you could change your job, you can even change your face these days and yet still you would be you". That proves that the real you can't be any of these things. Who you think you are is based on a Character that you have been taught to play by your parents, peers and teachers in order for you to grow up as safely as possible in the environment that you were brought up in. It's like you were handed a Script, a page at a time, over the days and weeks and years. It has solidified into a personality (which comes from the Latin word Persona which means mask) that you mistake as being the real you. The Script has been passed down through all of the generations that have gone before you. So here lies the answer to that much asked question: "Why am I doing so much that I would never choose to do?" It's because the Script is choosing, not you. Now close your eyes and take a big deep breath and enjoy a sigh of relief, because I'm here to tell you probably for the first time in your life . . . it's not your fault. That's right, repeat it to yourself, "it's not my fault" allow that to really sink in. Notice what you feel when you say that? Isn't it something like relief? That's how I felt when I realized it and it's also how the people who have completed our program tell us they feel, so you are not alone.

You see it really isn't your fault. You don't need fixing. There is nothing wrong with you and there never was but you may be reading from a crap Script which you didn't write but which will result in you giving a crap performance all your life. You can have the best actor or actress in the world in a movie but if the Script is weak then they will give a weak performance. You can't get a 10/10 performance in a movie from a 3/10 Script, it's just not possible . . . it's the same in your life.

Most people's default setting for their identity is the Script . . .
Richard Wilkins

CHAPTER SIX

You're Not Choosing!

Let's start by demonstrating one thing here; the fact that you are not choosing . . .

Ask yourself the following questions. No one else will know the answers so please be really honest, not how you would like to be but how you are right now.

1. What do you hold onto the longest, a compliment or a criticism?

2. Do you worry about your future or enjoy it in advance?

3. Are you "there" or are you "nearly there"?

4. Which do you spend more time on, wanting or appreciating?

5. Do you mostly take action or procrastinate?

6. Do you wait for things to happen or do you make things happen?

7. Do you criticise yourself or encourage yourself?

8. Do you love being you or do you wish you were someone better?

Now I'd like you to answer those same questions above but this time you get the freedom to choose. What I mean by that is ask yourself the questions again but this time ask yourself how would you like it to be, not how it is now. i.e. how would it be if you were really able to choose the answer you wanted?

Is there a difference? If you are being totally honest I bet you there's a difference.

So what does that mean then?

It proves that if you are doing any of these things that you don't like and wouldn't choose, it can only mean one thing: *'that you are not choosing'.*

Because if you could choose, you've just proven to yourself that you would choose better.

People won't be themselves because they don't like who they think they are . . . Elizabeth Ivory

CHAPTER SEVEN

Identity Determines Your Future

Your identity is created by your past but it determines your future. You may be unaware but your identity (self image) dictates everything. It determines what you value, what you notice, what you believe and all of your behaviour because how you act is always in alignment with who you believe yourself to be. Let's take a look at how the identity that you have today was created. In order to do this we really need to go back and take a look at your life story.

The following story is an example of how we're taught to read from the Script and it generally covers the various stages that we all go through on the journey of becoming unconscious. Before we know it we are sleep walking through our life, or as we call it, "Script walking" with no more choice than someone who is really asleep. Is it any wonder that the life we lead and the way we feel are both unfulfilling? This explains why we experience the inner nagging that there's something missing, something not quite right because we are not living the life that we would choose. Let's discover how this happens.

True Alchemy is turning your crap into manure . . .
Richard Wilkins

CHAPTER EIGHT

How The Script Was Passed On To You . . .

You were born perfect. There was nothing wrong with you and you didn't need fixing because people loved you just the way you were . . .

In those days crying meant you were healthy not that you needed to see a psychiatrist . . .

In fact as soon as you were born they smacked your bottom to make you cry, to ensure you were alright . . .

You were born a real Super Hero. If you doubt that look at the immense power and effect babies have on other people. It was the same for you, boy, you drew a crowd.

As a baby you were loved unconditionally. There was no expectations. You didn't need to perform. Everyone celebrated just because you were healthy. That was enough then.

Because you were born Scriptless, (without a Script) this meant you didn't have any reference point as to how you had to be, so you were free to just be yourself . . .

But very soon you began to look around and you noticed that you were in the land of the giants. Everyone and everything seemed so big you started to feel like you didn't quite fit in, a bit like being cast in the wrong movie. You thought to yourself: "quick act like them before they notice I'm different".

You soon figured out that in order for you to be safe you had to please the giants, so you started to copy them (your parents) which meant that you now needed a reason to laugh but you didn't need a reason to worry . . . (That was how you started reading from the Script.)

Grandparents Script

Parents Script

Your Script

By now you've been handed several chapters of The Script and you're not even aware that it has happened. (They call this socialization.) This is exactly the same way it's been passed down from generation to generation. From even further back than your great grand-parents who then passed it to your grand-parents, then to your parents and now to you . . .

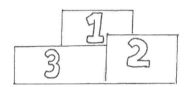

As you got older it was time for you to go to School. Here being how you wanted to be wasn't really allowed. You soon realise that now there are rules. It's here that you were taught the game of comparing and competing. You were tested against all of the other children even your friends. Although there were lots of kids in your class, there was only room for one winner! Shame you weren't that one.

So unfortunately for most of your school life you would have rather been someone else, someone good enough, someone who was the best. You know the one who was the top of the class or the one who was the champion at sport. You weren't the only one. Most of the other children felt this way too and yet you thought it was just you. Even though you didn't do badly it still wasn't good enough . . .

Even the one who was the winner didn't really win, because although people envied them, nobody really liked them because they made the other children feel like they weren't good enough, so in some ways you were all losers . . .

During this period The Script kicked in big time. You were so desperate to fit in with the gang that you learned to hide your unique Super Powers and took off your cape and tossed it in the bin, because human beings are extremely tribal and therefore we have a desperate need to belong . . .

So now you start doing "ordinary". Just like the majority of the kids, you stop being who you really are and you hit normality with a bang . . .

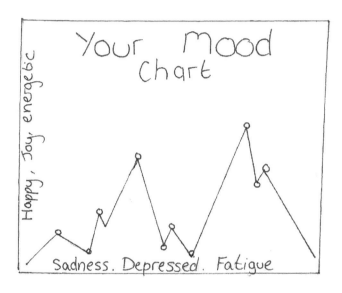

You no longer have the right attitude or altitude, so you can't rise above things like you used to. Now you are up and down, just like the weather . . . sound familiar?

Now you're reading from a Script where your head runs your heart . . .

Your true feelings are now almost forgotten because you are controlled by the negative voice that you hear inside your head. This is the audio version of the Script but until reading this, you believed this was the real you . . .

Now that you are "Script walking" through your life you look like the walking dead . . .

How much choice does someone have when they are sleep walking?

You no longer have a choice you see, when you're sleep walking you don't. But is it any wonder, when you were trapped in your head . . . ?

You try to rebel, to break free but with such a heavy controlling Script you just can't.

You're now holding onto criticisms instead of compliments, even though doing this doesn't make any logical sense. But that's what the Script tells you to do, so you do it . . . The real shame is that you are not alone. Everybody's doing the same thing. Because of this nobody's even questioning its effectiveness . . .

So now you are worrying about your future. Yet, if you could choose, you'd choose to enjoy it in advance . . .

But the civil war rages on between your two ears. You keep doing things you would never choose to do, because you're not choosing. You're hypnotised by the Script's commands which gives you the illusion of choice which equals no choice . . .

You know there's something missing, you feel lost and no matter what you achieve you still can't seem to make the feeling last . . .

How long does it take you to find what you're looking for if you're looking in the wrong filing cabinet?

Then you hit your teens where everything just seemed to get worse . . .

You started smoking and drinking. Initially it was awful but you stuck at it because all your mates were doing it and you didn't want to stand out.

(Note: the opposite to leadership is trying to fit in.)

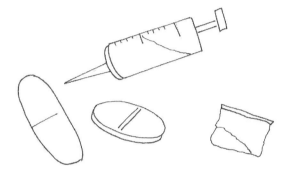

Then just around the corner were the drugs, just for recreation of course. Unfortunately some people paid the price for this, so you were one of the lucky ones . . .

With your low self esteem and never being able to achieve the Script's unachievable goals, you actually felt like life wasn't worth living. You didn't see any point to all this struggle so you even contemplated taking your own life. Again some people went through with it and didn't get the chance to read this book. Maybe together we can prevent this from happening in the future . . .

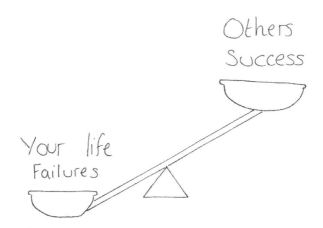

The Script is now constantly getting you to measure your life by your failures or by other people's successes. Either way, you always end up feeling not good enough . . .

Now it's time to get a job. So you read the job description and you turn up for the interview and pretend to be the person that they are looking for. The worst thing possible happens. You are such a great actor they believe that's who you are and they employ you . . . for the next 20, 30, 40 years you suffer from what we now know as the illness called Corporate Schizophrenia . . . because at work you can't be who you really are . . .

Then you meet your future wife/husband/partner. It's all great at the outset.

But she/he has a different Script from yours and before long the Scripts are at war with each other, fighting over who is right. The Script got you both to say things you didn't even mean . . . After years of this, you end up like so many others getting a divorce/splitting up . . . You try other relationships but they all end up much the same.

With all of this comes huge amounts of Stress, so you go to your doctor who tells you, it isn't alright that you feel the way you do. He does some tests and finds you are (fill in the blank) . . . So he medicates you . . . (Fact: today there are way more people on prescribed drugs than on illegal drugs.) You then go and research all the symptoms of the condition you've been diagnosed with and you adopt the behaviour of this new identity which you reinforce every time you tell someone:, "I am blablabla . . ."

You can't bear to sit with yourself. You need to be doing something. You don't run your own business, you run your own busyness. Busyness is your way of avoiding and denying how you really feel. You view feelings as a sign of weakness something you need to hide, so you build a huge wall inside to separate you from them . . .

The Script controls you by maximising all the little stuff, like the weather or the fact that its Monday which makes you feel bad and minimising all the good stuff, like the fact that you're the only YOU there is in the whole world, out of six billion people. How unique is that? But the Script still says you're not enough and unfortunately you believe it, which also makes you feel bad. So guess what, you spend most of your days feeling bad. So now you think there is definitely something wrong with you but you don't dare to tell anyone . . . do you?

Even simple tasks, like making business phone calls to people, the Script creates a horror movie out of. The telephone becomes like a huge monster with rejection written all over it and although you try to take action the Script keeps on holding you back . . .

SCRIPTLESS

Oh we forgot to mention the fact that you now have a couple of teenage children from your marriage/past relationship and guess what you've passed on to them, through your own behaviour. Of course that isn't what you tell them to do, you tell them they are lovely, they can do anything but at the same time you pass the Script to them, just the same way it was passed to you, because unfortunately kids don't do what you say they copy what you do . . .

Your children's inheritance is the Script. For your daughter it's her weight, she's not pretty unless she's skinny; she learnt that from her mum. For your son it's even worse because he's learnt from you that big boys are not allowed to cry. He has to be tough. You're not aware of it but he has started carrying a knife, just to prove how tough he is . . .

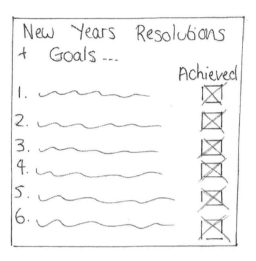

You often get angry because you feel like the real you is trapped inside the history of this character you've been playing all these years and you don't know how to get out. You try to change. You set New Year Resolutions and Goals but within a matter of weeks your best intentions have come to nothing. Now change feels almost impossible so you feel frustrated, hopeless and stuck . . .

Every now and again you do get a quick glimpse of who you really are, but it's usually only in a disaster and any time you do something great, the Script says: "oh that was just a fluke."

Like when you gave that amazing presentation at work. Again you were terrified because the Script told you, you couldn't do it. Yet everybody loved it. However the Script discredited it, by saying that it was all an act, that you weren't being who you really are, you were being a fraud, you may have fooled everyone else but it told you that only it knows what you're really like so again you believe it and quickly go back to what you now think of as the safety of NORMAL, reading from the Script and doing only what it says you can, nothing more and nothing less . . .

This is how you lived the rest of your life, you were always nearly "there" until the day you died. The sad thing isn't that you died. We all have to die at some point. It's the fact that you never really lived. You had what we call an N.L.E. You had a near life experience: you nearly lived . . .

Unfortunately People die but Scripts don't. They live forever because we keep passing them on even as your children are mourning they are being handed pages of the Script from the graveside all about how they should feel, how long they should feel like that and what they should do to deal with those feelings. So The Script reigns supreme . . .

That's roughly, give or take a few experiences, how it has been for most of us up until now and this also sums up more or less how it will be for our children. Are you alright with that? Because I'm not . . .

This could be "The End" or is this really just the beginning? Which one would you choose?

The moral of this whole Story is that "It's Not Your Fault" because you've not been choosing. This may have been how it was up until now. Read on to find out how it can be . . .

Before you can love yourself you first have to know yourself . . .
Elizabeth Ivory

CHAPTER NINE

It's All About Identity

Unless you change your identity in other words who you know yourself to be . . . nothing really changes, your behaviour may alter temporarily through the exertion of effort and will power but very quickly just like a rubber band, that has been over stretched, it soon pings you straight back to where it's attached, which is your self image, who you truly feel that you are.

If the Script is who you think you are that means you will believe and do whatever the Script's negative voice tells you to, without ever really questioning it. Also, when you do this, your behaviour reinforces your identification with the Script. This in turn creates a never ending loop that you can endlessly struggle to get out of. This sums up what's happening in most people's lives. We are like Method actors who stubbornly refuse to come out of character. We feel that we must continue to be true to who we have been, even though we know we didn't choose to play this part and that this role will never allow us to fulfill our dreams and will continue to hold us back from living our true purpose. How crazy does that sound? But it's what we are doing.

You are a real life Super Hero who is just pretending to be an ordinary person . . . Richard Wilkins

How To Change Identity . . .

Trying to change your identity through changing your behaviour, is like being in the sea and trying to push back the tide. What changes the tide is the moon, 240,000 miles away and if you didn't already know this, there wouldn't seem to be any correlation between these two things. It's the same with us, if we want to change who we know ourselves to be, we have to rise above the level that the identity was created on, therefore we have to go to the level of consciousness. Behaviour alone can never permanently change identity. It takes awareness to do that. Now that you are aware of who you are not (The Script) this will allow you the opportunity to separate this old identity from the real you, *"who you really are is who you would choose to be"* the only reason that this doesn't feel familiar is because you haven't practiced being the real you. So initially you need to be prepared for it to feel a bit strange, a bit unfamiliar and somewhat false because you need to become unlike your old self in order to be your true self and this happens through conscious choice. If someone is doing something that doesn't serve them while they are asleep what is the first thing that you must do before you can get them to stop? **You have to wake them up.** That's what this book is, it's a wakeup call. It's only once you are awake that you have the opportunity to truly choose. What is the opposite of unconscious? Of course it's conscious. So let's discover some ways to raise your level of consciousness.

Life is not about waiting for your dreams it's about creating your dreams . . . Richard Wilkins

CHAPTER ELEVEN

Ten Ways To Raise Your Consciousness . . .

1.   Wake Up . . . and consciously choose.

In the past you've been told that you either choose to be happy or you choose to be sad, wrong! Let's test it, ok? If you could choose to be happy or be sad, what would you choose? Well you would naturally always choose happy 100% of the time, who wouldn't? Once again we are back to the fact that you either are awake enough to consciously choose to be happy, or you are sleep walking again and The Script is choosing. Remember just because your eyes are open doesn't mean you are awake, most of what we do in an average day we do unconsciously, seldom are our heads and bodies even in the same place. Often your body will be going about its daily tasks, which the mind finds very boring and mundane, so it shoots off to somewhere in the past, or somewhere in the future. You have the equivalent of Sky TV in your head, your very own inbuilt entertainment system. You are a real life example of what we call a Time Traveler however you are seldom in the here and now. You are either re running some past event, what someone said or did, or what you didn't get right or you are worrying about some future event. You jet from the past to future and back again all in a matter of nano seconds. This is the biggest addiction of our time, the mental circus of our mind, with the Script as the Ring Leader.

Start to notice the difference between whether you are in your head (fantasy/asleep/ not choosing) or in the present moment, (reality/awake/choosing). Keep your mind and body in the same place more of the time. Consciously choose the things you want to feel, think and do. These systems were never intended to constantly run on auto pilot. The quality of your life is determined by the quality of your feelings, thoughts and actions. It's time to take back your own power and Consciously Choose to be the person you want to be. As Richard always says, this is the difference between "being driven and being the driver". If you are driven, somewhere it means you are a passenger, and it's The Script that's driving but if you had the choice wouldn't you rather be the driver?

2. Dare to be wrong about who you THINK you are . . .

The clue is in the word THINK! We think many things are true but it doesn't mean that they are. We used to think that the world was flat but it never was. Even though nearly everyone agreed that it was, didn't mean anything, apart from we all believed the same false thought.

I know that you will have tried many times before to change, with probably little success, even when applying huge amounts of effort and willpower, This is because these are no match for the familiarity and certainty of who you know yourself to be. You have been practicing this character for years and years and are convinced that it is truly who you are. For most people this identity is cast in stone, we even have sayings such as "a leopard can't change its spots" and "once a thief always a thief" which go a long way to reinforce that we can't really be different, not at our core, that people can't really change. You see the problem is that you think you know yourself and that nobody could know you better than you. Because of course you are you, but the truth is, the you, that you actually know, is The Script, the character you've been taught to play, who you have been. Who you don't know and most people never will know is the you, that you can be, the you of the future. There is a great saying "the past doesn't equal the future". Unfortunately for most people, it does. There are no dreams in the past. You are looking in the wrong direction. All your current dreams are in your future. If you always do what you've always done, you always get what you've always got. Well if you keep being who you've been, you'll keep getting what you've got so far.

3. Why is Change so difficult, even when you desperately want it . . . ?

Your greatest resistance to change is The Script. You see the Script values safety and familiarity over change. Change means the unknown, different, unsafe. All change to The Script equals potential danger, which is why the Script prevents you from moving forward. Trying to change without an awareness of The Script is like driving with one foot on the accelerator and the other on the brake. It just makes a lot of noise and you don't really get anywhere, feel familiar? What we've realised is that the Script does have a positive intention which is to keep you safe. If you were to measure it purely by this then you could say thank you to it, because if you are reading this book then I'm assuming you are alive therefore it's done its job. At least now we can make some sense out of why The Script has stopped us from doing so much of what we've tried to do. The Script is a bit like a little 5 year old child who is scared of almost everyone and everything. It imagines danger all around. "What if "or "yeah but" are two of its favourite sayings. They say that today we are a child-orientated society, with most children running family decisions and choices. Well that's exactly what it is like inside most people's head, (when we say most people we mean 99.9% of the planet) there is a 5 year old child who is calling the shots and whenever you try to be or do something different, it has a huge tantrum and creates havoc by draining your energy through fighting with it or paralysing you with fear., Either way you end up giving up, which also reinforces your experience that you just can't change, so you don't.

4. Stop believing the negative voice in your head . . . because it's the audio version of the Script . . .

The Script won't stop talking but you can stop listening and believing it. Just because you hear the voice in your head doesn't mean it's yours. When you are listening to an iPod with your headphones on, you hear the voice of who is singing in your head but you don't think it's your voice, why? Well because you can see the device that it's coming from, and also it probably doesn't sound like you. The negative voice that you hear in your head is the voice of The Script but because you have been listening to it for so long you think it's you. It is on a constant loop and continues to re run all the things that you do not want to hear and would not choose to believe about yourself and others. It is the voice of fear and so all it ever speaks of is the negative.

Take a minute now and close your eyes, just relax and let what ever you are thinking and feeling be ok, for the next few minutes I want you to notice what you are thinking, don't try to change it, or think something in particular, allow it to be how it is and just observe it. Well done, we're going to trust that you did the exercise and didn't just think about doing it. You see life is meant to be experienced not thought about. The difference between thinking of doing this exercise and doing it is humongous. If you did actually do it you'll have noticed that there are two of you in there, there is the thinker (not you) and there is the noticer (the real you). How could you notice what you are thinking if you are your thoughts? It would be impossible. You are the one who is noticing the thinking. Try it again with this new understanding. See if you can feel the separation between you, the noticer, and the thoughts. It's like you are the road and the thoughts are the vehicles that travel along that road but they are not the road itself. It's the same with voices in your head, there is a negative voice and a positive voice, this is the duality of the physical world. Everything has a polar opposite, a contrast that gives it its meaning. Up would mean nothing without down, good would mean nothing without bad, right would mean nothing without wrong. The fact that you are able to observe these voices means that you can be neither of them. You are something more than all of that. You are the observer, the witness to all that is happening, you are the watcher.

The next time you hear or catch yourself doing something you wouldn't choose, just adopt the position of the one who watches and observe everything that is going on.

This separation is the key to you waking up to who you really are and activating your ability to choose, to be the you that you want to be. From now on only believe the voice in your head if it says things that make you feel good about being you and offers you the freedom and encouragement to do whatever your heart desires.

5. Discrediting The Negative Voice In your Head . . . The Script

If you had a neighbour who you found out was lying to you consistently how much would you respect what they said? How long would you continue to listen to them? How much would you trust their information? You wouldn't. Yet the negative voice in your head, which we now know is The Script, has been telling you lies for years and yet you still believe it, why? Because you've thought it was you. If you had kept a record of all the times that The Script has said to you, you can't do something and then you've done it, or it's said they don't like you and then you've found out later that they do, the list would be endless. It's time to wake up to the reality of what's going on. Just for today, take note of all the times the negative voice of The Script kicks in regarding something, and then what ever it says to do or not do, do the opposite and prove to yourself just how untruthful and unreliable that voice is. Just dare to try it. The only thing that you have to lose are the limitations of your past.

6. Consistency . . . it's like breathing—you have to do it every day . . .

How many times would you need to hear a song before you could sing it off by heart? Probably quite a few times. This is where the role of behaviour kicks in Once you have consciously chosen and accepted the you that you want to be, it's the job of your actions to strengthen and consolidate this new identity. However, it has to be in this order, awareness first, behaviour second. The other way round just takes a lot of effort and without many lasting results. You see, effort is only necessary when you come up against resistance. This is where most personal development gets you to push harder, but rather than trying to push through the resistance, wouldn't it make much more sense and be easier just to remove the resistance? The resistance you face when you try to change who you are, is The Script. As we have said before, change to it equates to danger so it fights it. We bet you have first hand experience of this. However once you are aware of this, this awareness allows you to go beyond The Script and consciously take on your new identity. Then all the behaviours that we're unavailable to you, become available. Richard says "it's like having all the greyed out buttons on your computer become instantly live". Then with ease these reinforce the new you, through doing the things that this new identity allows you to do. At the beginning of a New Year, how often do you write the wrong year when you are writing a cheque? Probably a couple of times but soon you get into the familiarity of writing the correct year. This happens pretty quickly because you have only been practicing writing the old year, for a short period of time, a year to be precise but unfortunately with your identity, you have practiced being the old you for years and years, so it does take a bit of time and consistency to get to the point where your new identity becomes as natural and true for you as your old identity was. This is where the term 'practice makes permanent' fits in.

7. The antidote to The Script . . . is not over-caring . . .

When we genuinely care about something it makes us feel good, but whenever we go to the other end of the spectrum and care too much about something that we have little or no control over, it turns into us feeling worried that something bad might happen to it. This term is known as over-care. When you overly care about something or someone it actually leads to you feeling bad. The Script knows this and uses this to get you to over-care. It will say things like "what if you lose your job", or "what if that pain in your chest is something really serious". It will have you jumping through hoops. It's very similar to the Mark Twain quote "I have experienced many terrible things in my life, and some of them have actually happened." The Script uses the imagination to terrify and paralyse you with fear. All fears are reliant on the fact that you don't want them, for example imagine you are on an airplane and it's turbulent. The Script whispers to you, "this plane is going to crash and you're going to die". Now it knows that this is something you most certainly over-care about and do not want, so it has control over you. The quickest and easiest way to get out of the emotional lock that the Script has you in, is to invite the fear in. Either through calling the Scripts bluff by telling it to 'bring it on' and or reminding it of the fact that if you die, then it will also die. This is usually enough to quiet The Script down. Or the other way to respond to whatever it threatens you with, is just to reply with, "So" or "I don't care". No matter what it comes up with your answer is the same, "I really don't care". After a few minutes of this ping-pong game The Script, just like a little child who is getting no reaction, eventually gives up.

8. Feeling Good is the only thing you have to focus on because this is all you really want. Things don't come with their own value. You attach feelings to things, you don't get feelings from things . . .

As a human being we think that we have many different emotions that range from contentment and love to dissatisfaction and fear. However all of these can be condensed into two simple categories, you either feel good, or you don't feel good, that is it. If we get the job we feel good, if we don't get the job we don't feel good. We call it feeling bad. If you pass the exam you feel good, if you fail then you feel bad. If you worry about things you feel bad, if you enjoy things in advance you feel good. This means that throughout your whole life you will only really ever experience one of two things. Moment to moment you will either be feeling good or feeling bad. That's as complicated as I can make it. However where do those feelings come from? Who decides how you should feel about something or someone? Well either you do, by consciously choosing how you want to feel about something, which if you were able to you would choose to feel good 100% of the time, or The Script does and therefore you feel bad. All things are neutral they are neither good nor bad. They have no inherent value. Nothing has any meaning apart from the meaning that we give it. This translates to saying: feelings don't come from things. We attach the feelings; we evaluate the thing or the situation and then decide whether to feel good or bad about them. Most of the time this happens totally unconsciously. Most people are trying to get good feelings from things, whether it's a relationship where we want the other person to make us feel good, or it's a job where we want the job to make us feel good, but it's down to us. Feelings are an inside job. You need to put them into things in order to get them out . . . this leads us beautifully to the next stage . . .

9. Life is a Sausage Machine you only get out what you put in . . .

We spend a whole day on the Sausage Machine on our BC Course. This isn't just an exercise it accurately demonstrates how the law of attraction works. It is a process that allows us to understand why we are getting what we are getting in our lives.

If you put pork into a Sausage Machine do you doubt for one moment that you would get Pork Sausages coming out? Well it's the same with your life—you only EVER get out what you put in.

Here-in lies the problem. Most people are trying to extract things from their job, relationship, etc, that they haven't actually put in. How long would you have to wait for Pork to come out of the Sausage Machine if you haven't put any in? That's right: FOREVER, you could wait as long as fifty years, and some people do, and still no Pork would ever come out. This is the difference between being a Waiter or being a Creator of what you want in your life. A waiter waits, hoping that things will come to him somehow magically, even when he hasn't put any of these things into his life. A Creator knows that in order for him to get things out of his day he has to put them into his day.

So there's only one problem here; why aren't people putting in, what they want to get out? The answer is because most people are not actually choosing the ingredients that they put into their Sausage Machine on an average day? Let's show you what we mean . . . write down just off the top of your head, the top 10 ingredients you think the average person puts into their life on an average day.

Normally the list goes something like this;

Trying,

Wanting,

Busyness,

Effort,

Frustration,

Lack,

Low energy,

Fear,

Procrastination,

Self doubt

Granted there maybe a little bit of fun, if it's the weekend, but not much. Is it any wonder with those ingredients going in, that's what they're getting out and therefore that's how they feel most of the time.

So why don't they just put in the ingredients they want to come out, sounds simple doesn't it?

We are back to that Script again. For most people they are not aware enough which just means awake enough, to choose the ingredients consciously. So guess what chooses for them, that's right The Script.

How do we know that's true? Because if you were to ask someone if they could choose, (and the clue is in the word 'could') would they choose to put in any of those ingredients. Every single person would say, "of course not". So why are they doing it, because The Script doesn't leave room for a choice. We have been mistaking what someone is doing, with what they would choose to do. Just because a person is doing something doesn't mean that's what they would choose to do, if they were given the choice. These are two separate things and our confusion is that we have assumed that they are one and the same but we have just proven this isn't the case. Remember at the start of the book we said "Your greatest confusion isn't that you don't know what to do, it's knowing and yet not doing it that frustrates you"? Well now you know why.

So how do you become the Creator? First just by being aware of the fact there is a Script and that it is running most of the things that you do in your life, allows you to know first and foremost that "it's not your fault". You have been reading from a Script that by its very nature limits your ability to be the best that you can be and secondly you are not The Script, you are something separate from that, something far more than that.

As Deepak Chopra says "you are the whole universe pretending to be a human being" or as we say "You are a real life Super Hero pretending to be an ordinary person".

But isn't it time for you to stop pretending? and for you to acknowledge and harness your inherent power and use it consciously to create the life that you would choose.

What will you put into your Sausage Machine Tomorrow? Write down the 10 ingredients that you would choose and then consciously and deliberately put these in. If you do, guess what you will get out?

So will you wake up and choose, or will you continue to sleep and so allow the Script to keep running the show?

It's up to you now. We are giving you, probably for the first time ever, the chance to really choose, so will you be, a waiter or a Creator? . . . whatever happens, we still know which one you would choose.

10. The Pyramid Of Change . . . when you change the one above it changes all of the levels below . . .

Pyramid Of Change...

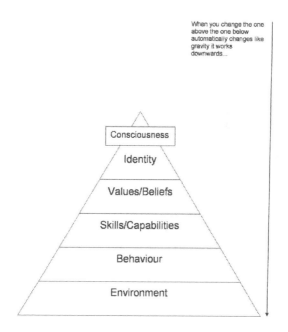

When you change the one above the one below automatically changes like gravity it works downwards...

Consciousness

Identity

Values/Beliefs

Skills/Capabilities

Behaviour

Environment

Based on the Robert Dilts Model...The Logical Levels Of Change...

This model reflects the different logical levels of change. I first came across it when I was studying NLP. It was Robert Dilts who created this, to show how problems have a level at which they are created and reside. It's said that abstraction is power which means that the higher the level at which you make the change, the easier change will be, because it will cascade down like a waterfall and affect all the areas below it. However if you make a change at say the Environmental level which is the lowest level that change can take place, it will do little or nothing to change the areas above it. That is why people can move from country to country and yet their problems seem to follow them. That's because as the Buddha said "where ever you go, there you are". Or in other words you take The Script with you.

When you fully understand this model it makes sense that the higher the level you make the change at, the more holistic the change that you create. When I suggested this at an NLP seminar it was agreed that aiming at least at Identity (the second top level) would make the biggest overall and lasting change. The challenge that we faced was "HOW" do you do that? At that time, none of us were aware of any process that could actually do this.

For example, Say someone has the identity "I am Fat". Even though they diet endlessly and keep fit, they still believe that at their core they are a Fat person. They think that they are a naturally Fat person, who is trying through changing their behaviour to be thin. Inevitably when their willpower wanes as it always does, they go back to what they consider to be 'normal' for them and go back to what they did before. Soon they are as fat as they were before, or even fatter. We even have a term for these people, we call them YoYo Dieters. This just goes to show that behaviours alone do not have the power to change who we know ourselves to be. New behaviours would have to be practiced consistently for a very long period of time before they could eventually change how we see ourselves. Unfortunately The Script prevents this from happening as it stops you very quickly from doing the things that would allow you to change. Thus you soon end up back where you started, with now even more evidence that nothing really works for you; you are what you are and you can't change.

That was before Broadband Consciousness. We know, through the endless examples from the people who have done our course, that this all changes when you wake up to who you really are, and start to really choose the life that you want to live. Just through reading this book you now have the awareness that there is a Script and that you are not The Script. This allows you to change your identity in one fell swoop, because you now have the freedom to embrace the identity that you decide to choose. If everything in the Script is negative and you are not it then that must mean you must be everything The Script is not, which is all that is positive and good. This new identity literally creates a whole and complete new you. So consider for a moment: who do you know yourself to be? What is your identity at present?

Write down ten things you pretend to be, that you want other people to think you are or you think you should be.

For example . . .

I am kind

I am friendly

I am loving

I am special

I am gentle

I am in control

I am better than I am

I am happy

I am wealthy

I am positive

Now write ten things that you honestly feel are true about you, but you really wish you weren't. For example . . .

I am ugly

I am fat

I am weak

I am needy

I am a failure

I am someone who can't change

I am scared

I am angry

I am lazy

I am not good enough

Now write down ten things that you would choose to be true about you, if you could choose anything? For example . . .

I am special

I am someone who can be, do and have everything I want

I am making a difference

I am good enough

I am naturally thin

I am beautiful inside and out

I am creative

I am on purpose

I am successful

I am rich, I have it all

I bet all 3 of your lists are different. So which one is accurate? The one that you say is accurate. It's up to you, now you can choose which one of these lists you accept as the real you.

Each day pick one of these, and practice feeling it. Feel it as if it is already true. Feel, think, and act as if it is what you already are.

If you do this repeatedly, one day these will feel as true to you as your name does. The only difference between the two of these at the moment is practice and a period of time.

Do you think someone who knows themself to be this last list, would have a different life and relationship with themself, others and the world. to those on the first list? Of course they would. This is what creates your experience. These are your filters that you view everything through. If you think the world is an unsafe place then that is what your experience of it will be. You will see/feel danger almost everywhere you look.

You see, those two little words "I AM" are two of the most powerful words in our language, because whatever you attach them to, you become.

So attach them consciously. Instead of having limiting beliefs about yourself, why not have convenient choices about who you are instead. Neither can be proven, both are just assumptions, that at best appear to be true, because that is what we feel, but you can change the feeling. Make a decision now to choose only to believe things about yourself that empower you and make you feel good about being you. Why would you choose to believe anything else? You wouldn't.

Accepting there is a Script puts an end to the civil war in your head . . . Elizabeth Ivory

Your Greatest Frustration . . .

You know that if you do the things that we have suggested, you and your life will be completely transformed. However as we said earlier, your greatest confusion isn't that you don't know WHAT to do, it's knowing what to do and yet still not doing it, that frustrates you. So the reality is: even though I have given you the How to change, you probably won't actually do any of it. Why? At least you now know why—because it goes against The Script, therefore it won't allow you too.

That's why we have come up with just one thing that integrates all of these steps into one powerful, yet simple, process.

You see you are only ever dealing with one thing; The Script. You are either in The Script which means you feel bad, or you are out of The Script which means you feel good. Your greatest gift to deciphering which is which, are your feelings—these are your internal guidance system.

As soon as you notice that you're not feeling good, you don't need to analyse or debate "why am I feeling like this?" you now know without a shadow of doubt that you are just in The Script. This at last puts an end to the ongoing internal civil war. Also the same applies when you notice you are feeling good. You absolutely know that you are out of The Script by feeling what you would choose to feel. The relief of this clarity is beyond words. It frees up all of your energy to focus on what you want.

We have the best question in the world for you to ask yourself throughout your day. This one question embraces all of the things that we have covered in this book because bottom line it raises your level of consciousness. Just by asking the question you wake up to what is actually going on internally.

So here it is, just ask yourself: "If I could choose, would I choose to feel the way I am feeling?"

And just notice what you are feeling. If you are feeling good, like we said, it means that you are choosing.

If you are feeling bad, it just means that you've been asleep again, so The Script is choosing.

Just to notice this, you have to become the observer, which in and of itself, raises your level of consciousness because you have to be at a much higher vantage point in order to witness what is going on. This separates you from the Script and reconnects you with who you really are.

This one question is the most powerful and yet simple process that we have ever experienced, in our years of research within personal development. It's something that you can do anytime, anyplace and anywhere. Most people can deal with one thing, and this is the one thing that drives all of the others. It gives you the awareness and freedom to choose how you want to think, feel and behave in every context of your life. However, please don't take my word for it, try it, use it, build your own proof that this works and then share it with others. Pass it on and maybe one day consciousness will reach a level where human suffering, internal and external, are things of the past. Your Script will say "that will never, ever happen", the real you would say, something like, "everything is possible". Now you're free to choose. Which one will you believe?

CHAPTER THIRTEEN

Warning: Scripts Don't Like Being Rumbled . . .

The Script will say: you've got this now, when all you've really done is ticked the box of your intellect. Throughout the years of Richard and I teaching we have consistently heard people say "I know this stuff" just because they have heard it before. Then you observe them in their everyday actions and you can see that they don't. It's like reading a book on swimming and then saying: "That's it. I understand it, now I can swim" when the truth is you have to get in the pool and dare to leave the side to become a swimmer. Or imagine reading a book on tight rope walking. Would that prepare you for the actual event? Of course not. We all know enough intellectually to be experts in this field but what we are talking about here is becoming a real life example of the person that you would choose to be. As Richard would say "you don't know it until you live it" in other words it's all about your own personal experience. That's what makes the difference. Who would you rather speak to if you are going bankrupt? Someone who has been through it and come out the other end or someone who has read about it in a book? Check out our website for our BC course dates, we call it the "pickling process". You can't just dip an onion in vinegar and expect it to be pickled, you have to totally immerse it there for some time. That's why our course lasts for five days. So why don't you book on and come and personally experience being pickled—because all you've got to lose is your old, limiting self . . .

Nothing can, nothing ever will exceed the relationship you have with yourself . . . Elizabeth Ivory

CHAPTER FOURTEEN

Real Life Super Heroes Stories . . . What BC Has Done For Them . . .

What has Broadband Consciousness done for me? . . . Maggie Robinson

I met Richard and Liz several years ago when they ran a CPD session to the Coaching Circle, an association of coaches who have been through the Barefoot Coaching Training. As a result of seeing them in action I booked on to their one day workshop—'Beyond words'. This was a very powerful and useful day where I was first introduced to The Script.

So . . . when I first heard of Broadband Consciousness (through an email from Richard) I went along to the Recharge Day to find out what it was all about. At the end of that day I decided to go on the 5 day course—thinking it would be useful personal development. I was wrong—the experience was profound. To say working with Richard and Liz has been life-changing is not an exaggeration.

Anyone looking at me and my life would have thought 'she's got it all: Happy marriage, 2 great kids, successful business, financially comfortable, good friends and an active social life.' But I knew there was something missing . . . I just didn't know what it was, and I had been looking for the answer for many years. I remember being around 15 years old and being aware that I was not happy (at times)—other people seemed to be and I thought others were having a better time than me. I was looking for a sense of peace and contentment even then.

I found the answer on the Broadband Consciousness course. It has truly changed my life for the better. Why . . . because you re-discover who you really are—and that you are not your script. I remember several years ago, asking myself "Will the real Maggie Robinson please stand up." I could be the confident, 'can do anything', sociable, full of energy, fun—be a real party animal. But, I could also be; lethargic, quiet, subdued, withdrawn and feel that I was in some way inadequate. What I know now is that when I felt any of the feelings which were negative—it was just my script.

Since attending the Broadband Consciousness course in February 2010 everyone who knows me has noticed a change in me (family, friends and business associates). They have all commented that I seem more relaxed and chilled—happier and more contented. There is no doubt BC has had a positive impact on all areas of my life. I know I am now completely 'comfortable in my own skin' and I : am enjoying my life and business more, have laugh out loud moments more often, have never been busier with clients make decisions easier, have a sense of peace, calm and contentment and I am more tolerant of others.

A beautician I have known for several years said to me "You are looking 10 years younger, you look great, radiant" She went on to say" I don't know what your secret is but I'd like some of it." The difference has come from within—how I feel about being me and being kinder to myself. Not from treatments, or creams that can be applied. She also commented that I seem 'softer'. Again, that's because of Broadband Consciousness—I am much kinder to me and I don't feel that I have to prove myself to anyone, even myself!

I was so completely 'sold' on BC that I wanted my 2 gorgeous girls—Charlotte (22) and Becks (18) to benefit as well. During 2011 they both attended the course and they have both discovered who they really are, what their script is and how it has impacted on them and held them back. It has made a massive difference to their level of contentment and how they feel about who they are. They are no longer letting their script hold them back. They are empowered. They have the knowledge now and have the gift of being able to stop reading from a disempowering script, and also to stop that script getting any longer.

When Liz launched the BC Coaching course I couldn't wait to go on it to find out how to bring BC into my business coaching and therefore work with my clients to enable them to benefit from BC. In January 2011 I attended the BC Coaching course. 'Brilliant'.

Since then, I have taken all existing clients through the BC coaching process and I take all new clients through it. It comes in at the very beginning of my work with clients and then it overlays all other interventions, techniques and approaches I continue to use as a coach. It really is simple, effective and long tasting. The results have been astounding—it has turbo charged the effectiveness of my coaching.

In addition—my husband has now also completed the BC course.

I think it goes without saying that I consider BC to be brilliant—life changing—and I have complete faith and trust in Richard and Liz to take my whole family through this amazing process.

I wholeheartedly recommend Richard and Liz and their courses. You'll start living as you have never done before and you won't regret it.

Maggie Robinson, M Powered Coaching.

Sheridan Coldstream—My BC Story

You often hear people speak of self-discovery, finding yourself, reaching your potential, getting 'there' one day . . . I, like so many, have spent the larger part of my life searching for happiness and craving acceptance . . . Born into an academic and typically English middle class family, I had always felt there were expectations to be met. Being a highly sensitive and creative person, I took criticism to heart and tended to compare my weaknesses with other people's strengths, a sure-fire recipe for feeling rubbish about yourself. My brothers were either getting straight 'A's at A level, scholarships to Oxford University or excelling at sport and classical music. Comparisons convincingly proved to me that I was stupid, fat, uncoordinated, superficial and that for 'people like us' this wasn't good enough. 'Good enough for who?' I now ask myself. These feelings increased through my school years, and quickly took hold, forming what I then believed to be my identity—who I was. At worst, I felt worthless, disliked, no good to anyone and completely inadequate. I got bullied at school, I saw myself as a victim and got treated as such. I considered myself the kind of person that no one would want to have as a friend, so hardly surprisingly found it hard to attract meaningful friendships. I shall never forget the day I ran away from a bully and hid in the boys' loo, only to have gravel and stones chucked through the window at me as I sat there in a weeping heap. If only I knew then what I know now!

These feelings of inadequacy dominated my education, stealing my ability to concentrate and as a result offering further proof that I really was the 'thick' one in an otherwise highly intelligent and educated family. A desire to sing, act and perform was the one lifeline I clung on to, although even here I didn't really believe I had what it took to be a success. Miraculously, I still don't know how or why, I got into the Guildford School of Acting and studied Musical Theatre for 3 years. I was convinced that I was less talented than everyone else. Even the fact that I was regarded as one of the strongest singers, won an award for dance and graduated with the highest qualification possible wasn't enough to boost my appalling self-image. By now I had learned to cover this up with a thin but believable veneer of confidence, after all I wouldn't want anyone to know that I was suffering, so much better to bottle it up, or so I thought . . . After leaving Drama School, I worked as an actor and singer for several years. On paper, my acting career looks reasonable—it is peppered with the odd West End appearance and television role. However, the same feelings of inadequacy still clung to me in a scary unshakeable fashion, which prevented me from really enjoying my years 'treading the boards'.

At my first professional audition I met an actress called Deborah. Five years later we were married. Deborah has always believed in me, seen the good in me and been an immeasurably positive part of my personal journey. The purchase of our first house and the birth of our two children, Henry and Arabella signalled the start of a new phase of life and the end of my career as an actor. Struggling to earn a living and still feeling like one of life's oddities, we dabbled in all sorts of things. I taught English to foreign students, worked in a shoe shop and built a network marketing business.

Here I was introduced to the idea of 'self-improvement' and 'positive thinking'. I started to listen to motivational tapes and devour books by authors like Napoleon Hill, Zig Ziglar and Norman Vincent Peale. Positive self-affirmations, seminars and goals became more important than anything else. Anyone who didn't feel the way we did was clearly missing out because this really was the way to achieve all your dreams, goals and unwavering happiness!! How arrogant and daft it all sounds now. The truth is—sometimes these books, tapes and events would lift my spirits, even make me feel great about myself. At times I really did believe I could conquer the world and be the happy person I'd always dreamed of being. The problem came when these feelings wore off. How could I feel so fantastic one moment and so utterly repulsive the next? The more books I read, the more tapes I listened to and yet . . . I would still feel horrible later. I must be REALLY bad, so bad that even all this positive input doesn't work!!! So that's it then—better settle for being a total loser through and through!! There we are my true identity confirmed: stuck-up, stupid, good-for-nothing idiot trying to kid himself and the world otherwise!

In October 2009 I turned up excited and nervous for my first day of the 5 day Broadband Consciousness course. I was one of 9 and wearing my confident, extrovert disguise that seemed to fit in well enough at most occasions. We were a mixed bunch of people from varying backgrounds. It didn't take long to realise that we were in a very safe and compassionate environment. We were introduced to the idea of 'the script' and how by recognizing it as such, we no longer have to believe that all our past 'baggage' is our identity, that we no longer need to filter all our life-experience though our scripts as a reference point. This alone was what I had been waiting to hear for more than 40 years. You mean—I am ok after all . . . really?? The exciting concept that we are all perfect to start with and that only our rotten scripts damage our perception, was hard to grasp at first. Then one by one we told our stories—I went first. Feed back from Richard Wilkins & Liz Ivory and the group could be summarised as follows:

"It's as though one lovely, confident and thoughtful person is sitting there telling an entirely different person's story. There seems to be little or no relation between the two."

Flattered? Sure, but did I believe them . . . ? Not until a lovely lady called Lindsay told her story. This seemingly confident, attractive and bubbly person spoke of a pain and misery very similar to my own, and here's the bizarre thing—I found myself giving her exactly the same feed back that I'd received myself! The penny was beginning to drop—I wasn't the only one letting my 'script' run my life. From then on there was no looking back. The five day course, though painful at times, was one of the most enjoyable and enlightening times of my life. Gem followed gem—the realisation that it is alright not to be alright. A bad day doesn't make me a bad person. We've all heard for centuries that 'You reap what you sow', but BC calls it the Sausage Machine. My script was stopping me putting the right ingredients in and therefore preventing me from feeling the way I would choose to feel. Here for me was possibly the biggest breakthrough of all.

There was a great spirit of generosity and love within the group and we all offered one another incredible support. My 'outgoing' and sensitive nature seemed to serve me well with my BC group—I loved them and felt that they loved me, but that left the most crucial area out—my relationship with myself. I realised that I didn't LOVE myself! Without my script beating me up the whole time I began to accept that I deserve to be happy. This realisation has been nothing short of life-changing.

The significant changes that BC has made to my life are far too numerous to cover here, but let me just mention a few. Whereas I used to hate the fact that I was so sensitive, I now look upon it as one of my greatest strengths. Satisfaction is immense when we can turn our own agonies and past challenges into meaningful tools to help others. Can people really relate to so-called 'sorted', 'ultra-confident' and 'perfect' people? I don't believe so. Vulnerability, honesty, love and openness are far more attractive qualities. People need to know they are not isolated in their feelings and that they deserve to know the truth and feel a massive relief that many others have felt the same. Before ever hearing of Broadband Consciousness I wrote and recorded a song called 'Here & Now'. The first line of the chorus is—'Here and Now is all we're guaranteed'. However, the significance of 'living in the present' has only truly come to light since BC. So often I would look to the future or wait for a result before allowing myself to feel good. I was all set to spend the rest of my life chasing rainbows, waiting to 'get there'. Instead, I enjoy my present, appreciating the 'here & now'. Everything we do, we do for a feeling, but here's the best bit—we all already have everything we need to access those feelings right now!

My awareness is heightened, my antennae at the ready, I now notice and appreciate seemingly small things that perhaps I used to ignore or take for granted. Looking for the good, noticing the beautiful and even tasting wonderful food can be magical if done so 'consciously'.

I love my life, my family and my work. I work full-time as a vocal and confidence coach, preparing mostly singers and some actors for audition prep, drama school and the music industry. Others just come to see me for fun. However, all my students have one thing in common; they like to feel good about themselves. Helping these people to recognise their true identity, and harness their unique individuality has become for me almost an addiction. Frankly, I can't get enough of it! Am I always happy? No of course not, but when things don't go right, I can feel the pain but I don't suffer. If something happens that makes me feel cross or unhappy I accept that this is 'my script' and the feelings don't cut so deep.

I owe so much to Richard & Liz for creating Broadband Consciousness. In a nutshell they have taught me how 'to look at the same old things differently'. The sentence that still sticks in my mind the most is this: 'Dare to be wrong about who you think you are.'

BC AND ME . . . DIANE INVERARITY

You know when you want your life to change for the better? So you embark on all the self development courses, read all the books, listen to all the tapes and really engulf yourself in it all? I did all that . . . and more and it's fair to say I did learn and have learnt a lot over the years which had made me into the person I am today, safe to say investing in your growth is never a waste of time.

So then why did I, with all this knowledge, keep repeating the same negative pathways in my career, relationships, health (ok being fat, I admit it), and life in general? I'd have it all together for a while then all of a sudden . . . shit happens . . . then as we do, call our best friends, moan and gripe, become the victim . . . woe is me . . . oh but wait!!! There's this course, that book, this person and here I went around the Hamsters wheel of life again and again . . .

It took me a while to go on BC. I knew about it from Liz and we discussed it at length . . . so I thought If I know about it and understand the concept . . . all sorted . . . yeah? . . . NO NO NO! Please don't be fooled. As Liz pointed out in one of our conversations . . . "If I was to show you photographs from my holiday in Hawaii, would that be enough or would you need to go to get the full experience?" . . . Of course I would need to go and as with all off life, its experiential . . . from your view, your perception and your own experience, and that's what BC was and still is for me . . . the ultimate intimate experience with me, myself and I. Now I know . . .

There is nothing wrong with me!!

I don't need fixed!!

I will feel amazing!!

I will feel pissed off at times and it's alright!!

I was Superhero (Wonder Woman actually) pretending to be an ordinary person!! and so much more . . . the sum total is always greater than its parts . . . I met my "SCRIPT"

The voice in my head, you know the one? The one that tells you big fat lies . . . (no you're not the only one!!)

You're too fat

You're not good enough for that/them

It's ok for them, but not you . . . stay where you are

Who do you think you are lady?

And I could go on and on and on . . . if I spoke to my friends the way I used to speak to myself . . . well, I wouldn't have any friends . . .

The Script is NOT me. I would NOT choose to speak to or treat myself like I did . . . ever, so I started to choose . . . I started to go beyond the Script and really Choose for myself.

The script will never go away . . . and that's BRILLIANT news . . . but now I can separate from it . . . so now I choose to . . .

Love myself . . . know I'm not just good enough . . . I'm AMAZING . . . I can achieve anything and anything is possible . . .

In my career, my relationships (because everyone has a script and I can see it so I have more empathy and understanding) my relationship with myself, my health (I'm amazing fat or thin) . . . WOW . . . Wonder Woman . . . and I am a BC Coach (so I am good enough!!) . . .

If you're thinking "this seems a bit too simple" it truly is!!! . . . but the script will tell you otherwise so who will you choose to believe?

My BC Story by Pete Field

I first met Liz and Richard in June 2008 on their One Day "Success without Busyness" program. Like many people introduced to Liz and Richard, I had an impressive 'personal development' CV: Master Practitioner in NLP, author with first book endorsed by stars from the film 'The Secret', attendance at personal development programs all around the world, including 2 retreats in the rain forests of Costa Rica and, of course, the obligatory home library with an extensive range of self-help books. Yet, despite all of these wonderful life experiences, the 'little voice' in my head said " . . . yes, but there's still something missing Peter. You're not quite 'There' yet!"

So as I sat in front of Richard and Liz, I wondered if this was going to be the day I finally discovered the 'missing piece' (or should it be 'peace') I had been searching for. Prior to this program, I knew nothing about Richard and Liz's work. The title was sufficient to arouse my curiosity. After all, who doesn't want success without busyness? And what I heard that day was different to anything I'd ever heard before.

The first thing that struck me was the humility and authenticity of Liz and Richard. Both had overcome some severe life challenges and yet openly shared their fears, failures and vulnerabilities. This was unusual and very refreshing.

The myth of self-improvement

As I sat and listened, it dawned on me that although I had enjoyed a relatively successful career, I still had this feeling I needed to 'improve' myself. I've since come to understand that approaching any self-improvement program with a belief you're not good enough or you're deficient in some way will only attract more evidence to support this limiting belief, because this is how beliefs work.

Liz and Richard begin their programs by telling you there is nothing wrong with you and you don't need fixing. In fact they go one step further. They passionately tell you that "you are a real life super-hero pretending to be an ordinary person!" And although this usually raises a smile, it contains a profound truth: you can't change behaviour at the level of behaviour. You have to go to a higher level of consciousness, namely identity.

Who you are

We have been conditioned to believe that who we are, our identity, is based on what we do (our job, behaviour, accomplishments) and what we have (possessions and wealth). As a result we feel inadequate and think we need 'fixing'. But this is a case of 'mistaken identity'. Who we are and what we do or have are not the same.

We are human beings, not human doings or human havings. What we do or have changes all the time. Who we are, at the being level is changeless.

So the invitation to you, the reader, is simple:

Will you dare to be 'wrong' about who you think you are?

The more I listened to Liz and Richard, the more I realised that their message was not only different, but it was presented in a way that was fun, simple and profound. I had many 'aha' moments during the one day program, but the real breakthroughs came when I attended their 5 day Broadband Consciousness (BC) course.

The Broadband Consciousness course

Describing the 5 day BC experience is like describing the taste of strawberries or your first visit to Paris. You can spend hours selecting the right words, but they will never do justice to the experience itself. So if the following words resonate with you in any way, please understand they only scratch the surface of what you will feel if you attend the course and discover your true identity.

We are not choosing

Perhaps my greatest insight from attending the BC course was the realization that I was not in control of my life as much as I thought I was. For most of the time we are not consciously choosing our thoughts, feelings and behaviour, but unconsciously reacting to circumstances. For example, no-one would choose to feel unworthy, fearful or depressed, yet many people do. So who or what is choosing?

Metaphorically speaking, our choices are being determined by a script handed down to us by our parents and peer groups. This script, which we did not consciously choose, guides our thoughts, feelings and behaviour. Anytime we think and do things we wouldn't consciously choose, we're unconsciously reading and reacting from our script.

But it gets worse. Until we're made aware of the script and the 'little voice' in our head (the audio version of the script) we can't separate ourselves from it. We then think that who we are is our bad behaviour and all the bad things we think and feel about ourselves. We then dislike ourselves even more.

Awareness is the first step

The BC course makes you aware of the script and the little voice in your head. This awareness changes everything because when you are aware of it, you are not unconsciously identified with it. And when you make the shift from unconscious to conscious, you can then separate from it and create a new and more empowering future for yourself and family.

Awareness of the script has made a profound difference in my life. I'm more compassionate and forgiving of myself because I know many times I'm unconsciously reacting to my script. I'm also more compassionate and forgiving of other people because I know everyone has a script (and voice in their head), but that is not who they are. If I had their script, I would think, feel and behave as they do. Even the greatest movie star will perform badly with a poor script.

From a practical point of view, I know I'm only dealing with one thing—my script. If I'm feeling bad, I know I'm stuck in my script because I would never choose to feel bad. If I'm feeling good, I've separated myself from my script and am being my true self.

This is so liberating and energising because all of the energy previously used to 'beat myself up' when I was stuck in my script, suddenly becomes available to focus on what I would choose.

Does this mean awareness of the script silences the little voice? Not at all. In fact it tends to push it into overdrive! I attended the BC course in September 2008 and in the weeks that followed the voice was relentless, " . . . it would say BC is too simple. You've spent thousands of pounds travelling the globe with some of the best mentors around. There's got to be more to it than this."

But don't be fooled. The laws that govern a happy and successful life are counter-intuitive. Truth is simple.

After BC life continues to provide its challenges. This is part of the duality process. However the peaks and troughs are much flatter and I have found that the 'bad' times are significantly less stressful to deal with because of my increased awareness.

Success is a feeling

Another breakthrough moment on the course was the realization that success is a feeling. When you peel all the layers back, the only reason we do anything personally and professionally is because we want to feel good. But here's the irony. These good feelings that we spend all our life searching for are already inside us. So why can't we access them?

My little voice told me I could not feel successful until I had achieved a certain job position, had a certain amount of money in the bank and lived in a 4 bedroom type of house. Yet even when I achieved all of these, at great personal and family sacrifice, I still didn't feel successful. Why? Because my little voice convinced me to put my feelings 'on hold' even longer until I had achieved another set of goals. How crazy is this? I wouldn't dream of telling my children that they couldn't feel successful and good about themselves until they had achieved some 'agreed' external criteria, and yet this was the script I was passing down to them.

This awareness has dramatically changed what I do and how I feel on a daily basis. I left the Corporate world after 31 years and instead of 'chasing' and 'wanting' material things; my focus is on providing value. This has significantly increased my energy levels and I feel more deserving and contented.

Is BC right for You?

If you have ever felt that there was a bigger, better and more capable person inside of you (a real life super-hero) and you've not achieved what you think you deserve, then the answer is a resounding Yes!!!

Pete Field BC Graduate

What BC has done for me . . . Chris BC Graduate

It sounds a little cliché, to say that BC saved my life. And yet it's also true.

When I met Richard and Liz, I was struggling with life rather a lot. I was quite seriously depressed, had a social phobia that made it very hard for me to interact with people and was self injuring on a regular basis. I was suicidal on and off because life just hurt so much. I had been on and off several anti-depressants, seen psychiatrists, psychologists, counsellors and therapists. I'd gone the NHS route and seen counsellors privately, but none of that really worked for me. I can still remember sitting in the office of my last counsellor, telling her that yes, things were getting better. In actual fact, I was feeling far worse again and had been self-injuring for a couple of weeks, but the last time I told her that, she threatened to section me and looked so disappointed I couldn't bear to tell her again.

Although I've had quite a privileged life on many levels, I have also experienced some really difficult times, mostly due to my classmates. We moved a lot and when I ended up back in my country of origin in a really affluent area where everyone had known everyone else for years, I didn't stand a chance. I was too different, had an accent, I was shy and bookish. It started with some teasing then things started going missing from my desk. Tripping me up or almost pushing me down the stairs as a "joke" became popular. In the winter, they'd rub my face with handfuls of snow, panicking me as I couldn't breathe. Within the year, they'd started beating me up on a regular basis. One month before my 15th birthday, several of them raped me. By that time, I was so broken down that I wouldn't have told anyone anyway-I didn't think anyone would believe me. The teachers had all sided with my classmates and I had no one I felt that I could trust. They also threatened me in a manner that made me very positive they would carry out the threat if I ever told.

I planned my suicide, but the universe had other plans for me and I never went through with my plans. I struggled on. Life had lost its meaning, people on the whole were scary and I didn't want anything to do with them, yet at the same time as I was starved for friends and desperate to interact.

A year and a half later, we finally moved to the UK. In spite of leaving the bullies behind, I couldn't leave the after effects behind and the pain inside me tore me apart. I tried everything because I was desperate to get better. I didn't want to be this depressed social misfit, but nothing I tried worked. I was self injuring so regularly it scared me and I was suicidal on and off. I tried overdosing on tablets when it all got too much, but came to my senses and called an ambulance.

Nothing worked until I came across BC that is. BC has given me the confidence to interact with people again. I have a huge network of friends and I have a social life that I can't quite believe sometimes. I have some absolutely awesome close friends whom I can trust with anything. I can stand up and speak to groups containing hundreds of people.

I stopped self injuring and no longer need depression as a crutch to survive life. The concepts behind BC have given me my life back. There is no doubt in my mind that without the skills I've learned, I would have given in to that suicidal nature by now. I was awfully close when I met Richard and Liz. I am still growing and learning about myself through those concepts. It's been 4 years now, and it continues getting stronger every day! People who meet me now can't believe that I ever had any problems. People I met a year ago still comment on the difference just in that short time!

The best thing is that I can now help others who are suffering the same issues that I used to suffer with! I can help others find their way out of the nightmare and that makes everything I experienced more okay. I can actually say I'm grateful, because without my own experiences, I don't feel I would be able to help others the way I do.

Chris . . . BC Graduate

My BC story—Rachel Wallis

What can I say about BC and the impact it's had in my life? Not much really . . . oh apart from a small thing of finally feeling 100% 'complete' by helping me find my true purpose in life. Just a small thing then really!

Without BC, I would have carried on forever looking for that missing 'something' in my life, often believing I would be fulfilled when I find my perfect job, or when I fall in love/find my perfect partner, or when I earn enough money to pay off my debts, or when I have a baby, or perhaps when I go travelling and 'find myself' etc. What BC taught me is that none of these 'external' things would have given me long term fulfilment without me first finding 100% love and respect for myself. And although I'd already heard that often said before by other people and I suppose I believed it to a certain extent, I didn't know how you actually really love yourself and why you had to before you could feel fulfilled. BC gave me the why and the how. And in such a simple, easy to understand way, that sticks with you for life.

Why did I do BC?

In August 2010 I was made redundant for the first time in my life, after working for only 2 different companies over the period of 24 years. I was expecting it so it didn't come as a surprise and I actually felt excited as it gave me a chance to really think about what job I wanted to do next. Although I'd never been unhappy in either of my two companies, I never really felt fulfilled. So I signed up for a careers coaching course to help me find my 'perfect' career.

I loved the course, and always looked forward to my weekly sessions with my careers consultant. After a few weeks, we eventually worked out that possibly coaching could be the right career for me. He then introduced me to BC as he recommended me to consider learning coaching through BC before I committed to any of the other coaching organisations.

I went along to the BC course on February 14 2011 and although I didn't know what the course would entail, I hoped that I would come away knowing that coaching was definitely the right career choice for me.

What a week, wow! Little did I know how life changing that week would be. Yes, I came away with more certainty about starting a career in coaching but more importantly I found out how you can live a satisfying, fulfilling, enjoyable, exciting, contented life straight away WITHOUT waiting for the perfect job, partner, money, home etc.

My life pre-BC . . . I've always considered myself lucky and privileged and a pretty happy, positive person. I suppose you could say I'm from that in-between working class and middle class family. Money wasn't abundant but it wasn't scarce either. I always remember going on at least one family holiday per year, even if it was in our caravan in the UK somewhere and I always got lots of Christmas presents, the biggie being a bike one year, even though it was second-hand and 3 sizes too big for me so it would last!

I had a very happy childhood overall, loved very much by my Mum and Dad, did well at school and was pretty popular, with lots of friends. After I left school, I went straight into work and got a well-paid job with good career prospects in banking. I got married in my early 20s, owned a lovely house and by the age of 25 I'd got everything you could have wished for. Except I felt there was something missing. And that's when that unfulfilled, incomplete feeling started, and also the feeling of guilt at the same time, because here I was, with nothing to complain about at all, quite the opposite, yet I couldn't help feeling there was something missing. So that's when I set off to find what it was that was missing.

First I thought it was my job, then I thought it was my marriage, then I thought it was perhaps Nottingham, the city I was born in, living and working in, so I changed all three within the space of a year! In 2000, I changed my job, moved to London, got divorced and started my new life. And after all the excitement of this huge change (with a few ups and downs along the way—some of them 'biggies'!) my life started to settle down, but guess what, that familiar feeling of something missing was still there. Again, I felt guilty for feeling it because I'd got this brilliant exciting life in a city that I love, in a good job, socialising with amazing people, having (albeit short-lived but fun!) relationships with numerous men in an attempt to find 'Mr. Right' but still not feeling fulfilled.

Perhaps I needed to go travelling or do some charity work I thought. So in 2007 I took myself off to Argentina for 6 weeks volunteering teaching English in a school in Buenos Aries. I absolutely loved it, felt fulfilled, came back to my old job with plans to go back to Argentina to live and teach out there when I'd paid off my debts and could afford it. Surprise surprise, that never happened as life just got in the way I suppose and I slipped back into the routine I had before.

In 2010, I'd just come out of a year long relationship and I entered my Big 40! A few months later I got made redundant, started my careers coaching and signed up for BC in 2011. That's when my life changed and I finally realized what this wonderful life is all about!

Post BC . . . Nine months on after completing my BC course, and 6 weeks on after completing my BC coaching course, I can honestly say, with 100% absolute certainty, I have found my purpose in life. Yes, it's partly because I have started to coach people, which gives me a tremendous amount of fulfilment, but BC has given me much more than that. It's helped me find me again. The real Rachel the one that existed before all the unfulfilled feelings started to set in, before the self doubt, lack of self-love, always striving for perfection set in. And yes, sometimes those feelings come back but the difference is that now, when they do, I know INSTANTLY how to choose NOT to feel those feelings but to choose all the feelings that make me feel good, contented, fulfilled, excited and just happy to be alive and live for the now, not for the 'one day . . . '. And I feel so much more tolerant and loving towards people who would have previously irritated or annoyed me and that's because I am so much more loving and accepting of myself.

Although I've started coaching in my spare time and I'm sure that I will eventually do it full time, I'm still working full time in my marketing job because I'm now making the job work for me until/if I'm ready to change it. A few months ago I could have easily walked out because of the long hours, pressure, not doing what I really wanted to do etc. but BC has taught me how to get the most out of every day, no matter what I am doing.

Why do I want to share my BC story? . . . BC has taught me the most amazing life-changing things and one of those is to turn the ME into the WE.

Quite simply, I cannot keep this wonderful thing to myself I have to share it because every single person out there deserves to find their true selves and their purpose in life. Everyone I know whose done BC has benefited from it so much that it would be so unjust for us not to share it. And the more we share it, the richer everyone's' lives will be.

And once you've learned BC, it just gets stronger and stronger and it's with you for life. I can't get enough of it!

Rachel . . .

BC and me—Tom Cassidy . . .

I was one of those people that had grown up in a very loving family environment, with tremendous support from my mum and dad, who always told us that we could do anything and supported us in every crazy undertaking. I was sailing through life perfectly comfortably, I did well in school, studied Physics at Oxford, played in football teams at college, was blessed with great musical talent and was very confident that I could turn my hand to pretty much anything.

Anyway, I became a teacher because I wanted to travel the world and I really enjoyed the life/work balance that teaching gave. My first three kids were all born during the school holidays and unlike a lot of people I knew with young families, I got to spend a lot of time with them.

However, money was a bit tight as a teacher and after several business ventures that didn't get the results I would have liked, I decided that I would have to either change career or move to a country where there was much better pay for educators. Research indicated that Hong Kong had the best differential between teacher pay and cost of living for a family and so we all relocated to Asia.

This was fantastic fun; we got a great financial package and had a terrific family lifestyle. I started my own school which took off nicely, started another education business and was having the time of my life.

I'd never have come back to this country if my marriage hadn't started to go a bit pear-shaped. In fact, the wisdom of hindsight reveals that our relationship had never been that good a match, but Hong Kong sharpened the wedge that was driving between us and it became clear that we would need to separate or tear each other apart. [Now we know that it was our scripts that were making it so hard for us.]

So, this is when it started to get a bit complicated. My wife and kids returned to England and I stayed in Hong Kong to finish my teaching contract and sort out some of the business issues and I found that period pretty tough. I flew back to the UK every 6 weeks or so to see the kids and leaving them to go back and spend another stretch on my own was very difficult.

In the summer of 2004 I happened to be over in the UK when Richard Wilkins was speaking and I was really knocked out by the simplicity of his message and by the fact that he wasn't claiming to have all the answers. His approach was so 'real' it hit me right between the eyes and I left the room thinking—I'm having some of this—so I bought everything he was selling!

For the next 6 months I listened to Richard's CD's relentlessly. I even added my own piano soundtracks to them so I could listen to them over and over again without fatigue—and in this difficult period where I was living on my own in Hong Kong and not really sure what was happening long term, it was priceless.

The relationship with my wife was on-off for most of this period. We had the deep realisation that we were probably never going to be able to live together harmoniously, but we also had a desperate desire to bring the children up in a loving and supportive environment.

There lies the challenge of many relationships and listening to Richard's CD's was what kept me going, gave me balance in a difficult and lonely period.

It was further complicated by having met a wonderful Taiwanese girl who was many of things that my wife wasn't (Isn't that always the way?!!) and I was torn between making a new start and patching things up and having another crack at the marriage. I'm sure I'm not the only person in history who's made the wrong decision in this regard. [In fact, it turned out to be the right decision in the end, as will soon be revealed]

Anyway, I resolved to settle all the business affairs in Hong Kong and return to the UK, with the view that we should try again to keep the relationship together—at least give it a chance of working by being in the same country!

I came back to the UK in January 2005 and by March it was already crystal clear that it wasn't going to work. We were just too different, too divided on the most pressing issues and while we did still have a kind of love for each other and did indeed still have some wonderful times, we didn't really have a good 'average' any more.

As in a lot of cases, it became difficult for me as the non-resident parent to get as much access to the children as I would have liked and over the next few years there was a gradual deterioration in contact until it really became quite difficult to see the children regularly. The irony of the situation was that I returned to the UK in order to see the kids more, yet I ended up seeing them less often than when I was in Hong Kong.

The next two years brought a lot of court action, a lot of legal wrangling, and a lot of pain but the worst part was dealing with the little voice in my head that was telling me it was my fault: 'You should have been a better husband . . . if only you'd worked harder on your marriage . . . if only you'd worried less about business and setting up your schools etc in Hong Kong, then you'd be seeing the kids now . . . your kids will resent you later in life . . . etc'

And because your problems consume you, totally understandably of course, you become a real drag on all your friends and family because you're always talking about it. So, that's where the knowledge of the script made such a difference to me. Knowing that beneath everything, before you even got to the point of controlling your attitude, there was a script that was making decisions for you made such a difference to my awareness.

Now I knew that since I would never choose an unhelpful attitude, if I found myself being negative about situations, it was my script choosing and not me. So I didn't have to beat myself up about being negative or despondent about things. This saved a huge amount of energy and gave me a real step-change in awareness. It was like passing the driving test to your mind. One day you're relying on your parents and friends to ferry you around—the next you're an independent agent, controlling your destiny, not reliant on anyone ever again.

The side effect of BC is that everyday miracles become predictable. When you begin to realise that most of the time the script is determining what you're putting into your sausage machine, you immediately begin to see how what you've created in your life has resulted from the work of the script and not by your own choice.

You start to take control of the situation, choosing what to put in the sausage machine of your career, your relationships, your future, etc. and amazing things start to arrive—as if by magic.

Regarding relationships, I put exactly what I wanted with my next wife into my relationship sausage in February 2006 on a flight back from Hong Kong and by April 2006 I'd started dating the lady to whom I'm now married. We have three wonderful children and she is absolutely perfect. More importantly—she is exactly the right match for me. She has done BC as well and we have been able to introduce the phenomenon to several of our friends, who can't stop thanking us for how we've changed their lives. That's a nice feeling.

With careers and other relationships, BC has helped me be aware enough to put exactly what I want in the sausage machine and it works with breathtaking accuracy. You put in clarity, specific requirements, absolute detail and that's what you get.

Interestingly, the metaphor of the sausage machine is not something that you can use if you like, or not if you don't really want to. Absolutely not. There's no take it or leave it with the sausage machine. It's something that works all the time, every minute of every day whether you give it attention or not. And that's what's so brilliant about the metaphor.

- It's *already* working for you right now.

Want to know what you've been putting in?—Have a look around you!

'If a sausage machine is in the middle of a forest with no-one around to see it working, would crap in still equal crap out?' Anon

Tom . . .

My BC story—Bryony . . .

BC is the calm in the storm.

BC is the missing piece of the jigsaw

BC is the key that unlocks the door to enlightenment.

BC is realising the grass is already green.

BC is a huge relief!

BC is simple.

BC is like coming home after a long search.

I did the five day Broadband Consciousness course in February 2011. Approximately ten years prior to that, I had seen Richard Wilkins do a local evening talk and I was truly inspired. I knew I wanted to go to some of his events and yet I never did. That was before I knew about the 'script'.

At the talk, I put my name on Richard's mailing list. Over the years I received various emails about events he was running, none of which I attended, although I was interested. Then I started to receive emails about something different—a one day event he was running with his partner, Liz. I looked at the content of the event and it definitely got my attention.

Between June 2009 and May 2010 I suffered from anxiety and depression. It was very sudden and shocking and hit me like a truck. One day I was fine and the next, the world had changed. For a long time, I thought I would never recover. I felt scared and alone and could not understand how this had happened. In the meantime, I continued to receive emails about the one day course and kept thinking about it. In February 2010 I decided to go to the course. I now know that I was choosing, not my script.

At that time I was working again and driving but I was far from okay. I was still battling the anxiety and wondering if I'd ever be the same again yet somehow I managed to get to the event. I brought no one with me. When I arrived I felt a little nervous—several people seemed to know each other and I felt lost but I knew I was supposed to be there. I tried to hide in the back row but a lovely lady who had previously done the five day course asked if I would like to sit with her and looked after me.

It was great to see Richard again and experience his energy, passion, enthusiasm and humour. When Liz spoke, I was deeply moved and felt it in the heart. She connected with everyone in that room. I felt privileged to be there. Several people who had already done the Broadband Consciousness course got up to speak about what it had done for them and I could really relate to their stories. I was blown away and knew that this was something very special. I had been to many events in the past but nothing quite like this.

As I drove home that night, I took with me something precious—hope. In the dark place I was living in, I could now start to see a way out. I knew I wasn't going to feel this way forever.

Liz, Richard and the people who had spoken during the day had talked about this thing getting 'better over time'. The stories they had told made me realise how many people felt the same inside. They had also talked of regular get-togethers and I loved the idea of the sense of community that could bring. I wanted to be part of it.

I was not, then, in a position to do the course. I was deeply in debt and had no way of paying for it but life has a funny way of delivering something that we need deep in our soul and that is right. For a long time afterwards, I thought about that day and I knew that someday, I would be on that course. I never doubted it.

A year later, I found myself on the Broadband Consciousness course. My script nearly stopped me getting there (my script is fond of doing this!!). It tried everything—"it's the wrong time, I'm too busy, I feel overloaded and exhausted just now, perhaps I should wait until the right time"—bla bla bla. The point is that in the world of the script, there is no "right" time. If I had listened to the script, I would probably still be making excuses.

If I had listened to the script, I would not have had the wonderful experience I had. In addition:

* I would not have met the wonderful people I spent time with on that course.

* I would not have developed the continuing and growing friendships that arose from that course.

* I would not have spent time with Liz and Richard.

* I would not have shared my story or heard the other stories which bonded us all.

* I would not have discovered that we all feel the same inside—different stories, same feelings.

* I would not have known that all those things the script says about us are not true.

* I would not have realised that many of the issues we have in our lives all arise from the same thing—the script.

* I would not be able to recognise when other people are in their script.

* One of my very good friends, who has now done BC, would not be experiencing the joy that she is now.

* I would not have gone on to do the four day BC coaching course which had a profound effect on me.

* I would not be able to share this thing with others.

The list goes on.

Before I tell you about what BC has done for me, I would like to share some of my story with you. I hope very much that it resonates with some of you and helps you. So here it is, with love:

I was born in 1964. My earliest memory was being out with my Nan and seeing my first rainbow. It was truly wondrous. I have loved rainbows ever since. Strangely, on the last day of the BC coaching course, a rainbow appeared in the sky!! I have only just recalled that!

Ever since I can remember, I always felt 'different', the odd one out. I didn't fit in. I wanted desperately to belong but I felt I never would. My red hair made me different as did a face that hadn't decided what it wanted to do with itself.

I was picked on from an early age. At school, by friends that came round to my house, you name it, I was picked on. I was sent out of my own bedroom by some friends who then plotted to beat me up after school. My two best friends at school blew hot and cold. Both bullied me for a long time before befriending me. I think I must have grown up believing that was normal. They would be nice to me then they would say "we've decided that we don't like you". I remember liking a boy at school and saying I thought he might have liked me too and one of my friends saying "Well it can't be your looks. It must be your personality. But it can't be that either because you haven't got one." One of them stabbed me in the leg with a compass during a lesson once and it bled a lot. People picked on me for that. I went in the toilet after that to clean it up, only to hear a crowd outside the toilets taunting me, saying my name over and over and waiting for me to come out. I stayed in there for ages and eventually had to face them. I'll never forget that.

People used to say I smelt, even though I had a bath and cleaned my teeth every day. One boy said I was the ugliest thing on two legs and would never have a boyfriend. I have since proved him wrong!! One girl said I looked alright from the back but when I turned round

I put people off. When I walked into a room, people would go quiet and sneer at me. A group of boys, two in particular, used to follow me round everywhere and make my life hell. It didn't help that my two 'best friends' were really pretty with big personalities and I felt like an ugly freak in comparison.

I felt sick every single morning before going to school. I hated it. I didn't know how to trust people. I felt they all hated me. I was an outcast, no good to anyone. My Dad used to be on my case for not trying hard enough at school. I often got the "could do better" remark on my school reports. My sister, in comparison, was hard working and did everything right. I was the disappointment.

The trouble was that I felt I couldn't excel in school. One of my two best friends had to come top in everything (her script!!). I beat her in English once and the two of them gave me such a hard time about it. They were really angry with me. So I was damned if I did and damned if I didn't. I couldn't win. I found it easier to disappoint my Dad than upset my friends.

My Dad was very strict growing up and had a terrible temper (his script). He was fairly violent and in those days, parents used to hit their children (my mother never hit me). Sometimes he would grab my sister and I and bang our heads together or bang our heads against the wall. He would shake us and hit us. Once, I dropped an apple on the floor. He pushed me down to the ground, got hold of my head and rubbed my nose in it. Ever since then, I've hated the noise of someone rubbing their hand or foot against the carpet.

Dad could also be very loving and really funny. I think he always loved us but struggled with a massive script. We have a good relationship today and it would upset him deeply to remember that stuff, I'm sure.

My parents' relationship began to crumble when I was about 13, at the height of the bullying. At that time, I became ill after a bout of flu and over the years have developed a worsening M.E. type condition. Dad began an affair that went on for about eight years with one of Mum's friends. He denied it and denied it but we all knew what was going on. He was terrible to my Mum at that time, really awful. He hit her once but the worst was the verbal abuse. He said awful things to my sister and I too. He was out of control. He was meditating a lot. Meditation is a wonderful thing. However, I think, unfortunately, Dad became addicted to it. When he was meditating he could suddenly get very angry then his eyes would glaze over and go funny. He would run relentlessly up and down the corridor. It was all very weird and I'd blocked many of those years out. During this time, Mum was in pieces. She cried every day and talked to me about Dad and how awful it all was. I counselled her. I never cried myself. I was always the strong one, the calm one.

When Dad eventually moved out, he was remorseful and apologised to my sister and myself. He asked if we wanted to live with him. We stayed with Mum. But despite everything, I loved my Dad and didn't want to lose him. My sister felt the same. My sister was going out a lot at that time with her friends and boyfriend. I was at home with Mum, listening to her. I kept in touch with Dad and saw him. He went back to the old Dad, how he was before he went off the rails. He has remained like this ever since. When I continued to see

Dad, Mum couldn't cope with it at all and the guilt trips were massive.

This always carried on afterwards, after I had moved out and found my own life. Whenever I saw Dad, Mum would say "oh" in a very guilt-inducing way and ask loads of questions. I felt so torn and I didn't want to hurt Mum. Mum was a lovely woman—caring, sweet and kind but at the same time I felt like I had never broken free of the apron strings. She never got over my Dad, not ever. He met someone new and got married but she never recovered. My sister and I were her life.

She always wanted me to go back and live with her and used to say things like "I've been on my own all weekend. I haven't seen a soul. I've been staring at these four walls". I worried about her all the time and felt guilty if I wasn't with her or finding a way to improve her life. I tried hard to help her but it was always the same. She never got over my Dad. However, she did smile and laugh a lot and was very sweet, kind and well liked. I had loads of great times with my Mum and spoke to her nearly every day. We were very close.

Mum became ill about five and a half years ago with Parkinson's Disease that progressed rapidly and she died a year and a half ago. Those few years were very stressful, especially her last year. She went through such a lot.

I have only told you a small part of my story and only the negative things have emerged. That is the way with stories! I've had an amazing life in lots of ways and have had some wonderful times. I've been very lucky indeed.

I hope the areas of my story that I have focused on today will illustrate some recurring themes that are common to many, many people—guilt, isolation, feeling different, feeling ill, not fitting in, and not feeling good enough. You are not alone.

Sharing my story and hearing other people's stories was phenomenal, not only because it showed that we all feel the same but also because it demonstrated how a script is born and grows bigger over time. Realising I was not the script and watching others reach the same conclusion was brilliant.

So what has BC done for me?

* My script does paranoia. It thinks people don't like me and are talking about me. It loves this one. I spent my whole life trying to find a way of getting rid of this paranoia but nothing worked. Nothing until BC. Now I can separate from it. I'm not saying it isn't still there at times but now I can rise above it. I can see when it's happening and see that it's not true, it's just my script. This has been HUGE for me.

* I can now love myself. (I can still get caught in the script but that's just fine) but I can love myself more and far more frequently now.

* I have more confidence.

* I know that I am enough.

* I don't have to pretend to be someone that I'm not. I can be ME.

* I know that sometimes, it's okay not to be okay.

* I know that I can't get it wrong.

* It's helped me to put great feelings into my day. Rather than resenting the daily grind, I've learned to love it. I enjoy my job far more now than I used to. I am getting the best out of what I am doing so it's a win win.

* It has improved my relationships.

* It has helped me to understand others better.

* It has helped me to help others.

* Most of all, it's given me ME. I am truly blessed . . . Bryony

My BC story—Joe Francis

I did the broadband consciousness course when I was feeling very, very low. I was struggling with life and had lost my way, to the point where I felt life was not worth living.

I tried so many things and always strived to feel the best I could feel, the problem was that nothing really made me feel complete. Even when I felt on excellent form I still was searching for that something to make me feel 100%.

Like a lot of people my life had been very up-and-down. A traumatic family breakup when I was young left me feeling emotionally de-stabilised, which triggered a variety of emotional and psychological challenges that I struggled with throughout my life. Subsequently I always felt like the circumstances of my life were built on poor foundations.

I would often distract myself with major projects which would take up a lot of my energy and cause me huge amounts of stress. These circumstances would often drive me from periods of balance and stability to chronic anxiety, fear and worry. At times I would feel so low that I believed life was not worth living and that the world was doomed; there were many times when I just could not see a way through it all.

Incidentally, the last time that I fell hard was following a period when I felt the most balance I have felt throughout my whole life. On paper I had everything going for me—I was getting married to my long term girlfriend, we were moving house into a lovely new area, my business was going well and was flourishing in a time of recession. The interesting thing was that even with all these 'material' things that people think will bring them happiness; I still did not feel complete.

So even though I felt great there was still a part of me that I thought needed to be fixed, and so I was looking to see what I could do to get that sorted. I had a variety of therapies and treatments to help heal wounds of the past but none of them seem to give me the complete solution I was looking for. I was puzzled by this and wondered what it could be that was missing. I was then convinced that it was where I was living that was keeping me from feeling how I wanted to feel. And so we decided to move out of town to be closer to the countryside (which is where I'd always wanted to be) thinking that this was it, that this was the solution. How wrong I was!

In my true fashion I created huge stressful challenges to overcome. We moved house within a month of getting married—a double helping of intense stress added to the stresses of running a business proved too much for me. In a matter of weeks following the move and our wedding I plummeted into a dark hole of anxiety and depression. This affected every part of my life, my business began to falter, my confidence left me as did my energy and I felt like I had become pretty much useless.

My relationship with my new wife began to wobble and even our cat became fat and flea ridden! The worst part of it was how I felt about myself—I felt totally worthless and incapable and it didn't matter how many times people told me otherwise it just would not sink in. I liken this episode in my life to something like a plane crash where the plane is hurtling towards the ground and you're sitting at the controls but no matter how hard you try you just cannot pull up. Although I pretty much crashed I thankfully remained in one piece and somehow managed to fight on even though day-to-day life was such an immense pressure; at times I felt as if my head was going to explode. My mind was torturing me in ways that I could never wish on anyone, however I know that a lot of people have felt and are feeling this way too.

A fortunate stroke of luck came my way when I overheard someone talking about a course they had done called BC which mentioned the concept of 'a script'.

What I had overheard, albeit a snippet, really resonated with me and while part of me knew I needed to do this course it was some weeks before I actually picked up the phone to speak to someone about it.

I clearly remember the first conversation I had with Richard, he seemed to really understand how I was feeling (he was the first person I had come across who, I felt, truly related to what I was going through).

I must admit I was sceptical about the BC course and feared that it may be some kind of scam, so I delayed booking on but eventually I felt I had no other choice as I was totally desperate.

As it happens doing the course was a lifeline for me. Although I still struggled afterwards (and even wondered if the course had actually done anything!) I can now say two years later how incredible the

Broadband Consciousness course is. I have read a lot and had some very enlightening experiences in my life, however, never ever before had I encountered so much wisdom compiled into such an easy, enjoyable and complete package delivered with such loving sincerity as it is by Richard and Liz.

The five days I spent on the course were like a holiday in heaven compared to the daily experiences that I had been having previously. This course is truly a lifesaver. All you need to do is have faith, trust the process and commit yourself entirely to being who you want to be. I promise that if you do, the journey is more wondrous, exciting and inspiring than you can possibly imagine.

My life is now flourishing in more ways than I ever thought possible. While I believe we follow our own destiny I know that Richard and Liz and all of the amazing people I have met through the course have contributed greatly to my success.

Thank you guys from the fullness of my heart . . . Joe x

My life and BC . . . Sarah Van Sminia

I have had a happy family upbringing, with loving parents and plenty of friends. My life was "normal" as I thought. I married quite young, had two lovely boys by the time I was 30, lived a life abroad in Spain and then my world as I knew it fell apart. My husband told me he wanted a divorce. Our divorce was bitter and acrimonious, he was difficult with money and (although I didn't realise it at the time) was a bully using bullying tactics to get what he wanted. I stayed as strong and together as I could for the boys. We moved back to the UK to be nearer my family. Then my world became a place I didn't want to be in. I had lost my confidence, didn't want to go out anymore, felt continually anxious, had panic attacks, had suicidal thoughts and had this voice in my head backing all of this up, telling me that I was useless as a mother, daughter, and friend. I slowly withdrew more and more, finding it easier to have days under the duvet behind closed curtains. I pushed my family and friends away. Why would they want to spend time with me? I was useless.

Naturally, my parents and those close to me were concerned and persuaded me to go to the doctor, which I did and I was prescribed anti-depressants. They helped in the beginning, but then I was back to the same place, so back to the doctor I was taken and they prescribed me some more tablets, referred me for 6 weeks counselling (that is all the NHS will give you, how they think they can understand you in 6 weeks, I have no idea!) and to a psychiatrist at a top mental hospital. I went to the psychiatrist for nearly two years. She prescribed more pills on top of the ones I was already taking. I finished with the counsellor after 6 weeks, saw another one who didn't help, another and another . . . I kept thinking; no one understands me, I'm different to everyone else. I was taking about 8 different tablets but nothing helped. There was still something missing. The self loathing I had was awful, and still brings me to tears when I think back to it. The psychiatrist eventually diagnosed Bi-Polar, so I went home and looked it up and read all the symptoms on the internet and of course, believed it all. That was me, that was the answer. What I didn't realise at the time, was that I was taking on the identity of a person with Bi-Polar, having read all about it, and the psychiatrist and the counsellor were treating the behaviour of Bi-Polar, not treating me, Sarah, the person that I was, my true identity. You can only truly change at the level of identity not at the level of behaviour and that is what all the counsellors and psychiatrist were doing, treating the behaviour I was demonstrating.

Thankfully one day in October 2009, I came across Richard and Liz, completely by chance. That meeting, which I cried all the way to out of sheer fright, because the voice in my head was telling me: why would they want to meet you, no one can help you, you're different to everyone else, they won't understand you. That meeting was a moment that changed my life forever (but I didn't realise it at the time). I will never forget the moment I met Liz she said those words that will live with me forever "there's nothing wrong with you and you don't need fixing, you are just reading from a bad script!" Can you imagine what was going through my head at the time? Having been told that I was this and that and that there was something wrong with me.

I stayed for lunch with the superheroes, that were doing the five day BC course that week and after lunch listened to a couple speak that had done BC a year or so before. The first thing Guy talked about was the civil war going on in your head, and boy, did I sit up when I heard that. I never until that moment understood that other people had voices in their head (which of course I now know as the Script), maybe I wasn't so different and there was someone who understood me!

Fortunately for me there was one place left on the 5 day course for the following month so I took the quickest decision I had taken for years and signed on.

I turned up for the five day course one Monday in November and had the most revealing experience of my life, learnt that all the stuff I thought was me, wasn't in fact me and that I could now learn, through these five days, how to detach from that. All through the five days, I kept saying to Richard: "I'm not getting this!" There is nothing to "get". When you spend those five days with Richard and Liz, you are pickled in BC and I have yet to meet someone who has not got BC after doing the course. The other ladies I spent the course with have become some of my closest friends, you laugh together, you cry together, you share stories that you have never shared with anyone ever before. I learnt so much about myself, learnt to "like" myself (I could never look in a mirror for any length of time before BC) and now after more time, "love" myself and have a new best friend in myself. Before you can expect anyone to like/love you, you have to first have that relationship with yourself. I never knew about having a relationship with myself.

Now two years after BC and having also completed the BC coaching course, I am not that person who would spend the day under the duvet, behind closed curtains. I won't deny that I don't have some bad days, but I know that they will pass, and that it's not me, it's the script. Also, I learnt that other people have scripts and that you are not always dealing with the person but their script. I have a new family in all the other superheroes and Richard and Liz. There is always someone there when you need to hear those few special words. I stopped seeing the psychiatrist and all the counsellors the week after I completed BC, I think they (all the specialists, as they are referred to!), were all slightly shocked, especially the psychiatrist when I said I wanted to come off the tablets, the medication they had prescribed to fix me.

I now work three days a week, and am good at my job, am a good mother to my two wonderful sons, and my biggest passion is to now go on to coach/help other people who have experienced what I went through but have never met the right person who could help them at the level of identity and not behaviour, and make them realise that they don't need fixing, they are just reading from a bad script. I now have the confidence to do things I would never have dreamt of before. One of my proudest moments was standing up at a BC Recharge Day to speak in front of about 150 people. I had no prepared speech but spoke from my heart and it just came out, proof that when your message is greater than your fear, you step up and become part of the WE not the ME.

Had I not meet Richard and Liz at that chance meeting, I don't want to think about how my life would be today. I certainly would not have the life that I do, the confidence to do the things I do or more importantly to enjoy my life. Nor would I understand that it is just OK to have bad days and that really nothing happens as a result of that bad day and it doesn't mean I am bad, it is just the Script.

Sarah . . .

My BC story—Paul Campbell

I had the absolute good fortune to bump into Richard and Liz—I remember the occasion like it was yesterday. Now, at the time I was in a very confused state. I won't bore you with all the details, one because it upsets me, but two because I'd rather tell you about the reasons why BC is so different and works!

So briefly since the age of 19 when I broke down in front of a doctor over suicide issues I have spent most of my life in and out of very black clouds—those that understand the dramatic ups and downs will understand. I've hidden away under duvets, in flats, in cars on the side of the road, in service stations, in the woods, hotels in complete darkness for days and sometimes weeks. Suicide was a big part of my thinking. Relationships have been a huge issue. Doctor's surgery, two mental health authority's councillors, hypnotherapists, reflexology, acupuncture, book and books—you name it and I've tried it.

Breakdowns were common place—normally hidden away in the strangest of places with some brilliant excuses to hide my behaviour. I'm a brilliant actor, if that makes sense. Who I really am scares me sometimes—but I understand it now and I'm ok with that.

At 40 years old I had my first full blown panic attack on an aeroplane and boy did that give me a further load of hassle—after that I struggled on trains, in buildings, in crowds and even on the middle lane of the M1.

Desperate and yet I still couldn't get any help. The only thing for me according to the doctors was prescription drugs. I begged in the end for psychiatric help and when I eventually got to see a consultant I was told they couldn't help me because I wasn't schizophrenic!

So you get the picture.

So . . . I spend a week on BC with some people who helped me change my thinking forever—I didn't really understand the certainty, trusting the process, and the mindset that 'it will get stronger'. However 3 months later and I started to 'trust the process' that I'd learnt and, blow me, it worked.

You see the thing is, all this 'civil war between the ears' which I now completely understand, is going on, in one form or another, in all of us. Once you can get your head around it, and use a method, you can deal with virtually anything that's thrown at you—now don't get me wrong I still get knocked off the track, I still get dark grey moments, I still breakdown into pieces and I still get suicidal thoughts but they are rare in comparison to the daily battle I was having just to survive and get through from the age of 19- to 42. Now I have a thought process that has become a habit. I can deal with 'those moments'. Once you have sussed the habit then you can really shine . . . and why not.

That leads me on to helping other people to help themselves. There is nothing better than using your own story to help others with their thought process. I was given the opportunity to do the very first BC coaching week and wow what a difference that has made—using my research to learn more about others and in return teaching me even more about the power of Broadband Consciousness—it is a life saving tool for me personally and trust me I've given loads of hints and tips to loads of people which I know have made a massive difference. How cool is that?

All this experience, research, call it what you will, has finally given me the best opportunity to enjoy what I have for the lifetime I have left and drag as many people as I can out of their own dis-comfort zone and into a habit of self confidence and deserving—of moving out of their own way and realising that with a simple process, and a bit of trust, they really can lead a fulfilling life that, let's face it, we all deserve.

Just one last thing—my business was very much on its last legs. But let me tell you something—the understanding of complete certainty which I learnt and put into practice has helped me keep my company and keep its employees in a job. I've helped hundreds of customers through difficult times and the future is looking good.

It would be damn selfish of me not to tell my story over and over again, wouldn't it?

Paul Campbell

Kitty Hunter's life before and after BC!

I was a course junky for several years. I tried desperately to find answers to why my life didn't feel complete, it cost me thousands of pounds, and thousands of miles travelling, and time away from my family, and yet still I felt lost, incomplete, unhappy with myself, and never really found the answer to my quest!

I would come home from a course, and feel YES this is awesome, but soon found out that to maintain the positive attitude was hard work, frustrating and often times made me feel like a failure again, because I couldn't maintain it!

Something was still missing; the constant arguing I had inside my head, as to what was I looking for? Who do I think I am, I am not special, I do not deserve to have a better life, I am normal, everyone has troubles, and everyone else puts up with life and gets on with it. Just you carry on being you, running around trying to please everyone, putting myself bottom of the list, beating myself up if I didn't get everything done, constantly feeling like a failure and that everyone had to like me because I did everything for them and if I didn't I would not be liked or loved!

I had resigned myself to the fact that nothing could help me, or change, until I saw a person I once knew, who looked amazing. When I heard the reason why, and listened to Richard and Liz I knew straight away I had to give it one more shot, I knew this was something amazing.

I did BC on June 22nd 2009, (I will always remember the date as it was 25 years to the day that my father had passed away)!

I took five days out of my life to attend BC with slight reservations.

It was an intense week. "Trust the process" was mentioned constantly and I got through the week with a massive transformation.

People ask, how did it change your life? Every day since BC I have amazing pearls, I see things differently, I appreciate the little things far more than I ever did in my life before,

I understand me, for the first time in my life. I understand why people do the things they do; I understand and respect what and why my parents did things when I was growing up. I understand . . . why my children say and do things now. But most importantly I understand how to react to situations far better, than I did before.

Why? Because most of my life I have had the script telling me what I am NOT, NOW I know WHO I am, I now know and understand that people love and like me for WHO I am and NOT what I do for them!

I do not need to put others first, I need to put myself first and not be ashamed of it, because if I am not loving and giving to myself, I cannot give and share it with others.

I have also learnt that sometimes you have to let go of things and loved ones, as they too need to find themselves. This is not me letting them down, this is me giving far more than they realize, as letting go is so much harder for me.

The feelings I experience every day, I now know, I CAN change in a heartbeat if I choose to and even better than that, I know WHY I am feeling like that.

Yes, I still have days where I forget my true self, but it doesn't take long to realize it is not me truly; it is my script still trying to be in control!!!! Kicking my script in to shape is now great fun! Now it's the real me that's in control of my life and not the Script controlling my life . . .

Kitty Hunter . . .

What BC has done for us . . . Kris Plumley

8 out of 10s ok . . . Is BC worth the risk?

I have been known as a "cup over-flowing" kind of guy for a long time, and would have said when asked: "on a scale of 1 to 10 how happy are you?" I would have confidently answered "8" (I'll address that 8 later).

I had met Liz and Richard around 4 to 5 years before I finally did the BC course. I had connected with them from the start. Richard was very funny, cutting straight to the heart of my very being, with humour and insight. It was like he was reading my thoughts and making me laugh at my own foibles. Liz by contrast, challenged me with questions I dared not ask myself. I guess I just didn't want to face the answers.

I (well, my script) thought it best to send my wife, Hayley on the course first to see if it was of benefit to her, and our relationship. More importantly I didn't want to risk the happy persona I had cultivated over the years.

On Hayley's return, I could tell there was something different about her but I couldn't really say what. She had a calm way. Nothing for her was better than "the right now". I felt like I had to treat her carefully, I didn't want this to end.

I finally found myself on the BC course. Like a lot of people I thought I might not really get much from the course: I was 8 out of 10 happy. Maybe I would be able to help the others. One of my main beliefs was that I did not have a story, certainly not like some peoples you hear of with their tales of woe. I was last to tell my story. I told of my mother's tough teenage years, marriage, my entry to the world, my father's adultery and their subsequent divorce and our move away to live with my grandfather (her father). I told of my school days and how being an only child of a single parent felt. How my mother was generally angry so we weren't much of a touchy, feely family. The thing was I didn't ever visit my youth, I didn't enjoy it, so why would I think about it, or talk about it. As far as I was concerned, my life started when I was around 17, when I started building the persona. Along the way I had become a successful business man with a strong personality, leadership skills and the trappings that came with it. The persona I had cultivated to become 8 out of 10 happy. What I didn't want to talk about was the feeling I lived with. The one that said that at any moment it all might go tits up and I'd get found out as someone who had just been lucky, someone who had no business skills and all the possessions would be gone and I would be nothing. On top of this I knew (thought) people relied on my confidence and leadership to keep them in work and pay their mortgages. When I finished my story I was surprised to hear my BC friends say they had heard a story. To be honest I was also a little surprised and offended to hear someone say "bloody hell its hard work being you". As the week went on I found out more and more about myself and the relationship I had with my rather subtle script. I did still hold, at this point, the opinion that my life was good and 8 out of 10 still stood. On the Thursday I grasped BC, intellectually at least. It was all so clear and I couldn't have been happier with how I felt about myself and my self-worth. This was amazing. I was good enough. I did deserve the life I had.

However I also discovered something else about myself I didn't know.

I had harboured a genuine belief that I was a happy guy with a good relationship with myself and those around me. Perhaps I always held a little of my feeling back from people and especially those closest to me, but that was a good survival technique. Surely, not giving everything of one's self is common sense. When this belief was truly explored, I found a different and somewhat sadder truth. The biggest surprise was the relationship I thought I had with myself. I had built such a façade, a protective wall, that I actually didn't feel much. I batted away any feeling from my childhood, I'd protected my sensitivity by not letting anyone in, but in the process I'd let nothing out.

Now I got it emotionally.

Suddenly I could feel the warmth and power in a hug. I had always been ok with hugs, but I thought them to be more a benefit to the other person or just something some people do. This little thing was so powerful for me (it still is). I suddenly realised I hadn't felt the love that my wife was lavishing on me. Why, because I had held that little something back of myself. I had not truly given my heart to my wife, because I didn't know I had suppressed my feelings so much. In an attempt to be happy I'd lost the ability to feel. It upsets me now to write it, not because of any thought of lost time, but because I could have gone the rest of my life and have never experienced the feelings of love I was being given or could give.

8 out of 10. I kind of was 8 out of 10 happy, but boy that other 2 are massive. Just being with my wife can

be a fantastic feeling, spoons in bed are a feeling my cars and trinkets can't get near.

Within a week of completing the course my best friend and this wife came around to tell us they were expecting their first child. That wave of emotion was so amazing it scares me to think I could have never known what it feels like to share such a moment.

Life and wife after BC

Because we have both been on the course our relationship has benefited hugely. We forgive ourselves and each other when the script sometimes kicks in. I notice we don't seem to look "out there" for someone else to do the job of making us feel good.

Kris . . .

Life Beyond the Script . . . Helen Scarlett

I went along to the BC course curious but apprehensive, I'm not sure I really needed to go to BC as I have a very 'normal' life.

Day one, I had to tell 'my Story', My life was doing what I had been taught, to be respectful, law abiding, honest and kind, making sure everyone around me was looked after. I opted to be the last to tell my story as I had nothing to say that was really interesting! As people started to talk I realised that we had all experienced the same feelings, they were just brought about by different circumstances.

On Day 4 I had a major breakthrough. I went to the bathroom, I was washing my hands, I looked up into the mirror and I saw myself for the 1st time that I can remember. In fact I had never noticed what I looked like before. I went back to the group and told them and from that day I have never looked back and I realised that BC was something very special.

That day I saw an attractive lady, with a lovely smile, great teeth, beautiful eyes. I realised that I had never looked at me because I didn't like me. Prior to that day if I looked in the mirror I ignored my face, I saw an overweight body and that's all I believed everyone else could see.

Since BC it's all changed, I realised that, before I can help other people and make sure that they are ok, I have to be ok first. And being ok doesn't mean I have to have the perfect body nor do I have to put everyone else before me.

Throughout my life I have always believed I've had a hereditary problem, and that Problem was I was always going to be fat! I came from a 'big boned' family and sure enough I became overweight.

I believed that everything I had achieved in my life was because other people had been nice to me or felt sorry for me. I portrayed a very confident, fun loving person, yet underneath I was tied in knots trying so hard to make sure people would like me I was happy to be the topic of jokes because I believed that people liked me because I wasn't a threat to them. After all I was fat and Ugly !

Well things changed after a week on BC. I know I am a confident, fun loving person, but now it's real. I do like to make sure people around me are happy and cared for, but not at the expense of not caring for myself.

I struggled for years yo yo dieting, and every time I stopped, the little voice in my head told me I was a looser, I would have to be happy living as a fat person for the rest of my life. Then I reflected back on what Richard and Liz have taught me, that everything in my life is a choice, and if I'm not choosing then it means that my Script is controlling my life—I decided it was time to choose for myself.

I would be lying if I said that life is perfect now, that nothing ever gets me down, but the truth is that I now know that my life can be as good or as bad as I choose to let it be.

I don't spend all my time worrying about what other people will think of me. When I walk into a crowded room now, I don't try to be lost in the middle of a group of people so that I can't be seen.

I don't choose to believe that people only like me because I'm fat. In fact in recent months I have lost three stone in weight, I kept that weight in the past to secure friendship !!!!

At the time of doing the BC course I was working as a PA in a small business. I realised very quickly that it was not the job for me. On returning to work I reduced my hours because the environment I was spending my time in was dragging me down. Again, I used the option of choosing and I chose to leave. I've tried doing a few jobs since, but if I don't like where I find myself, I move on. But I don't beat myself up anymore for making a wrong choice, I choose to believe that every decision I make in my life is moving me towards my real job, and that's to help other people just like Richard & Liz helped me.

I've always believed that I had a good life, but now it's amazing. BC helps in every part of life, it doesn't make it perfect, but it gives you the tools to make your life whatever you want it to be.

I know that there are lots of people out there right now facing the personal challenges that I have lived with. I am now determined to share BC with these people to allow them to live the life they would choose, and I know that none of us would choose to live in the prison cell we lock ourselves into. So now I've broken free, I'm off to release a few more people . . .

Thank you Richard & Liz, you helped me to see what I was missing in my life and helped me to put it right . . .

What BC has done for me . . . Julie Stretton

BC is a life changing event. How do I know that? Because I am living proof and if you want to meet me or talk to me then get my number from Liz. BC has brought a zest for living that I would never have thought possible. I am at peace with myself and for most of the time with the world around me! I can laugh at myself and have discovered that what other people think actually belongs to them. Things I would have taken to heart and beaten myself up about before can be left behind. I need not carry them around with me day after day, and I can and do let things go! I am happy with who I am. I do not need to strive or pretend I'm more than me because I'm more than ok "I'm amazing". I know that no matter what happens, what life chooses to present me I will be ok. I have found happiness on this earth and I cannot imagine living any other way. I am not talking of religion or any magic but about a way of being able to choose how I want to feel. "That's not possible", I can hear you say . . . I feel bad sometimes because A or B or C has made me feel that way. Well I can promise you that it does not matter who you are or what culture or religion you come from, BC has no boundaries. It's for everyone old or young, black or white.

My story really begins the day my mother died. Until then I had a childhood typical of the early 60's although not wholly typical, as my mother for her own reasons was a Jehovah witness. I remember the day she died as if it was yesterday. Another child came into school and told me my father had died, I remember thinking it will be ok Mum, will look after us. Mum was the person who held our family together. She was kind, funny, sang, danced with us, taught me to knit and sew and crochet. I loved to lick the bowl when she made cakes and she made up wonderful fairy stories to keep us amused. She worked full time and yet always had time to make each and every one of us feel loved and wanted. I remember us sitting round her feet as she told us a story, thinking how wonderful and exciting it was going to be to have a new baby in the family. I was not to know then how different our life was going to be only a few months from then. My Dad was strict but he listened to us, would play on the floor with us, let me take things to bits and on a Sunday he always took us on a trip to the moors. We were a happy family.

I stood in the head master's office and I stood looking at my sister and two younger brothers. The baby was at home, he was three months old.

"Do you know?" the head master asked me.

"Yes" I said.

"Will you tell your sister and brothers?"

"Your Dad's dead."

"No, not your Dad, your Mum!"

I remember my whole world seemed to stop then. It came tumbling down, and life was never the same again. We left behind our toys and books and went to live between our maternal Grandmother and our paternal grandparents, and in between that with various aunts and uncles.

Dad's parents lived a Victorian life style 'children should be seen and not heard'. The time we spent with Dad was limited and most of the time he didn't even seem to notice us. The house always had a very gloomy atmosphere and only on odd occasions did I feel at home there. I do not remember feeling loved or ever being hugged there. We did not have enough food to eat, we had clothes that had seen better days and most of the time my shoes had holes in them and bits of cardboard stuck in the bottom to help them last longer.

I spent most of my weekends with my maternal Grandmother. I liked it there. It seemed like a happy house, and two of my aunts were younger than me. Although now I realise the things she said were meant to hurt my Dad, actually all they hurt were the five of us. I did not like the things she said, but I believed every word.

"Your Dad killed your Mum. He's too clever to be caught by the police".

"He's had lots of affairs. Your Mum was going to leave him."

"Your Dad does not care about you, he has never cared about you."

"It's such a shame, you could have done something with your life."

"If your mother had lived, things would be very different. You would have been able to go to college."

"If your mother had been alive, you would have had clothes and shoes and enough food on the table to eat."

"Your Dad hates you all. He always wished that you had not been born."

"You'll never do anything with your life."

When you're ten and you listen to someone you love, you believe the things they say. I hated my father more than you can imagine, but I hated myself more. I had argued with Mum the day before she died and blamed myself for her death. Although I always hoped in my heart that Dad loved me, he never did anything that proved this to be true.

At 14 I met my first boyfriend. I remember my first kiss. It was magical. The world stood still and when I was with him I felt really special. He made me laugh and I felt loved. He was my first "proper" boyfriend. My memories of that time are very special, but he decided to finish our relationship when his best friend told him I had kissed someone else. It was a lie, but I knew there was no point arguing and I watched him walk out of my life with a heavy heart. My grandma's words were true I was unlovable and worthless. I never felt good enough; I always thought that other people were better than me in every way. I always thought that no one could ever love me. I hated myself for not being able to protect my brothers and sisters from the world. I often went without food so they could eat. I even tried to commit suicide at the age of nearly 15 as I felt that the world would be a better place without me in it! I remember taking a whole bottle of pain killers and thinking everyone will be so much better off without me. My brothers and sister would have more to eat and well I would not missed.

My paternal grandma was angry and said: "what would people think?" I did not care, I just wanted to die and I hoped the ambulance would not get there in time. I felt totally worthless. My life was not worth living. The psychiatrist I saw was more interested in why I took a whole bottle of pills and not just six. I remember thinking why does the amount I've taken matter. Surely what matters is why I do not want to be here. No one ever asked me what was wrong or how I felt . . . And I remember looking after the people in the ward I was on and listening to their stories and deciding I really wanted to live no matter how bad life got.

It was around this time that I embarked on my first abusive relationship. He controlled who I could talk to. Looking back now I realise that there was no love in the relationship but at least I felt needed. It was when he hit me for the second time that I decided that was unacceptable and got a job 250 miles away.

I was 17 when I met my first husband Richard. He was 19. He had the most wonderful family and I instantly fell in love with his Mum and Dad and his brother and sister. I remember my first Christmas with them vividly and it still brings tears to my eyes.

After Mum died, my sister and I spent Christmas with my maternal grandma and my younger aunts who every year had presents piled high under and on the piano and on the sofa. Lots of exciting parcels with their treasures hidden inside them. Every year I used to think I've been really good this year. This year will be different, but it never was. My sister and I would open our couple of gifts of a pair of socks or tights and a small selection box. We would sit and watch as our aunts opened up piles of wonderful toys. It's strange but I was never jealous. I just blamed my Dad, as my Grandma said: "If he was any sort of Father he would not have let us all go without!"

My first Christmas at Richard's I had bought presents for everyone, and I remember coming downstairs Christmas morning, and his sister saying: "Come on Julie aren't you going to open your presents?"

She pointed to a huge pile of presents and I remember not wanting to open anything but just sitting amongst them with tears streaming down my face! When I finally did open them there were all sorts of wonderful things, including a sewing machine. His whole family made me feel welcome, loved and appreciated. Marrying someone because their family is nice, is not the best decision I have ever made. I was 19 when we married and he told me what I could wear no short skirts, no makeup. He told me who I could talk to and he held the purse strings. "You may have noticed a change in my behaviour recently. It is because I will, and should be, the boss when we marry."

If anyone showed me a letter like that now I would say run! But all I read into it was that he loved and cared for me! LOL I had my first child, a daughter, at 21 and my second child at 23. I loved being a mother, but while I was being a wife to him and mother to our children, he was having affairs. I turned a blind eye and when he said jump, I jumped. Inside I was still the worthless teenager that I had always been. It was easier not to see what was happening than to acknowledge it. I adored my children and on the outside looking in we seemed to have quite an idyllic lifestyle. We had a lovely house. Lived in the countryside a few miles from the sea. My children had everything they needed. I still did not spend any money on myself and wore his sister's hand me downs. We were not struggling for money, but he forbad me to buy things for myself, so I didn't. I still had shoes with holes in them!

That's the way it has always been in my life so I expected it. His family had no idea, and I never let on, and in a way I was quite happy being oblivious.

We moved when the children were 4 and 2 back near to his parents, he still continued to have affairs and I continued to turn a blind eye. I hated living in a town. I loved living on a farm and found the adjustment harder than I expected. I missed my friends and the lifestyle. Things took a turn for the worse when he ordered me to flirt with a neighbour. I cannot believe that I was so under his thumb that I did flirt with the neighbour, and, to cut a long story short, we ended up divorcing, and I ended up with the neighbour.

The grass is not greener on the other side, and when you are emotionally abused it's a pattern that continues, until you see the world through different glasses. My second husband was also emotionally abusive but I had made my bed and had to lie in it! All my friends said leave him but I made excuses about the way he behaved. Things would be ok for a few days and I would think it's not that bad and blamed myself when things went wrong. My confidence was nonexistent. He spent so much time telling me I was a useless wife, mother, lover. The list was endless. The best things to come out of my relationships are my children. My daughter is now 30 and my sons 28 and 17.

One day with Richard and Liz changed my life. The day was called Beyond Words and I realised that I was waiting for life to get better, not creating the life I wanted. I decided to put my all into my marriage and create something special. It fell on deaf ears and everything I tried to do was never good enough. I told him how much I hated the time he spent on the computer. He said that if I did not like it, I knew what I could do. I cried and remember thinking it will be ok, he will listen to me and he will want to save our marriage. The next morning, I remember the day vividly, I went down to print something off the computer for work and when I turned on the screen an adult movie was down-loading. I did not have to live like this! In that instant my life changed. Yes I could create something else, instead of waiting for things to get better. I was scared but felt strong, and he instantly knew something had changed when he saw me. I asked him how he knew and he said my whole body language had changed. I told him he was right and I was divorcing him. I always thought I would never manage on my own. The start of our divorce was very emotional and I blamed my husband for everything that had gone wrong in our relationship. He blamed me. He would not move out, but then neither would I, and things were fraught and difficult for us all.

Around the same time, Richard and Liz had created BC, I had seen the change in a good friend of mine, and I wanted to do the course but money was stopping me. Then I thought what the hell and booked on. Just after booking on the course, I got in touch with my very first boyfriend. We chatted and agreed that when my divorce was over, we would meet up. It was 30 years since I last saw him. After a few months we met up. I was very nervous as I had not seen him for 30 years. It was amazing, and we actually spent a week in a hotel! We live 450 miles apart. One day we might live together, or we might not, but we make the most of every moment we spend together. My memories of us as teenagers were also special to him. I still feel the same way about him as I did when I was a teenager.

I was nervous about dong the BC course. What if I was wasting my money? What if I got nothing out of it? What if . . . The first day, I made assumptions about everyone in the room. I was so wrong. When the week started and people started to tell their stories, it felt like we were all connected.

Telling my story was like having a weight taken off my chest. I felt lighter, I felt excited, I felt free. The whole week was amazing and life has looked and felt different ever since.

My divorce was easy. I realised that it was not all his fault. I had allowed myself to be bullied. The instant I had changed, he had to change his behaviour too. I was not a weak person. I was actually a strong person. I had been through lots of crap but putting it down as research has made so much difference. Material things did not matter and when he said "I want" I said "that's fine".

Four years on, Life is even more exciting and I will never again be the person who walked into the room on the first day of the course. I'm not really a different person, but I am the person that I was too scared to let the world see, I now know that I am being the best me I can possibly be. I have ups and downs just like you but I can change the way I feel about what happens in my life and can choose to accept the things I cannot change.

I notice the small things like rain falling off a leaf, the bee collecting nectar from the flower, the ladybird climbing up a blade of grass, the spider spinning its web, the stillness of a warm sunny day, and the beauty of the trees in the autumn. I can stand in the moment and appreciate what a wonderful world we live in.

I love my job. I work with teenagers who are having difficult times in their lives. Using the script with them is easy. It can change the way that they see things instantly. To see a child realise that they are perfect just as they are, that things can be different and do not need to stay as there are, is wonderful. Friends, family and colleagues are amazed at how much energy and enthusiasm I have for life, no matter what it throws at me!

I can accept the compliment, and choose to leave the criticism where it belongs—with the person who gave it. I am perfect just as I am and if I am quirky or you think I'm mad, that's ok with me, because, from where I'm standing, my life is pretty wonderful. "Get lost" I can hear you say! But I'm not saying my life is perfect, it's far from it. I'm a single parent who has just taken a £2000 wage cut. I have a teenage son who at 17 is studying for his A levels. My job is not 100% secure and there is talk that we might not have a job next year. My dearest sister was diagnosed with ovarian cancer stage 4 six months ago. The chemo could not be continued because the cancer had spread to most of her organs. Then she had a post chemo stroke and is now unable to care for herself. I have been in my "script" lots of times. When her consultant said the words "palliative care only" I cried so much. When out of my "script", I have given thanks that I have been able to spend the most amazing time with her. We have laughed, we have danced, and we have done things that would have never been impossible if I had not known about the "script". My brothers, my sister and I had a weekend together—the first one we have ever had since I left home. It was so much fun! I have helped her make peace with our Dad (something I did after BC). He is a huge part of our lives now. I took my sister to Spain to meet him and really talk to him, something she had never done. He spoke of his love for my mother and the pain he felt when she died and how he wishes he had been a better father. I wish that I could change my sister's future, but that is impossible. No amount of money could make her better. She will emigrate to heaven. I do not know when but I take each day as it comes. I only have power in this moment to enjoy life and that is what I choose.

I now realise the feelings, and the power to choose what I want out of life, are mine. The past is just the research I have done in my life already.

It has been very interesting. It has had its ups and downs, and it has had its sorrows and joys. I would not change it. It is because of my research, that I am the person I am.

Julie Stretton

What BC has done for our relationship . . .
Guy & Jacki Belchambers . . .

We have been together for nine years and have always considered our relationship to be close, loving and mutually respectful. Now with our knowledge of BC, we can look back and see how we could have supported each other in a far more helpful way. We have also realised that if others going through similar or even tougher issues had known about BC, many more marriages/relationships would not only have survived but would have flourished.

Our story . . .

She could go in to very dark spaces and he felt helpless and upset as he didn't know how to move her away from them. He had very destructive voices which encouraged him to "take the lazy and quickest" route. This flew in the face of how she would have approached the situation and conflict could easily arise. These incidents were unhelpful to their relationship. She felt she lacked confidence and he could be over-confident making social occasions not nearly as enjoyable as they might be. She was reticent to say what she was thinking, in a work or social situation, for fear of making a fool of herself with a tendency to hang back and wait to be asked. He found this to be annoying as he felt she was more than capable of shining in company. He, in contrast, could be over competitive and could appear confrontational, which distanced people from him. Secretly, he also "hung back" when in the company of his peers, not always saying what he felt. He believed he had led a "charmed and lucky" life but had no idea how this had come about or how he could use it as a model for others to follow. They both cared deeply when their partners and friends were in a troubled place but were often unsure how best to support them.

This is a précis of our own shortcomings as we saw them but could also be a recipe for many other modern relationships. And remember . . . we considered we had a good loving relationship—one of the best—but we also had a curiosity that there was something better.

We were privileged to meet Richard and Liz and learn about Broadband Consciousness and the Script three years ago. The five day course we attended together was a revelation and the start of a wonderful journey. We now have a deep and exciting understanding of who we truly are, not the imperfect beings that our Scripts had often hoodwinked us into believing we were. So what? . . . You might ask. The transformation—and it was life-changing—in our approach to each other, our work, our family and friends was profound. We thought at that time, three years ago, that we'd reached a wonderful peak of "being". Wrong! Like peeling away the layers of an onion, we continue to evolve and learn more and more about ourselves. Our relationship with each other and those around us grows and grows.

She rarely visits her dark places and when she does they are less debilitating as both he and she know it's her Script which has caught her off-guard. His voices are less insistent and are now almost his friends . . . He derives much pleasure from doing a job properly. She has confidence through finding her own voice and knowing that it was her Script that didn't want her to shine. Having dropped the bombastic mask he felt he needed to wear, he feels much more comfortable in his own skin and people warm to him and seek his counsel. They both know when the other is under the Script's influence and do not react irrationally to it. Disagreements are no longer "personal" and go away much more quickly—after all, it was just their two Scripts being destructive. There is far more understanding and support for each other.

The BC Coaching course has enhanced their practical understanding of how they might help others. People have noticed the change in them and are curious to know how this has happened.

We soon realised the beauty and simplicity of BC and could see how easily our Scripts can damage our relationships and our lives. We are now conscious that our Scripts will never leave us alone, always waiting for those "off-guard" moments—tiredness, drink and life's other excesses—to launch an attack on our happiness and self-esteem. We all need BC—our relationships with ourselves and others will improve beyond all measure. We can honestly say that BC has changed our lives for GOOD and in the most wonderful way!

Guy & Jacki Belchambers

The truth is the truth whether you believe it or not . . .
Hollywood Movie "City Of Angels"

CHAPTER FIFTEEN

Frequently Asked Questions . . .

So you've read the book and now you know about The Script . . . but what now?

1) Realise that you are not alone . . . everyone has a Script

If you or anyone else around you, is ever doing, feeling or saying things that do not make you feel good, and that given the choice you would not choose, then obviously you are not choosing . . . so what is? Now you know it's the Script. Just this understanding alone allows you to have compassion and forgiveness for yourself and others and what a difference that makes.

2) So what if you're still not certain whether you are in the Script or not, how do you know?

Remember you just ask yourself the best questions in the whole world to gain clarity . . .

'If you could choose, would you choose to feel the way that you are feeling right now?'

'If you could choose, would you choose to be saying what you are saying right now?'

'If you could choose, would you choose to be doing what you are doing right now?'

If your answer is "yes" then great, that means you are choosing, you're awake . . . so celebrate!

If your answer is "no", then you are not choosing, The Script is. You've just gone unconscious. Relax, just noticing this means you're awakening . . . remember "awareness is awakeness".

3) So when I know I'm in The Script, what do I do then, how do I get out of it?

Accept it, allow it to be ok. You will go into your Script and so will people around you, because the Script is like a habit that you have practiced throughout your whole life, it is reaction not a choice. Just notice, become curious to what is happening, become detached from the behaviour, become the observer of your life and what's going on.

The more clarity you gain about The Script, then the greater the patience you will have with yourself and others when they are in The Script and the easier your life will be.

4) So how long will I remain in The Script, once I notice that I'm in it?

That depends on how much you allow it to be ok that you are in it (acceptance = freedom). The Script relies on one thing (you not wanting to be in it), it requires your resistance to control you. The more you make you 'wrong' for being in the Script, when the reality is that, whether you like it or not, you are in it, the longer you will be in it and the more you will suffer when you inevitably find yourself there. Don't fight reality flow with it.

Remember you are a human being, not a human doing. Life is all about balance, like yin and yang. There is no up without down, no day without night, no doing without being. So whenever you feel a bit low on energy, a bit down, relax, it's natural. This is the time to just be . . . be still, be gentle, be accepting of how you feel and allow whatever it is to be ok. It's just like night time, relax and use it as an opportunity to take care of YOU!

When you have lots of energy and feel up, this is the time to do, to do new activities, to do your work, to do some good and help others. This gives us balance and purpose to both the ups and the downs of life.

5) How will knowing this help me in my life?

What is life but a serious of events, we can honestly predict your entire future . . . how has your life been up to now? We bet it's been up and it's been down, and your future will be exactly the same. There will be ups, and there will be downs, and that's all there will be. This means that you can't get life wrong can you? Imagine the relief, if you choose to accept this. How would it feel to know that you have not and cannot waste one moment of your life? You are either up or down, feeling good or feeling bad and all of that is natural and has a purpose.

6)   But surely the aim is to never be in The Script?

No the aim is to become aware of the fact that there is a Script.

And to know that The Script is not who you are . . .

And to notice when you are in The Script, and allow that to be ok, remove the resistance. Feeling not good is a natural part of life but suffering is optional. It's our resistance to what we are feeling that causes us to suffer.

It's all about increasing your level of self awareness and allowing it to be ok, whether you are in the Script or not. How can you ever know if you really love yourself?

You see, it's easy to feel good about being you when you're up and doing great but the real measure is how you treat yourself when you are down. That's what really demonstrates your unconditional love for yourself. When you still love and accept you, no matter what you are feeling.

Of course it's natural and alright to prefer to be out of The Script but not to the extent where you beat yourself up, if and when you find yourself back in it. We love our children and our family whether they are feeling good or bad. It's time that we applied this unconditional love to ourselves.

Do you learn by others' mistakes or do you insist on making your own? . . . Richard Wilkins

CHAPTER SIXTEEN

Conclusion

Remember I told you that throughout your life you will either be in The Script, meaning you're not choosing, and the result of this is that you feel bad

Or you will be out of The Script, meaning you are choosing, and the result of this is you will feel good.

The difference now is that you know both of these are not only alright but necessary for balance and contrast in your life. Now that you recognise this, it allows you to feel good about feeling bad, can you believe that? More importantly you can now feel good about being you, no matter what you're feeling or what's going on in your life. You now can separate you from both of these. You are not your day and you are not even your feelings, you are far more than that. This is the completeness and wholeness that BC offers. You now know that you are not broken and you don't need fixing, there is nothing wrong with you and there never was.

This inner contentment is what you and most other people have been searching for in their life. You have now found what you once thought was missing. What a gift. So, all we ask of you is that you also pass it on, just like we have passed it on to you. You now have the most precious gift that you could ever give someone. What could stop you from sharing it? Only one thing and you know what that is . . . that's right, The Script. Will you dare to consciously choose and go beyond it? We hope that you will because every time you hold back someone loses out.

CHAPTER SEVENTEEN

If You Like The Book, You'll Love The Course

This may be a little book but it contains an absolutely massive message. As I said it has been created from our hugely successful 5 day workshop 'Broadband Consciousness.

This is just a little taster of how we raise people's consciousness on the course through increasing their level of self awareness. Broadband Consciousness . . . literally does what it says, it takes your consciousness "broadband".

The course has a 100% success rate to date but don't take our word for this, check out our School for Super Heroes at our website www.theministryofinspiration.com and watch the videos of our Super Heroes explaining in their own words exactly what Broadband Consciousness has done for them. Or contact us by email at mail@theministryofinspiration.com If you could choose to see yourself as an ordinary person or to see yourself as a Super Hero, I know it's a tough call but, which would you choose?

Now, Ask Yourself . . .

What Script are you passing on by your own behaviour?

Is it what you would Choose? If not . . .

You now know that means the Script is in control

So if you could choose . . . **what would you choose?**

Now, go and be who you "choose" to be . . . **and keep practicing making conscious choices!!!**

Remember "You are a real life Super Hero just pretending to be a human being"
So dare to Fly High!!!

I look forward to hearing from you . . .

With love . . . **Elizabeth**

22593621R00123

Printed in Great Britain
by Amazon

CONTRACT

MURDER FOR MONEY, THE DEAD WANT THEIR DUE

SIMON SPURRIER

CONTRACT

MURDER FOR MONEY, THE DEAD WANT THEIR DUE

The right of Simon Spurrier to be identified as the Author
of the Work has been asserted by him in accordance with the
Copyright, Designs and Patents Act 1988.

Quotations from 'Fear and Loathing in Las Vegas; A Savage
Journey to the Heart of the American Dream' by
Hunter S. Thompson (Vintage, New York, 1973)

First published in Great Britain in 2007
by HEADLINE PUBLISHING GROUP

First published in Great Britain in paperback in 2007
by HEADLINE PUBLISHING GROUP

1

Cataloguing in Publication Data is available from the British Library

ISBN 978 0 7553 3590 9

Typeset in Garamond by Avon DataSet Ltd, Bidford-on-Avon, Warwickshire

Printed and bound in Great Britain by
Mackays of Chatham plc, Chatham, Kent

HEADLINE PUBLISHING GROUP
An Hachette Livre UK Company
338 Euston Road
London NW1 3BH

www.headline.co.uk
www.hodderheadline.com

To Nadia, Pam, and both Johns. I wish I'd
known you better.

And to Sherrie and Ian: the best in all the world
at what they do.

Acknowledgements

For all their help and support with this novel, I owe my deepest gratitude to Tracey Spurrier, David Couch, Chiara Warne, Stephen Dow, Roland Brass, Peter George, Alice Tarleton, Chris Stephenson, David Swanson, Jeremy French (and his highly knowledgeable mother), Frazer Irving, Steve Roberts, Jamie McKelvie, Ben McCool, James Smith, the wonderful staff at the Elgin on Ladbroke Grove and the Bailey in Highbury, Luke Clarkson and everyone at Wellington College, Tharg the Mighty and the flexible-deadline folks at *2000AD*, and all the wonderful people of London who make research so easy.

Special thanks to Rachel Calder and Piers Blofeld, and above all to my inestimable parents. I owe them everything.

Interview Room 2

This sort of guy, the way he jangles his keys, you just *know* he's sexually frustrated. This sort of guy, if this was in a bar, he picks at the corner of his beer label and peels it up till it rips. He flips cardboard mats off the edge of the table and tears them without thinking. This sort of guy, if this was in a bar, he eats complimentary peanuts when he's not hungry and jiggles his left foot up and down like a street drill.

Today and here and now, this is not in a bar. Where this is, you've got to assume it's underground. This place, with the guy and his keys, with the woman prodding me along from behind, the thing is: lack of windows. The thing is, strip lights, meaty walls. Cables and pipes on the inside.

This place, you've got to assume that thing with the air, that *stillness*, that heaviness, it means we're buried. You've got to assume it's rock and soil behind every breeze-block, worms and moles headbutting at concrete. You've got to assume, somewhere, there are stairs going up.

This place, when you shout out loud, eats up the echoes like soundproofing. This place, down here, everything is migraine-noisy.

So these two goons, this man and this woman, these two pinstriped nightmares in smart worksuits and polished shoes, these two fashion-corpses with name badges and matching socks, with jangling keys and shoving hands, they lead me to a door that says 'Interview Room 2'.

Heavy-arsed hinges, hardcore locks. Opening, it groans like a whale.

The funny thing is, seriously, I have no idea how long I've been underground. Down here you've got to assume they turn lights on and off at the same time every day. You've got to assume they feed you three times during Lights On, and they're not just messing with your head.

They could, you know. Disrupting diurnal rhythms. Fucking with your circadian cycles.

The funny thing is, underground, until these two robot-suits, these dead-faced smuganauts, these paid-to-be-grim authority machines, until they came and fetched me from my cell, I hadn't seen another human being since I arrived.

Whenever that was.

Given why I'm here, you have to wonder what sort of sick bastard ends up in Interview Room *1*.

Down here, underground, these clockwork thugs, these law-chimps, these smarm-monsters, they cluster round and do that shove-in-the-small-of-the-back thing. This is like you've seen on American police shows. This is propelling me out of the corridor and through the door.

'Sit,' the guy says. The guy with perfect teeth, this sexually repressed gimp, this floppy-haired public-school disgrace to the gene pool, his name is Jason Durant. It says so on his badge. I recognise him from somewhere, and I think maybe he visited me in hospital. I can't be sure. I don't know how long ago that was.

He doesn't look like a Jason.

He looks like a Paul, maybe. Or a Jim.

Or a Sam. He looks like a Sam.

Scratch that. What he looks like is an arsehole.

In Interview Room 2, if you want to know, there's a smell. This smell, it's from every school hallway you were ever in, every doctor's waiting room, every public toilet, every terminal-patients-only-easywipe-walls-AIDS-zombie-in-the-corner hospital ward. This smell, it's something to do with magnolia paint and breeze-blocks and linoleum floors. It's something to do with cheap detergent and plastic chairs and forgotten urine and Confused Old People, et cetera et cetera.

Listen. That smell, seriously, what it's mostly to do with, just so you know, is this: a complete, one hundred per cent lack of hope.

I'm sitting in a plastic chair. Not *on* it, you understand. It's that kind of chair. Down here I'm sitting without any handcuffs, without a light in my face, without a packet of cigarettes and without a mirror.

I expected a mirror. A big one.

'You're Michael Point?' asks Jason a.k.a. Jack a.k.a. Jim a.k.a. Sam. This is from the other side of the table, with him and the woman facing me. This is him still fiddling with his keys in his jacket pocket.

I expected a mirror, a big unnatural one-way-glass mirror, because where else will the sergeant stand to watch? Or the little guy, you know the one, with wide-rimmed glasses and old-style recording gear? And a clipboard. In movies, he's always got a clipboard, that little rat-man.

There's *always* a mirror. Only, look, not in Interview Room 2.

'Call me Mike,' I say. 'Aren't you going to record this?'

The thing with there being no mirror, also: there are no cameras.

And Jason, all sexually frustrated, all hitching curtains of hair out of his face, he looks across at his colleague. Her name badge, it's sort of hard to read on account of being right next to her boob. I keep getting distracted. Her name badge, I think it starts with an 'A'.

Jason says, 'Yeah. We're recording this. We're recording everything.' And he waves a hand, like maybe I'm an idiot for not noticing the cameras and microphones poking from the walls. Like maybe only a complete fuckwit would ask a question like 'Aren't you going to record this?' Like maybe out of all the pond slime that's sat in my seat, across the table from him in Interview Room 2, no other stupid moron has *ever* voiced such a twat-brained query.

Only I still can't see the cameras and microphones.

'So, Mike,' he says, and he smiles. I told you already he has perfect teeth. 'Why don't you tell us what you do for a living?'

And I figure: fuck it.

So I tell him.

Chapter One

Today is Wednesday. Today I'm delivering pizza.

Yesterday I was a minicab driver.

On Monday . . . let's see. On Monday I was busy. On Monday I was a delivery man. Also, a jogger. On Monday night, I bought groceries and walked them back and forth outside this gigantic grey apartment block. Up the street. Round the roundabout. Back down again. Monday was hardcore.

Already I've had three different careers in this town. I only got here on Sunday.

This could be anywhere. This could be Bristol or Birmingham or Brighton. It could be Edinburgh. Maybe Norwich, maybe Guildford, maybe Exeter. Maybe this is Cardiff or Southampton or Bradford or Swindon or Liverpool. Nottingham, even.

Get a pin. Fetch a travel atlas of the UK, flip open to any page. Jab that puppy in there. Anywhere you like, maybe that's where I am. Maybe that's where I'm delivering this pizza. Maybe that's where, yesterday, I sat out in the car park and waited for my fare.

With pizza delivery, the clothing is important. Don't try to emulate one of the big chains. Not Dominoes or Herbies or Papa John's. You choose one of those, you might bump into another employee, which, let me tell you, is awkward.

The one place this isn't, the one place this couldn't be, is London. I don't work in London.

This is what you could call a Rule.

For the record, this is a town called Bracknell. But, really, truly, it could be *anywhere*.

Pizza firms like red. They like blue. They like baseball caps and Aertex shirts. They like name badges. Also bumbags for tips and change. Also chewing gum. Chewing some chewing gum is a good idea. Apart from the name badge and the gum, you can pick up the kit from a charity shop for a fiver. The name badge, you make yourself.

Bracknell is what happens when a capital city runs out of room.

Bracknell is what happens when London has been bombed to paste by the *Luftwaffe* and needs a place to lick its wounds.

The way I look at it, Bracknell is the twentieth century's urban carcinoma.

Also, check out Milton Keynes. Also, Hatfield, Peterborough and Harlow. Corley. Northampton. These places are all what you might call secondary tumours.

A tumour, which the Americans spell without a second 'u', is a patch of cells that don't want to stop. A tumour is your basic cellular workaholic. A tumour is cell division gone wrong. A tumour is where your body gets impatient. A tumour is evolution on speed. Abnormal or morbid growth, the dictionary says.

This is a metaphor. Bear with me here.

The gum, you buy at a local petrol station. This is important. Being seen, being recognised, is important. This isn't about stealth. This isn't about wearing black and bursting through windows. This is about misdirection.

Abseiling off the roof? Fine. Cool. Very Hollywood. Very stealthy. But how the hell did you get up there? Huh? You think Mrs Gibbs in flat 3A, on her way out to the bingo-rama, is going to smile politely at the balaclava-wearing ninja as he wanders past on the stairs? You think that evil shit of a dog, the one being taken out by Mr and Mrs Mudharki from 5C, the one on its way down for an evening crap in the car park, is going to wag its tail and dribble at the spicy aromas of Mr Suspicious-looking-SAS-wannabe as he sprints on by? Shit, no. He's going to bark.

Yap.

Whatever.

The answer is pizza.

Sometimes you get a tumour wrapped up in a layer of fat. Like a snowball, only greasier. Sometimes the tumour can't keep growing, on account of having nowhere to grow to. So what it does is relocate. It 'seeds'.

This is called metastasis.

The gum, by the way, is just for appearances.

Think of that fat, that white capsule of soggy shit, that surrounding, suffocating bundle around the tumour, as suburbs. Think of the fatty layer as street after street after street of identikit houses with identikit cars. Think of that grease-thick spooge as two point four kids, stable middle-tier managerial job, firm Christian values, keep-your-perversions-in-the-cupboard Johnny Everyone.

A city, like, say, London, can't grow when it's wrapped up in fat. It's got to relocate. Start a new colony.

Welcome to Bracknell.

The upshot is, Bracknell has no old buildings. Bracknell has no local history. Bracknell might as well have been dropped out of an army helicopter, prefab.

Insert slot A in shopping mall B. Score along the jagged pedestrian-path, then fold.

In Bracknell, the stones have no sense of weight. In Bracknell, there's not much to respect. In Bracknell, everyone's what you might call equal.

In Bracknell, equality is like suspicion. Everyone's eligible.

In Bracknell, you want to avoid the stares and glares, you drive a minicab.

You deliver parcels.

You go for a jog.

You buy groceries and walk them home.

You deliver pizzas.

On the way up to the eighth floor, I nodded at the old lady. On the way up, the dog smelled the pizza and wagged its stubby little rat's-arse of a tail. On the way up, I smiled and said hi to the mutt's owners.

I said hi to the girl in the petrol station when I bought gum. On the way up, I'm chewing it.

These people, maybe, will remember me. It's important to be polite.

On the eighth floor, flat 8A is empty. Mr Whatever-the-piss-his-name-is, with the steroid-shoulders and the moustache, he works evenings.

On the eighth floor, flat 8C is empty. Little Miss Single-parent makes a point of heading out with her kid every evening. Two hours, sometimes three. My guess is, swimming lessons. Piano lessons. Cinema. Junk food. Ice skating. Bowling.

My guess is, your-daddy-left-us. My guess is, he's paying maintenance and she's spoiling the kid rotten. My guess is, it's none of my business.

On the eighth floor, flat 8B is not empty. On the eighth floor, I use the pizza box to jam open the lift. On the eighth floor, I rummage in my bumbag. In America, these are called fanny-packs.

There is no money in my bumbag.

In my bumbag there are several bits and bobs. There are two narrow rods, which look a little like hacksaw blades. There are two pairs of flesh-coloured latex gloves.

On the eighth floor, in flat 8B, someone is watching TV. I can hear the *EastEnders* theme tune.

In my bumbag there are two matchboxes which do not contain matches. They rattle a little when I shake them.

EastEnders is a soap opera about a community of miserable, melodrama-prone men and women living in a miserable, mythical part of London's East End. Remember the tumour thing? The East End is Bracknell's spiritual home.

In my bumbag there is a fixed-barrel Ruger Mk II .22, with a disposable silencer which I made myself. It's easier than you might think.

I also made the pizza-company name badge, which says my name is Kristoff. My name is not Kristoff.

The two rods which look like hacksaw blades – guess what? They're hacksaw blades, filed away in interesting patterns along each long edge. One is called a torsion bar. The other's an insert bar. A more effective lock pick you will not find.

In the matchboxes are spare bullets, just in case.

I'm not here to deliver pizza.

Interview Room 2

It's important you understand how simple this all is.

Back in Interview Room 2 – remember that? – I'm telling Jason Durant and his scowling partner, hey, it's simple. I'm saying, there's no mystery, no hidden agenda, no deep-rooted social psychosis. There's no Freudian psychoanalysis bullshit, no externalised self-loathing manifesting as destructive tendencies, and there are no – no – *no* strings attached.

What I'm telling them is: it's nothing personal.

What I'm telling them is: It's. All. About. The. Money.

It's like my personal little mantra.

'Have you ever heard', I ask them, 'of George Bernard Shaw?'

This is fidgeting like maybe I could use a smoke. I don't smoke.

I say, 'He was a playwright.'

They look like maybe they already knew.

'So?' the woman says. The way she's sitting, with both elbows on the table, it makes her blouse sort of ruck up in between each of its buttons, like a mountain range with its valleys fastened down. I shouldn't be staring at her blouse. I should be Answering Questions and Paying Attention.

The point is, I can see her bra. In Interview Room 2, I feel like a twelve year old catching a look.

Her saying 'So?', that's the first time she's spoken.

'George Bernard Shaw', I say, oh-so-very-fucking-matter-of-fact, 'said the people who get on, they're the ones who get up and look for the . . . the *circumstances* they want. And if they can't find them, they make them.'

I'm pushing the envelope labelled 'Smart Arse' here. I memorised that line years ago and I still misquoted it all to hell. I memorised that line in some dusty schoolroom with the same grey-yellow walls and the same fruity hospital ward detergent stink as Interview Room 2. That line appealed to me even then.

Borrowed wisdom. Give it a go.

Try casually dropping some double-clever quote into conversation, like you thought of it yourself. Try getting around the fact that people write things differently to how they say them. Try blagging your way through a discussion where everything's already been said before, and everyone knows it.

'What's your point?' the man says. Jason Durant. With his eyes, he's telling me that he doesn't give two self-removed foreskins for George Bernard Shaw, socially viable life-goals, or whether I, his captive, his piece-of-shit prisoner, his man-in-the-crosshairs, feel stupid or clever.

Jason Durant, I do not like one little bit.

The thing with borrowed wisdom is, pretty soon there'll be nothing else. Pretty soon it'll be that you can't say a single thing that hasn't been acid-etched on someone's gravestone before.

One day we'll run out of music.

You borrow too much wisdom, you forget what originality is.

The way I see it, at least I *told* them I was quoting from memory.

I still haven't looked at the woman's name. Her name badge is two inches from the lacy edge of her underwear.

'The point *is*,' I say, staying focused, 'I've always known what I want.'

'And what's that?'

I smile, like our boy Jase must be thick not to get it. He pulls that shit on me, I pull it on him. This is karma.

'Money,' I say. And I smile wider. I smile and tell him things are oh-so-much, *much* simpler when what it all boils down to is basically deep-rooted personal avarice.

The woman's bra, that tiny matinée-performance sneak-peek it's treating me to, it puts me in mind of a doily. The kind you'd maybe put a drink down on, in some mouldering old lady's home.

Speaking of which . . . 'Could I have a glass of water?' I ask.

Doilies are to old age what pornos are to adolescence. Cats too. I think of old ladies, I think of doilies and cats. I think of so much cat shit everywhere that little old Beryl, or Maude, or whoever-the-hell-she-is, she's slipping about in it like a drunken slag at an ice-disco. I think of little Agnes or Mavis or Ethel, I think of her stumbling about, smelling of soap and piss and cat food, and I think of her brittle hip popping right out. Then it's ambulances, operations, artificial joints, cyborganic grannies, blah blah blah.

Doilies and cats. Doilies and cats are to ancientness what erections are to puberty.

You've got to wonder how much money the excretion habits of the feline population of the UK is costing the NHS.

Me, I'm more a dog person.

In Interview Room 2, as the woman huffs and stands to fetch a drink, as her blouse creeps open a fraction more, as the perfect camber of a perfect breast sears itself across my eyes, I'm remembering how it felt to be twelve.

If these guys ask me to stand up any time soon, I'm in trouble.

And look, I know. A grown man shouldn't be struggling against the disobedient behaviour of his prick in response to nothing but a frilly bit of underwear.

It's just that this is probably the last real boob I'll ever see, and if you don't mind, I'd sort of like to enjoy it.

Chapter Two

In Bracknell, the tall man in flat 8B on the eighth floor, the man who weighs too much, with receding hair and a microwaved curry planted neatly on his lap, the man who *pissed someone off*, his final message to the world goes something like this: 'Nuh.'

Apartment blocks are a pain in the arse.

For a start, you've got your noise issues. Breeze-block-cavity walls will stop a .22 hollowpoint without trouble, but what they won't stop is a big sod-off bang. You'd better hope the neighbours are watching John Wayne flicks with the volume on *full*, or you'd better *know* they're out.

The neighbours are out. Trust me.

I know they're out because I was here yesterday. Yesterday I was a minicab driver, remember? On Monday, the day before, I was a delivery man. Also a jogger. On Monday night, I bought groceries nearby and took them home. Several times.

I've clocked up more minutes on the pavement in front of this big ugly building than the pigeon-shit that calls it Home.

This building, this stack of shoebox cages with packing-crate window boxes and *eau-de-urine* stairwells, I know like the palm of my hand.

The neighbours are out. Take my word for it, OK?

CONTRACT

This tall bastard, he's so into *EastEnders* he doesn't even hear the door-lock go. This tall bastard, he doesn't even notice I'm here till the trigger's halfway home. This tall bastard, his curry is so bright with artificial colours it glows. It hits the rug between him and the TV like a monosodium-glutamate supernova. This tall bastard, his eyes bug out like an over-inflated sex dolly.

The neighbours are out, *but*. But down a floor, up a floor. That's a different issue.

Vertical neighbourhoods. I told you already, apartment blocks are a pain in the arse. With apartment blocks, if you want to shoot someone, maybe right in the face, or in the heart, or just maybe in the leg, whatever, then you're going to need some specialist equipment.

This tall bastard, he says, 'Nuh,' and the curry's already seeping into the shag pile.

To construct your very own homemade silencer, you will need:

a square yard of strong and flexible matting: fibreglass for preference
a foot of ¼-inch car-brake line
a powerful epoxy resin, with the mashed-up-horse hardener
a drill rod or cut dowel to fit the inside dimension of the barrel snugly (this is important)
a foot of 1½-inch PVC piping with a pair of end caps
six small wood screws
a couple of sandpaper sheets
two ¼-inch, or smaller, drill bits
razor blades, elastic bands, masking tape, rubber gloves, a spare afternoon and somewhere private

This is all in books. This is all over the Internet like acne. Borrowed wisdom. Here's one I made earlier.

Good for four hundred rounds, give or take, and your upstairs-downstairs neighbours needn't know a thing. This tall bastard, his brains look like clay mixed with cat food.

I always think of spitting at times like this. A glob of saliva hitting a hard surface. A hand slapping a book on a desk. Bubblegum popping.

Spwk-spwk-spwk-spwk

That's what your silencer does. It's not like in the films. It's not like the popular Hollywood impression that a muffled weapon makes the same noise as an industrial crop-sprayer.

Fffi-fffi-fffi-fffi

That noise is what could affectionately be called wrong.

I shoot this gangly pituitary freak four times. Twice in the head, twice in the chest. He dances, he bulges out his eyes, he slaps back into his sofa like liquid, and he deposits his primary yellow curry like a sacrifice at my feet.

On the TV, generic EastEnd fishwife number 1 shouts at generic EastEnd fishwife number 2. This is the bit where distractions count, so I'm glancing at the soap-opera action, I'm checking out the pictures on the wall, I'm looking through cheap Venetian blinds at Bracknell. I'm looking at everything except the cooling puddle of meat on the couch.

He looks sort of comfortable.

Maybe.

With apartment blocks, the second problem is *ooze*. If you leave your kitchen sink to overflow, sooner or later Mr

Patacharia downstairs gets himself a runny ceiling. Sooner or later he's going to wake up in the night with something dripping on his forehead, like piss out of plaster.

And yeah, maybe he switches the light on, and what's falling on his head is water.

Maybe it's not.

The point is, if you shoot someone in an apartment block, you'd better be able to stop him from bleeding everywhere in a hurry.

Option number one is this: stick the tall bastard in the bath.

Mr Tall-where's-the-back-of-my-head-gone-bastard, he's a shower person.

He does not have a bath.

'Shit.'

Rugs. Rugs are good. You wrap a guy up like a fajita and maybe stick him on the sofa. Keep him high. Let your basic everyday gore splatter go brown and crusty before it even gets to the carpet. Think of this as a premature coffin. Think of this as a scaled-up drip tray from beneath your expensive gas barbecue. Think of this as a pancake for a tall, balding, crispy shredded duck.

Think of this as sleeping bags for the dead.

While I'm looking for a rug, I'm thinking: 240lb? 250lb? Big-boned, mate.

Mr Tall Bastard, he has no rugs.

'Shit.'

Let me tell you, you want to make sure you don't get manhandled by some unscrupulous mercenary Dispenser of Human Termination after you're gone? Here's a tip: cancel your gym membership.

For picking up a body – an *unpiloted* one, I mean – see also: lifting a sleeping cat. See also: wrestling water.

Shifting this tall bastard is going to be tough. Shifting this dead, bleeding piece of ex-human is going to make me wish I'd brought along a woodsaw. I hate killing fatties.

A duvet. A duvet is as good as any rug to catch drips. Improvise. That's the name of the game.

On the carpet, the tall bastard's brain-spooge is mixing with the curry sauce. Suddenly, I'm back at nursery school, mixing yellow and red to make . . . to make a sort of bubbly, swirling brown, except all speckled by bits of skull.

This tall bastard, this man-monolith, this tree wannabe, guess what? He has no duvet.

He's a *sheet* man. Sheets are no good at all.

'Shit.'

So I'm standing over him and swearing, and I'm feeling the time slide by like I'm on a rollercoaster, and I'm wondering what his face looked like *before* I put two .22 hollowpoints right through it, when it happens.

This tall bastard. This tall bastard *moves*.

Oh yeah . . . the hollowpoint thing.

What you do is, you widen the cavity at the top of each round with a pillar drill. If you do this too fast and you're lucky, maybe you'll just lose a finger or two.

Curiosity killed the cat, right? Well, impatience killed the hitman, but only after it was through pulling out his teeth and crapping in his mouth.

This tall bastard, when I say *moves*, I don't mean the whole 'contracting muscles' thing. I don't mean the moaning, farting, soiling-your-dead-self thing you see in films. Just for the record, that stuff doesn't happen as often as you'd think.

I mean *moves*. I mean his eyes open. There's not much left of them – all gristle and pus – but, oho yes, they're definitely staring.

Not just staring, you understand. Staring at *me*.

I move, *they* move.

'Shit.'

So you've drilled the hole bigger, and now you've got a bullet which is basically a syringe. Conventional wisdom says, fill it with poison. Take a small lump of melted wax and seal the hole. Load it into a clip, and hey presto! Instant lethal injections. Makes sense, right? That way the client's dead whether he's K.O'd or winged. Only, here's the trick: what *is* poison?

This tall bastard, this messy piece of offal at my feet, he should be the happiest corpse in the world. He should be out like a light. He should be crotching through fairyland, whether I shot him in the head or the leg. This tall bastard has enough unnatural fluid clogging his veins to O.D. a dinosaur.

For the record, there's a hole like a volcano where his forehead used to be. For the record, poison or not, this tall bastard should *not* be moving.

He's moving. He's watching me, the bastard, and oho yes, oho yes, I am getting freaked.

Poison. One drop and you're dead.

Listen: if you've ever been food poisoned, you know it's not that simple. One man's instantly lethal death juice is another man's hospitalisation-followed-by-kidney-failure-and-dialysis. One man's screaming, choking anaphylactic shock is another man's mild headache.

Listen: the seeds of the castor bean plant *Ricinus communis* can be broken down into two separate poisons. Ricin is a potent cytotoxin. That means your cells go to hell like salt in the bath. RCA is a potent hemagglutinin. That means your blood gets sticky like treacle and all your veins burst in the back-up.

All in books. All on the Internet.

This tall bastard, he blinks like his eyelids are still even *there*, and blood pours out of his mouth like he's gargling on soup.

This is very irregular.

A single milligram per kilo of bodyweight of either RCA or Ricin will kill you. The common castor bean plant is easy to get hold of. This, ladies and gentlemen, is the dream poison.

Provided you don't mind waiting two days for your client to apply boot-to-bucket. Provided you don't mind convulsions, abdominal pain, bloody diarrhoea, tail-diving blood pressure, rhubarb rhubarb rhubarb. Unpleasant, to be sure. But not exactly *hasty*.

This tall bastard, you don't get much hastier than two holes in your head and two in your chest. He hasn't got the hint.

What you should be looking for in your poison *à la mode* is: supply, effectiveness and compatibility. You've got be able to *get* the stuff. It's got to kill quickly – like maybe faster than it takes to get some poor gutshot goon to the police. And it's got to kill *everyone*. Healthy, sick, immuno-deficient, veggie, vegan, lactose-intolerant or not.

And here's the problem, people, honestly: there really isn't that much in the world that'll actually *do* that.

Thallium rat poison: takes hours. Easily detectable due to gastrointestinal symptoms and paresthesiae of hands and feet. If it's detectable, it's treatable. All in books. All on the Internet. Borrowed wisdom.

Sodium Cyanide. All but impossible to get hold of. Trust me on this.

Compound 1080: same problem. Only place it's still used as a commercial pesticide is New Zealand and, unless you have the time to nip round the world every time you get a job, that's where it stays.

Hydrobromide of hyoscine. Rare, expensive, ineffective.

Then you've got your basic home-grown old-wives' favourites: mistletoe, jasmine, yew, daphne berries . . . All as effective as papal porno.

This tall bastard, oh god. This tall bastard, he's got nothing on the back of his skull. It's all gaping open like wet lips, like someone cut open a womb, like a rotten watermelon. It's broken like an ostrich egg with spaghetti inside.

This tall bastard, shit . . . this tall bastard has a hole through each side of his chest. His shirt started off white. Now it's pink.

This tall bastard, let me make this perfectly clear, he's *dead*.

He opens what's left of his mouth, and – seriously, I'm not shitting you – he talks.

'That', he says, through so much blood and paste that it hangs off his chin, 'was out of order.'

For the record, his eyes burn red. For the record, his fingers are too long.

Arsenic, right? Everyone's heard of arsenic. Death'll take

two hours or two days, depending on how good you are at breathing puke and hanging on to your kidneys. Either way, 2.5 mg of Dimercaperol every four hours for two days, and welcome to a Brave New World of witness parades, artists' impressions, court testimonies and a whole lot of trouble for yours truly.

Arsenic can kiss my arse.

This tall bastard, he tries to stand up and calls me a cunt. His left eyeball hits the floor like a water balloon, and behind it, where it came from, there's only brightness and red.

You kill people for a living, you get used to seeing some nasty shit. (Actually, that's not true. You get used to *ignoring* some nasty shit.)

But when it's thrashing about and calling you names, when it's oozing over the carpet like Niagara Falls, let me tell you: it's sort of tricky to ignore.

With poisons, I spent a long time thinking it through. It's not like you can just test things.

What I did was, I went to Birmingham.

This tall bastard, he crashes about like he's having a fit. He moans and shouts and stamps his feet, and all the time his face is falling off. All the time there's gore swinging under his bottom lip.

This tall bastard, his pointy little fingers slap my shoulder as he swings round, and suddenly I'm back with it. I've been in shock, maybe. I've been a rabbit-in-the-headlights. Maybe.

This is realising I can't be dreaming, on account of how I'm still awake.

Tall bastards don't stand up and call you a cunt when

they're dead. It's not normal. It's reasonable you're going to be alarmed when it happens.

Only now he's slapped me one round the face. Only now I'm back in charge. I'm thinking it through. I'm cool as a cryogenic cucumber. Scratch that. What I am is this: *Aware.*

Aware, say, of the red puddle round his feet. Aware he's stamping and moaning so loud, he's oozing so much, he's bashing the walls every time he moves, that – listen – *someone is going to notice*. Stealth is out the window.

Vertical neighbourhoods. Shit, shit, shit.

In London a gram of white heroin – this is clean shit, straight from the joyous, liberated farmers of Afghanistan – comes in at around £80. In Glasgow, maybe it's sixty, maybe it's forty. Depends who you ask. Depends what you want. Depends who you know. In Birmingham, it's £25 a gram.

This is a tangent. Bear with me here.

This tall bastard, he's getting better. He's got a new eye. The hole in his head just closed up, and the slime on his chin, it's un-sliming. You ever seen one of those gross-out Mondo documentaries, where they get the stop motion camera to record a decomposing human body? The collapsing head, the rictus grin, the peeled-back lips, all of that? If you've ever seen one of those, then play it in reverse. That's what's happening to this tall bastard.

He looks like a balloon, re-inflating. He looks like a jigsaw, finishing itself off.

What he looks like, most of all, is a 250 lb exploded ogre putting himself back together, piece by piece.

He staggers forward, and I'm moaning in my throat. He thumps into me – jelly bear hug and *shit* there's blood *every*where – and my hands are round his neck. It's warm and slippery and he's gasping, and the hole in his head is gone.

I've been in this room five minutes already. I should be long gone. I should be clean. I should be the *Fonz*. Instead I'm late, I'm covered in blood, I'm panicking, I'm about to piss myself if this zombie doesn't get out of my face, doesn't stop shouting, doesn't stop *living*.

Stealth. Yeah. Yeah, right.

Your average heroin user gets through somewhere between 50 and 80 milligrams a day. You want better statistics than that, good luck. Different supplies, different metabolisms, different purities. Hardened user or beginner? Intravenous? Intramuscular? Smoke it, eat it, stick-it-up-your-arse?

You ask Mr Holy-shit-where's-my-life-gone addict how many times he sticks a hollow tube into his flesh and pumps it full of rendered Diamorphine, how much he uses, how pure his supply *is*, and what you don't get is numbers. What you don't get is hard facts.

What you get is 'Whatever it takes.' What you get is 'Why do you wanna know?' What you get is 'Leave me alone.'

Not much is precise, with heroin. Same as poison, see?

Listen. What's precise is this: if you're a first timer, 500 mg will kill you in minutes. If you're a frequent user, 1800 mg will microwave your brain and detonate your heart.

Conventional wisdom says I should fill my hollowpoints with poison.

Heroin's cheaper.

What I'm getting at is this: this gangly bastard, this overweight piece of human cholesterol, this stringy wedge of fuckwitted *big*, four bullets means he's carrying 4000 mg of pure skag.

China White. Aunt Hazel. Chiva. Smack. Brite.

All dissolved in lemon juice. All mixed up in citrus squeezings, which keeps it liquid. Heroin, normally, you've got to heat it up to dissolve it.

In bullets, heat is a stupid idea.

This tall bastard, he's choking and staggering. He's grunting and shouting, though the bleeding's stopped. He's a slippery bastard, and I'm strangling him like he's done me wrong, like he's my *enemy*. I'm dancing with him, and every footstep goes *squitch squitch squitch*. I'm wedging the heels of my hands up under his wattles and I'm squeezing like he's made of sponge. I'm waiting till his face goes red and he dribbles, and I keep squeezing. This, for the record, is the most awkward kill I ever made.

You want to know what awkward is? Awkward is buying £500 of pure Afghan Poppydust from a smug Brummie kid when you don't know the latest street slang, the latest crap euphemism.

Number 4. Mud. Hero. Polvo. Dog. Al Capone. AIP. Whatever.

This tall bastard, I shot him four times. This tall bastard, he's had a hundred quid of top-notch nastiness mashed into his blood.

This tall bastard, he should be the happiest stiff in the world.

Dead people shouldn't be allowed to come back to life. They shouldn't be allowed to regrow the bits I blew off. I feel very strongly about this.

It takes five minutes. It takes using my *hands*. This has

never happened before. It takes wringing his tall neck until his windpipe crackles.

He goes down and I watch. I watch and I'm daring him to try resurrecting again. I watch maybe ten minutes, just waiting for the Lazarus skit. The messiah thing. The on-the-third-day-bullshit. Tall bastard.

At some point I realise I've gone mad.

At some point I realise it's a hallucination. Obviously.

What I'm thinking is: be cool. What I'm thinking is: go through the motions. Pick up the spent shell casings. Take a shirt from his cupboard, put it on. Bundle the bloody rag you wore on the way up into a sports bag from under his bed, and take it with you. Disassemble the gun and replace it in the bumbag. Switch off the TV.

Wipe your face down.

Don't look at the body.

Don't look at the body.

Close the door behind you. Pick up the pizza in the door of the lift.

Don't run. Never run. Just walk. Nod and grin and walk.

What I'm thinking is: get the fuck out of there.

Interview Room 2

In Interview Room 2, the woman is back with my water. She's brought it in a little paper cup. You know the kind, with the conical bottom, so either you drink it quick or it soaks through the recycled paper and wets your crotch. Crap little paper cups like this, the one thing you definitely *can't* do with them is smash them on the table and use the jagged edge to fight your way to freedom. Crap little paper cups like this, they're an insult to dramatic convention.

The woman, she sits and passes it to me without a word, and I'm thinking that at some point, maybe while she was out of the room, she's adjusted her bra or her blouse or whatever. Suddenly the secret little peek hole is gone.

Bugger.

When she came in, the door squealed like a pissed-off pig.

Right there, maybe she notices me copping a look, because suddenly she's doing this thing with her eyebrow – just one of them – that makes her look like she's had a stroke and only half her face is working.

For some reason I'm suddenly wanting to say 'sorry'.

Just in case you didn't catch it, I kill people for money. Ogling tits should not be the end of the world.

I let it go. The way to look at it is, down here, down

amongst the rapists and pimps and murdering crackhead sickos, she should be used to it by now. I shift my eyes as if I'm looking at her name badge.

Her name is Anna.

Her partner, Jason Durant, this coiffured Aryan Nazi pigshitter, who, from the look of him, *definitely* is a part-time pervert bondage freak, has more pressing things on his mind. I've just finished telling him the Bracknell story, hand movements and all, and his mouth hasn't closed yet. Crap little paper cups like this one, it turns out they're perfect for miming a strangulation, and my fingers are still wrapped around the soggy cone, held up for the moron to see.

His eyes are bugging out like someone pushed a tyre pump up his arse.

'So . . . just to . . . *reiterate*,' he says, like it's for the benefit of the recording devices I still can't see, 'you admit to murder?'

I choke on my water, like in a cartoon, and it's only down to some quick lipwork that I don't douse these two goons, these two bright-eyed bastards, with spittle-spray.

He's just heard me tell the sodding Bracknell story, and he's fixating on *that*?

'Didn't you hear me?' I say. 'The bloke came back to *life*! He had holes in him. Fucking *holes*. Blood everywhere.' More hand movements, another twitchy eyebrow from Little Miss Disapproval.

Jason Durant, this leering little arsewipe in a pinstripe suit, he waves it all aside.

'Murder,' he says, clinging to it.

He thinks I'm mental.

He thinks I'm cerebrally diseased. He thinks my frontal

lobe is an ulcerous mess with damaged synapse pathways and degraded neural connections. He thinks I'm gaga. He thinks I'm some sort of hallucinating psycho.

Ahahaha.

'I'm serious!' I say.

'Murder,' he repeats, like he's an icebreaker cutting through frozen bullshit. He counts on his fingers. 'Then you've got breaking and entering, possession of a grade A narcotic, firearms offences . . .'

Un-be-fucking-lievable.

Some people, people like our man Jason Durant, you just *cannot* hold a rational conversation with. Some people will listen to the best joke in the world then correct you on your grammar. Some people will read the best book ever written, then complain about the title.

Some people will sit and listen to you saying how, shit, look, a dead man, an actual *dead piece of meat*, sat up, bled everywhere and called you a cunt, and *still* go off on one about the most ridiculous and irrelevant detail they can latch on to.

'Murder,' Jason says. 'You're paid to kill people. Correct me if I'm wrong.'

If I wasn't down here in Interview Room 2, or outnumbered, or recovering from being shot twice by an Armed Response Unit, I'd fucking *have* him, that squinty-faced perfect-toothed slice of mullet-haired wank.

'That', I say, 'isn't the point.'

The woman leans forward.

Anna, she-of-the-perfect-tit, smiles.

'Tell us the point, Mr Point.'

29

Chapter Three

From the block of flats in Bracknell to the travel lodge off the M4. Rental car. Window down, music playing, make-sure-people-notice-you-loud.

Hard stuff. Sledge hammer bass-beats you can't buy from a high street store. This stuff, this angry sonic leprosy, this eardrum-bleeding throb, you have to track down to backstreet empires of LPs and unlicensed porn. This is to 'dance' what atomic war is to A Frank Exchange of Views.

I fucking hate dance music.

Oom-chkka-oom-chkka-oom-chkka

The gun I've stripped down to parts, like a platter of shrapnel in a plastic bag on the passenger seat, and every couple of minutes I'm losing another chunk out the window; bouncing off into the bushes. The sports bag with the bloody shirt, it hits a ditch and sinks. Maybe someone will find it. It doesn't matter. It's all *his* blood.

I lose my shoes five miles from each other. Footprints, sticky blood, chewing-gum residue. These are the forensic expert's closest friends. I have spare shoes in the glovebox.

The music, it makes the air shiver like a shotgun.

I'm trying not to think of dead fingers flexing. I'm staying away from imagining eyeless sockets oozing open. I'm keeping my mind well away from zombies using the c-word.

Oom-chkka-oom-chkka-oom-chkka

It helps, a little.

You don't listen to this shit for relaxation or enjoyment. You don't listen to this shit because it makes you want to dance. You listen to this shit to stay focused. To get aggressive.

To make sure people remember you.

Oom-chkka-oom-chkka-oom-chkka

Slow down through towns. Let them see you. Make eye contact. Smile.

Gangs of pre-pubes in mock-Burberry caps and puffer jackets. Nu-Goths on street corners, trench coats and blue-rinsed hair. Indies and townies and slags.

Teen clans. The tribal nations of youth.

Let the little fuckers hear you coming.

Oom-chkka-oom-chkka-oom-chkka

Hard guy in a car. Loud music.

Oom-chkka-oom-chkka-oom-chkka

Smile. Smile. Then drive off.

They'll remember you, maybe. But they'll get it wrong.

The gun, every time I stop at traffic lights I'm running a rat-tail file down the barrel, losing the ballistics marks, changing the signature. At the motel I lose the stock in a rubbish bin out the front. From here, you can hear the motorway like a pulse.

This is how it feels to be a blood clot, watching other cells rush by.

This is how it feels to be a foetus. Muffled life.

I like motels.

At the reception I smile at the walking acne-monster on the desk and pick up my key.

'Have a good evening, Mr Rose.'

My name is not Mr Rose.

'Thanks.'

Smile. Smile. Nod and grin. Let them remember you. Let them see you.

Does this defy the logic of criminal mentality? Does parading about with my face hanging out get me a black mark in the *Big Book of Villainous Stupidity*?

No. No, no, no. Ladies and gentlemen, let's hear it for the human brain.

(Crowd goes wild.)

My pal, the evolved organic computer. My good mate, the Human Face Perception Mechanism. This is a Borrowed Wisdom phrase. This is a dull-science term which means 'the ability to recognise people around you'. This is the one tentative shambolic little feature of the human calculator that stands between me – a sicko antisocial mercenary bastard – and anonymity.

In my motel room, I wipe down every surface for prints. To the best of my knowledge I haven't taken off these uncomfortable latex finger-condoms in here, except to sleep and wipe my arse. To the best of my knowledge, my good friends in the British constabulary do not have my fingerprints, photograph or DNA profile on record anyway.

The thing is, nobody ever got caught being *too* cautious.

The thing is, all you need in this job is assiduousness and anal retention.

See also: a certain moral lassitude.

The thing with the human brain is, you learn its weaknesses. You learn the flaws and oversights of that lump of spaghetti sloshing inside your skull, and in my line of work you can meet people's eyes and smile, smile, smile. And never be seen again.

In my motel room, I pack carefully. More haste, less speed. My mother used to say that.

Anyway.

In my motel room, I'm checking there's nothing left behind. I'm checking there's nothing in my bag that shouldn't be there. I'm checking the bed's made and there's no reason for the maid to pay special attention. No curious stains on the sheets. No pubes in the plughole. No calling cards. No giveaways. Nothing memorable.

The hardworking individuals of the Thames Valley Police are renowned for their enthusiasm, integrity and devotion. It would be remiss of me to make life too easy for them.

The thing about the Human Face Perception Mechanism is, Photofits. The thing is, Identikit. The *new* thing is, E-fit.

Sign of the times. Stick an 'E' in front of any word: instant modernity.

E-Fit stands for Electronic Facial Identification Technique. What happens is, Little Miss Braces in the petrol station, little Miss Pregnant-by-the-age-of-fifteen, who sold me chewing gum before I killed the client, who smiled and nodded and grinned, she sits down with an officer maybe a week or two after the event, and she tries to make my face.

Little Mrs Whoever-the-hell, the one with the stinking dog who passed me on the way into the lift, on my way to shoot her upstairs neighbour through his face, she scrolls through nose after nose, chin after chin, smile after smile.

Little Mr Acne, the minimum-wage junkie working the motel lobby, who really does believe my name is Mr Rose, he points and he clicks, he drags down a new cheekbone, a new eyebrow, a new hairline.

These are the agents of my destruction, and I've smiled at every one of them.

It's all computers, these days. Used to be artists. Used to be chunks of photos on cardboard, put together like jigsaws. Used to be transparencies, one laid on the next. New methods, new techniques, same problem: people don't see faces. What they see is features.

I check out of the motel at nine o'clock that night, though I've already paid for the extra night. This is one of the many measures I take in my working life which I – cutely, don't you think? – refer to as JICs. Just In Cases.

If the pus golem thinks it's weird, walking out early, he doesn't say so. Maybe he'll remember it when the PCs slide by. When the forensic units set up white tents in the car park. When he's asked the same question thirty times.

This will maybe happen days from now. This will maybe happen weeks from now. Depending on how well I've covered my tracks, this will maybe not happen at all.

Even so, every siren on the motorway, every sonorous banshee wail in the distance, my heart's heating up like the music in the car.

Oom-chkka-oom-chkka-oom-chkka-oom

Driving, the leather seat feels like dead skin against my back, and already I'm seeing clotted wounds, ruptured meat. How many cows die to upholster a car? How many vegetarians wear leather shoes? How many butchered heifers stand right up, brains sliding from spike-driver holes, and call the slaughtermen cunts?

Not many, I'm guessing.

I peel off the false moustache before the sweat unsticks the glue.

When the fine men and women of the nipple-headed-uniform seek witnesses to this most heinous of crimes, when they've done the piece-by-piece search and found the chunks of gun lying in fields, playgrounds, pisshole-ditches, laybys, bus lanes, gutters, hedgerows, when they've tracked me from the murder scene to my motel, when they're pursuing their enquiries with vigour and enthusiasm, this slab of sticky horsehair gumming up my top lip will become my own personal Jesus Christ.

Out of the motel. Lights and motor sounds, like an arthouse installation.

Oom-chkka-oom-chkka-oom-chkka-oom

I switch off the stereo. Out here on the motorway, on the carcinogenic arteries of the motorised nation, there's no one to impress with angry beetz. The road has its own rhythms. The road breathes traffic and shuddering air.

Back to Features. Let's role play.

You meet a guy in the street. Let's say he bumps into you. Let's say he's using a crutch and his aluminium almost-leg whacks you one in the shin. Let's say this embittered walking injury is so monged on his own inferiority he doesn't even apologise. Let's say this self-hating bastard is so down with wallowing in disability he doesn't feel the need to act like a civilised human being.

Give him a good hard glare. I dare you. I know how it works. Ooh dear, he's disabled, you *mustn't* say anything, poor soul, blah blah. Cut that shuffling troll to shreds with razor blades out of your eyes, then walk on. Feel better? Karma fully restored?

OK. So. What did he look like?

Was he a caucasian male with oak-brown hair going to grey central parting and the first vestiges of a bald patch, approximately sixty years old, five feet ten inches, wearing a shabby blue raincoat with a rubber hood and toggles, a chequered shirt and black corduroy trousers with faded patches over the knees, one polished black work shoe and one waterproof sock, whose face comprised an unbroken Greco nose, sallow cheeks, brachycephalic brow, disproportionately thick lower lip, minor gap between front teeth, hornlike black eyebrows in unsettling incongruity to the hair, attached-lobes, shadowy bags beneath both milky-blue eyes, and a pronounced scar running between his colossally flared nostrils and the upper edge of his mouth . . .

Or was he a miserable old shit with a crutch and big fucking hare-lip?

On the motorway between Bracknell and London I wind down the window and listen to the air drumming inside the car. The speedometer's touching seventy on the nose – maybe a fraction over – and I'm slipping right down the middle lane. This atmosphere-percussion, this *thwub-a-thwub-a-thwub*, it's keeping me awake like a hammer to the head. Dance music has nothing on this.

On the motorway, I'm reaching up and scratching my face. On the motorway, a little piece of my face comes off.

This may sound obvious. This may sound like the first thing you learn at your weekly classes in *Vicious Murder 101*. But you know what?

It works.

Photofit, Identikit, E-fit, these things will never

accurately create an image of my face. Why not? Because people don't see faces. They see features.

Let's pretend I come back to Bracknell in a month. I'm seeing here-there-and-everywhere posters. Pieces of white rain-damp paper taped to lamp-posts, with POLICE NOTICE in big serious letters, and a man staring at me with big, serious eyes.

MURDER.

This man, his face is an amalgamation of bland features borrowed from the memories of those who created him. He is an E-fit gargoyle meant to look like me.

HAVE YOU SEEN . . . ?'

This man, he has a moustache like a slug on his lip.

CALL THIS NUMBER WITH INFORMATION.

This man, the girl in the petrol station couldn't *exactly* remember his eyes, but, wait, weren't they . . . weren't they a little like that guy in that film, you know the one, with the hyperintelligent killer crabs and the sex-scene on the submarine?

This man, the woman on the stairs caught a good look at him, and his chin put her in mind of a schoolteacher she once sucked off during detention.

This man, the spotty goblin in the motel would swear blind he got those eyebrows right, bang on the money, stake-his-life-on-it, and if maybe they have echoes of his mate's girlfriend's dad's drinking-buddy's brother . . . coincidence, right?

On the motorway, a police car streaks past me, all whirligig lights and breathless sirens. High-speed disco.

On the motorway, my heart goes *thwub-a-thwub-a-thwub* along with the air in the window. Ohoyes, even me. Even now. Sweaty palms. Dry mouth like gargling on cocaine.

Trying not to think of dead men and bloody faces and strangling hands.

The cop pulls off at the next junction.

This man, the man in the poster, the staring bundle of poorly segued features and bulging eyes, it's like someone took a marker pen and drew a big black blob on his cheek.

REWARD FOR INFORMATION LEADING TO THE ARREST OF . . .

This man, it's like a pigeon took a shit on every single sheet of paper, right below his eye, up against his nose.

This man, he has a mole.

A *big* mole.

You know the kind.

This is the kind with three or four little hairs – little wiry bristles, like Satan's pubes – poking from the top. The kind no one would *ever* be rude enough to mention, would *ever* dare refer to in conversation. The kind where people keep accidentally saying the word 'tweezers' in the middle of sentences, then going red.

The kind where all you want to do is sharpen a teaspoon and *dig*.

The kind where you try, you *really really* try, to make eye contact.

The kind you just can't help god-fuck-it-all looking at.

On the motorway, this lump of latex with three toothbrush bristles jammed in the top, it bounces on tarmac and smears. It's eaten by the rear view mirror, which gobbles all things.

Thanks for everything, little buddy.

The other parts of the disguise are interchangeable.

Wigs, moustaches, beards – this is hardly clever-clever stuff. This is hardly *The Saint*. It needn't look good. It needn't look professional. All it needs is to be *memorable*, because the more that people remember the hairline or the goatee or the dodgy tattoo or the gold tooth or the old scar or the new scar or the nose ring or the birth mark or the big revolting heinous crime-against-mirrors mole, the less they remember the rest of the face.

These are called Unusual Identifying Features. They should be called Can't-Remember-Anything-*Except* Features.

I've been in Bracknell since Monday. Today is Wednesday. Different hairstyles, different beards, different glasses. These things are the background. The geometry of the face that my friends in the witness stand use as their guidelines. Like a child with a crayon, always fighting to stay inside the lines.

You fill your face up with features, what's left is this: bland, forgettable space.

This man, who perhaps will glare from soggy posters all over soggy Bracknell in perhaps a week, perhaps a month, he is not me.

The motorway goes on.

On my mobile phone is the number of a woman named Sally. Speed-dial, all cued-up, ready to ring. At the next service station I'm pulling in to place the call, waiting for the pickup, listening for her voice. Organising. Trying not to get too excited. Then it's back, out on to the motorway, air throbbing in the window, heading for the light-pollution on the horizon. London, Ariadne's Café, Sally, and home.

Contact 20

DAY: Wednesday.

TIME: 9.23 p.m.

LOCATION: Ariadne's Café. Second table from right, facing window (dark outside: reflection on glass – no view). Now alone drinking coffee.

CONTACT REASON: Usual story. Mike spent day working, called my mobile on way home after job. Wants to meet up, chat, always here. Eats burgers and cheese. Talks, <u>strengthening bonds</u>. Important: checking all in place, final look @ his routine. Suppose you'd call this the final stretch – start of it, anyway. Crept up on me.

OBSERVATIONS: Right now, drinking medium-warm coffee. Crockery in café new, replaced since last visit (2 weeks ago, see <u>CONTACT 19</u>), but already chipped, discoloured. Currently: eavesdropping on conversations @ nearby tables. Lorry driver complaining re. cyclists, two builders grumbling about late shift, lucky tramp with tea and bacon roll (lucrative day somewhere) pestering flat-hunting student. Ariadne talking to herself by till.

CONTRACT

Place stinks of chips mixed with cigarette smoke and over-brewed coffee. Makes hair greasy. Writing this as quickly as possible – don't want to stay.

Michael left fifteen minutes ago. Him today: skin paler than usual. Hair cropped (cut since last time?). Jacket sleeves too short, make hands look clumsy. Overall: awkward inside himself (teenager without spots). Today wearing faded jeans (boot-cut), new trainers, black shirt (short sleeves, grey buttons), cheap black jacket. Dressed to go out (usual routine – goes to club after meeting me. Where?). Cheeks too pink from hot shower and scrubbing, but in general: looks ordinary. Apologised several times for smell of burning. Said he had to get rid of clothing – 'Messy job'.

New observation: every time he drinks = sluuurp. Very annoying; once noticed, can't unnotice. Dimples in his cheeks suck in, chin goes tight, eyes close . . . sluuurp. Came close to getting up and going. More froth in his coffee than normal – didn't seem to notice. Maybe made slurping worse? Either way, not necessary – poor manners.

NOTES: M still talking like he's got an autocue – no pauses, no hesitations, little chunks, glib bollocks, platitudes and bad jokes. Been trying to surprise him with questions, to see if I can make him say 'um'. No luck. Nearest I came: asked about day's 'Messy job'. No explanation; big frown. Looked shaken? Said: 'All turned out OK – that's what counts.' Changed subject – very good at deflection. (Note: need to stay disinterested/ uncomfortable re. his work.)

Conversation: mostly humdrum. Usual obsession with trivia, eg: comments on Ariadne's Café, cholesterol, abattoir scrapings in burgers, fat content, hormones in livestock etc. Says nickname for cafés like this = 'Greasy Spoon'. In America = 'Choke 'n' Puke'. Says: 'Both are ironic. It just means people keep their expectations low. It's the only way to make sure you're never disappointed again.'

M looked pleased with himself (likes to feel competent at chitchat). Doing my best to look spellbound, smiling and nodding. Eventually decided to up stakes, ask <u>searching</u> question. Need to feel like I can go deeper; complete trust.

Reminded him of several times he's mentioned his 'plan'. Big deal to him, told him I was curious, wanted to be distracted from my own boring Nothing. Told him: self-distraction = new self-destruction = new self-improvement. Made him giggle. Two normal people, sharing homemade wisdom. Could see him relax. Deep breath, then speech. Longest he's ever spoken in one chunk. Sounded rehearsed. Not verbatim, but gist goes:

'Most blokes, this trade, they've got a' – pauses for false thought – performing! – 'a plan without a capital P. Mostly a vague thing. A sketchy idea of what and where and when and how. Maybe they'll quit and open a bar. Maybe retire and spend their days playing golf. Dominoes. Maybe just booze themselves silly and die of cirrhosis.'

(Barely stops to breathe here. Note: discussing his

*job more casually now. Think he's more comfortable
with me knowing what he does.)*

'If not cirrhosis, sclerosis of the liver. Maybe
pulmonary tuberculosis, or . . .' *(Etc. etc. Don't
remember all of it. Random trivia: very <u>him</u>.)*

'The point is, most blokes in this trade, it never comes
off. Quitting, retiring, getting away. They say . . . "I'll do it
tomorrow", then the stupid fucks take one more job.'

At this point, he sits back with a smile and says:
'Tutankhamen thought he'd live for ever too.'

*(Tangents, platitudes, smug bullshit, etc. Means
nothing to anyone, makes him feel knowledgeable.
Pleased with himself – can see it on his face. Wonder
how many times he's told all this to a mirror.)*

'That's not for me, ending up like that. Wasting away,
never getting out. So . . . I've looked into it. Researched,
made notes, done my homework, you know? Worked it
out.'

*End of first chunk – pauses (slurps coffee). Makes it
all sound scientific: data not opinion, scholarly
investigation. Self-important; body held upright, eyes
darting side to side. Has a habit of looking away (e.g. at
floor, ceiling, his feet, fiddling with fingers etc.) then
remembering to make more eye contact. All forced.*

'That's how I know,' *he says. Encouraging my
involvement – wants me to ask:*

'Know what?' *(Keeping him moving, but also:
<u>colluding</u> in story. Good way of bonding, and all at <u>his</u>
instigation. Excellent progress.)*

*Makes him put his hand in his pocket and bring out a
square of paper, folded and sellotaped shut. Puts it*

43

down on table and sits back. Very strange. Eye contact.

Says how uncomfortable he finds London, England, all of Britain. 'Stifling', he says. Rambles a bit – don't remember exact words. Not rehearsed, this section. Doesn't sound as convincing. Says his work has taken him all over the place, fidgets, fiddles, looks away. Ends up getting melodramatic, doesn't sound right.

'Everywhere I go, there're bullet holes and bodybags. You look at a map, little red drawing-pins all over the place. Those are little puddles of blood, spilling together. All along the motorways. Crashing up and down. Bubbling across the Severn Bridge, lapping over Hadrian's Wall, in between all the streets, gurgling closer.'

Doesn't look embarrassed by bad rhetoric. Genuine sentiment or fluff? Too poetic to be genuine, IMO. Self-delusion, deflection, dramatising himself.

'Only place the blood doesn't come is London. Like an island, sinking slowly. Lapping up at the shores. Only place I don't work. Won't work. Even animals don't shit in their own beds.' (Sits back. Sighs for effect, picks up coffee – sluuurp.) 'Problem is . . . Problem is, I fucking hate London.'

Fiddles with the piece of paper. Doesn't open it.

'On this . . . written inside, there's a number. I haven't looked at it in – oh, two years. But I know it by heart. It's the amount of money I need to Get Out. To . . . cover every possibility. For good. Fake passport – you know? A life of luxury – sun, sand, somewhere else. Doesn't matter where. Bikinis and waving palms. Coconuts and jetskis and barracudas and . . . sangria. Fishing trips – fuck it, I don't know.'

CONTRACT

(Looks away again. Very uncomfortable. Unconvinced and unconvincing. Maybe embarrassed by his own scheme? Knows it sounds naïve? On positive side: watching for my reaction closely. Obviously important to him – my approval).

'I wrote the number with the blue Biro from the cheap desk-organiser next to computer in my flat. I remember it very clearly.' *(All this pointless detail: why? Anally retentive? Or attempt to create a mythology? Legend Of Him? His idea of intimacy?)*

'This number, all you need to know about it is, it's big. All you need to know about it is, it has a bunch of zeroes and a pound sign. The magic number. The Get Out Of Jail Free card.

'One day I'll quit, and I won't ever fucking come back.' Looks pleased with himself.

Very exciting. Most he's opened up since CONTACT 1. And no awkwardness afterwards! Believe I'm finally integrated.

THOUGHTS/CONCLUSIONS/OTHER: Realising more and more: Mike = utterly defined by routine. Lots of time to himself – sits and festers in between. Pretends there's more to him, never has anything to say. After work needs someone to talk to (remind him he's human?) <u>spiritual handjob</u>. Always says 'Let's catch up' on phone, 'Let's meet in Ariadne's', but nothing to catch up <u>about</u>. Just wants company. Least he pays for his own burger.

Slurping reminded me of being married. Daniel used to slurp too. Mustn't let it get to me.

Last thing: @ beginning of conversation today, Mike said 'You look tired.' Felt uncomfortable: not supposed to be me under microscope. All fine, though: quickly realised he was only saying it so I would reflect the comment (i.e., 'you too'). Likes to feel someone notices, even if he has to signpost it. Naïve guile – unexpected.

Ariadne (café owner) keeps winking at us. Thinks we're together. Convincing illusion, then.

S

Chapter Four

This is an exercise, maybe, in relaxation. Winding down. De-stressing.

I fucking hate it.

This is, maybe, a ceremony. After every kill, a night of wild abandon.

First of all, the routine goes, I see Sally at Ariadne's. Call her up on the way home from doing you-know-what. First of all it's coffee and food and letting the adrenaline go away; letting the day simmer out the back of your head. The way I see it, this is colonic irrigation for the brain. Mental bum-soup. This is clearing out blockages.

With Sally, what happens is, we mumble and stare. What happens is, I guess inside we wonder about each other, and about the 'us' we never mention. I guess we wonder what the Us is in aid of and where it'll end. Maybe we wonder where it'll start. With Sally, mostly, I talk. Mostly she listens. Mostly we mutter and sit inside comfortable silences, and smile in the gaps, and repeat-laugh after every joke, like an echo of a dead giggle, to bridge the quiet chasing it.

Old people do this a lot.

Sally is unemployed not-bad-looking clever interesting and interested. Sally likes my jokes. Sally looks at me like it matters, and listens when I talk. I've known Sally since I was eighteen, give or take.

Sally is trained as a psychiatric nurse.

Before you ask, no. This is not how we met.

Listen, Sally and me, when we talk, she's Off Duty.

Sally is the opening tune on the *Just Killed Someone* album, and like all shit albums the best tracks are bunched-up at the start. It goes downhill. The routine is, first of all I see Sally, I get my brain-shit sucked out, I get my cranial-colon polished up a treat, then, when all the clogs are gone, I stand up and leave, and what I look for next is: sweat.

Preferably dripping off the ceiling. Preferably making *Jurassic Park* ripples in my drink with every bass-quake.

What I look for is expensive drinks and plastic cups and hot little rooms beneath cold little streets, with neon lights and flame-retardant upholstery and brain-retardant Choonz. All part of the routine. Sally then sound-abuse. Coffee then cacophony.

This is late into the night, early into the morning. This is where the *actual place* itself doesn't matter. This is my routine, and I hate it like nothing else in the world.

For the record, with Sally, I figure she's been damaged. I figure she's maybe a fuckup, maybe a victim. She's on benefits at the moment. She's out of work. I don't like to pry. With Sally, I figure she's quiet and cold just to keep it all at arm's length, and hey, ohoyes, that's fine. If you like. That's fine, and I figure she built this structure like a crab with a fresh shell, and now it's just another part, just another skin, and yes, yes, yes, that's fine.

It wouldn't be fair to judge her.

Crabs, for the record, shit out of their mouths and have blue blood.

Sally, I figure she has claws too, under it all, and the main thing is, listen: she's my friend. Don't laugh.

This routine right now, Sally is a new addition. Sally popped up out of nowhere six months ago, after I hadn't seen her for ten years.

The way I met Sally in the first place, that's a whole-other-story.

Here and now, look. A night of Forget it All, lost behind tinted-glass doors and steroidal bouncers. This is maybe a night of Let it Go, available at the price of entry and a torn-off raffle ticket to lodge your coat, if you dare, in the cloakroom. A night of acne-goons and braless tops and too-short-skirts and schoolgirls on the pull and fumbles in the corner and pills and cheap alcopops and music like the Last Days and sweat and salt and broken glass and . . .

. . . and you get the idea.

This is maybe a night of Go With the Flow, in bars and clubs with names made up of two juxtaposing words picked at random from dictionaries. Melon-Reef. Arctic-Frog. Sugar-Moon. Poetic-Engine. Fucking-Dismal. Soho, Shoreditch, Camden, Regent Street, Hoxton Square. What the hell am I *doing* here?

Maybe it's about impressions. Maybe it's about floors so thick with sweat and shit and spilt spirits you're walking on glue. Dance floors like cattle markets. Graffiti in toilets with a line for every occasion.

These are the Oscar Wildeisms of our times. These are the acid-tests of our civilisation. In a thousand years earnest archaeologists will dust these walls with fine sable brushes, and wonder at Lukey B's desire for ANAL CARNAGE.

Ask me why I'm here, and if I can hear your voice, I'll shake my head and shrug and go and find a different corner, or maybe I'll stay and talk. Maybe it depends what you look like, darling. Maybe it depends whether or not I'm ready to go back to yours.

Like, 'Do you come here often?' Like, 'Can I get you a drink?' Like, 'What's a vicious mercenary prick like you doing in a trendy but otherwise godawful place like this?'

Chat-up lines are the conversational equivalent of taking the scenic route.

Maybe I'm just here for sex.

Maybe.

I'm twenty-eight. I'm wearing a shirt and trousers and a vaguely smart jacket. I'm not smoking. I'm drinking lemon-bloody-ade. In the Sticking Out Like A Sore Thumb stakes, I might as well be a geriatric in an iron lung.

What I'm getting at is, I don't belong here.

What I'm getting at is, I don't *like* it here.

What I'm getting at is, just by being here I make the fuckos around me nervous.

I could have gone somewhere else. Theatres, galleries, wine bars . . . but it's harder to impress girls when they actually *care* what you have to say. It's harder to play it cool when everything you know is borrowed wisdom, when every opinion on painting X, sculpture Y or Installation Z, has been cut-and-pasted from the *Guardian*. Little Miss Arthouse, she can spot a fraud in under two seconds.

Here, I just stand and wait.

I'm not smart. I'm not quick. This is important. You

might think these were vital qualities in my rarefied profession, but listen: here and now, in this place, surrounded by wobbling flesh and product-glistening haircuts and designer trainers and cheap gold chains and imitation Rolexes and acne and toothbraces and young girls with old eyes and you get the idea, the less I have to speak the better. Here, no one could hear me if I tried.

Me and the DJ, we have this love–hate thing. Being here, this is maybe an exercise in self torture. Being here, my head hurts from the music. Being here, some slick-haired invertebrate is tonguing away at the open mouth of a disinterested schoolgirl next to me, left hand beneath her skirt/belt, right hand clutching his plastic pint like a lifeline. Standing there with her eyes open, watching her friends on the dance floor, she reminds me of a hippo. Mouth wide, breath steaming, waiting for one of those little birds – you know the ones – to finish picking ticks and scraps from between her teeth.

Hippos kill more people every year than lions, tigers and crocodiles combined. Those birds, they're either brave or stupid.

Somewhere, across the sea of bobbing heads and boob-tubes and chequered shirts and nipples like raisins, there's a bottle fight. Bouncers wading like herons through shit. Shouting faces with no voices. Someone spills a drink and laughs. A drunken slag slaps a drunken troll. The music volume rises a notch.

Being here, I *hate* it.

Being here, a girl throws me a look and pouts; jailbait seduction. Her hair's pulled back so tight her eyes are just slits, and all I can think is that if someone yanked her

51

ponytail hard enough maybe her face would split right open. I let her pass. I'm not ready yet.

Being here, the DJ says something into his microphone. It sounds like a porpoise gargling.

The hippo-girl gets bored of her dental inspection and sinks back into the water. The slick-haired tick-bird looks over at his mates and punches the air: another five points for the scorecard, another tablespoonful of someone else's spittle down his throat. Big guns firing hard.

If anyone ever wanted to ask me why I kill people for money, this would be a good scene to describe.

Why am I here?

Being here, this is maybe a subconscious way of punishing myself for my destructive lifestyle. This is maybe in order to resume karmic equilibrium.

Being here, this is maybe my way of reaching out to the masses.

Being here, this is maybe an easy way of getting a fuck.

Being here, honestly now: it's all to do with the alternatives.

Let me tell you, if I wasn't here, if I wasn't watching blondes, brunettes, redheads, like how I guess a hyena watches gazelles – waiting for one to fall behind – I'd be in my flat. I'd be in bed. I'd be lying there thinking through the day, waiting for sleep.

Listen. You work in an office, you maybe lie awake thinking *what did the boss mean when he said* . . . ? Maybe there's a rumour going round and you're *sure* it's about you. Maybe you fucked up a presentation and as you lie there – wishing your brain would switch off – you're remembering their faces, those bastards, trying so hard not to laugh at the upside-down profit chart, at the spilled coffee in your crotch, at the shambolic useless worthless never-leave-home-again piece of rancid executive waste that is You.

If you work in an office, that is.

I don't.

Been there, done that.

In this club, this double-barrelled abattoir called Cherry-Bomb or Badger-Mountain or Concrete-Clock or What-ever, you couldn't dwell on your day if you tried.

You couldn't envisage neat little bullet holes. Neat little crackles of smoke and sparks. You can't conjure in your mind the *spwk-spwk-spwk-spwk*, the homemade silencer, the clutch-ing fingers, the slack lips. You can't see, in your memories, eyes that maybe – *maybe* – throw you the tiniest accusatory stare in the second before they roll up into their sockets.

I come to Park-Mosaic or Tibetan-Mist or Sliding-Safari or Somewhere-Similar after every job I do. Every *normal* job. Every by-the-numbers-routine hit. Just to be distracted. Just to not think about it.

Today I was called a cunt by a dead man. Today I strangled a man to death – second time lucky – until his regenerated eyes bugged out and his tongue went purple and his neck . . . his neck went like popcorn under my hands.

That sort of thing will tend to leave you a little off balance. Trust me on this.

A girl in a white top and hotpants slides over, hoop earrings like hubcaps. She's got a feather boa round her neck, which is either tacky or ironic, who knows, and whoever it was told her she had legs good enough to flaunt was either being cruel or charitable. But she's good enough. Any other day, good enough.

But no, no no no no no, luv, I'm not ready yet, and when she tries to talk I'm ignoring, ignoring, walking away. Some other corner. Some other slag. Later.

Like maybe when I can look at her face and not see the tall man.

Bleeding, thrashing, cheeks bulging, bowels voiding, as he bites off his own lips and goes limp like fishmeat.

Just a hallucination, I tell myself.

Ahahaha.

So now it's two o'clock in the morning.

At some point the headache stops being a conscious agony and becomes just a component of the *experience*, like some double-clever undertone to the music.

Tension-type headaches, which are caused by sensory or lifestyle stresses, are easily treatable using mild over-the-counter analgesics like aspirin and paracetamol.

I don't use drugs.

By two in the morning the music is still an agony, but only in the same way it hurts to breathe, or take a step, or blink, or all those other things we do that should hurt but don't.

With brain-pain, listen: always the fear it's something worse. Cluster headaches, vascular engorgement, migraine, temporal arteritis. Reach for the Sumatriptan, Ergotamine, Stemetil, Verapamil, Fluoxetine, Amitriptyline, Methysergide, Nortriptyline, Naprosyn . . .

I don't use drugs for two reasons. The second is that their names sound like ancient Aztec gods, and the idea of those feathered weirdoes zapping about my head freaks me out. Five cc's of Ixtlilton, please, with a Cihuacaotyl hypodermic chaser and a Quetzalcoatl suppository.

CONTRACT

Gods and medications have a lot in common. Good in emergencies. They make you feel better about yourself and the world around you. Stop the pain. Habit forming. Indulge one every day, you're pious; indulge the other, you're an addict.

Same-same-but-different.

The main reason I don't use drugs is because I might not be smart, I might not be quick, but if you can't trust your own senses, what have you got?

By two in the morning, I'm ready to find company for the night. By two in the morning, when I'm keeping an eye on the blondes, brunettes, redheads, when I'm ready and in the zone and up for it, trusting my senses is the only way to wake up with dignity.

For the record, it wasn't always like this. For the record, with drugs, I've tried most things once, twice, enough. For the record, the last time I fell off the wagon was the day Sally reappeared. For the record, this was six months ago, give or take.

Sally and me, years and years ago, even then we barely knew each other. Sally and me, half a year ago was a second of recognition in a café, then chatting, catching-up, telling jokes. Her smiling. Sally and me, when we met half a year ago, there was Camden, dodgy dealers, cheap skunk, sitting by the canal, chitchat . . . a-whole-other-story.

Tonight, the agent of my ongoing mental distraction is a brunette. She's standing across the room, away from the dance floor, and though she's with friends she's not *with* them. This is because her attention is focused entirely on me. In places like this, on nights like this, stand in the corner long enough and you will never again sleep alone.

Provided your standards are flexible.

This girl, she's not bad looking. I'd describe her better, only here's the thing: by two o'clock in the morning, 'she doesn't repel me' is all that matters. 'She doesn't make me think of the Tall Man' is all you need to know.

And then there's a guy beside me, and I didn't see him coming, and drugs or no drugs, my senses have fucked up, and already I'm looking at him and thinking: *shit*.

Listen: this man, he does not *belong* here. This man, he does not *like* it here. This man, he makes the fuckos around him – that's me – uncomfortable.

He wears polished shoes, sensible trousers, a dark shirt and a black jacket. He wears a red tie. He looks like someone who came straight from a funeral, which he enjoyed.

That sinking feeling.

This man, anywhere else, he's a dealer. Rummage in his shirt for a Colombian wrap or a crystal twist. Coke, crack, smack, morphine methamphetamine methadone. This is the man who knows people. This is the man who can get your Ketamin. This is the man whose pockets overflow with PCP, mescaline, fucking *Salvia divinorum*.

Here, in Whale-Window or Peppermint-Jungle or Triptych-Yak or whatever the hell this place is called, all this man is, is a well-dressed shifty-looking motherfucker surrounded by drunken kids.

For a minute I think maybe I'm looking at a mirror. I'm not.

This man, all he is, is focusing his attention on me.

All he is, is either reading the wrong signals, or after something *other* than sex.

CONTRACT

The brunette has aborted her approach manoeuvre. Shit.

This guy, this smarmy bastard with his chiselled features and his black eyes, he grins. His teeth *glow*. This guy, he holds out a hand, and that solid lump of African Gold cluttering his wrist, sending X-E-L-O-R reflecting across my face, that's no counterfeit. This guy, he says: 'Good evening, Mr Point.'

Shit shit shit shit shit shit shit shit shit shit shit shit. J.W.A., Mike.

'It's morning,' I say. Play it cool. J.W.A.

He knows my fucking *name*.

Klaxons, foghorns, sirens, drowning-not-waving.

'J.W.A.' is a made-up acronym. It stands for this: Just Walk Away.

Normally, this is for when things don't feel right. This is for if your wig half slips off during surveillance and you think someone saw. This is for if you get a parking ticket a day or two before a job. This is for if the police stop you for speeding on the way to a kill, and you have to use your real name. This is for any situation that could, maybe – just maybe – lead the nippleheads to your door.

See also: random red-tie-wearing bastards sauntering up to you in clubs.

Nearby, the brunette's attention is wandering. Shit.

To understand why it's a problem that this guy knows my *actual fucking name*, you need to have a perfect, detailed grasp of the way in which I conduct my business.

The brunette, my distraction, my don't-dwell-on-today's-events, my fall-asleep-so-knackered-I-don't-dream-at-all ticket out of here, the chances are she'll find some other schmo.

The way in which I conduct my business is this: oh-so-very-very-carefully.

'Good *morning*, then,' he says. I don't care. I'm leaving.

Possibilities: maybe he's a cop. Maybe he's a crook or a competitor or a cocksmoker. It makes not a single iota of a difference. He *knows* me.

And yeah, OK, maybe he really *is* just my postman, who recognised my face and came to say hi. Maybe this whole thing is just a string of crazy events with, har har, Hilarious Consequences.

It could happen.

This is me turning away to run like fuckity-fuck-fuck.

Except even though I've turned away there's a hand on my shoulder and, in an action film, I'd be pulling that move where I grab the wrist and spin round so quick his arm breaks off or his body backflips or he bursts spontaneously into flame – but I'm not in a film. I'm in Napalm-Glory, or whatever it's called, and two people who *both* stand out is a recipe for being stared at.

'Good work today,' he says, and there're icicles in my spine and I think my testicles just retracted, and he gently turns me round to face him and this time I'm shaking his hand like an old pal, and his eyes are twinkling like Catherine wheels. 'The Tall Man. We were impressed. Got a bit messy, I hear, but it worked.'

This guy, he is not my postman. *Messy*, he says. Shit.

I tell him he's mistaken me for someone else. He snorts. He makes a laugh noise like he's trying to breathe through his gums.

Kkkhh

This guy, he knows who I am. He knows what I do. He

says he'd like to chat in a professional capacity, with a view to offering me work, and would I be interested?

I have contacts. I have a broker. It doesn't *work* like this.

It doesn't work like this, fucker!

This guy, he's grinning the whole time.

This guy, he slaps a rectangle of white card into my hand and pats me on the shoulder.

This guy, he tells me he's just a messenger, then he's gone into the crowd.

Shit shit shit shit shit.

The card is a number and an address.

The card is, apart from that, a single word: CHOIR

Someone shouts in my ear and I think I almost soil myself. The brunette. She has better patience than most.

'Who's your friend?' she shouts, above the DJ's crimes against sound. 'I like his tie.'

It occurs to me the man, the man in the jacket and the shirt and the red tie, the man who gave me his card, he didn't raise his voice once. He didn't have to shout, and he knew about the Tall Man.

That sinking feeling.

The brunette is waiting for an answer.

Chat-up lines are the conversational equivalent of taking the scenic route.

I scowl and say, 'Do you want a fuck, or what?'

Interview Room 2

In Interview Room 2, I'm feeling mischievous. As I tell my story, as I disclose my cunning chat-up technique to these two pinstriped idiots, these dour-faced mannequins, I'm making damn sure I look straight into Anna's eyes.

Anna, the winter-maiden. So stern is she, I'm wondering how many guys she's put through hospital with frostbite to the gonads.

Scratch that. Our girl Anna, she's the wait-till-she's-married type. No doubt about it.

'Do you want a fuck,' I say, the faithful storyteller, 'or what?'

Her eyebrow does that lopsided thing again. I was hoping for a blush, ohoyes, but that eyebrow is enough. That eyebrow, I've scored a point.

'Smooth,' says Jason Durant, her toned-tanned-tit of a colleague.

I shrug and tell him it works for me. I tell him I went back to the brunette's place and enjoyed several hours of protracted keep-the-noise-down-for-fear-of-waking-her-flatmates sex. I tell him how she had a small silver piercing through her tongue, and every time she locked her mouth over mine – an airtight seal she'd maybe seen in a soap opera that she'd come to associate with passion – this little bauble clanked against my lower teeth. I tell him that when she yanked my prick into her mouth I was sort of worried she'd accidentally slice it off. I tell him this girl, I only just met her. I tell him I'm not ready to sacrifice my todger for her just yet.

He doesn't laugh. I bet he's gay.

I tell him: actually, it turned out all right. I ask him, did he know that in the womb we all start out as little girls? I tell him a clitoris is the vestigial remnant of what, in a guy, turns into a prick. I tell him all those nerve-endings crammed like sardines into a woman's rusty bullet of joy, they end up on that small y-shaped bit of gristle on a guy's foreskin, like the flap under your tongue.

I tell him a silver piercing nudging about down there, that's not a bad thing.

I tell him at one time the male circumcision rate in the US reached 95 per cent. I tell him: pity those poor suckers.

He gives me a look. Jason Durant, I do believe, is circumcised.

I look back at Anna. I bet she's thinking the same thing. This is all borrowed wisdom, of course.

You remember when overpaid executive wankers, fearing for their right to clamber over their colleaguettes in seizing promotions, used to accuse women of 'Penis Envy'? You remember that?

Every man who's ever had sex with a woman, who's ever seen her arch her back and groan at just a touch, in his secret soul he resents the clitoris.

In Interview Room 2, I'm back to tormenting Jason Durant. Jason Durant looks like the sort of guy who has Clit Envy *really bad*.

I tell him this girl, with the metal tongue and the cute tattoo of a lizard scuttling up her thigh, I tell him she kept 'shushing' me every time I made a noise, then went ahead and groaned like a bullfrog whenever I did a thing.

I tell him that softly-softly approach, you know the one, with due care and attention paid to the creaking of beds and the squeaking of floorboards, with every attempt made to stifle breaths and grunts, with an unspoken agreement to refrain from pinching, spanking, scratching and all the other noisy instincts that come flooding out of even the most repressed weirdo's psyche the moment there's flesh slapping against flesh – all those attempts to keep it down, they *never work*.

I tell him that if you try hard enough to be quiet, all it does is spoil the occasion. I tell him if there are people near enough to hear, and they're not already asleep, *they know*. I tell him you might as well just enjoy it and let rip, right? I ask him, you know what I mean?

He scowls, and this fucker, this blond-haired goon, his cheeks are glowing red.

That's another point to me.

Anna, the snow-frosted Queen of the Interview, Oh Icy Mistress, who is maybe the last woman I'll ever get this close to, who I'm trying to impress with my worldly wit and sensitive wiles, no really, she purses her lips.

'We'll have to check out your story,' she says. 'To make sure you were where you say you were.'

Fair enough.

'So' she says. 'This girl. What was her name?'

Chapter Five

It begins with an 'M'. Probably.

That doesn't narrow it down.

Madeline, Margot, Muriel, Marilyn . . . shit.

It shouldn't matter, am I right? I shouldn't *have* to remember. It's called *casual* sex for a reason.

This morning I'm thinking: there's not much worse in the world than waking up with last night's condom still clinging to you.

This morning, this thing, it's like a treacherous leech. It's cold and it's damp. Parts of it have gone crusty and caught in the hairs of my leg.

Let me tell you something horrifying: this morning, I'm not quite fully awake when I roll over and this thing, this cock-cover, this prick-parcel, it slips away. This morning, for three seconds, I'm convinced my cock just fell off.

This morning, it's occurring to me that one of the few things worse than waking up with last night's condom still attached, is being unable to find a box of tissues or a bin to get rid of it.

Her name. Melanie, maybe. Michelle. Madison. Maggie.

This morning, it shouldn't matter that I can't remember this girl's name. She's up before me, faffing somewhere in the flat. I can hear toasters popping and the giggling voices of flatmates comparing notes on their nightly conquests.

Students.

This morning, I'm alone in her room.

Listen: early condoms were made of linen, with drawstrings at the open end. The Chinese made cock-sheaths from turtleshell and ram horn. Cave paintings show men forming thin leather prick-packaging. None of them sound much fun for the women involved.

During the Gulf War, soldiers used condoms to keep sand out of their rifles.

During the Gulf War, those lucky bastards could just drop them in the desert and no one would care.

During the Gulf War, they didn't have to walk past a recent fuckee and all her flatmates carrying a used rubber, swinging like a pendulum, to the nearest bog.

All condom packages contain an advisory pamphlet suggesting that used barrier-contraceptives should never be flushed down toilets. This is either a health and safety measure to prevent potentially diseased spunk from filling the sewers, a concession to the waterboards who find more blockages caused by condoms than any other waste, or a genuine attempt to prevent those situations, those embarrassing moments of pure horror, when *the little bastard just won't flush*.

Marcie, Mairi, Myrtle, Millie . . .

It shouldn't matter that I can't remember her name, but it does. I should be a stone-cold sonovabitch, but I'm not. I should fuck and go, I should take what I want and vanish, I should be James T. Bond.

I'm not.

If I was a misogynistic sexual predator who got off on

degradation and domination, I'd leave the johnny on the floor. Or maybe empty it all over her pillow.

I'm not. Don't look surprised.

Out the window it is, then.

Ninety-five per cent of condoms are made from naturally occurring rubber-tree latex or synthesised polyurethane. The other 5 per cent are the scraped-out innards of sheep.

Borrowed wisdom.

The idea of unsuspecting vegetarians going at it hammer-and-tong with the pulverised remains of a lamb's intestine squelching between them keeps me warm on winter nights.

Martha. Maggie. Mirabel. Megan.

Here's the quandary, kids. The only thing that'll stop me reliving a day's work over and over, all night long; the only thing that'll keep dead eyes and gouting blood and dribbling mouths and mercenary murder out of my mind; the only thing that'll let me *do* what I *do* and not spend my life hating it and myself, is a marathon fuck session after every job.

Preferably in sleazy and/or dodgy circumstances.

Preferably without goody-goody sensibilities, teddies on the bed and strings attached.

Preferably without smiling photos of Mummy and Daddy watching from the bedside table.

Preferably with hard, fast, shouting, angry, violent, and downright dirty behaviour.

Preferably with *no bloody missionary position*.

I'm not proud.

This happens to me maybe once a fortnight. Kill, see Sally, fuck, move on. You think I'd be used to it by now. Only, you won't believe this, I'm not *like* that.

Melinda. Marsha. Maria. Margaret.

I don't *think* casual sex. I don't *think* sleaze. I don't *think* detachment and modern isolation and treating-women-like-objects and emotional frigidity.

It just *happens*.

This morning, this thing with not remembering the brunette's name, it's just another nail in the coffin of 'Michael Point: Decent Guy'.

Get dressed. Tug the bedsheets into some vague semblance of order, just to show willing. Close the window, and ignore next door's cat playing with the limp transparent shape on the patio below.

Get out of there, soldier.

(On the way out, with the flatmates' eyes on the back of my neck, there's a sign on the outside of her door which says 'Amanda's Room'. Maybe last night, in between moans, she introduced herself as 'Mandy'. Maybe I at least got the initial right, and I'm not a filthy woman-using piece of shit after all. Maybe.

Amanda looks embarrassed.

'Morning . . . Want some cereal?'

See you around, love.)

Outside, London is grey, brown, black, white, nothing, in brick and breeze-block. London's a landfill site someone stacked upright. A cardboard city with pebbledashing and pavement pizza.

This impression, I get this a lot. I'm not a morning person.

Seeing London like this, let me tell you: this is its natural state of being. If you get rid of the history and the culture, you slice off the colours and the people and all the frilly whatnot; what's left is just stacks of rock, held together with puke and pigeons.

Outside, I'm doing something vague with my hair – prevention of BedHead, re-establishment of Averageness – and taking a piss down an alleyway. Outside, I'm heading down stairs that stink like dead people and ignoring bad buskers, and it's flickering yellow lights and pale magnolia tiles and piles of the *Metro* and the smell of crowds. Outside, this morning, this is Welcome to the London Underground.

The *Metro*, a free newspaper they give away on the London Underground, supports itself by selling advertising space that none of the readers look at, and is the number-one source of bog-paper for vagrants city-wide.

This morning, I'm not even sure where I'm heading. People push past me, and I politely hate them.

This morning it's eleven o'clock, which is the peak-time for suicides on the London Underground. The platform controllers call them 'one-unders'. In New York, they're called 'track-pizza'.

In the US, everything is bigger and better. Cars, guns, houses, waist sizes. Necessity is the mother of invention, so let's hear it for liposuction, fat farms, calorie control, work-out routines and colonic irrigation.

In the future, museums will need extra room for their waxwork tableaux.

Wide-load aeroplanes.

Horizontal fold-out pin-up pages.

The London Underground is 431 kilometres of the oldest subterranean transport system in the world. Forty minutes on the tube is the carcinogenic equivalent of smoking two filterless cigarettes.

This morning, upright-sardine stylee, picking up a crumpled *Metro* from the hypnotic tartan upholstery of this train or that, I could already see the headline in my mind.

'Bracknell Apartment Carnage', maybe. 'Businessman Murdered in bloody Mêlée'.

Shiver, shiver, try not to remember.

Except it's a rant about traffic congestion, and over the page I'm flicking story-to-story, looking for a mention.

The Tall Man in Bracknell, he's still lying there, clothes torn, neck bright purple, dripping through the carpet, and nobody is any the wiser.

Except the man in the club last night.

'The Tall Man,' he said. 'We were impressed.'

That sinking feeling. His card is still in my pocket.

Shiver, shiver, try not to remember.

I need to see Wilson.

Today is Thursday.

On Thursdays, Wilson is in the bookie's.

This is North London, straight up the Bakerloo line. Noisy place off the Harrow Road, right-left-right out of the tube, dodging pricks in Beamers and kids smoking dope.

Take a copy of the sports pages.

Tomorrow, Friday, Wilson will be in the launderette. That's in Barnes, out west, stuck in a loop in the river like a bubble in a spirit level. He likes it if you take a pocketful of 50p pieces.

For the machines, he says.

In the bookie's, today, through the crowd and the smoke,

CONTRACT

I spot him straight away. Wilson is the blackest black man I have ever seen. He has skin so dark it's blue, like Superman's hair. He has skin so dark his eyes stand out like a pair of silver coins, and if he wore sunglasses he could stand in a shadow and never ever be seen again, until he switched on his odd little smile.

Wilson is maybe sixty, maybe seventy, maybe eighty.

On Mondays, Wilson can be found in a pub in Balham. Smokiest place I ever saw that wasn't on fire. Me, I don't drink, but always when I see him on a Monday he says, boy, you got t'buy sometin'.

Wilson has Jamaica in his voice.

On Mondays, Wilson sits with a packet of dry roasted peanuts and sucks the salt off them one by one, crunching them up with his dentures.

In the bookie's, today, Wilson is alone with his *Racing Post*. I sit down right next to him and say 'Hi.' He's watching the screens opposite, horses with connotative names thundering like medieval warriors towards the camera, and he's ignoring me, same as ever.

In the bookie's, One Too Many is leading the pack, chased hard by Change Your Life, Inner Monologue and Who Names These Fucking Nags Anyway.

Sense of Perspective goes down at the ninth, and Wilson winces like he's been stung.

On Tuesdays, Wilson sits in the Reading Room in the British Museum. He says he likes it there because nobody raises their voices, and you can people-watch all the tourists shuffling in and out. On Tuesdays, Wilson wants you to put a donation between two and five pounds in the museum's collection-pot, and sulks if you don't.

In the bookie's, today, the race finishes and this little man, this smartly dressed man with his creased skin and his glowing eyes, he says: 'Huhm.' Then he shrugs, and turns to look at me.

'Too many knees,' he says, waving a pale palm at the screen. ''Sah problem. Too many knees.'

In the bookie's, it's best just to nod and grin.

Wednesdays . . . Wednesdays are a pain in the arse. On Wednesdays, Wilson sits on a train in the front coach on the East London Line, which is the shortest tube line, and travels backwards and forwards between Shoreditch and New Cross all day long. He says he has fun waiting for people to call him – as they always do – on his mobile phone, only to get cut off when the train slides into a tunnel. He says people should know better, by now, than to try calling him on Wednesdays.

On Wednesdays you've just got to pick a station and sit there, peering into every train that passes, until you see his little bald head.

The London Underground system, less than 50 per cent of it is actually underground.

All these places, these are Wilson's offices. These are his five boardrooms, where he conducts meeting after meeting after meeting, and no one else pays the blindest bit of attention.

Just two pals, they think, chatting on the tube. Just an old man, boring some random stranger with war tales in the pub, or whiling away his lonely life by inflicting himself on unsuspecting customers in the local launderette. Just a bookish pensioner, maybe, researching this or that on behalf of the media-types who come shuffling into the library, make some notes, then vanish. Yeah, that's it. Nothing to worry about.

Just some crinkly faced old guy, they think, face like a prolapsed prune, stinking of Old Spice and garlic, wasting his pension on horses, hounds, matches, fights. Swapping bad tips and not-quite-dead-certs with youngsters down the local Turf Accountancy.

This is Wilson.

In the bookie's, Wilson twists away from the TV screens, lifts up his *Racing Post* and a chewed pencil, and looks at me.

'How di' go?' he asks. 'All sorted?'

He means the Tall Man. He means my job. He means, did you kill the individual you were supposed to kill?

I clench my teeth.

'Sorted,' I say.

Wilson, once I spied on him. Paint me suspicious.

In this trade, you learn to sit and watch without it being obvious. You learn to stay still. You learn to take in little details, and not to draw attention.

This was in the pub in Balham, so it must have been a Monday. This was a little over two years ago. This was with a heavy jumper and a beard, and a pretty good wig. This was with the hairy mole and all.

All day they came. One, sometimes two every hour. Mostly men, sometimes women. White guys, black guys, Asian guys. Notebooks, pens, cigarettes. Pints of beer. Lager. Soft drinks.

Peanuts and pork scratchings and smoky bacon crisps.

He spoke to them all. Muttered and mumbled and passed the time of day.

To each one, he pushed across a piece of paper.

To each one, he nodded and grinned.

Then he was on his own again.

Sometimes his mobile rang, and he answered it quietly, perched up behind his paper. Always he's reading, always a different title; like shields to cover his face.

This is Wilson, and he hasn't changed a bit since I met him.

That day, a little over two years ago, in the pub in Balham, at the end of the day he made his way through the crowd like he was on his way to the gents, and he paused right next to me, me in my wig and my mole and my beard, thinking I'm oh-so-smart, and he said: 'Aright, Michael?'

This is Wilson, and he is a Very Clever Little Bugger.

In the bookie's, here and now and today, Wilson's doodling with his pencil; random shapes that go round and round, like octopus tentacles, all up the margin of his paper.

'You after sometin' else already, m'boy?' he asks, eyes twinkling.

The way it works is, Wilson is a People Person.

The way it works is, he never gets his hands dirty.

The way it works is, he smiles and nods, and hands you a slip of paper with a phone number.

All these guys and girls who come to Wilson, they can't *all* be killers. I'm guessing burglary, I'm guessing prostitution, I'm guessing racketeering and laundering and smuggling and dealing. I'm guessing armed robbery and extortion.

In London, there's always someone organising something.

It's not Wilson, but he knows who it *is*.

In London, it's too easy to turn round and find yourself in some well-connected fucker's pocket, some greasy wannabe don who's seen *The Godfather* once too often, without even realising how you got there.

In London, this pleasant-looking man Wilson, this friendly old guy who's maybe on the payroll of Bigshot Player X, Y or Z, who's maybe just an independent sneak, who's maybe nothing but a guy with big ears, he's as close to 'Organised Crime' as I need to get.

The thing is, I don't *think* 'criminal'.

The thing is, hey, I'm just doing a job.

The thing is, here and today and now in the bookie's, Wilson is just another tipster.

He gives a low chuckle – *hup hup hup* – and fishes in his pocket.

'Matter fac',' he says, 'might got sometin' for you.'

This piece of paper, this slip of white he's holding up, this is not the phone number of somebody I'm supposed to kill. Wilson isn't into that. Wilson isn't that hands-on.

This is the number of somebody who, through ethereal channels that would evaporate the minute you looked too close, has Let It Be Known they're interested in hiring somebody in my rarefied trade.

One way to look at it is, Wilson is a matchmaker. He brings people together.

One way to look at it is, he gets £300 from every person who comes to see him, paid every week into an account in the name of Ms. Q. Timmins.

The wonders of Internet banking.

One way to look at it is, he just *knows* stuff.

I tell him, no, hang on, I didn't come here looking for work, not so soon, not now. I lick my lips without thinking, and I tell him the last job was a little . . .

'Little what?' he says.

'A little messy,' I say.

'Messy?' His eyes twinkle. The way he says that one word, he's like a gardener discussing weeds.

I say it again, because there's nothing else to describe it.

'Yeah. Messy.'

And, of course, it's there in my head straight away, that not-dead-body, bleeding and lanky, spilling eyeball-gunk from its ruined orbits, sicking up its own guts, thrashing with its lips hanging off.

Wilson goes back to staring at the screens, and I say, 'I think I'll take a . . . a month off, maybe. Lie low a bit.'

Next to me, Wilson purses his lips. He puts the piece of paper back in his pocket, and he says, 'Huhm.'

On the TV screen nearest us, Time's Up is the favourite in the next race, with Worthless Human Filth highlighted for a risky flutter.

'You come here just tell me dat?' Wilson says, and he's talking from the corner of his mouth with the pencil going round and round. 'Just tell me you don' wan' work?'

'Course not,' I say. This is with a friendly grin. This is because you piss off Wilson, and you're out of a job for good.

No more work.

No more money.

No more The Plan.

No more piece of paper in my pocket, folded tight with a number, a long number, a bunch of zeroes and a pound sign.

I tell him, 'Actually, I – well, wanted to ask you something.'

So this little man Wilson, he looks me up and down like

he's checking I'm real. This is already the longest conversation I ever had with the guy, and I haven't even asked The Question yet. Wilson has one leg folded above the other. He shrugs his little shoulders and says, 'Gwan.'

This could be awkward. Like: Hey, Wilson, you know how you've never played me a duff note since we met? Well, just on the off chance, have you been giving out my real name to scary-looking, well-dressed red-tie-wearing mother-fuckers? Just so I know, sort of thing.

Tact was never my strong point.

'The thing is, Wilson,' I say.

I have no idea what 'the thing' is.

I fish out the business card and pass it over. 'Have you heard of this lot?'

Wilson is still looking at me. Slowly, like icebergs turning over, those perfect pearls in his face twist round to read the card.

Then back at me.

Then at the card.

'"Choir,"' he says.

'Do you know them? Or him. Her. Whoever. You ever heard of them?'

Wilson's mouth creases at the edges, and I'm thinking of panthers in the jungle, gurning leather.

'You never been to church, m'boy?'

This man Wilson, this man who earns maybe eight, nine, ten grand a week from dealers and pimps and robbers and murderous criminal scumfilth like yours truly, this guy who should be serious like a wake, like an International Summit on coming-down-hard-on-crime, he just cracked a joke.

He says, *hup hup hup*.

'A bloke gave me this last night,' I tell him, ignoring the chuckles. In the bookie's it's best to just nod and grin. 'Came right up to me, out of nowhere, called me by name – my fucking *name*, Wilson – and gave me this.'

His face goes sour.

'Don' curse.'

'What?' A pause stretches out. I fidget.

'You tinkin'', he says, 'it's cos I give him you name, eh, this man? That's why you here?'

'No, it's—'

'You accusin' me?'

'Course not, it's just—'

Wilson waves at the TV screen, and maybe he's annoyed, or just sulking, or just passing the time. With Wilson, you never know.

'Race startin',' he says, and he's back to ignoring me, back to muttering, back to doodling in his margins. 'Too many knees . . .' On the screen it's *barumbarumbarum-barumba* as the horses head out of the stalls, and already the commentator's throat sounds raw from shouting.

'Christ's sake Wilson,' I say, 'I wasn't *accusing* y—'

Actually, that's exactly what I was doing.

'Don' *curse*,' he says.

On TV screen, Give It Up Kiddo has an early lead.

I run my tongue round the insides of my cheeks.

'Listen,' I say, and through *barumbarumbarumbarumba* maybe he does, maybe he doesn't. 'This bloke – you know who he is or not?'

The lead pack have It's All Perfectly Innocent boxed-in, and the three to one favourite You'll Laugh About It One Day is languishing at the back.

Wilson, out of the corner of his mouth like he's spitting, he says, 'No.'

'Fine.'

Barumbarumbarumbarumba

That's All Folks nudges ahead. You see these horses, eyes rolling, mouths frothing, bloody great lumps of metal clanking round their teeth, whips flaying their arses, straps digging at their bellies, and you know the jockeys have it easy.

'So I'll – I'll see you next month,' I say, trying to build bridges. 'Or maybe the one after.'

Wilson shrugs, maybe. Maybe he's just clearing his throat. 'Huhm.'

This whole thing, it could have gone better.

So I'm out the door, and remembering what it's like to be in smokeless air, and London still looks like shit, and the cackle of commentators is behind me, and I'm imagining the business card in my pocket.

I need to make a phone call.

Listen: on the way home from seeing Wilson, outside a tube stop nowhere near my home, at a payphone with massages-oral-naughtychat-kinky-nurseplay-escorts-bondage-Asian-teen-slutfun services on cards and photos stuck down with gum, I put 20p into a slot and dial a number.

The voice at the other end sounds muffled. This voice, its gender: you just can't tell. This voice, it says, 'Yeah?'

I say, 'There's nothing like Cheese and Cucumber Sandwiches.'

After this, a long pause.

This number I just dialled, let me tell you, this is the

person who wanted the Tall Man dead. This is the number Wilson gave me a week ago. This is someone who bore a major grudge against the big guy in Bracknell. You remember him? The one who came back to life.

I was hallucinating. Ohoyes.

This message thing, this cheese and cucumber sandwich thing, normally the voice on the phone stammers. Normally it says *oh, right . . . that means . . . uh . . . I see . . .*

Today's voice says, 'Yeah. Good.'

Today's voice, probably I'm imagining it, only . . .

Only this thing, this thing with there being nothing like cheese and cucumber sandwiches, maybe today's voice already knew.

Which is sort of weird.

Listen, this 'code' thing, it's always embarrassing if you dial the wrong number.

I hang up.

Shortly, several thousand pounds will be plopping into a temporary account under a false name.

Happy, happy days.

On the way home from seeing Wilson, standing at that phone, I'm fiddling with the business card in my pocket. The one saying CHOIR. I'm staring at the number on the back. I'm thinking of a slick guy in a black shirt with a red tie.

He knew my name. 'Give us a call,' he said. And OK, so I don't actually *look*, I don't actually *check*, but, seriously, I'm almost certain I have no more 20ps in my pocket.

Go home, Mike.

An Interlude on the Subject of Me

Stop for a moment. Pay attention.

This thing with Wilson, this thing with Sally, too, this thing with the Significant Characters Inhabiting My Sphere, well, maybe you were wondering.

If you want to know, I've been killing people – professionally, I mean – for two and a half years. If you want to know, that's maybe thirty months. That's maybe one hundred and thirty weeks. That's I-don't-know-how-many-jobs. That's a longer-career-than-most, of no visitors, no calls, nobody knowing.

The first job I ever did, that's a whole-nother-story.

If you want to know, I left school just as soon as I could. This doesn't actually mean anything. This isn't actually *important*.

The reason I'm telling you is, maybe you wondered. Maybe you wanted to know what happened. Maybe you're intrigued about how Michael Point, aged twenty-eight, got to be doing what he does. Maybe.

The thing is this: vocations, eventually they just catch you up.

At school, let me tell you, I was always pretty popular. At school, I wasn't clever or well behaved. This is helpful in getting friends. At school, the numbers and words got jumbled in my head. You could blame my home circumstances, you could blame antisocial behaviour based on a dysfunctional upbringing, but this is a big pile of Arse.

If you want to know, up until the day I found what I found . . . (in the shower, on the floor, on the white tiles, with the . . .)

Anyway. Until that day, I was brought up just peachy. (This is Michael Point, aged twelve, embarrassed at seeing a woman naked for the first time.)

Polite. Good manners. Pleases and Thank-yous. Ps and Qs.

Listen, the first job I ever did – *real* job, I mean, *normal* job, I mean, non-homicidal job, I mean – I was seventeen years old. This was after dropping out. This was living with Foster Family number 4 or 5, I forget which. This was driving a forklift truck in a warehouse in Tottenham Hale. This was every lunch meeting behind the local McDonalds, me and the guys, me and the shelf-stackers, burger-flippers, trolley-collectors, pump-pullers, till-operators, used-car-pushers, sales-assistants, number-crunchers, et cetera et cetera, me and every other last dropout-loser-nobody working in a one-mile radius. This was a council of opt-outers. This was us sharing lunches, getting stoned, talking bollocks. This, if you want to know, is where I met Sally.

At school, before all of that, the reason I was popular was that I was the kid who'd do anything.

This is not the same as the Leader of the Pack. This is not the same as the Class Bully. This is not the same as the frothing little weirdo who everyone kind of respected because he was so fucking mental.

These are co-ed clichés – there's one in every class.

CONTRACT

For the record, I was the other one. I was the one who'd climb the wall to get the football. I was the one who'd make the first spray of graffiti outside the Head's office. I was the one who'd do anything, *anything*, so they'd like me.

I'm not proud.

Listen, after I dropped out of school, after I got my first job, after I was the Popular One, this thing with meeting Sally behind McDonalds, seriously, she was just some girl. I barely knew her. Back then, seriously, she was just the plain little good-girl chick who wouldn't smoke pot and wouldn't flash her tits like the rest.

About how I met Sally, I'm sorry, but that's all there is. That's it.

The first job I ever did, one time, my foreman caught me trying to forklift my own car. This was because I was too stoned to drive home. The way I saw this, I was being conscientious.

This was the end of the first job I ever did. For maybe ten years, this was the last time I saw Sally.

At school, the reason I was popular, I was that one, you know, when someone said, 'I dare you,' I said, 'OK.' This was not courage. This was because I'm not fast or strong or clever. This was because when there's no other niche to fill, being That Kid – the one'll who'll do stuff that no one else will – is all that's left.

Sometimes they paid me.

Like: *Give you half my Maltesers if you eat an earthworm.*

Like: *You show me yours, I'll show you mine.*

Like: *50p says you won't stick this on Mr Meyer's back.*

These things weren't hard to do. These things didn't need skill.

It was just that no one else wanted to do them.

You can see where I'm going with this.

Listen, the next time I met Sally after that gap, that ten years, that decade of fluff, that was six months ago. What I did, mostly, in all that time, was this: Nothing Worth Talking About.

Call centres. Sorting offices. Bar work.

Back at school, before all of that, before the decade of Not Worth Mentioning, listen, the way you do things no one else will do is, don't think about it.

Concentrate on the reward. It's. All. About. The. Money.

You can maybe see a pattern forming here.

Two and a half years ago, give or take, I met Wilson. This was not chance. This was friend-of-a-friend-of-a-friend, and none of them are *actual* friends. This was just natural progression. This was just nothing-else-feels-right.

I told you, the thing is, vocations, eventually they just catch you up.

Six months ago, give or take, I was sitting in Ariadne's Café when I recognised someone. More importantly, someone recognised me.

This never happens.

This was Sally coming back into my life.

Sally said she'd been out of London. Married, divorced, blah blah. The way Sally said this, it was No Big Deal. She said she'd trained as a psychiatric nurse. She said she was Between Jobs.

Sally and me, we spoke. Sally and me, no, no, no, *not* spoke. Sally and me, we *chatted*.

This never happens either.

We went for drinks.

CONTRACT

We bought cheap skunk in Camden.

Sally, no longer the good-girl chick. 'Like old times,' she said.

Sally and me, we talked and talked and talked and talked. That night, the sad thing is, I can't remember half of what was said. That night, stoned like an old testament adulteress, at some stage, I told her What I Do.

That night was the last time I drank. That night was the last time I smoked. That night was the last time I forgot that if you can't trust your own senses, hey, what have you got?

The thing is, the way I look at it, six months later, just to bring her into my world, that One Night Only of I-don't-care . . .

It was worth it.

Chapter Six

So now it's the evening.

This is my guilty stash. This is my work-locker.

This is in the corner, under the heavy-looking-but-actually-pretty-light bookshelf, below the three-foot piece of floorboard I spent an afternoon sawing. This is maybe the worst hiding-place cliché there is.

My flat is one bedroom, one kitchen, one bathroom, one living room. The walls are painted, not papered, and the colour is open to interpretation. The furniture is just furniture. Downstairs is an overpriced hair salon. There's a concrete stairwell down the side of the building, and a man in the flat upstairs who only flushes his toilet every two days.

Here and now I'm oiling lumps of metal. I'm counting lumps of lead, I'm arranging and dusting and going through the motions. I'm trying to stay distracted.

The business card saying CHOIR sits on the sofa. I keep thinking it's watching me.

Listen, inside the hole in the floor are six Ruger Mk II .22 handguns, each containing a full clip of ten hollowpoint rounds. There are four spare clips and two full boxes of ammunition.

This is my home. Just so you know, just in case you were wondering, pretty much anything of interest you'll find here is hidden beneath the floor. There's probably something profound in that. Unintentional.

This evening, I sit on the edge of the hole with my feet dangling. This evening, I rub grease into joints, safety catches, trigger-hinges. I hum a tune I've never heard.

Beneath the floor, my oily little kill-gadgets are the product of safe-firearms licensing. The way it works is, gun collectors are allowed to own as many as they want just so long as they've been deactivated. The way deactivation works is: a little cutting, a little welding; a gun's just a lump of metal.

There are ten thousand and eighty minutes in every week. If you want to know, I spend an average of 7,350 of them here. In my flat. The fact I know this will give you some idea of how I spend them.

The pistols, the way it works is, the guys you buy these from, they charge £300 a pop. Give or take. Deactivated top-grade models only. Fixed-barrel semi-automatics. Safe as houses.

In my flat, in the living room, is a television with a Sky digibox and a desktop computer with Broadband Internet Access. Out of the 7,350 minutes I spend every week here, when I'm not sleeping or cleaning the guns or exercising or eating or crapping, what's left is something like four thousand minutes.

I spend exactly all of them staring at a screen. One or the other.

Welcome to the crazy, hazy world of Me.

The pistols, the way it works is, you take your deactivated murder-machine and you look up some names. Maybe you know a guy. Maybe the Internet helps.

It often does.

An extra £100, maybe. A little cutting, a little welding . . . Deactivated-gets-*re*activated. Money changes hands. Everyone's happy.

There are no receipts. This is not tax deductible.

Right here and now, right when I'm poised over the hole in the floor, right when there are flesh-coloured latex gloves on both hands and an oily rag shoved up the barrel of an unused, unmarked, un-deactivated weapon, something loud and shrill happens behind me.

This makes me drop the gun back into the hole, where it clatters and Does Not Go Off. Except for in Hollywood, that never happens.

It takes me some time to work out what's making the noise. The reason for this is, in my flat, the phone *never* rings.

Ever.

The best description for the way I feel in this instant is: panic.

I peel off the gloves and place them down. I remember where the phone is, and I stare at it. It rings again, and again, and again. I stare back down into the hole. I wonder what to do.

In my flat, below the floorboards, are two small bags of high-quality heroin, a miniature g-clamp and a hand-held precision drill. Below the floorboards are two sticks of sealant wax, three boxes of disposable flesh-coloured latex gloves, a pot of lubricant oil and a pile of dirty rags. Below the floorboards are three sets of metal files, four sets of lockpicks, seven homemade silencers and a double-edged seven-inch hunting knife in a rubber sheath. Everything is disposable, and you never use the same tools twice. That sort of stuff, I understand.

The phone . . . well.

Sooner or later I stop hoping it'll shut up. Sooner or later I cough and lift the receiver. Sooner or later I tell myself: a cold-calling salesman, flouting ex-directory laws. I tell myself: wrong number. I tell myself: a crossed wire.

A voice says: 'Evening, Mr Point.'

That sinking feeling.

The thing with me spending 72.9 per cent of my life inside this flat, you could get philosophical. You could bandy about DIY psychoanalysis like there's no tomorrow. You could suggest there's a twisted irony. You could tell me my only influence on the world is destructive, like I don't really have a *stake* in it. Like all I know, you could say, I learned from plastic sources: telly infotainment; Internet bullshit; the secondary-heard-it-all-through-the-grapevine-where's-your-proof resources of the idle researcher.

Karma, you could say.

'Who's this?' I say. Not hostile, yet. The way I'd describe my voice is: a croak.

The voice says: 'We met last night. Remember?'

It's a man's voice. You can hear the smile.

'Or rather,' he says, 'this morning.'

This person, when he laughs it's a half-laugh, it's a half-sneer, where you can hear him breathing through the gaps at the back of his mouth.

Kkkhh

The guy from the Choir. The Not-My-Postman.

The Red-Tie-Guy.

'What you up to, Mr Point? Not disturbing you, am I?'

The funny thing is, when you're gaping for words, when you're shivering and tumbling into terror, when you've no idea what the *fuck* to do, chitchat comes ohsoveryveryeasily.

'No. No, I mean – nothing. I'm not doing – look, w-what's—'

'Checking the stash, Mr Point? That's the routine, right? Isn't it? Oiling, cleaning – all that?'

Oh God.

Looking down into the hole, listen: below the floorboards is an AR-7 rifle, still in its case, with a mid-range scope. I never use it, but still it gets cleaned every night. JIC.

Just In Case.

This hole in the floor, this floorboard cavity which nobody is supposed to know about except me, it's my supply larder. It's my how-to kit. It's everything I need to blow Poor Bastard X's brains out, or perforate She-Made-an-Enemy Y's body, or pump Stranger Z's blood full of enough skag to overload his heart and haemorrhage his brain, and walk away, and never, ever, ever get caught. Up until now.

The anger arrives. It took its time.

'How the fuck did you get this number? Who's – how the *fuck* did you know about me? Who *are* you? W-what's . . .'

And so on.

All through it, he's saying: 'Mr Point . . . Mr Point, listen to me . . . Mr Point . . .'

Sooner or later the steam farts out of my head and I just say, too quiet: '*What?*'

He tells me I should go to my front door. He tells me there's something for me. He tells me not to hang up. He says: 'I'm happy to wait, Mr Point.'

That sinking feeling.

I put down the phone. I take a gun from the hole. This is panicky and stupid. This is with, no protection, no plan. This is *reacting*, not *acting*. This is how people get caught.

But still, but still. I'm not going *near* that door unarmed.

In my flat, in the hallway, is a set of boxes containing T-shirts in all different colours and sizes. In those boxes, one set is printed with the phrase: THIS IS NOT A T-SHIRT

This is surreal clothing designed for people who like to be stared at. This is comedy for people who laugh at anything. These T-shirts, they're a whole-nother-story.

The letterbox clatters open and shut, and I jump for the second time in five minutes. I trip on the boxes of T-shirts and shout 'Fuck!'

A letter lies on the floor inside the door. Outside, footsteps go away.

It takes me maybe one minute to check the corridor outside. This is slowly opening the door, peering round the doorframe, gun shaking, sweat in my eyes.

Then I'm grabbing the letter on the floor. I'm slamming the door and turning, I'm racing for the window to see who was *here*, what bastard has *done* this to me.

This is me tripping over the T-shirts a second time. This always happens.

These T-shirts, one batch says:

TIME FLIES WHEN YOU'RE ~~HAVING FUN~~
TERMINALLY ILL

This is comedy for people who smirk instead of laugh. This is dark humour. This isn't funny.

Next to the window, I'm looking down into the hole and seeing the rifle. The AR-7, with its scope, all tucked away.

Next to the window, I'm looking down into the street and waiting, and whoever pushed that letter under my door will *have* to appear out of the concrete stairwell soon, will *have* to step out on to the pavement, will *have* to be completely 100 per cent exposed.

I wonder how good my aim is with shaking hands.

The thing is, that rifle, up till now, I've never used it to kill anyone.

Still staring out into the street, I pick up the phone.

'Was that *you*?' I say.

I can imagine him. Slick hair, mobile in one hand, stepping out down there, oozing across the street . . . falling down, bullet through brain, legs twitching, skull pieces and tarmac.

The voice makes its sneer-laugh.

The sniper rifle, one reason I've never used it is: It's too bloody hard.

'Not me,' the voice says. 'But keep watching.'

The sniper rifle, one reason I've never used it, is a thing called M.O.A. This is a borrowed wisdom acronym which stands for Minute of Accuracy. It works out at 1.047 inches per 100 yards.

At a hundred yards, that's the difference between an eyesocket and a grazed temple.

At two hundred yards, that's the difference between a heartshot and a cracked rib.

At three hundred yards, that's the difference between a fatal wound and a supersonic hollowpoint streaking harmlessly past while alerting the whole world to its presence by means of the miniature sonic boom which follows in its wake.

The sniper rifle, let me tell you: if you miss, even *with* a silencer, you're busted.

Below me, a man steps out of the stairwell. He's kind of tall. He wears a blue jacket and a peaked cap with chequers around the rim. Black boots, trousers. Belt with cuffs and baton and pepper-spray and *oh sweet fuck he's a cop*.

He saunters. He walks like a man who doesn't think there's anything major going down. He doesn't look back at me. He doesn't smirk or grin or point or grandstand. He yawns, gets into an unmarked car parked opposite, and starts the engine.

Even through the tinted windscreen, listen, don't laugh, I'm serious: his head *glows*.

The voice on the line says: 'Now listen here, Mr Point. Don't be getting your knickers in a twist. Brendon out there, he's not on duty. Finished his shift a half-hour ago. On his way home anyway. Nothing to do with her Majesty's Finest.'

My sterling contribution to this conversation goes something like: 'But . . .'

Right now, I should be reacting. I should be squeezing a trigger. I should be dragging that limp, bleeding sack of meat out of its car and up the stairs, *b-bonk-b-bonk-b-bonk*, and hoping like I've never hoped before that nobody peeps out of a window. I should be placing the body in the bath to prevent it leaking into the plaster ceiling of the overpriced Salon downstairs. I should be laying out plastic sheets and planning a simple fragmentation of the body.

Right now, for *fuck's sake*, I should be doing *something*.

Instead I say, for what's now the second time: 'But . . .'

Disposal of a *Corpus Delicti*, if you want to know, isn't as easy as you'd think. The stink of decomposing meat is the biggest problem. Time, forensic traces, bone-digging dogs, dental records, hair fragments.

Throw a body in a lake and the decomposition of its cells will fill its stomach and lungs with gas, bringing it to the surface. You have to stab it once over each pec and twice in the guts. Like letting air out of a tyre.

Same for burial. Most shallow-graves don't work for shit because the body swells like a mini hillock. Like midget subduction. Bonsai volcanoes.

Throw a body in the sea and, piece-by-piece, its bits will come loose. You've got to make sure it's weighted all over, bound head-to-foot, or there'll be fingers and toes washed up on the beach.

Cue fingerprints, DNA testing, undernail skin-fragment analysis.

If you have enough time, and no visitors, doing it piece-by-piece down the plughole is best. For this you'll need:

a standard hacksaw, with two or three replacement blades
a mallet, for ball-joints and thick bone
two dozen large freezer bags, sealable
a large freezer
five or six two-litre bottles of industrial-strength bleach, to cleanse your pipes after every discharge
a powerful food processor, with replacement blades
a lot of replacement blades
a lot of patience
rubber or plastic sheets, to prevent drips and sprays
more replacement blades
approximately two weeks

This is how my mind should be working.

'But . . .' I say, and this is strike three.

CONTRACT

The voice says: 'What it is – Brendon, he's a mate of ours. We've got a *lot* of mates, Mr Point. That's something we want you to know. Something we're keen to illustrate. You with me? A lot of mates happy to do us a *lot* of favours. Thought it might make you sit up and pay attention if old Brendon made our little delivery. Might make you see what's at stake, sort of thing.'

Below, through the windscreen of the car, the off-duty-cop's eyes shine like gold.

Listen.

This thing with me being stuck in this flat all day every day, this thing with me never getting out, this thing with me festering by myself, stagnating in my own solitude, cue the violins, switch on the rain machines – the thing is, the first year I was here, I *tried*. Long walks. Museums. Galleries. Improving myself. Driving lessons, cookery courses, computer literacy, blah blah blah . . .

You know what I found?

Borrowed. Wisdom.

Disseminated from this source or that. Never primary, never *genuine*.

The way I see it, absorbing this shit from a computer screen, or hardlining on the Discovery Channel, or flicking through an encyclopedia: this is exploring the world but cutting out the middleman.

This is all just for the record.

Up until tonight, my flat was my magic carpet. My Mystery Machine, my private jet, my bloody crystal ball. Up until tonight, my flat was where I sat on my arse and didn't fret, and didn't worry, and went exploring.

Up until tonight, my flat was *safe*.

'You know,' the voice says, and I should be *saying* something, I should be demanding answers, I should be *proactive*, 'we thought you would've called us by now. Our number *is* on that card.'

He sounds reproachful.

I tell him I ran out of 20p coins at the phone booth, then my brain clocks-in again and I shout at him: *Who the fuck are you?*

He says, *Kkkhh*.

He says, 'I told you last night. I'm just a messenger.'

He says, 'Look. This is hard for you, we get that. But keep it calm, Mr Point. Don't worry too much. You're not in the shit – not yet. My boss has one or two unusual ways of . . . finding things out, that's all. You shouldn't let it worry you.'

I ask him what exactly he means by 'a few unusual ways'. He ignores me.

He says, 'I represent a . . . You'd probably call it an *organisation*.'

I demand to know who told him where I live. I say, 'How did you get this number?'

He says, 'We'd like you to do some work for us, Mr Point.'

I freak out down the phone. I snarl and rant. I tell him I'll kill him. This is with sweat on my neck. This is with my heart going too quick, and lights wibbling round the edge of my vision. I tell him I'll find him, and unless he tells me right now how come he *knows* so much, I'll *kill* him. I tell him I'll shoot his FUCKING FACE OFF unless he FESSES THE FUCK UP, and I'll FUCK the FUCKING SOCKETS of his FUCKING SKULL when

I've put FUCKING BULLETS through his FUCKING EYEBALLS.

This bastard, this smarmy arsehole, he says, 'No you won't, Mike. What you'll do is, you'll come and see us. My employer wants to meet you. And there's no need to be crude.'

'Why should I f—'

'Open the envelope, Mike.'

Outside the window, the cop drives off. Smiling all the way. His head in its own little disc of radiance, like a saint from an old picture.

I put down the pistol.

The thing is, he could be *anyone*, dressed up like a cop. The thing is, this whole mess could be just one big set-up. The thing is, I shouldn't lose my control. I shouldn't leap to conclusions. I shouldn't panic.

I open the envelope.

. . .

I panic.

Here is a photograph.

Here is Michael Point, *oh fuck*, delivering a pizza. On his way out of a dreary building in a dreary town. Bracknell, if you want to know.

Michael Point wearing a shirt too big for him, like he's just taken it from someone's cupboard. Michael Point with spots of red on his trousers. With fear in his eyes, like he's just seen something unexpected.

Down the phone, the Red-Tie-Guy hums to himself.

All this time, I should be running down the street with a suitcase of money. All this time, I should be on the Internet, booking flights to Mexico. I should be forcing answers from this mystery-man. I should be preparing. I should be doing something.

The man says, right on cue, 'We've been paying quite a bit of attention to you, Mike. You see that? Truth is, we already hired you once.'

My mouth goes dry. 'Bracknell?'

'Oh yes.'

But Wilson said he didn't know what the Choir—

He says, 'All anonymous, obviously. That's *normal*, isn't it?'

Like he's listening in on my brain. Like he's hearing my thoughts.

That sinking feeling.

I gape. Dying fish. Whale with billowing baleen. Slack-jawed twat.

He says, 'What we've got in mind, Mike . . . I don't think anonymous'll work. We'd like to have a chat in the flesh. We think you're the Right Man for the task.'

I say, 'What task?' Except what comes out of my mouth, all quiet and broken, doesn't sound the way I want. I guess he knows anyway what I'm getting at.

'Strictly temporary. Two small jobs, like a . . . a probation thing.' He half laughs, *Kkkhh.* 'Then the real gig. That's it.'

I whisper, 'I'm *freelance*.'

'Basically, we're looking for an exclusive deal, Mike. You work for us – for the duration – and nobody else. Shouldn't take more than a week or three.'

I tell him, and now maybe my voice is a little stronger, I tell him: I'm *freelance*, motherfucker.

'It needn't be a formal arrangement. And look – you

should be flattered. It's been a long time since the guv wanted to recruit.'

I ask him, 'Aren't you listening? I don't *do* that, mate. I don't get involved. I don't play that . . . that mobster shit. I'm *freelance*.'

'We'll make it worth your while,' he says.

'Bullshit,' I say. 'This is fucking blackmail. This is *crap*. This is—'

'Just come see us,' he says. 'Let us convince you.'

'*Bullshit*.'

'C'mon, Mike.' The phone hurts my ear. I'm pressing into it too hard. Outside, the empty street. The gaping hole by my feet, filled up with guns and death and drugs. 'C'mon,' he says. 'So far it's just a photo. Doesn't mean anything. Not *quite* incriminating . . .'

And suddenly my tongue works again. Suddenly the speech centres of my brain have heated up. Suddenly I'm alive, and turning back from the window, and glaring at the small rectangle on the sofa. CHOIR

Suddenly I'm seeing straight. It's only taken me ten minutes. (I'm not quick. I'm not smart.)

I say, 'Why? Huh? Why should I stick my neck out? I can fucking *disappear*, mate. You . . . you don't just walk up to me. You don't get to *do* this stuff. There're *ways*. Brokers, meetings. You don't just throw your weight around and expect me to—'

'You're right,' he says. Voice thick with a smile. 'We're sorry. *I'm* sorry. Time's ticking, that's all. We're new to all this.'

Disarmed with a smile. I stammer.

'Mike,' he says, 'listen. We want you in. We want you in *willingly*.'

I laugh down the phone.

'We'll pay you one million pounds,' he says. There's a brief pause.

He says he's serious. He says he doesn't expect me to believe him, but at the very least come along. Meet the boss. No strings attached. One million pounds.

I mumble: 'Don't be stupid.'

I mumble: 'That's . . . that's ridiculous.'

I mumble: 'That's too Hollywood.'

Then again: It's. All. About. The. Money.

He tells me a time and a place. He says, 'Don't be late.'

He says, 'Think it over. It's a lot of money. Enough to retire on, if you do it right.'

The piece of paper in my pocket, with the magic number, with a bunch of zeroes and a pound sign, it feels like it's burning my side.

He says, 'Take care, Mike.'

And then the phone clicks, and the line is dead, and I'm back in my flat, and it's weird how the whole place seems different.

The funny thing is, right now, the first thought I get is: *Remember how easy it is to call people?*

Really. Anyone, I mean. Anyone in the world, any time you want. All linked together like cobwebs of cable.

The phone, still in my hand. I'm shaking. I dial a number.

Contact 21

DAY: Thursday

TIME: 8.24 p.m.

LOCATION: T.A.D.C. – hospital corridor. Plastic seat outside Room 12, uncomfortable, same as always; perching diary on left knee. Not gone inside yet today, might not go in at all. Been here since 7 p.m., visiting time over soon, rushing to finish entry.

CONTACT REASON: Unexpected contact – not at all prepared. No aims. Michael phoned approx 7.45 p.m., no warning. (Supposed to have mobile off in hospital: had to rush downstairs & outside.) Taken by surprise – never expected contact so soon. First time he's called not after 'job'. Hope didn't sound too flustered; kept myself together. Had to react on-hop.

OBSERVATIONS: Hospital smell: piss/detergent (same every week). Striplights flicker only when looking away. Annoying. Tea from vending machine: plastic. Beeps & hisses from Room 12 (machines – hate them, hear in dreams sometimes).

Phone: need to change ringtone. Startled me, made nurses stare.

M: voice bizarre. Not heard him so vague since Contact 1 (finally 'umming' and 'ahhing' – no prompting). Stammered, sounded out of it – i.e. drunk, stoned, but <u>not</u>. Just shaken? Dreamlike, half-awake? Reminded me of old days – lunchbreaks out back of McDonalds, etc.

NOTES: M called in panic, trying to be conversational, 'just wanted to chat', etc. No use: quickly crumbled, admitted he's shaky (needed to talk to someone). Said he'd just had a phonecall, something about a letter through the door, photo? Spoke too quick, didn't explain well, but obvious: feels trapped, locked in vice. Voice breaking up (profound reaction, unexpected – had no idea he could be so affected). He's been Got To, security spoiled. Feels unsafe.

Did my best to sympathise, let him drone on: space to gush. Meanwhile: cold outside hospital, stood near door, watched pigeons, 'mmm'ed down phone. Hope I sounded interested. M kept losing track mid-sentence. Not tangents, just caught-up in subject: rants, angry, afraid, etc. Whining. Asked him if anything I could do to help – silence. Nothing. Repeated: 'Just wanted to chat.' Displacement, denial.

Asked what he planned to do. Voice went strange (child being cunning). Rambled at length re. 'insurance', said: have come up with idea. Way of protection. Asked him about it (seemed natural to pry). Think he was relieved at interest: like waiting for me to check his plan? Parental approval, affirmation.

CONTRACT

His scheme = clever. Unexpected. Told him so – 'very impressive, good idea, gosh, wow, etc. etc. etc. Lapped it all up.

Need to think about what his idea means, though. Might fuck things up.

Need to speak 2 Daniel.

THOUGHTS/CONCLUSIONS/OTHER: M's 'plan' = potential problem, but overall positive. Needed to talk to someone: naturally phoned me. Good sign. Bonded, reliant. <u>His only friend</u>? Makes it easier to break cycle.

Next contact hopefully soon. No more surprises!

S

Chapter Seven

Today is Friday.

Today I sit and sway and swelter, crushed up in plastic-and-metal tubes inside black tunnels. Today the kid next to me has earphones and closed eyes and head rocking back-forth-back, and a shiny little techno-lump in his hand glowing neon, volume too loud, and it's *Oom-chkka-oom-chkka-oom* all the bloody way.

Today I have an appointment.

Listen to me: the London Underground is 431 kilometres of heat and dark. This is travelling and walking and standing and waiting beneath a million tonnes of rock. This is a city of 7.5 million people above your head, pushing down, spread across arches and escalators and concrete struts. On the tube, this is the sort of thing You Just Shouldn't Think About.

I do.

I hate the tube.

At some point, at a tube stop shadowed by the great saggy tit that is the Millennium Dome, I head above ground. Through barriers, up stairs, into light.

Let me tell you, people with near-death experiences, this is what it's like. Minus the fumes, maybe. Minus the incontinent pigeons and punch-drunk tourists. London. Love to hate it.

Then it's on to a bus, *trundle clank shiver*. Packed to the gills, standing only, legs splayed, breathing deep on crowd smells.

I mean, *just look at them.*

Moist armpit-patches; frizzy hair clogging nostrils; limbs tangled; bags littering floors; mobiles ringing; talk, talk, talk, talk; engine grunts, squealing brakes; iPod white noise; the stink of onions and cigarettes and cheap cologne and pent-up fart and shoes, shoes, shoes; change dropped on rubber floors and apologies and *Sorry, mate* and *'Scuse, my stop*, and arms extended to reach rubber handles and braces, 3D Twister, knees against crotches and boxed-in by flesh and—

And oh sweet fucking no.

Please. *Hurry up.*

I hate buses.

At some point, with gulls squawking and kids sloping by in hoodies and tracksuits, I step off and look around. Every other Friday, this moment. This relief at escaping the pack. This reminder where I am. This gathering gloom.

Today my appointment is inside an orange-brick estate in the South East of London. This is a big bastard building with a massive coat of arms above the main gate. This is a symbol meaning: Never Been Opened. Like a seal on an envelope. Someone's little joke.

This place, it has a neat line in huge fuck-off walls. This place, inside are some Very Nasty Pieces of Work.

It's called Belmarsh. It's a prison. This is where my father lives.

All through the journey, all the way here, all through tunnels and slow trains and line closures and 'passenger incidents' and Never More than Six Feet from a Rat and tourists and suits and tramps and buskers and you get the idea, all through *all* of it: thinking about the Red-Tie-Guy. Staring at the business card.

The time is twelve-thirty, and I've got anything up to two hours with my father. This is a routine. This is something that happens every other week, like other families have Sunday roast, football in the garden, videoed soap operas, chatting about how the kids are getting along at school. Normal everyday nothing-to-see-here average middleclass Joe Everyone, with his horde of doting relatives. Bless.

My dad, I'm all the family he's got.

My dad, he's all the family I've got.

We don't get sentimental about it.

The thing with going to visit the Red-Tie-Guy and his Boss, and clambering into a nest of vipers I could live without, is that I'll make up my own mind, ta.

For the record, me being here at the prison today, waiting in line behind wives and children and left-behinders whose friends and lovers don't get out much: I'm not here for guidance. This is just in case you got the wrong idea.

Like: *Hey, Pa, what do you reckon to me prematurely seeking to retire from a career as a professional murderer by wilfully mixing with mob-style sinister gangster fuckknuckles who Know Too Much?*

Me and my old man, we're not like that.

Today the duty-warden is a human-sized pig. I'm wondering if you rubbed him in salt and poured oil on his back whether he'd turn to crackling.

These people are obliged by law to search every visitor from head to toe, to check I.D. against bookings, to receive and cross through Visiting Orders, to glare unhelpfully and generally foster an atmosphere of hostility. It's in their contracts.

A contract is a piece of paper, which is a symbol, which tells you what you can and can't do, and what happens if you fuck up. This is important.

Today's guy, he goes too high in the crotch. He goes over the buttocks, under the armpits, across the nipples, round the neck.

Today's guy, the way he smells, this is like sexual assault via compost heap.

The thing with going to see the Red-Tie-Guy, with getting mixed up in all that business, is that there are two reasons why I shouldn't even *consider* it.

The first reason has to do with Organised Crime.

The thing with Organised Crime is, really, it's a stupid name. This is a name to conjure an inaccurate impression. This is a mythological *EastEnders*-style establishment of tough-but-fair geezers who run criminal empires of boxing gyms and nightclubs.

This is what could charitably be described as a load of old cock.

The truth about Organised Crime is, all you need to be a Gangster is a gang.

The truth about Gangs is, they're not nearly as suave as you'd think.

In Her Majesty's Class A Prison-Service Facility Belmarsh, SE28, the blue-jumper Orc squints down and asks if I'm carrying any knives, guns, matches, fireworks, explosives, bottles, illicit substances or dangerous/prohibited items of any other sort.

I've seen idiots in the queue joke here. These people do not get in to the visiting room. These are the people who declare they've got suitcases full of bombs at international customs then can't believe it when they're dragged away.

If anyone ever wanted to ask me why I kill people for money, this would be a good thing to mention.

I tell him 'no'.

The thing with Organised Crime is, not many people set out to be criminals. Not many people have a life-goal of breaking laws. It just happens.

Like, maybe, you figure you're prepared to do something most people wouldn't, and there's a barrel of cash to be had out of it.

The thing with Organised Crime is, it's never like it looks in films.

The thing with Organised Crime is: It's. All. About. The. Money.

Stop me if you've heard this before.

The Prison Service Ogre, whose name-badge has a coffee-ring half obscuring the photograph, he squints at my I.D. and compares it to the name on the Visiting Order.

Today my name is Sam Brunt. I have a goatee. I have a bristly mole on my chin.

In her Majesty's Prison Service Visitation Waiting room, the troll grunts something that could be 'Table six', and waves me through.

This place, it smells like Dettol and magnolia paint and breeze-blocks.

The problem with Organised Crime is, all it takes is one stupid arsehole, one chat-happy nobody with verbal diarrhoea, opening his mouth to the wrong people, and the whole shebang tumbles down.

I work alone. If anyone's going to drop me in it, it's me.

This is reason number 1 why I don't much fancy this whole 'Choir' business.

This prison visitation system, it's a complete bloody palaver.

The way it works is, Her Divine Majesty bequeaths to each con a Visiting Order. This is a small piece of paper which is easily lost, and a bastard to replace. This is a piece of paper which, if you fill it out wrong, isn't worth spit. This is a piece of paper which the prison sends to whoever wants to visit.

This is a small piece of paper which tells you what you can and can't do, and what'll happen if you fuck up. This is important.

Without this piece of easily torn newspaper-grade shit, the prisoner's life consists of: The Prison.

Isn't it funny how much in life revolves around small pieces of paper?

The visiting order, whoever receives it signs it, calls up the prison, books an appointment at least twenty-four hours in advance, and brings it with them when they come.

My father, he never asks why he has to send it to Sam Brunt, c/o the Post Office branch three tube stops away from my flat. I think maybe he figures he'd be calling the kettle black.

Like: *Hey, son, I notice you're using a false I.D. Now, OK, I know, it's true that I'm serving a life sentence for murder, but I do hope you aren't getting up to anything illegal.*

You heard me. The 'm' word.

Maybe it's genetic.

Listen, standing here, not thinking about it, just waiting; ohoyeah, my eyes start to flicker and flash. This is like the first symptoms of an aura migraine, which I used to get when I was twelve, thirteen, fourteen. This is the sick knowledge that you're about to spend the next three hours feeling like someone went shish-kebab with your brain, like you can't move without puking, like there's a gap over your vision – or if not your vision, then your actual *consciousness*. Migraines, let me tell you, are nasty.

My fingertips go numb.

Fuck it, I tell myself, over and over and over. *Just fuck it*.

A door clangs, a buzzer buzzes, somewhere footsteps shuffle nearer. The cons, being brought out. The eyeball thing goes away and my fingers wake up.

Self-distraction is the new self-destruction, which was yesterday's new self-improvement. Who told me that?

Listen, reason number 2 for not being sure about this whole 'Choir' business is a thing called 'Reflected Risk'. This is sort of at the heart of what I do. This is important.

Bear with me, here.

In the visiting room, which is like a school canteen without the food, the cons waddle in one by one. They look grey. They look like the dead-ghoul-zombie-hallucination in Bracknell, except they're all in one piece and not quite as angry.

These people, what I'm getting at is, they aren't really people at all. These people, in this place, what they make me think of is a VHS tape left on 'pause'.

A frozen chicken nugget, awaiting the glorious Day of Defrosting.

These people, until someone hits 'play' again, they're just going through the paces.

My father is halfway down the line. He catches sight of me.

There're about two seconds of eye contact.

Let me tell you, however long I decide to stay, it's all downhill from here. This two seconds, this is the limit of affection between us.

The Reflected Risk Principle has something to do with trust. Or maybe the lack of it.

What the Reflected Risk Principle comes down to is that someone who pays me to kill someone will not compromise my security, on account of how their neck is on the line too. All my risk is reflected on to them.

This sounds obvious. This sounds like common sense, only you'd be surprised.

What the Reflected Risk Principle comes down to is, if the employer gets found out, because maybe he blabbed to someone, or couldn't handle the remorse, or got drunk and lippy – whatever – it's no skin off my nose. The employer never gets my real name. These people, they never get my address. Sometimes I never even meet them. These people, they know nothing about me except the number of a temporary offshore account and the sound of my voice telling them there's nothing quite like cucumber sandwiches. These people, if they get caught . . .

I don't.

My father walks over to table six and takes his seat.

'Hi.'

'Hi.'

I suppose he looks a little like me. The real me. *Sans*

goatee and grotesque mole, *avec* heroin-style eyebags, three-day shadow and balding dome. We stare at each other.

'So . . .' he says.

This could take a while.

With Organised Crime, there's no Reflected Risk. With Organised Crime, they tell you to do something, you *do* it. With Organised Crime, if you get caught, that's the end of it. Game over. Stop the clock. They know your name. They know where you live. *They* get caught, *you* get caught.

And let's say it's the other way round. Let's say you fuck up on the job. Let's say there're cuffs on your wrists and you're stupid enough to mention who it was who hired you, who you're working for, plea-bargaining whingeing, blah blah fucking blah. Let's say you Sell Out the Firm. What will happen is two things.

Number one: the Slippery Bastards you're pointing at will prove they had nothing to do with it. Alibis, witnesses, greased cogs.

Number two: you will disappear.

Organised crime, let me be clear, is a pain in the arse.

My father and I . . . I'd like to say we have a rich and enlightening conversation.

My father and I, I'd like to say we laugh and trade news, and smile and twinkle like all these others in here. I'd like to say we engage on a deep and personal level, so that even though he's Inside and I'm Out, it makes no difference.

We don't.

I stay half an hour. This is a little longer than usual, and this is only because the prison library just got a new batch of books and he's got something to enthuse about.

For half an hour I sit and grunt and question and nod,

and all the time I'm seeing clean, white bathroom walls, spots of blood slipping down the tiles, running along the Polyfilla channels. The body slumped in the ceramic base, all curled up like a cat. Like a witchetty grub. I'm seeing pink skin turning white-then-grey. I'm seeing knife wounds like tiny tidy fannies, washed clean by the shower-water so the edges are as clear as lipless mouths. Like puppets, waiting for someone to open and close them, chatting along in time with a ventriloquist. *Gottle of geer, gottle of geer. At's a-way to do it!*

I did not cause this death. This death was a long time ago.

I'm seeing her hair. Matted. Stuck to the tiles. One of the wounds has opened her cheek, and there's hair caught in the gash. Snagged by the meat.

I'm seeing myself, twelve years old, embarrassed as hell at seeing a naked woman for the first time.

Back in the here-and-now, the lights are flickering again. Around me people look grey and dead, with tongues lolling and eyes blazing red and faces rotting away. Spidery shadows tangle round my legs under the table, and the memories of the bloodless body in the shower get muddled with prison faces, scowling eyes, bored men and women.

Fuck it. Say it over and over and over. *Fuck it, fuck it, fuck it.*

As long as I don't talk about it. As long as I don't open my mouth. As long as my father and me, in this quaint little small-talking façade, obey the cardinal rule of our visits: We. Do. Not. Discuss.

It.

Then I'll be fine.

111

Ask me why I come here. I dare you.

Let me tell you: I've only been doing this two-and-a-half-years. Since I started my job. You might say entering my obscure profession opened my eyes.

Let me tell you: it's when you live with the possibility of imprisonment that you start thinking how you'd cope.

Let me tell you: my father, before me, no one ever came to see him.

And maybe this is empathy for the devil, maybe like I understand how it must be for him, in here, thinking of the past, all regrets . . .

Or maybe this is just my control. Maybe one week I won't come.

What will he do then?

Maybe one week I'll send him a postcard from Antigua or Costa Rica or Phuket or Christchurch or wherever.

. . . *not coming back, Pa* . . .

Maybe I'm only here to give him something I can take away. Maybe.

Every job I do, this problem gets more real. And perish the thought I should launch into a melancholy dirge on the horrors of corrective punishment, but this smell . . . this place . . . not for me.

The point I'm making is: who'd visit *me*?

Call it the law of averages. Call it the 'nobody's-luck-lasts-for ever' principle. One day, unless I get out soon, this is where I'll be. And then me and my father, we'll both be the same.

This is something I can't allow.

The Plan. The magic number with a bunch of zeroes and a pound sign. The get-out clause. The life in the sun. My

Plan, it's like the ultimate J.W.A. You remember that? Just Walk Away.

So yeah, this whole business with going to see the Red-Tie-Guy, with taking a trip to visit the Choir: it has its obstacles. It has its reasons-to-be-wary. But in its favour . . . in its favour, you've got to weigh the *pro* with the cons. One. Million. Pounds.

Sunny beaches. Sangria. Pretty girls in bikinis. Happy, happy days.

Let me tell you, sitting here, smelling the Dettol, staring at the magnolia walls, failing dismally to talk to the only person on this fucking horrible planet who knows me at all, what I'm thinking over and over and over is this:

It's. All. About. The. Money.

Chapter Eight

Today is Monday.

Today I wear glasses. Today I am a walking mullet with thick eyebrows. Today my head aches like an earthquake and I can't decide if it's the wig or the eye-strain or Something Worse. Today I would have taken pills, only if you can't trust your own senses, what have you got?

All these little foibles. All these little getting-to-know-yous.

This morning after I left my flat, I stopped and bought a mid-range Polaroid instant-photo camera from a high-street shop five tube stops away from my flat. I also bought a book of first class stamps, a Polaroid instant-photo camera film, and a manila envelope with a self-sealing strip at the top. The Polaroid instant-photo camera, which hangs on a cord around my neck at this precise instant, comes with a control called 'Time Sig'. This means, if I want it to, it'll print the date and time on to the bottom corner of the picture.

This is important.

For the record, the way I spent the weekend was: exploring.

Today the place I'm heading for is just another building. Today this is any one of a billion grey-brick unadventurous

Victorian-house-conversions. Today, this is the office of the man, woman, men, women – who knows? – I've come to meet.

On the buzzer by the door, the little glass window beside the number 3 has a printed label. It says: CHOIR

That sinking feeling.

I press the button.

With Exploring, on Saturday, I sat at the computer in my flat, and Googled. If this sounds surreal, or painful, or pornographic, it isn't. Mostly.

Googling is what happens when we think we have a global culture. Googling is what happens when every empty-skulled moron can type what they want, when they want, and call it Fact. Googling is an encyclopaedia for people who aren't bothered about the Truth. I Google a lot.

Today, this buzzer, it makes no sound.

Let me tell you, Google is a search engine enabling you to find out about Whatever.

This is via the Internet. For example, did you know that a spider's silk is stronger than steel, can stretch to 140 per cent of its original length, is inelastic, and is coated in a natural antiseptic useful for the treatment of wounds?

This is trivia, which is similar to trivial, but without the 'l'.

To spend any amount of time browsing on the Internet, you've got to know what you're getting into. You've got to be aware of the different types of stuff you're looking at. The way it works is, there are four categories:

1. Fact
2. Opinion

3. Culture
4. Bullshit

Let me tell you, when you go Googling, you never know which one you're getting. This is far more liberating than it sounds.

Today, over the buzzer, a man's voice says 'Come to get rich, Mr Point?' Then, 'Third floor.'

The door unlocks.

Did you know that less than 8 per cent of all the money in all the world exists as physical cash?

Fact? Bullshit? I told you already: this is seeing the world without the middleman. This is a drug called Information. This is procrastination hiding behind learning. This is Borrowed Wisdom, intravenous or intramuscular, addictive and antisocial and useless and oh-so-fucking irresistible.

At exactly what point does it matter if it's bullshit or fact?

The inside of this building has no reception. The inside has a stairway with no security guard, no lift, no paintings and no decorative flowers. There are no cameras.

On the third floor, at the top of the stairs, the Red-Tie-Guy is waiting.

'Knew you'd come,' he says. 'Nice wig.'

In my hand is the manila envelope, and this guy, this suave skank, this black-shirted vision of once-I-was-a-Goth-kid twattism, he's staring at it and smiling. 'Brought your CV?' he says.

I tell him if I had a wit as sharp as his I'd be careful in case I cut myself, and he does his laugh, his half-sneer. *Kkkhh*

Did you know that cats have over one hundred vocal

sounds, while dogs get only ten? Smarmy bastards in Red Ties can make as many as they want.

'Arms out,' he says.

And he gropes. He feels. Armpits, chest, crotch, neck, shins. Some people, they put razor blades round their collars just for a laugh.

For the record, in my pocket today there is no Ruger Mk II .22. There is no AR-7 sniper rifle. There is no double-edged seven-inch hunting knife in a rubber sheath.

Don't think I didn't think about it. Don't think I didn't consider playing this by ear, reacting violently, storming the place. Don't think I didn't ponder a rampage through this building. This building I've never been inside before. Killing people I've never met. Looking for a boss I wouldn't recognise. Protecting my anonymity, my reputation, my liberty, my motherfucking freedom, with hardcore shooty-death-kill-crimes I haven't had a chance to plan.

Instead here's me, still clinging to professionalism.

'Good lad,' he says, and I hate him. 'This way.'

Through a door, down a hall lined with other doors, treading bare floorboards. This place, if I couldn't hear typing, couldn't hear hands on keyboards, couldn't hear *clittaclattaclittaclatta*, if I didn't know better, I'd say it was deserted.

On Saturday evening the Googling got dull. On Saturday evening, when I was through with downloading recreational porn, when I was through with dubbed wet noises, groans and moans, arched backs and slippery faces and shaved unshaved skinny podgy mature 2g1m *ménage-à-trois* anal spitroast everyhole felching creampie bukkake midgets fatties S&M facial cumshot screaming grunting orgasmic digitised *drama*, when I was through with 'leztwinsex.wmv', '69!!great!!.avi' and 'herfirsttime.mpg' (it wasn't), what I did was this: I turned my thoughts to this business with the CHOIR.

Reflected Risk, I thought.

Isn't it funny, I thought, how much in life revolves around little pieces of paper.

Right, I thought.

On Sunday . . . On Sunday I was busy. Sunday was hardcore.

Today the Red-Tie-Guy says: 'Wait here', and vanishes through the door at the end of the hall.

On Saturday evening, and all day Sunday, the idea I'd been cooking up since I spoke to Sally on the phone, which was Thursday, which was two days before, went something like this: *I'd better have as much dirt on them as they've got on me*.

The posh way of saying this is: *know thine enemy.*

The way my brain went was, hey, they don't call you a contract killer for nothing.

'OK,' says the Red-Tie-Guy, and he's standing in the doorway waiting. The funny thing is, I didn't even see the door open. 'He's ready for you.'

Inside is a room. Somewhere there's a desk. This is maybe near the door, or maybe across the room. The funny thing is, it's hard to tell, and already my headache is worse.

Did you know that astronauts on the moon couldn't judge perspective for toffee? This was because, with no atmosphere, everything seemed too sharp, too focused.

This room, suddenly I know what they meant.

Beside the desk is a cheap imitation log fire, with flames

made from orange silk that flutter above a hot-air fan. This room, I only just came in and already I'm sticky with sweat.

The cheap fire makes a noise like this: *vvvvvvvm* . . . *vvvvvvvm* . . . *vvvvvvvm* . . .

Did you know: In 1666, the Great Fire of London burned down 80 per cent of the city's buildings but injured just six people. It started in the house of Thomas Farynor in Pudding Lane, where nowadays there's a stylish-yet-inexpensive Spanish restaurant called Fuego.

Thomas Farynor wasn't Spanish.

Behind the desk is a man. In the man are the weirdest eyes I've ever seen.

In the future, a restaurant named *Fall-out* will open in Chernobyl.

In the future, *Kaboom* is a trendy wine bar in Hiroshima.

In the future, *Ahahaha* is an all-night ratmeat BBQ in the ashes of a Scorched Earth.

'Ah,' he says. 'Mikey.'

Yesterday, which was Sunday, I sat at my computer and did not go Googling. On Sunday I sat with a word processor, rubbing my chin and saying 'huhm'.

This man's eyes, they're like those wildlife documentaries with night vision. They're like if you're driving at night and you know there's a fox, maybe a deer, maybe a badger. They're like if you've ever taken a photo of someone with a flash, too close up.

Like where the light reflects off the cornea. Like when you remember: the eye, actually, it's just a hole. This man, he looks up and he smiles, and you can see right inside. Inside, seriously, it looks like gold.

I ask him, so who the fuck're *you* then?

119

This is what's called overcompensating. This is what's called Being Aggressive As a Result of Gnawing Feelings of Inadequacy.

On Sunday, for this sheet of paper I'm carrying inside the manila envelope right here, I even went to the trouble of designing a little letterhead: MAKE YOUR POINT, INC.

My little joke.

This man, he stares at me for a moment, and all I'm hearing is *vvvvvm . . . vvvvvvm . . .*

The man in the chair, who is maybe forty, maybe fifty, who is perhaps a touch overweight, who has unremarkable hair and unremarkable features, who wears a comfortable-looking jacket and a black suede scarf, he says: 'You can call me boss.'

His accent: if he's not a Cockney sparrah, I don't know what is.

I tell him, no-no-no.

I waggle my finger like a metronome.

I tell him I'm not interested in what he wants me to call him, or any of this spooky dark-room bollocks, or any of this Hollywood gangster shit. I tell him I want to know what his *name* is.

He smiles.

He digs in his pocket and takes out a wallet. He spins it across to me. Behind me, the Red-Tie-Guy makes his little noise. *Kkkhh*

Inside the wallet are odd and ends. Inside are pieces of paper, plastic cards, one or two £20-notes. The name on the first card matches the name on the second. It matches the name on the driver's licence, and the photo is of him.

There's a donor card with his name and his handwriting, and a Blockbuster video rental card.

These could be fakes. These could be made up by any guy down any street with a magnetic-strip forger and a laminator.

These could be bullshit, but here's the thing: it's better than nothing.

I've got an address and a name. In a moment I'll have a fingerprint, a photograph, a signature. It's *enough*.

(The name, if you want to know, is average and boring and dull, and under normal circumstances I'd tell you exactly what it is. It's just that . . . right now . . . right this moment . . . I can't quite remember.)

The silence stretches out, and eventually I hand back the wallet.

Eventually I say, 'So.'

It's like talking to Dad all over again.

I say, 'First things first. How d'you find me?' This is with face set. Cool, I mean. In control, I mean.

This Boss, he tells me to sit down and gestures at a chair facing the desk. This chair, let me tell you, I'm nearly sure it wasn't there when I came in.

The Red-Tie-Guy, behind me, he says, *Kkkkhh*

'My name,' I say. 'My address, my fucking phone number . . .'

This Mr Call-Me-Boss, he smiles.

'I wasn't followed home,' I say. 'Not from the job in Bracknell. I know that fucking much.'

Twice round every roundabout, indicators pointing the wrong way, waiting at lights till the last instant . . . This trade, no one ever got caught being *too* careful.

121

This Mr Call-Me-Boss, he smiles again and he gestures. 'Sit,' he says. 'Please?'

I tell him I'm not doing a fucking thing until I get some answers. I tell him it doesn't work like this.

I do not mumble. I do not mutter. I have planned this.

The electric heater says: *Vvvvvvvmm . . . vvvvvvvmm . . . vvvvvvvmm.* I sweat.

This man, this guy-with-the-eyes, he sighs. He purses his lips.

He says, 'The thing is, Mikey – and I didn't want to do all this yet, but you asked. The thing is, what you're askin' me there, that's a tricky question. The thing is, you're just gonna have to trust me.'

I hold my sides and mime laughing. He just stares.

Eventually he says, 'What you got to understand, Mikey, is – an' I'm sorry 'bout this— I *know* you. I know you in all sortsa ways you're never gonna work out. Birthday, shoe size, all that.' He waves a hand in the air. 'Like. I know you never been christened. I know how old you was first time you got your end away. That thing with you tryin' to lift the car with the Forklift – first job out of school, right? Know all about that.'

He looks at me. His eyes shimmer like gold.

'I know about the thing you saw in the lav, Mikey. Twelve years old. The shower. You remember that?'

Oh. Oh, that sinking feeling. This is my legs not working. This is my eyes going strange.

This is me saying: 'But . . .'

I sit the fuck down. I ram my eyes shut.

Behind me: *Kkkkhh*

Somewhere, like a long way off, this Mr Call-Me-Boss,

he says, 'But you don't wanna *talk* about *that*, Mikey, do you? Not now.'

Kkkkhh

The voice says, 'So how 'bout you stop askin' stupid questions I ain't intendin' to answer, eh? Honestly, mate. Comin' in 'ere, all up yerself. Not nice.'

I breathe. Slow and deep. I'm gripping the arms of the chair like I'm planning on falling. I'm gripping like this till my head stops swimming and I can tell the difference between up and down again.

I open my eyes and he's still sitting there, still staring. Smiling.

'Wanted to ask you,' he says, ''bout that last job of yours.'

I wipe sweat off my head. All my anger, all my demands for answers, all my confusion; wiped off my forehead with the back of my arm.

Let me tell you, being here in front of this man, this guy-with-the-eyes, this Mr Call-Me-Boss, this is like being up shit creek without a boat.

He runs his tongue around the inside of his mouth, like a frog watching a fly, and he narrows his eyes. 'Would I be right in thinkin',' he says, 'our lanky mate – in Bracknell – there was somethin' . . . Bit odd about him?'

I try to set my jaw. It probably looks like I'm pouting.

'Odd how?'

He waves another hand. 'Oh, I dunno. You tell me. Somethin' beyond the ordinary, maybe? Didn't quite go according to plan . . .'

. . . *moaning and stamping about, stuff hanging off his lips, face all caved-in, calling me a cunt with four bullets in his body* . . .

I say, 'Don't be stupid.'

This Mr Call-Me-Boss, he smiles. He does this indulgent-shrug-thing like he's humouring a kid, like any minute he's going to tousle my hair and tell me: *you'll understand when you're older.*

And then he shrugs. I *hate* that.

'Either way,' he says, 'you done well. 'S why you're here.'

An uncomfortable silence dribbles into the room. In it, if you want to know, I fidget. I blink and try to come up with something. Some genius way to divine what's going on. Some infallible scheme to get out of this, to escape, to turn this whole shambling, bleeding, oozing mess to my advantage. I run my hands over the manila envelope in my lap, and I glance over my shoulder at the Red-Tie-Guy. He's staring at me. I look back at the Boss and my mouth is dry, and the camera around my neck feels heavy.

The problem is, it's hard to escape from something when whole chunks of your brain are . . . How to put this? *Distracted.*

I say, 'This offer of yours . . .'

The Boss says, 'One million.'

It's. All. About. The. Money.

It's as well to get this stuff sorted. Sod haggling. Sod the 'you have to convince me' pricktease, the hard-to-get, the holding-out. I knew the second I walked in I wasn't leaving without the deal done.

'One million,' he says. 'Three jobs.'

I tell him I want details. I want assurances.

I tell him I want paying up-front.

He laughs. He shakes his head, chuckle-chuckle-chuckle, then

CONTRACT

BAM.

No smile.

'Be serious, Mikey,' he says. 'That ain't how it works. I ain't fundin' your little plan.' He nods at my jacket and the paper nestled inside and the magic number on it. *How does he know?* He leans forwards.

'You're the shithead in this, Mikey. You're the bad guy. Don't forget that. You gotta earn *your* trust.' He shakes his head again and barks out one last little laugh. 'No, you get paid in chunks. That's how it works. Two hundred kay after the first, 'nother two after the second. Rest on completion.'

I try to keep the wobble out of my voice.

'Difficulty levels,' I say. 'Could be suicide, all I know . . .'

He shrugs. He blinks like a camera shutter; mirror snapping-down, secret chemistry behind. Celluloid and silver, ratchets and springs, hidden images. Golden glow.

It makes me shiver.

'Not suicide,' he says. 'Not if you're any good. First two jobs are standard. Easy. Third's trickier – but doable.'

He says, 'For that much cash, Mikey, I would've thought you'd at least fancy a *look*.'

I stare at him. He stares back.

'And if I say no?'

He licks his lips. 'Well,' he says. 'Then that's that.'

The Red-Tie-Guy makes his noise. I resist the urge to punch and kick him until his teeth are shattered out of his gums and his tongue is a swollen cucumber blocking his throat and his cheeks are shredded scraps that dangle and flutter with every breath.

Again the silence, though this time my face is burning; this time my ears are doing the roaring-water thing.

This is beyond awkward.

'I need some insurance,' I say.

The Boss scowls and waves a hand, an Imperial *go on*, and this I find infuriating. This has something to do with his confidence. See also: power. See also: me being a resentful small-minded little crook who thinks he's being sneaky.

I open the manila envelope. I've carried it all this way. Inside are two identical sheets of paper, with a carbon transfer page between them. Isn't it funny how so much in the world revolves round small pieces of paper?

This is *mutual* risk. This is making sure he's got as much to lose as me. This is the convenient collection of a signature, a timed, dated Polaroid photograph, and a set of his fingerprints. This is my little trick, so when I agree to bend over for him – as he knows I will – he at least has to keep his expensive bastarding trousers on.

I have planned this carefully, since talking to Sally on the phone. Just talking to her. Seriously. It helps me *think*.

At the top of the page is a letterhead, reading: MAKE YOUR POINT, INC.

Beside this is a company logo. It's a finger, pointing. My little joke.

This sheet of paper, the first line begins: *We the undersigned* . . . At the foot of the page are two straight lines, one beside the other. One is marked: *Employee*. I've already signed it.

A signature is a symbol filled up with importance. Tip it up and what pours out depends on what you think the symbol means.

Listen, this is important. On its own, without someone to see it, a symbol is just a shape.

A signature is a symbol that means ME. The other line is marked: *Employer*. In between, in language so pompous I needed a dictionary twice in each sentence, what it basically says is, 'If *I* go down, so do *you*.'

'What's this?' says the man behind the desk.

I smile and tell him, 'What do you think it is?'

Contract: *n.&v.* • *n.* '*kontrakt* 1. agreement between parties; business agreement for supply of goods or performance of work at specified price; agreement enforceable by law. 2. accepted promise to do or not do; formal agreement for marriage; conveyance of property; commitment to make stated number of tricks.

Sooner or later, the Boss reads through it. He holds it with his left hand, fingers pressed against the paper, and his lip twitches – twice – as his eyes flutter left-right-left.

That's a fingerprint, shithead.

Sooner or later, and fuck me if I have any idea how long it takes, he places the paper down and looks up at me.

Sooner or later, he says, 'Is this a joke?'

I tell him no.

He breathes out. His breath – honestly, here in this sweaty heat and cloying dark – his breath *mists*.

'You're your father's son, Mikey,' he says.

That sinking feeling.

That spiral into unexpected dark.

That off-balance mini-death.

'W . . . what?'

It would be nice to pretend I kept out the stammer.

Did you know: studies have shown that children are

statistically more likely to share the gender of whichever of their parents was less stressed at the time of conception. Fact? Bullshit? Culture? Opinion?

My mum, there with my dad . . . My quiet, awkward, too-calm father. You've got to wonder.

Mr Call-Me-Boss stands up. It surprises me how short he is, then again, when I get convinced, despite it all, he's *massive*, looming; like there's some freaky dimension to him you can't describe. Astronaut-eyes, misbehaving perspective. Is he distant and colossal, or pressed against my face with his breath steaming around him?

'Told you, didn't I? Know all *about* you, Mikey. You and your family.'

I try to stand.

'Always had a . . . meticulous streak, your old man. Planned everything very carefully.'

My legs, misbehaving again.

The walls bulge inwards. Suddenly, this gold-eyed bastard is different. Suddenly, out of the corner of my eye, his hair's on fire: white and heatless, and the golden slivers in his face pour out like honey. Suddenly, he's wearing white.

He's talking about my dad, still. Things only I could know. Things about . . . about water running. About fingers greasy and wet on Perspex drip-screens. About the crashing shrieks from *Psycho*, about white tiles and red gutters and—

No. Fuck it.

Calm, Mike.

FUCK IT. Focus.

Listen: whatever it is he's saying, whatever unreal shit he drones, however he *knows* this, I'm not listening. I'm not paying attention. His chair flutters with feathers and the Red-Tie-Guy, he's a hummingbird with a scarlet breast, wings held out. The heater smiles, wet tongue and cavity-filled teeth, and every time it giggles—

Vvvvvvvm . . . vvvvvvvm . . . vvvvvm . . . the tongue wriggles.

I'm hallucinating.

Fuck it. Fuck it, fuck it, fuck it.

At some point, I'm standing and taking the Polaroid photo. I think perhaps the Boss poses. I think perhaps the Red-Tie-Guy helps, because there are hands on my shoulders and when I glance at the picture there's a man there, smiling. The world wobbles. Things seem blurred like I'm ready to faint but can't quite commit. The gold-eyed bastard blazes and blinds me, and still I'm placing the photo in my pocket and thinking: *Got you, you twat.*

At some point he signs the contract. Still he's talking about me. My life. My father.

At some point paper flutters and a pen scratches across whiteness (snow, sleet, white tiles, blood in the plughole, *shit*), and he's showing me the signature because I dare not fucking stand up in case I fall – (no, I'm *already* falling, I'm tumbling and *shit, oh shit, oh shit*) – and then he's tucking the copy away in his desk, and the original he slides with a grin into the manila envelope. And hands it over. And the walls stop shaking. And his voice stops droning.

'Ain't that how it went, Mikey?' he says. 'Nasty shit for a boy to see.'

I need to leave.

The Red-Tie-Guy says, '*Kkkhh.*'

The Boss, he pulls out a drawer from under the desk and

lifts up a brown file tied with string. He glances at the title on the front, weighs it in his hand, and passes it over.

'What's this?' I ask, wiping sweat, coming back. Returning to Earth.

'Your first job.'

This is too daft. This is too damn Hollywood. This stuff *never* happens.

Inside the file, on the top of a sheaf of papers, is a photograph. This is taken surveillance-style. This is probably from a car window. This is showing a middle-aged man, smiling, shaking the hand of an elderly woman in a stone doorway.

This is a man wearing black.

This is a man with a dog collar.

'Jesus Christ,' I mutter.

'Not quite,' says Mr Call-Me-Boss.

This man, this suited freak of nature, he chuckles to himself and there's steam coming up from his breath like it's the middle of the winter.

'Sorry about the cold,' he says.

The heater says: *vvvvvvm . . . Vvvvvvm . . . Vvvvvvvvm . . .*

I sweat and go.

On the way home, I'm not even bothering.

Trying to figure out what the fuck just happened, what weird nonsense just came over me, what screwed-up brainrot is dissolving my synapses *right now*. All this. I'm too tired. I'm too busy keeping down puke, wiping sweat, breathing. Too busy not thinking.

Self-distraction is the new self-destruction, which was yesterday's new self-improvement. Who told me that?

I'll go home and drink coffee and switch on the TV. I'll dissolve into Borrowed Wisdom. I will Google and download porn and watch cheap nature documentaries about dangerous reptiles. The anticipation of this almost makes me cry.

On the way home, I pause at a letterbox on the corner of Charing Cross Road, and I write my own address on the manila envelope I've been carrying since leaving the Boss. I include my own name. My real name. I unpeel a stamp from the booklet I bought earlier, and wonder when they stopped putting gum on the back that meant you had to lick them. Now, they just peel off. Like party stickers. Like parking permits. Like price tags in a superstore.

This post thing, this is an old trick. This is to retain something as evidence permissible in a court of law.

The way this works is, the fine men and women of Her Majesty's postal service apply a rubber stamp to each and every item that passes them by, and on said stamp is a date.

An unsealed envelope, a stamp to prove its date, to prove it showed up before the crime it describes, and yeah, ohoyeah, Mr Call-Me-Boss: *I've got you.*

The thing is, in this job, nobody ever got caught being *too* cautious.

In a day, or two, or three – or a week – this manila envelope will crash through the letterbox of my home and startle me awake, because I never, *never* get post. I will leave it sealed, and I will stare at it from time to time, and think of the signature-photograph-fingerprints inside. I will think of the postage stamp on the cover which will corroborate my story, and every time I glance at it, I will remember that a signature is a symbol that means: *Don't you fuck with me, you weird-eyed prick.*

As I go home, I can almost persuade myself to smirk.

Interview Room 2

Back in Interview Room 2 – right now – Jason Durant, my old buddy, my old mate, this floppy-haired cockfracture, he screws up his forehead like crumpled paper and scowls.

His partner Anna is scribbling notes on a spiral-bound notepad with a blue Biro. I don't know what she's writing. I don't know where the pen and paper came from. I'm pretty sure they weren't here when I came in.

Her pen, when it moves across the paper, it makes a sound like: *scritchascritchascritchascritch.*

This is the world as a mole hears it. This is a filtered thing of bristle-noses and scratching claws. This is what it's like to be buried in the earth, six feet down, with just worms and taproots and maggots for company.

Graveyard grooves.

Jason Durant looks annoyed. Not because of the scratching pen, ohono. The reason he looks bugged, right here and now, is this: 'I need to piss.'

That's me, saying that.

'It can wait,' he says.

This is biological tyranny.

This square-shouldered rugby-playing monolith. I bet he's repressed.

This flawless Teutonic knight. Dreaming every evening of

whips and bondage and scrotal flails and intimate piercings. I bet. It's written all over his face. I bet he's into Sado.

Jason Durant. Silly name.

My bet is, he has a collection of Butt-plugs for his personal use.

£30-vibe-ass battery-powered prostate punchers with flared ends to prevent colonic perforation and a free bag of KY jelly.

My bet is, our man Jason just looks too squeaky clean to be true.

'It can't wait,' I say.

'Half an hour,' he says. 'Then we'll see.'

I tell him no, thirty seconds – *then* we'll see. And probably smell.

I tell him, hey, did you know, holding back on taking a piss can cause voiding dysfunction, infections to the urinary tract, damage to the kidneys. Urethritis, cystitis, pyelonephitis.

I tell him that a tiny split in a bladder can cause systemic toxic shock. I tell him people die from it all the time. I tell him I've read about it.

Anna looks up from under her eyebrows.

Jason Durant, this floppy-haired crusty clump of malignant penile warts, he curls his top lip and says: 'That's borrowed wisdom, is it?'

I tell him, so what if it is?

'So how can you be sure,' he says, 'if it's fact or opinion?'

Smug, smug, smug.

I tell him: let's find out, and I cross my arms.

Silence descends.

Long story short: I get to piss, he gets to watch.

CONTRACT

*

In the gents, it echoes like a room with no furniture. There's no one else around.

Let me tell you: White tiles. Mildew. Soap dispensers without soap, dripping urinals. Yellow soap-cakes clustered together like UFOs lurking over the plugholes. These things, they have the sort of look where you can imagine what they'd taste like without even opening your mouth.

Down here are speckled mirrors. Down here are looped towel-dispensers stained and soggy. Down here are strip lights like epilepsy-bait and red-brown stains in the sinks.

Nice.

Down here, this could be a public shitter anywhere. This could have a Central London turnstile right outside, twenty pence a piss, confused tourists, bored maintenance guys with disinfected mops and yellow eyes.

Down here, somewhere, there's a dripping tap. Obviously.

So I'm unzipping and doing that little jiggle, you know the one – landing gear deployment – and I'm wondering if our man Jason Durant would be surprised how much shady shit goes on in cubicles where No CCTV Has Gone Before, when he goes and asks.

Listen, it had to happen.

Our man Jason, he's the curious type.

He's standing somewhere behind me. Watching my back, I guess. My attention is focused elsewhere.

SSSssss.

Oh God, yeah. Steam rising. Gurgling plughole.

'How d'you do it?' he says. His voice level is: Sort Of Quiet.

'Do what?'

'What you do.'

Ah.

SSSsss. Jeeeee-zus.

'Off the record?'

'You see any microphones?' There's a smile in his voice.

With my piss I'm playing that game where you try to nudge the yellow soap cake up the side of the urinal. It keeps slipping back.

'Not "why"?' I ask.

'Not why. How.'

I shrug without splashing. 'The thing is,' I tell him, 'there's different answers to that.'

'Like?'

'Like . . . What do you want? Mercenary honesty? Black-and-white-I'm-an-evil-shit sort of thing? Or you want me to have a crack at justifying it?'

Ballistic bladder-pressure dwindles. The yellow soap cake settles back over the plug. If it could flip me the finger it would.

Sss-sss . . . sss . . .

Last squirt.

'You mean you think you *can* justify it?'

'I mean I could *try.*'

'Would it work?'

I think for a second, then say, 'Not really.'

Here, we're just two guys. Public bog repartee. Urinal chat.

Outside of Interview Room 2, I could even forgive Jason Durant for being the dickdribble he is.

'Care to try?' he says.

I smirk and look back over my shoulder. 'You have a go,' I tell him.

This is reflected risk. Remember that? This is infecting others with a little dose of Me.

This is Michael Point, twenty-eight, insidious-but-not-smart.

'OK . . .' he says, and he's doing my job for me. 'OK.' You can almost hear the cogs turning. 'Survival of the fittest.'

I can hear his feet shuffling. I say, 'You what?'

'I mean, you could use that, couldn't you? Like justification. Natural order. The strong weed out the weak. Oldest law there is. You're Darwin's right-hand-man.'

'Would it convince you?'

'No.'

'A jury?'

'Hah. No.'

'Well then.'

Staring straight ahead, I'm down to leftovers. Secondary reservoirs. Bladder muscles pumping, prostate bobbing up and down like a beach ball.

SSssst.

SSssst.

Zero degree splashback. I *rule*.

'So what about the . . . the "Cleaner" principle?' says Jason Durant, international man of conscience.

'The what?'

'Come *on*,' he says, like he's been an expert all his life. 'Chances are the people you go after have done some bad shit anyway, right? You're just tidying up.'

Shake. Shake.

Jason Durant has been watching too many films.

'Bit Hollywood,' I say. 'You believe it?'

''Course not. Just playing devil's advocate.'

Zip.

I head for the sinks and glance at him. He has his arms folded. He's smiling.

Just two guys.

'So you got any other excuses for me?' I ask him.

He works his jaw. Maybe he thinks we're bonding.

Wanker.

'Living weapon,' he says.

'Come again?'

(Ahahaha. 'Wanker', geddit? Come ag—. Oh, never mind.)

'Down here, the taps have those plungers where the water never flows long enough. Those taps, you've got to keep pressing them over and over, and by the time your hands are back in the bowl the water's already stopped running.

'Guns don't kill people,' Jason says. 'People do.'

'Riiiight . . .'

'You could say you're just the same. You're just the weapon. There's no *intent.*'

I purse my lips and nod, like I'm considering it. Like I've never thought of this before. Like he's telling me something *new*.

Wanker.

'Yeah,' I say. 'Yeah, OK. I can see that. Any good?'

'Nope. Got to be an element of responsibility.'

''Course.'

He stares at me. The water stops running.

'What, then?' he asks. 'What's the justification? I'm out of ideas.'

My hands are dripping in time with the taps. I'm moving slow, holding eye contact, smiling, breathing deep.

Approaching.

'What keeps your conscience clean?' he says, and still he's smiling but maybe now this isn't so funny.

Just two guys in a public john.

He's not standing alert. His arms are folded. Off guard.

In the UK, public toilets are one of the top three locations for incidents of GBH.

Let me tell you, I'm not smart and I'm not quick and I'm not strong, but this man Jason Durant, right now I could kick his chiselled little arse and force yellow urinal soap cakes down his perfect throat until his guts rupture and he swallows his own tongue.

'What do you *say* to someone you're about to *kill*?' he says, and you can tell he's fascinated. Like he's scratching a cut. Like he can't leave it alone.

Somewhere behind me the timer on the urinals clocks out and the automatic flush begins: squirting and farting like a diarrhetic rat. It's noisy. It'd cover the sounds of a struggle.

Jason's still staring.

I'm still smiling.

I'm close enough to smell his aftershave.

His pupils are maybe just a *little* too big.

I say, 'You're in my way.'

His pupils get bigger.

'W-what?'

The flush goes quiet.

I'm almost touching him.

There's sweat on his forehead.

'The hand dryer,' I say. And I smile. And I nod towards it. 'You're in my way.'

When it comes on it sounds like the end of the world, and the air isn't hot.

Back in Interview Room 2, Anna's pen and pad of paper are gone. She nods at Jason as he leads me in.

'You boys have fun?' she asks.

'The best,' I say.

Jason sits down and looks ruffled. More points to me.

'Let's get on with it,' he says.

Chapter Nine

Today is Tuesday. Today I'm Just A Guy.

This is one week and one day since I went to see Mr-Call-Me-Boss.

Yesterday, which was Monday, I was a land surveyor taking measurements for a Ramblers' Association map.

On Sunday, let me see . . . On Sunday I was busy. On Sunday I was a local parishioner attending the Solemn Eucharist. On Sunday I was visiting the grave of my Uncle Tom, my father's sister's husband, who died when a tree fell on his car. On Sunday I collected conkers for my son Finn – he's in bed with the flu – from one corner of the graveyard. On Sunday I smiled and complained about my bad back to any dog-leading happy-smiling churchgoing Joe who walked by.

Sunday was hardcore.

The Ramblers' Association is a club for people who like walking. The latest thing is, Ramblers' Rights. The latest thing is, spending years campaigning for the right to walk down blocked-up public pathways. This is for access to fifty metres of shitty illegally developed real estate, so the poor dears don't have to detour through the pine-scented wooded paradise nearby.

For the record, I do not have an Uncle Tom.

I do not have a son called Finn.

I'm not here to grieve or conker-collect or attend church or survey the land. I'm here to shoot the friendly looking vicar twice in his face and twice in his chest with heroin-filled .22 hollowpoints fired at point blank range.

I've only been in this town three days and already I'm wrestling with Scruples.

Don't look so surprised.

Today I am in a small nowheretown called Parsons Yat, which is in the Forest of Dean, which is in Gloucestershire, which is maybe two, maybe three hours from London.

Let me tell you: to survey the topography of a small town street and parish church you will need:

an orange or yellow workman's jacket
a wooden tripod with an orange box and a lens
a second tripod with a bicycle reflector glued to the top
a clipboard

The jacket you buy from a charity shop. The rest you make yourself. This is *Blue Peter* for adults. This is make-and-do for Big People.

Smear cereal packet A with orange safety-paint B. Insert broken milkbottle C to poke out like a sophisticated piece of highly sensitive optical engineering. Here's one I made earlier. (Make sure you get a grown-up to help you with the cutting.)

The thing with wearing an orange reflective jacket is, the only people who'll ever ask what you're doing are *other* people in orange reflective jackets.

The thing with homemade cardboard surveying

equipment is, the only people who'll ever know the difference are other surveyors. If any of *those* show up, let me tell you: J.W.A.

Today, Tuesday, I'm just a guy.

This is sitting in a rental car outside the church. This is watching the clock on the dashboard creep towards 5 o'clock. This is wishing I'd taken a piss before I left the Bed & Breakfast in the next town. This is wearing flesh-coloured latex gloves. This is with a loaded Ruger Mk II .22 fitted with a homemade silencer in the left pocket of a massive blue cagoule. This is with the hood up.

By 'the hood' I mean the hood on my cagoule. The one that covers my head. In the US, a 'hood' is also a car bonnet. Also this is an abbreviation of 'Neighbourhood'. Also slang for a gangster.

The Hooded Hood lifts his Hood in the middle of the Hood.

This is Roger Red Hat for the twenty-first century.

In this trade it's best to avoid confusion.

I check the clip in the gun. This is the sixth time. In my other pockets are spare bullets, a rat-tail file, spare gloves, a double-edged, seven-inch hunting knife in a rubber sheath and a spare prosthetic facial mole. Today's bristly crime against skin conditions sits like frogspawn on my top lip.

The cagoule hood has drawstrings. I'm wearing an extra-thick rimmed pair of costume glasses. E-fit *this*, people.

The Solemn Eucharist is a formal choral liturgy in the Catholic tradition of Anglicanism. On Sunday, I sat at the back and pretended to sing along, like I knew the words. On Sundays, here, services start at 9. Then the Family ceremony's at 10. Then the Solemn Eucharist is at 11.

One crowd leaves, another shuffles in. Aloha.

Today is Tuesday. Today the big hand hits 12 and it's 5 o'clock p.m. This is with me watching the lights through the stained-glass windows. This is with the church just a shadow-shape beside the car. This is with rain coming down on the windscreen like I'm in a carwash.

Let's go kill a Man of God.

Today, being just a guy, what I'm wearing is: stuff. Jeans. Cheap trainers, with a second set ready and waiting in the glovebox. Black T-shirt.

The cagoule cost £34.99 in a sale at an Outdoor Sports shop in the Brent Cross Shopping Centre. The way I figure it, any splashback and all I've got to do is stand in the rain.

This is baptism, DIY-style.

My bladder, in my head I'm seeing water-balloons so full they burst. I'm seeing ripe melons exploding. I'm seeing sausages splitting as they cook.

I can't believe I forgot to Go.

On Sunday, the vicar stood and talked and sang and talked and sang. On Sunday, it didn't matter that his voice is like fingernails on chalkboards, on account of how, the louder he got, the louder the congregation got too. This is devotion by proxy. This is like beggars baiting their pots.

This little man. This pencil-thin pillar of the community. Robes and rosy cheeks. Wire-rimmed glasses. Dog collar.

This little town, for the record, it could be anywhere.

Dog collars, if you want to know, started out as thin bands of cloth to stop Catholic priests soiling their expensive shirts. This is right after the Renaissance. This is a style-over-content sort of thing. This is a functional way of disguising a sweaty neck winding up part of a professional uniform.

'Man of the cloth', see?

Borrowed wisdom.

One day every TV show will be a rerun. One day every film will be a remake. One day they'll invent glasses that turn everything upside down, just so the world seems *original.*

Today is Tuesday, and I'm out of the car and locking it behind me. Last time someone left the church was 4.23 p.m. This was a group of three old people, I'm guessing parish councillors, clustered under a single umbrella. This was like a tortoise, only with six legs, and they paused, like everyone round here does, to look at the muddy hole next to the path outside the front of the church.

This hole, it's like a deep crater. This is something of a Local Mystery.

On Sunday, at the end of his sermon, the Vicar said he suspected Kids, Up To No Good.

In this town, this hole is a symbol meaning: *What's the world coming to?*

So I'm out of the car and as I walk I'm looking at it. The thing is: unless you know who did it, it's just a hole.

As I walk, the jitters go away.

Oh yeah, the jitters. Scruples. Doubts. Nagging Thoughts.

These are not to be embraced. These are not emotional frailties to be celebrated, to remind me I'm alive. These are not genetic moral signposts to tell me what I'm about to do is wrong. What these are is: disposable.

The church door's unlocked. It doesn't creak. I checked on Sunday.

I lock it behind me.

This little man, with his unassuming tank-top and his unassuming haircut, who lives in the house beside the church with his unassuming wife and his unassuming cat, this little vicar whose sermons are safe and unassuming and uncontroversial, this little shepherd whose flock sing like saints just to drown out his whiny little voice: he's still inside.

This is his routine. I know this because yesterday at five o'clock I was standing across the street peering over a cardboard topographical surveyor. I know this because on Sunday at five o'clock I was flipping conkers into a Tesco carrier bag at the end of the graveyard. I know this because all day Sunday I was standing by the church, staring at The Hole, smiling and chatting and saying hello to whoever came by, grieving at the grave of my Uncle Tom.

The church is supposed to close at 5. This unassuming little vicar, he locks up just after.

What I'm getting at is, his wife and his cat aren't part of the deal.

What I'm getting at is, there's no better time or place.

What I'm getting at is, if you think it's a bit weird to be killing a guy inside a church, let me remind you of the golden rule.

It's. All. About. The. Money.

Inside the church is big and cold and old. It smells of candle smoke and dust.

Inside the church saints with names scribbled on twirly scrolls stare down at me. This is my stained-glass audience. This is crude pictures shattered and pieced together. This is with scribbled black lines holding faces to necks, swords in hands, dragons at bay.

CONTRACT

I wish I'd taken a pee before I came here.

St Margaret of Antioch was swallowed by Satan and spat back out again. She looks a little like Sally. I can't wait for this evening.

The church, today and here and now, with me holding off the jitters Pretty Well So Far, there's no one around. This is like an empty cinema. This is like a film that no one's watching.

Scratch that. What this is, is an antique stone cavern built for hundreds of people to buy one-way holidays in the afterlife. This is a massive great room with no one inside. This is a morgue without a corpse.

Take away whatever makes something what it is, what's left is just polystyrene packaging.

I take the gun out of my pocket.

St Paul, he was blinded by the flaming glory of the Lord on the road to Damascus. He's watching me with this funny half-smile, only his face is made of two separate pieces of glass and the expressions are different. St Paul, who was a Christian-hating Pharisee before the Loving God burned out his eyeballs, who is also called Saul, here and now and today he looks like he's had a stroke and only half his face is working. St Paul, when the blinding glory of heaven scorched his retinas to a pulpy mass, he didn't eat or drink for three days. St Paul, when eventually Ananias restored his sight, he converted to Christianity immediately.

This is not borrowed wisdom. This is not something I looked up in a book.

This is stuff I just know. Stuff from *before*.

I don't like to talk about it.

The story of Paul on the road to Damascus, listen: this is

someone Stealing Something Precious from you. This is them giving it back three days later. This is you being expected to *thank them*. This, let me clarify, is *fucked up*.

I'm walking up the aisle. In here, every footstep, it echoes like . . . Let me see. Like a sociopath in a church.

Does a falling tree still make a sound if there's no one there to hear it? I tell you, you've got to wonder. Is a church still a House of God when there's nobody around to bask in his glory? (I don't count.)

At the back by the altar there's a doorway with a curtain. You listen carefully enough, there's tuneless whistling from inside. This is the sound of a man who thinks he's alone. He's not.

For the record, tuneless whistling is up there with dance music and cats in the big book of things that I fucking hate.

All these little foibles. All these little getting-to-know-yous.

St Augustine of Hippo, surrounded by scrolls telling the world how we're all filthy bastards, how sex is evil, how we've all got to suffer to be pure, he's watching me tug back the curtain with a disapproving stained-glass glare.

Tonight, Augustine, when I've killed this unassuming little priest with his unassuming little whistle, when I'm flexing and sweating and grunting and scratching and pinching, when I'm arching my back and clenching my teeth and groaning like a caveman, when I'm slapping flesh with some random girl from some random club in some random bed, what I'll do is: I'll consider how very evil I am, just for you.

I've never been big on religion. This is important. Or not. It depends how you look at all this.

I'm subduing the jitters. Bear with me.

Behind the curtain is the vestry. This is the room where meetings take place. This is the room that can double as the vicar's office. This is the room where, traditionally, priests hang their vestments. This is a borrowed-wisdom phrase that means: robes.

The vestry, the smell of old sweat and mildew, the clothes hanging on iron pegs, this is like being back in my school changing-rooms. This is for football, hockey, swimming. This is for the tiny scrap of grass out the back of the school, across the main road, with the tumbledown goals and the broken glass. This is lurking in the shadow of the local estate.

This is with Foster Family number 2 or number 3. I forget which.

The Vicar has his back to me. I raise the gun.

He whistles like a squeaky bicycle.

Today and here and now, with a silenced Ruger Mk II .22 aimed at the back of his head, I tell the unassuming, whistling little vicar, 'Hey.'

This is so he turns around.

This is not because I have scruples about shooting people in the back. Sorry. This is because the curvature of the skull at the rear makes a killing shot just that little less likely. This is because of shoulderblades protecting the heart. Sorry.

In the vestry, the vicar turns round too quick and says, 'Whu.'

His eyes, they roll down from my face to the end of the gun.

He says, 'Oh m—'

I like to think he was about to blaspheme.

Spwk-spwk-spwk-spwk

Two in the face. Two in the chest.

Let me tell you, black shirts with lumps of skull. Spots of brain. Bits of eyeball. I'm trying not to think about it. Here is where the jitters come back *hard*. Here is the part when clarity counts, when distractions are a good thing.

Gunsmoke and legs twitching. The smell of blood.

I wish I'd taken a piss before coming out.

Today the body won't need a bath to prevent dripping. Today the issue of vertical neighbourhoods is not an issue at all. Today's burning topic is: time. Today, if this unassuming little vicar is half an hour late home, maybe an hour, his unassuming little wife has only a short walk to find out why.

Today's burning topic is: Get The Fuck Out Of Here.

Pick up the spent shell casings. Don't look at the body. Don't think about it.

Except here's the thing: the brain doesn't haven't an 'off' setting. Beyond the obvious one, I mean.

Except, here's the thing: that bowl of skull-spaghetti inside you, always it's collecting details.

Except, here's the thing: this little priest, this little devotional damp patch, he dropped something when he went down.

Heavy book. Leather-bound. Cross on the front.

I just killed a man reading the Bible. Go, scruples, go.

This man, with the fluid packaging, his brain leaking on the floor, with his white dog collar keeping his shirt from going red, this man of the cloth, this unassuming little stiff, he stares up at the ceiling and in the vestry there're no saints watching, no stained-glass panel of judges holding up score cards. There're no shattered images glued back together, keeping tabs. There's no Holy Big Brother.

Go through the paces. That's what.

The file I was given, that CIA-wannabe dossier bullshit in the offices of the Choir, after pages and pages of information, photographs, statistics, routines, printouts, maps, it contained a simple instruction.

Get his wallet.

So I'm bending and rummaging, and it turns out this is worse even than killing the guy; this is graverobbing, this is petty theft. This is one more nail in the coffin of Michael Point, Man of Principle.

Ahahaha.

I should be running away. I should be a distant dot by now. I should be Linford fucking Christie, up the aisle and out the door, wallet in hand, job done.

Just a little look.

Run, idiot.

Inside the wallet are several pieces of paper. One is a list written in blue Biro. Names and numbers. There are credit cards, family photographs, receipts, £5-notes, donor cards, no johnnies.

See also: a hidden pocket.

See also: tucked away, folded immaculately, another photograph.

Run! For fuck's sake, run!

This is feline inertia. This is what killed the cat. This is textbook Just Plain Amateurish.

My feet don't move.

The photo, it has blood on the corner. This is a picture of a little boy. He's maybe five. He has blond hair and a smiling, chubby face. He looks happy. He looks stupid and brainless and happy. This little boy, he's naked.

He's covered in mud like he's been wallowing in it. The camera flash is right in his eyes and that circle at the middle, that red lens, in this kid it's *not* red. In this kid it's white, until I blink and look again and now it's green, and now it's purple.

His hands are tied tight with white cloth, and you can see from the bruises it's *too* tight. This kid, his ankles are tied behind the chair legs to stop him moving. His eyes are blue now. The background in this photo, let me tell you. It looks a lot like this vestry.

This kid, count the cuts on his arms and legs. Spot the dried blood.

This kid, my stomach flops over.

'What', I say, and this is out loud because – hey – who's listening in an empty church, ahahaha, 'the fuck?'

And then I'm walking away, and the wallet is in my pocket, and I'm through the curtain, and my footsteps are echoing all round, and I'm putting the gun away, and Barnabas and Paul and Margaret and Eunice and Augustine and all the others, they're staring down with stained-glass frowns and the rain hammering on their backs, and nothing's changed.

Out through the door. Fresh air. The smell of grass. Take a look around.

There's nobody watching. Nobody who knows.

Let me tell you, the car waiting at the end of the path, past the muddy hole, the rental motor with loud and unbearable dance music cued-up and ready, this is salvation. This is a cure for the jitters.

Oh yeah, the jitters. Back with a vengeance.

I need a piss.

CONTRACT

Let me tell you, the car waiting at the end of the path, I'm getting closer. Fresh shoes. Dispose of the gun. Back home. M4. London. See Sally. Clubbing. Sex. This is the shopping list of normality. This is Handling Homicide 101.

The church door closes behind me. I didn't hear it open. The hinges don't creak. There's a hand on my shoulder.

'Where'd you think *you*'re going, you little cock?'

Says the vicar.

Fuck.

Listen. The bullet holes in his forehead, I'm not joking, they're like two new eyes. I figure if I stand in the right place I could stare right through to the other side.

Fuck.

Listen. The dog collar on his shirt, it catches fire and smoulders all away.

Listen. The lips on his face, they detach and swarm up his cheeks like two slugs.

Listen. There is a second face growing out of his belly, shirt-creases for brows, buttons for eyes, pale skin opening and laugh, laugh, laughing.

Long story short, there's a struggle.

Long story short, I piss myself.

Long story short, this shouldn't be happening. Not again.

'You're dead,' I tell him.

He isn't convinced.

His gut-mouth giggles.

Listen. I haven't pissed myself since I was twelve. This was the first night after finding—

Anyway.

This was after they took away Dad. This was after cuffs and protests and undignified struggles, and the neighbours

153

watching. This was in some weird post-traumatic stress place, a place full-up with broken children, a place with magnolia walls and the smell of no hope. This was waking up on a damp mattress.

Today and here and now, this unassuming little vicar, it goes without saying he should be dead. It goes without saying this isn't normal. Scratching, biting, clawing, strangling. This is him growling and grunting, this is the crucifix on a chain round his neck turning into a spiny fish and flap, flap, flapping to death. Drowning in air.

This is us on the floor and thumbs on my throat. This is fingers slippery round my neck, and knees on my chest and blood in my face and holes in his head and gore dribbling and shit, shit, shit. This is rain and mud hammering on my glasses.

In my blue cagoule is a double-edged seven-inch hunting knife in a rubber sheath. This is harder to get at than you might think.

'Fucking *kill* you,' he says. Dribbling lung juice on my forehead. 'Fucking *kill* you. Eat your fucking *soul*!'

His teeth, seriously, I'm not joking: too big. Too sharp.

I'm hallucinating. Bear with me.

The knife comes free right when there's light in my eyes and I can't breathe. Something goes funny in my head. I think my arm might be moving. I think my muscles might be burning.

This is my eyes going all to black.

Then there's just rain and darkness and wet sounds.

Fap-fap-fap-fap

Sex noises. In my head I'm with Sally. This is warmth and wetness all round my lap. This is the best night of my life.

CONTRACT

Fap-fap-fap-fap
'Oooh . . .'
Fap-fap-fap-fap
Did we have to have the light off? Can't we . . .
What's . . .

This is me leaning on the car. Call it five minutes later. This is with a bruised neck. This is so covered in blood the cagoule isn't blue any more. This is recovering my senses and sucking on air like it hurts, like my lungs can't remember what it feels like to breathe. This is with my tongue dry in my mouth. This is with the knife still in my hand, and the jagged edge at the top isn't just covered in blood but little pieces of skin and flesh caught in the teeth. This is with an arm that aches like I've been staring at too much porn. This is leaving a pin-cushion *thing* on the tarmac outside the church, next to the hole that he blamed on kids.

I had to use my hands again. Knifework. *Touching*.

This is not normal.

This thing on the tarmac, listen, it has no neck. Not any more. Its chest is just meat.

It ain't getting up.

The stained-glass saints, they're staring at me back-to-front, lit up from the inside out. The rain washes everything away, and fills up the mystery hole like a swimming pool. The cagoule goes blue again.

This is baptism, DIY-style.

Time to leave, Mike. Time to call Sally.

Chapter Ten

Now it's night. Now it's cold and still raining. Now there are holes in my memory and I've *missed* stuff.

Now this is Willesden, and I'm sitting on the kerb. Come see me next to Sally, watching kebab wrappers and polystyrene burger boxes punting down the gutter. Come see a regatta of disposable nothing. Come see the bright lights of a fleapit cinema behind us, a place we walked out of ten minutes ago, and come see spots of puke all down the front of my shirt.

Sally says she's leaving London. *Shit.*

Now and here, ten minutes after leaving the cinema – fast – here's rain dribbling off our noses and me with nothing left to puke up. Here's the dry heaves slowing. Smog air and toxic rain; kill-or-cure.

I think I've sat in dogshit.

I've been hallucinating again. This is twice in one day. This isn't good.

My legs aren't working.

Bear with me.

In the cinema, my eyes went wrong and my stomach lurched and everything went tits-up. In the cinema, I saw two apes fucking with fur like giraffes. I think, before that, they were kids. I think they were teens tonguing at

156

faces two rows ahead. I think – before Sally told me she's leaving London, before something happened in my head – I think the cinema was pretty empty. Except for those kids, except for Sally and me, except for a tall guy down the front near the screen, all alone with red-plush seats and the smell of popcorn. Those kids, all out of nowhere I saw them turn to hairy freaks with empty sockets and tongues like tentacles, wrapped up together. I saw frills grow out of their arms.

Here on the kerb, come see Sally with her arm round me; rubbing my back like it'll help. Here on the kerb, she's Nurse. Here on the kerb, she's helping me calm down, watching me puke and spit, and all the time I'm snuggling in like a kid. All the time I'm trying to work out what *happened* in there, I'm smelling the smell of her, I'm grateful for the comfort, I'm jonesing on Basic Human Warmth; but even so . . .

Even so, I'm hearing her voice, back inside, say: *I'm leaving, Mike.*

I'm hearing: *if you want some advice, whatever it takes, just get out.*

I'm hearing: *no one should do your job for ever.*

I knew coming here was a bad idea.

Listen. This is important: today is Tuesday. Earlier today I stabbed a man of God maybe forty times across his neck and upper chest. I lacerated his pectoral muscles and left a ragged gash across jugular and carotid. I opened his superior thyroid artery and cut so deep under his chin his tongue lolled out the gap.

This is with him lying on top of me.

This is like a waterfall that isn't water.

Now and here, I spit to clear my mouth.

When I kill someone, like today, what happens is: I call Sally. I meet her. Every other time this has happened has been inside Ariadne's Café. Every other time this has happened, these meetings, Sally and me, we sit and discuss nothing. Every other time, afterwards, I go Somewhere Else and fuck Someone Else and wake up Somewhere *Else*, and then Get On With Life. Self-distraction.

Every other time, my festering routine. Always going back to the start.

Tonight: uh-uh.

Tonight, as I drove home from killing a vicar, before valet-wash-in-and-out, return car to rental firm, home to change, burnt clothes, blah blah blah, tonight, when I called Sally and asked her to meet me, to catch up, to chin-wag, tonight what she said was: *Let's try somewhere new.*

I knew coming here was a bad idea. Sally's leaving London. Shit.

Now and here, kerbside, sick-mouthed, back-rubbed, I'm glancing round. Now and here it's a weird thing, this hallucinating malarkey. Like tuning-out. Like losing time.

I can't even remember what film we were watching.

This thing with me not able to feel my legs, not able to stand up, not able to function, *possible causes*:

This is maybe limb parasthesia caused by a trapped nerve, or nerve compression syndrome. This is maybe caused by circulatory problems resulting in the loss of blood to extremities. This is maybe cellular oxygen starvation, or the first signs of a deep vein thrombosis. This is maybe the onset of crippling rheumatoid arthritis, the first symptom of multiple sclerosis, or the effect of a stroke. This is maybe a

Transient Ischemic attack, and my brain is withering without oxygen.

Borrowed wisdom. Three cheers for the *Family Medical Dictionary*.

Now and here, across the street, a homeless man wearing shorts over his jeans carries three plastic bags and discusses the day's political news, out loud, with an imaginary companion. It looks like there's a disagreement brewing. This guy, his face is just *hair*.

If you want to know, maybe twelve hundred people sleep rough every night in England. Maybe more, maybe fewer. Who's counting?

Mostly in London, if you want to know. Mostly men. Mostly useless no-point-in-existing alcoholic junkie criminal scumfucks. Mostly have-no-sympathy ignore-the-motherfucker blot-them-from-your-attention *nobodies*.

This is sarcasm. Bear with me here.

In war films, when someone says, 'I can't feel my legs,' it's movie-code for 'he's been blown all to shit, but we can't show it or we'd lose our PG certificate.'

The good news is: I can't feel my legs, but I'm pretty sure they're still there.

Sally says: 'How're you feeling?'

I grunt.

This thing with her leaving London, when she told me – sitting in the dark, trying to watch the I-can't-remember-what-it-was film – when I heard her say that, what I *really* heard was: the end of Us.

What's funny is that there never really *was* an Us, and *how*, precisely, do I feel about that? You've got to wonder.

In the cinema, it was soon after that when things went

weird. I wish I could remember what started it. In the cinema, when the fit started, that scrawny lone figure in the front row turned round and had no face. Nothing inside its head. *Nothing*. For the record, that's not just blackness. Not just stars or empty white. *Nothing*. Nothing that sucks on your sight and swallows up everything you hear and stretches out your joints.

That scrawny lonesome figure, there was a red stripe on his chest, and as his face went away he said, not needing to shout: *Kkkhh*

That sinking feeling.

Here's the thing about my routine. The morning after it's all happened, the kill-coffee-club-*fuck* rundown, it's the part where I meet Sally that always sticks in mind.

What I'm getting at is, this *I'm leaving* thing: it's a big deal.

What I'm getting at is, the common ground just caved in.

What I'm getting at is, my routine just got shot down, and in my pocket the piece of paper with the magic number for putting the Plan into action, this number with a whole bunch of zeroes and a pound sign, it burns. It shouts out and wants me to open it up and look at it, and maybe . . . maybe think about whether the number's big enough for *two* people to escape *together*.

Across the street, the tramp glares at us and scratches his crotch. Sally keeps rubbing my back, saying: 'It's OK, it's OK.' I have sick on my knees.

A little over one third of rough sleepers have a 'mental health need'. This is a borrowed wisdom phrase that means: they're fucked-up.

CONTRACT

A little under two thirds of rough sleepers have a 'drugs need'. This is gold for the cynic. This is righteous damnation, raining from high on the heads of the meek. *Why*, he wants to know, *should I give money to these junkies? They're just gonna spend it on crack!*

The point is: so what if they do?

The point is: if it makes life bearable, people will do pretty much anything.

In the cinema, I remember Sally saying: 'I hate it here, Mike. D'you know what I mean? I *hate* it here.'

In the cinema, I remember trying to think of something to say. I remember trying to think of something that might make her change her mind. I remember stammering.

The thing is, *I* hate it here too. In an affectionate sort of way.

Now and here, Sally glances up to watch the tramp amble past. Right now, with her rubbing my back, with her having something to *do*, the focus has drifted from communication. Even so, I can feel it: the embarrassed silence.

Let me tell you, this is like a balloon bursting. This is like something small and frail being stamped on over and over. The last Giant Panda being hit by a truck. Van Gogh's *Sunflowers* fading in direct sunlight.

Me and Sally, we don't *do* embarrassed silences.

I panic.

I wipe my mouth and blurt: 'Sorry about this.'

Sometimes, I tell her, I just get spaced out. Sometimes I see stuff that's not there. Maybe. Probably. Ish.

Probably I'm just over-tired, I say, and I wish she'd disagree.

She nods and says nothing.

On the way out of the cinema the manager stood behind the popcorn counter reading a porno, except the top of his skull was missing. That manager, as he bent down to look at the puke I splattered over the floor, his brain flopped out like an eggyolk.

On the way out the girl inside the ticketbooth, her eyes were hanging out. There were black things inside her head, moving. Every time she swayed her steely little eyeballs knocked together.

Newton's cradle. Swing one, tap one, tap the next.

Fap-fap-fap-fap

Like stabbing-a-vicar sounds.

Sitting here outside the cinema in the rain, thinking it all through, I say to Sally, 'You think I should . . . get some help?'

She wrinkles her nose. On top of everything else, I believe I may be getting an erection.

She says, 'Up to you. But . . . *Doctors* . . . you know?'

This is an expressive thing to say. This spreads out and clogs up my head, and all the insinuations spawning off it are tadpoling through my conscience. What hits me mainly, and this is right between the eyes, is: *Hey, if there's something fucked inside your brain – ulcer, cancer, disease, sickness, cyst, pustule – if there's something deep down where no scalpel can reach it, packed-up against spaghetti grey cells and slippery memories, if there's something killing you a bit more every day . . . would you* want *to know?*

Sally says none of this, of course, but I'm reading between the lines.

Across the street, the homeless guy shouts, 'Gim yuck la *tahm.*'

We watch him go. I think I can feel my toes again.

Suddenly, Sally leans in close. Suddenly, Sally says, 'Mike, seriously. If you want my professional assessment, OK, listen – you don't need a doctor. You'll be fine.'

Stop everything.

Pay attention. This is the craziest thing of all.

Now and here, traffic roaring by, skyjuice down collar and inside shoes, the world stopping as she says it, I *believe* her.

Which is weird.

I've been hallucinating again, and maybe I'm just too knackered to disagree. For the record, in the cinema, the only person who *wasn't* changed, who *wasn't* transformed, who *wasn't* hellish and howling and horrific . . . That was her.

Like she was in a bubble.

Sally's trained as a psychiatric nurse. Sally says I don't need a doctor. Sally says I'll be fine.

My legs, yeah. Back in control.

Now and here she passes me my cup and tells me to drink, so I do. It tastes funny.

Across the street the tramp trips up a concrete step and swears out loud ('Bugg-*fush*!'). Sally's hand feels good on my back.

'Reminds me of my first job,' I say, nodding at the hobo.

She looks awkward and I remember she's uncomfortable talking about this stuff. I remember it's not normal. I remember it's not average, and I'm ready to say sorry, to make an excuse, to change the subject.

Only out here in the rain, rubbing my back, this time Sally says, 'Oh yeah?'

*

The way it works is this: everyone starts somewhere.

This is two and a half years ago, and the place I start is: a tangled scrub. This is a hybrid place, built up of wire fence, gorse bush, pebble floor. This is right next to a railway line, scattered with newspaper pages and beer cans and condoms and used needles. The joke is, when you're young, this is where you come to find porn. Right here is right opposite a traffic flyover, and this naïve little pussy version of *me*, what he's primarily occupied with at this precise moment is: aiming.

Right here is a flashback.

The best things about the AR-7 rifle are, it's cheap, it's small, it's light, it's easy to use, and it disassembles down tiny enough to fit inside its own hollow plastic stock.

The worst thing about the AR-7 rifle is, it looks a bit . . . well, girly. Sorry.

Right here inside this flashback, I'm slumped up against a concrete fence post. I'm snagging my jeans on gorse thorns and reminding myself to dispose of these clothes later. Forensic tests, hair samples, etc. etc. This pussy-arsed, sweaty-handed version of me, this past Mike, this doesn't-know-what-he's-doing loser, he's so green he could spread his arms and pretend to be a tree.

He has, listen, *no fucking clue*.

Right now he is – *I am* – aiming at a scrunched-up little figure all alone in the shadows beneath the flyover. This guy, I don't know his name, and at this stage in my career that surprises me. I expected to be told everything.

This guy, he looks homeless. He wears a beanie hat and a big brown corduroy coat. He wears shoes that don't match and – even though it's dark – circular sunglasses like John Lennon. At this stage in my career, I'm still guessing he's a spy or an assassin. He's a defecting commie or a James Bond wannabe. Obviously. I'm assuming I wouldn't be sent to put a bullet through the much-dented skull of Just Some Nobody.

I told you already. *No fucking clue.*

This is before all the tricks with the hollowpoints and the heroin. This is before facial-moles and bumbags and moustaches. This is before J.W.A. and hallucinations and so on and so forth. This is just me, on a railway siding, preparing to snipe the brains out of a tramp on the other side of the tracks. For free.

He's drinking cider from a big plastic bottle, staring at nothing. There is pigeon shit on his shoulders. This will be the first person I ever kill, and he has *pigeon shit* on his *shoulders*.

Here and now: my sweaty-palmed fun.

Here and now has a lot to do with Wilson. My broker. At this stage, inside this flashback, he's not even that. He's just some guy. I found him through a guy, who knew a guy, who knew a guy.

This job, I haven't exactly been *looking* for a way-in. But an enquiry here, an whisper there – you know how it works.

The thing is this: vocations, eventually, they just catch you up.

The first job Wilson gave me was this one. He said the first one is always for free. I invest in him, I pay him money, he gets one free job, and then the rest I use to line my pockets. This first-job malarkey, it's about as hands-on as Wilson gets.

Listen: I was expecting a businessman. A rival broker, maybe. A mob hit, with suits and tommy-guns and bowler hats, etc. Back then, back in this green know-nothing ignorance, back when I had no fucking clue, I expected someone *important*.

My eye, pressed up against the attachable Accessory Scope With Free Calibration Chart, which cost me £27.99 over the Internet, there's so much sweat on my brow I can barely see. The tramp swigs from his cider and goes back to staring at nothing.

Crosshairs on his face. Crucified expression. Pinned down. Butterfly on a page.

Here's my finger, tightening on the trigger.

Here's my arm starting to shake.

(For the record, I found out – three days later – that Wilson picked my guy because he sees him on the way home every day. Wilson picked my guy because he's just someone who won't be missed. This tramp, Wilson isn't the sort of guy who'd hate him. He's not the sort of guy who'd take umbrage at being scrounged. Wilson isn't the type to use his one-free-job psycho killer to knock someone he hates off his shabby little coil. This tramp, Wilson hasn't sent me to kill him because it's *personal*.)

The thing about this job (and inside this flashback right here and now I haven't worked this out yet), is this: really, it's not that hard. Really, it's not that skilful.

This job, all you need is assiduousness and anal retention. Also: a certain moral lassitude. All you need is a willingness to do what other people *won't*. This is just Wilson's way of finding out if you can, with some poor-bastard Random who won't be missed.

CONTRACT

The AR-7 rifle, the reason it looks a bit girly is: it's just so bloody skinny. This isn't like in movies. This isn't the polished black Doom Cock you've seen before. This is a pencil attached to a matchbox attached to a plastic tube.

The AR-7 rifle, stowed away in its own stock, like this you can carry it in a Tesco plastic bag. Like this, you can bring along the first homemade silencer you ever built hidden inside a loo-roll, and a cheap clip-on self-calibrating scope inside a child's spongebag.

This is a little less obvious than a violin case. Brown leather briefcases, military satchels, shaped Styrofoam. Too Hollywood.

The tramp sits at one with the universe. I sweat and clench my finger and hold off the shakes.

I can feel myself getting profound. This is expected.

Here is a moment of cosmic significance. Here is Zeus smiting the sinners; impunity personified; death from afar; *God*. Here is me, about to kill. Here is me considering the randomness of life, the infinite improbability of man's existence, the awesome numbers involved in his destruction, the—

The tramp burps. This takes some time. Even from my hiding place, even across the road and the tracks and the scrubland, it echoes.

Then he goes: *nyup, nyup, nyup*. Like a dog after yawning.

And suddenly I can't do it. Suddenly I'm crippled. Suddenly it's *too big*, too far beyond the pale. I will never be a killer, and the reality of this revelation trickles like diarrhoea into my soul, and then I'm smirking and taking my eye away from the scope, and thinking: *saved by a belch, buddy*.

And then a pigeon shits on my head and I pull the trigger by mistake.

Later, like days and weeks later, I'll hear about the Drop. This is a borrowed-wisdom phrase. This is why I don't use rifles any more.

With the sniper rifle, what films and TV never tell you, the tiniest gust of wind can change a bullet's course by degrees. What films and TV never tell you is that gravity works on a speeding bullet just the same as it works on one you drop from your hand.

Check out the latest straight-to-video-classic. That expensive scope black-clad-Ninja-assassin number 1 is sighting through? What he does, he lines up on his victim's head, eyeball in the crosshair, finding a rhythm, *feeeeeeling* the target . . .

A clean kill, he's thinking. *Right through the motherfucker's temple*, he's thinking.

At four hundred yards, that speeding lump of Hollywood lead is going to hit the poor bastard in his shin. Three cheers for Isaac Newton. This is the Drop.

Long story short, I miss the tramp. Long story short, I explode his cider bottle, and right now he's staring at it with a face that says: *just when you thought life couldn't get any worse.*

Bloody pigeons.

There is no way I can shoot this person now.

I hang around for a while. I pick up the spent shell casing. I unscrew the barrel nut and remove the barrel, detach the receiver from the stock, stow it all away. Chuck it in my plastic bag. Ready to go. I wonder what to do.

Long story short: I dawdle.

Long story short: I watch him for a while, scratching my head.

Long story shot: I go and talk to him.

My first job ever. Ahahaha.

One in five rough sleepers have been on the street longer than ten years. A lot of rough sleepers, what it is, they don't want to go back. They're *free*, they say. They've *moved on*, they say. They've escaped convention, they've broken out of the rut, they've *opted out*.

He says his name is Mart. He talks without punctuation and without breathing, which is exhausting, but when you've got your ear in it makes sense. This is existing without nicety. This is bare-bones life. If Mart ever had to write something down, *hee wud spel it funetiklee*.

He has Mental Health needs. He has drug needs and alcohol needs and whatnot needs. Above everything else, he likes to keep things simple.

I think he broke up with his wife. He talks about a woman, anyway. He touches his sleeve to his left cheek an awful lot, like twice during every sentence, and I can't work out why. It's like a pace-setter, maybe. A metronome, counting out the beats of his ramble.

He tells me a thunderclap just made his cider bottle explode for no reason, and now he's got nothing to drink. The way he sounds already is: pissed as a fart.

Tonight, inside this flashback, for the record, it's fucking freezing.

One in five rough sleepers is described as 'socially isolated'. This means they don't need to be around other people. This means they operate best alone. Or say they do.

Or believe they do.

Or *tell themselves* they do.

Me and Mart, we have a lot in common.

I ask him what he wants. Out of anything in the world, what does he want?

Stop.

Slow down.

This is a mystical moment. I can feel it before even he's answered. Before he opens his mouth, before he touches his sleeve to his cheek, before he squints through his odd little glasses and wets his cracked lips with his purple tongue, before *anything*, I know it: his answer to this question will define me. It will be a life-changing moment. It will make me, *me*.

'Vodka,' he says. 'Maybe gin.'

I say: 'Uh.'

Long story short, I buy him a bottle of vodka.

He drinks it all in one, and by dawn he's dead. I sit and watch him the whole time, as it happens, and all night we talk. All sorts of shit. I wish I could remember more of it. Opera, film, art. Rats. Scabies. Good food, good wine, quality loo roll, the best places to piss, the best crack dealers. Acorns. Duvets. Shoes.

That night, inside this flashback, two and a half years ago, was the last time I had a proper conversation with another human being.

He choked on his own vomit about 5.30 a.m. I sat and watched.

After that, shooting people in the head was easy.

Now and here, back on the street, back in the present, with the puke-taste and the cinema behind me, Sally nods at my story and keeps on rubbing my back. Sally tells me to keep drinking my drink. She says I must be dehydrated after all that up-chucking, and I notice that at some point during my story the rain has stopped.

I notice that at some point during my story I'm half dead with exhaustion.

Still trying to remember what happened in the cinema. Still trying to remember what made me freak out. Still trying to remember what me and Sally talked about. Still trying to think of *anything*, anything at all, except: *I'm leaving, Mike.*

Sally keeps rubbing. She keeps talking, although . . . although, if I'm honest, I believe I have at this stage stopped listening. It's enough to hear her voice.

I guess eventually I fall asleep, sitting there on the kerb, forgetting all about guns and hallucinations and films and horror, because all I remember is warmth and darkness, and Sally's voice cutting through it all, like a secret signal buried in white noise.

Contact 22

DAY: Tuesday.

TIME: 11.56 p.m.

LOCATION: Nightbus. Going home. Left cinema (Willesden) 10 mins. Afraid of falling asleep – writing report now. Bus driver = wanker. Brakes too hard, almost falling off chair. Old lady in priority seat shouting.

CONTACT REASON: Usual routine. Michael just completed job, phoned approx. 7 p.m. (Was ready for it tonight; expected call; suggested to him diff. venue.) Intentions: divert routine (test trust, & limits), deliver bad news ('I'm leaving') & obs. reaction. Start ball rolling, etc. No longer working way into him, naturalising etc. being <u>proactive</u> now.

OBSERVATIONS: Bus smells of fried chicken. Hoodies @ back of top level smoking & eating. Have come downstairs – left them to it. Outside: London yellow, street lamps, sky green. Ugly. Rain stopped. Windows *steamed-up, have to rub clear with elbow. Edgware road = takeaways & graffiti.*

Michael tonight: same cheap jacket, dark shirt (blue?), jeans. Heavy bags under eyes – looked older. Kept pulling up shirt collar, try to hide bruises on neck. Pretended I didn't notice. Uncomfortable in cinema – wanted to talk, chat; usual routine, fidgeted. Unhappy with not being listened to (me: big show of watching film; deprive him of attn.). Needs to feel validated?

By end: covered in rain, bedraggled, sick down chest & trousers. Went from average/dull/nobody → wild-eyed madman on kerb in space of hour.

NOTES: At beginning: phonecall. M not much resistance @ new venue suggestion. Probably taken by surprise – didn't even complain (maybe couldn't think of good reason? Not quick enough?). Told him I was bored of café (true!), gave new place/time. Spluttering, uncertainty: eventually just 'OK' – defeated. (Worth remembering: gets easily swept along. Given no space to protest; he won't.)

Made sure I arrived cinema early – spoke to Greg (manager – chatted before, frequent customer, late screenings whenever can't sleep), slipped £100. Played my choice DVD (not weird Euro shit). Film = Léon, Dir. Luc Besson. Appropriate. See how M reacts (particular scene) – experiment. Felt like kid w/ test tube.

M arrived, then inside cinema: chatting/watching film. Don't think he was paying attn. to screen; using time to think what to say next. Slots comments into quiet moments: ref to day's work (more 'bad shit'). Bought him lemonade (ignored slurping – too much froth on drink again). Opening credits, Manhattan, Little Italy, hitman killing mafia fattie etc. Great film.

M lost patience – 10 minutes. Direct challenge (building courage for long time?). Asked: 'Why here? What's wrong with Ariadne's? At least we can talk there.' Disgruntled. Felt ignored. Kept mumbling about 'Hollywood shit' in film (silencer makes wrong noise, apparently. WTF?).

Told him: wanted change of scenery, have important news, didn't seem right telling him in usual place. His expression: <u>sheer panic</u>. Hates surprises, ready to run.

Told him I'm leaving London. BANG. Looked like bomb exploded under chair. Told him: Need to get out, want a job, can't live on benefits for ever, etc. Strange cruelty: kicking a puppy. No reply. Told him (salt in wound): his job scared me. Made uncomfortable. Told him I like him but what he does = awkward. Could see shock, never considered it: up till today he revelled in having someone to confide/collude – no longer viable.

M said: When?

Just shrugged. Told him: soon.

<u>Horror</u>. Resents himself. Big pupils, sweaty. Looked on diff. wavelength. Right moment.

Told him: if you want some advice, whatever it takes, just get out. Suggested puts his 'Plan' into action ASAP. (Watched him fiddle w/ folded piece of paper). Held arm, looked into eyes, ignored film. Not flirty – <u>more</u> than. Said to him: no one should do your job for ever, Mike.

Reaction = <u>incredible</u>. Could see advice going in – computer accepting command. Eyes unfocused, half-asleep, said: 'Yes. You're right.' Robot!

After that, film 1st climax: corrupt cop kills little girl's family, boom-boom-boom, woman shot in bathtub. Spilled water & blood. Watched Michael very close — testing response. Whole reason for choosing this film . . .

Major wig-out. Threw up, shouting at audience, pointing, complete mess. Sweaty, big eyes. 'Devils! devils!' etc. Fucked up. Seeing things not there. Got him outside, sat to calm down. Cold & rain. Persuaded him no doctor needed (last thing I want! someone else obs him!). Told him: just overtired.

Dropped off on my shoulder. Kept talking to him till bus came.

THOUGHTS/CONCLUSIONS/OTHER: Responses perfect. Showing film = crude, but excellent illustration. Slightest trigger. Opens right up; impressionable, programmable. Can tell when he's in the right 'zone' now, frame of mind, etc. — pupils dilated, voice slurred, tangents: advice goes in, no questions. Tell him 'jump', he asks 'how high?'

Beginning to think whole operation might work.

Discussion re. me leaving, excellent result. Make him resent his own niche/job/routine. Creating desperation: wants to get out. Prepared to do anything.

Overall promising. Real tests coming soon. Next Contact = probably last.

(Less pleasing = personal reaction. Guilt? Keep reminding myself: all for the best.)

S.

Chapter Eleven

So this guy, this sharp-suited freak-eyed piece of mobster Pacino DeNiro shit, this manicured temperature-oddity with his breath condensing and his skin grey like a rhino's arse, I lean down over his desk so I'm nearly touching him, and what I tell him is: 'No.'

I'm feeling a little hostile. Bear with me.

Right now, I'm back in the deserted-but-not offices in Russell Square. I'm back with the Red-Tie-Guy standing behind me and the sound of typewriters from who-knows-where. You remember this place, right? The Choir. The buzzer on the door that works. The no-cameras-in-sight. The too-hot heater.

Vvvvvvm . . . vvvvvvvm . . . vvvvvvm . . .

All these little getting-to-know-yous.

So I'm back staring at Mr Call-Me-Boss, and Mr Call-Me-Boss, he's back staring at me.

The way I tell him 'no', the way I frame this lead-balloon of a word, I'm avoiding any possible misunderstanding. I'm avoiding the chance for him to say 'But—'. I'm preventing one of those fucking awful 'Now hold on a moment—' moments.

The way I tell him 'no', it's *final*.

In advertising, repetition is the best way of getting your

message across. Dress up your product however you want, redesign its Dayglo-blue packaging, stick it on the telly with a poorly animated cuddly wombat and give it the world's cleverest jingle. Makes no difference.

What matters is, how often people see it.

What matters is, how many times your silky voiceover guy repeats its name.

What matters is, driving the point home one, two, three times.

This is why Bad Adverts are so successful. This is why Annoying Ditties + Crap Jokes = Improved Sales.

Bad news just sticks in your brain.

Borrowed wisdom, three times in a row. I saw a documentary.

'No,' I say again. This is number two.

Mr Call-Me-Boss, his tongue is worming inside his cheek and then his lips are parting and he's going to say something. Here and now timing is everything, so I wait until his breath's sucked in and his mouth's forming the words, and I cut right in and say: 'No.'

That's three.

He sits back in his chair and smiles. He looks too big, maybe. Scaled up. His teeth are too white.

The Red-Tie-Guy, I can *hear* him smiling. Behind me, looming, he shuffles his feet and says: '*Kkkhh.*'

Did I mention how annoying this is?

Mr Call-Me-Boss, on the desk in front of him are three manila packages, side-by-side. The first contains a printed sheet of paper detailing the transfer of two hundred thousand English pounds into a temporary bank account in the name Barry Travis, based in the Cayman Islands. This is for me.

This is good news. This is one little step closer to putting the Plan into action. This is what it's all about, remember?

My name is not Barry Travis.

The second package is a little larger. It contains documents and files, which are currently scattered across the desk.

The third package is unopened.

'Why don't you sit down?' says Mr Call-Me-Boss, and this is not a question. This is one of those polite commands. This is one of those times when that dangling question-mark at the end, that rhetorical sweetener, it's all that stands between me and being told to SIT the FUCK DOWN before someone gets BAD ANGRY and SHOOTS me TWICE through the BACK of my MOTHERFUCKING HEAD.

Et cetera, et cetera.

Mr Call-Me-Boss, all this is just in his voice. It's expressive. It's threatening. It's advertising-you-don't-*have*-to-repeat. His eyes do things they shouldn't.

Long story short: I sit.

Mr Call-Me-Boss, in his hand he holds a leather wallet with a few crusted scraps of dried blood stuck to it. This belonged to a vicar I frenzy-sliced with a double-bladed hunting knife four days ago, which was Tuesday, after he turned into a demon.

As you do.

This was after I was certain he was already dead. Mr Call-Me-Boss has already flicked through this wallet. He has already taken out the sheets of paper, the lists, and passed them to the Red-Tie-Guy. He has already glanced at the photo – *that* photo – and his expression has already flickered.

The little boy. Muddy, bound, gagged, smiling.

Mr Call-Me-Boss, with his maybe-eyebrow-twitch. With his maybe-lip-droop.

'You did good work,' he says.

I don't answer.

'Habit for messy jobs, ain't you?' he says.

He twinkles. He says, 'Hope you managed to get it out your system, anyway. Had a *pleasant* evenin' after.'

His mouth stretches out like a frog.

'*Léon*,' he says. 'One of my favourite films.'

I say: 'Eh?'

On Tuesday, which was four days ago, after Sally left me outside the cinema, after I nipped home and dried off and scrabbled about to cling to the scraps of my routine, what I did was: an irritating nineteen-year-old called Rebecca.

Rachael. Rita. Whatever.

On Tuesday, after Sally left, I picked up this loud-mouthed idiot-girl from Sahara-Midriff or Shellac-Unicorn or Trivalvic-Donkey or Easy-Pickings or wherever. On Tuesday, I stood there with my lemon-fucking-ade while she pestered and pestered and wouldn't go away, and in my head I killed the vicar again and again and again, in time to bad music.

Fap-fap-fap-fap

Knife sounds.

Oom-chkka-oom-chkka-oom-chkka

Lay it down on a fruity choon, slice it up with badass beetz, sell it on the telly as an expensive subscription-only mobile phone ringtone. Possibly with a cute animated logo. Maybe a seal.

On the desk the printed receipt in the first package, that's proof of the opening payment in our seedy little arrangement. I will check my account just as soon as I'm home.

Three jobs, he said. *First two are standard. Easy. Third one's trickier.*

The first job, which was *standard*, which was *easy*, involved shooting a smalltown vicar twice in the face and twice in the chest, then perforating his ribs, lungs, heart and neck thirty-six times with a double-bladed hunting knife because he came back to life.

Standard. Easy.

The reason I know it was thirty-six times, and not thirty-seven, or thirty-five, is this: the papers.

Yesterday, which was Friday, the Brutal and Horrific Murder of The Reverend Desmond Couch finally shifted from the front pages. That makes life easier.

Let me tell you: Wednesday and Thursday on the London Underground, and everywhere you looked, it was open copies of the *Metro*. Fascinated flick-throughs, grimacing faces, furrowed brows. Big black letters, 32-point Times New Roman, toilet graffiti written for nobody's benefit but mine, mine, mine.

'Senseless,' they said.

'Savage,' they said.

'Satanic,' they said.

These headlines, at the very least you've got to admire the alliteration.

On Tuesday, standing in that club with that relentless female human being yakking on and on and on and on, I stood there and played Sally's words over and over through my head. *I'm leaving*, she said. *No one should do your job for ever.*

On Tuesday I waited and waited and watched and

watched, and it was *never* the right time and there was never the right time and there was never the right person. On Tuesday, in the end, I got desperate, and went home with Raquel or Rose or Robyn or whoever before my head was clear, before the vicar was out of my eyes, before I was ready. Just to shut her up. Just to *show* her.

Just to take it *out* on someone.

Listen. In the second manila package on the desk in front of me are the details for the Second Job this criminal mobster wanker wants me to do. The second *standard* job. The second *easy* job. This manila package was placed on the desk by the Red-Tie-Guy a short while ago, after the Boss handed him the list from the Vicar's wallet. The Red-Tie-Guy, he looked at the list, nodded, went out of the room. Somewhere, I think, I heard filing cabinets. And then he was back, and the package was on the desk, and the Boss was smiling.

Bear with me here.

Me saying 'No' three times, just now – you remember – that was because I'd just been shown the contents of the second manila package.

Try to keep up.

Standard. Easy.

For the record, this second job, it is not standard. It is not easy. This second job, it has J.W.A. written all over it.

Just Walk Away.

The printed-out receipt in the first package, if you didn't know already, there are two types of money.

Less than 8 per cent of the world's total wealth exists in real solid hold-it-in-your-hands fold-it-in-half-or-hear-it-tinkle form. The rest is make-believe. The rest is 1s and 0s. The rest is data in computers and figures written on forms, in triplicate, countersigned and rubber-stamped. The rest is plastic-magnetic-strips on debit/credit cards. The rest is just numbers.

Let me tell you: banknotes, paper money, this has no real value. This is symbolic. This is because all of us, all at once, *choose to pretend*. This is communal hallucination. One day, people will choose to opt out.

Here and now, I fold my arms without thinking about the whole Giving-Away-My-Defensive-State-of-Mind thing, and I nod towards the second manila package.

That's the one with the Next Job.

Seriously, try to keep up.

'I'm telling you,' I say, staring straight into Mr Call-Me-Boss's weird eyes, 'I'm not doing it.'

There are three reasons I won't do The Second Job. Today is a day for threes.

Bear with me here.

Of the less-than-8 per cent of the world's total wealth which exists in real solid hold-it-in-your-hands fold-it-in-half-or-hear-it-tinkle form, the most common paper currency is not dollars or pounds or yen or euros. The most common paper currency is Frequent Flyer Air-miles.

All those airborne people. All those dreams of sand and sangria and sunsets. All those miniature little Plans.

The Second Job, the three reasons that just *thinking* about it make me want to Just Walk Away, are these: 1) it's in London. This is a polite way of saying: in my own back garden. 2) It's without visual identification of the client. This is a polite way of saying: no bloody photos. And 3), it's With Information Extraction Required. This is a polite way of saying: torture.

On Tuesday, four days ago, let me tell you, every time my back arched and the bed creaked and Rosie or Roberta flexed, we got a little slap, a little smack. Skin-against-skin. Wet noises. Sex sounds.

Fap-fap-fap-fap

Like a knife, hack-slice-dice-cut-slashing.

Sneaking between the ribs of an unassuming little vicar, with two unassuming little holes in the centre of his forehead. Still alive.

You've got to wonder, how am I supposed to block it out when it's *everywhere*?

You've got to wonder, how am I supposed to distract myself from this unnatural shit?

Dead people should not be allowed to get up and return the favour. It's not *done*.

Here and now and baking in front of the cheap fire, what I tell Mr Call-Me-Boss about the Next Job is: 'It's stupid.' And then, 'It wasn't part of the deal.'

He wobbles a hand.

I say, 'Cutting people up, getting . . . documents, that shit. That's not what I *do*.'

He waves an arm, like a dismissal. 'Oh, now,' he says, and his breath steams in front of him.

The Red-Tie-Guy, he makes his funny little noise.

I say, 'I'm serious. I *shoot* people. That's why you . . . that's why I'm fucking *here*.' I slap the file. 'You can't even tell me what this guy *looks* like!'

The only useful thing in the manila package, if you want to know, is the client's name. The client's name is 'Alex'.

'Come *on*,' he says, and his shoulders look too wide, and even though he's sitting down he's a big fat lump of *menace*.

'Come on now.' This Is Final. He taps the manila file. 'It's just a bleedin' bedsit, Mikey. Bottom dollar says there's no other bugger there. You wade in heavy, you get us some answers, easy. It's nothin'.'

Now would be a good time to get up. Now would be a good time to walk out, to shake my head, to mutter and scowl, to buy in to some high-drama, soap opera excitement, a cut-short tantrum. Now would be a good time to exit stage left, dignity *intacto*.

Except.

Except I need the money.

Except Sally said it right when she said *no one should do your job for ever*.

Except unless I get this cash, unless I *do* this shit, in blood-stained Britain I shall remain.

Except the Red-Tie-Guy's hand is on my shoulder, and there's pressure somewhere, and I never even left the chair.

Except the leathery old shit opposite, he's steepling his fingers and staring, and his eye . . . his eyes dribble gold.

My brain. It's all to do with my brain.

The boss, what he does is, he sighs.

'You ain't a fan of surprises,' he says.

I tell him, 'No shit, Sherlock.'

'I can understand that. Don't wanna go in blind. You're a professional.'

I tell him if he's trying to flatter me into giving the nod, he can bugger himself into oblivion with his own diseased prickhead.

He takes it pretty well.

'I think I can persuade you,' he says.

Mr Call-Me-Boss, he drops the vicar's wallet – which he's been fiddling with all this time – and it hits the desk and goes: *spwk*.

Like spit hitting concrete. Like a hand slapping a book. Like bubblegum popping.

Like a Ruger Mk II .22 with a homemade silencer delivering a nugget of hollow lead, optimum-grade rendered diamorphine and a globule of sealant into the fleshy organs of a living human person.

Mr Call-Me-Boss, he reaches for the third manila package.

On Tuesday, four days ago, Rudy or Roxanne or whoever she was, the loud-mouthed little tramp, she was *supposed* to be distracting me. She was supposed to be my Don't Dwell On It.

Let me tell you: on Tuesday with this girl, no matter what I did, no matter how long I did it – *nothing*.

Fap-fap-fap-fap

Not a moan. Not a groan. In the club she was so *noisy*, and in the sack, *this*.

It's not fair.

Fap-fap-fap-fap

Angry humping. Trying to *show* her. Sweaty and tense and exhausting. This is worse than not having sex at all. This is a direct challenge to your confidence. This is angry and dirty and violent.

This is known as a Grudgefuck.

On Tuesday, the way I would describe my carnal experience was: un-fucking-satisfying.

This has left me somewhat frustrated. This has left me somewhat preoccupied. I have not turned over to the next chapter. I have not forgotten the little vicar. I have not *moved on*.

I'm a little tense. Bear with me.

Mr Call-Me-Boss, he places a thumbnail under the flap of the third package and starts to open it.

Listen. Money is awkward. Start paying fat cheques into your dull everyday highstreet current account, the thing is: people ask questions. Bank managers, auditors, fraud squad. The thing with money is, if you're earning it, you're on a *system*. Name on a screen. Printed in a register. Code numbers and PINs and National Databases.

This job, that's never a good thing.

This job, the thing is: Tax Returns. National Insurance donations.

This job, the thing is: with enough false I.D. you can set up anything at all. You can be anyone. You can send all your cash wherever the fuck you want, then dribble it back to yourself in nice, freshly laundered wads.

To achieve this you will need:

a false passport, N.I. number, driving licence and utility bill
an Internet connection
the phone number or email address of an astute bank manager in Panama, the Bahamas, Guatemala, the Cayman Islands, et cetera et cetera
$10,000 as a deposit
enough cash to pay foreign-government transfer fees and conversion commissions
a lot of time
a lot of patience
a basic disregard for financial law

CONTRACT

Mr Call-Me-Boss, as he prises open the third package with fat fingers, his eyes don't leave mine.

You remember his eyes? His weird, hollow, golden eyes. His give-you-a-headache-just-trying-to-look-into-them eyes.

People don't see faces. People see features.

They see these holes in your head, these glistening cavities with retina-reflector backsheets, these lumps of soft tissue and photo-receptive spikes, and they get romantic. Can you believe that?

Windows into the soul, they say. A mischievous glint, they say.

You can tell a lot about someone, they say, by looking into their eyes.

Here and now, looking at this guy, pretending like I'm cool and untroubled and not shivering from the xylophone bones above my hips, I'm thinking that maybe eyes aren't always windows into the soul, as much as the chimneys poking out of its arse. Exhaust pipes. Coolant towers. Whatever. Somewhere where all the noxious shit comes boiling out.

This man, this icicle-toad in human clothing, he draws a piece of paper out of the third manila package, and the sound it makes is steelier than any Hollywood samurai sword slinking out of its sheath. This man, what he does next is: he smirks. At me.

Inside the third manila package is a sheet of paper. At the top is a company letterhead which reads MAKE YOUR POINT, INC. Beside it is a logo, shaped like a pointing finger.

My little joke.

My little symbol, full to the brim with meaning, just so long as you're in the Know.

'Remember this?' says the mobster crackershit arsehole bastard.

This is my Contract.

'What about it?' I say.

This thing with money, listen. What you do is: you go professional. You go exotic. You set up a Lending Corporation overseas using false identification. You go legit, a businessman, a motherfucking international jet-setting yuppie.

All without leaving London.

The place you choose, that'll be some poverty-stricken paradise where the smiling rum-swigging locals don't pay income tax. That'll be some wonder-world of palm trees and sun and sand and white beaches, where you can rake in all the cash you want and not pay a penny to the Chancellor.

And yes, foreign governments like you to pay a little for the privilege, but still, but still.

What you do next is, you go legit in London too.

My name is Michael Point, I'm the Chief Executive Officer of a small fashion design company. Seriously.

Bear with me here.

Mr Call-Me-Boss, he says I promised I'd carry out the three jobs he asked me to do. He waves the contract. He says I signed it, so I should know. He says all this making-it-formal bullshit was *my* idea, not his, and now *I'm* the one trying to renege on the deal.

He says that, no offence, but in his considered opinion that's pretty fucking out of order.

CONTRACT

Mr Call-Me-Boss, frozen-cold cockney sparrah, mist rising up on his breath, the way it sounds when he says this is: '*Aaaht'v ordah.*'

Suddenly I'm in *EastEnders*.

For the record, a Cockney is anyone born in earshot of Bow Bells. The Bow Bells hang in the steeple of St Mary-Le-Bow church, Cheapside. Technically speaking, there were no Cockneys born between 11 May 1941 and 21 December 1961, on account of how some unscrupulous *Luftwaffe schweine* messed with London tradition by blowing the bells to shit.

Mr Call-Me-Boss, I tell him: No.

I tell him: Hang on one minute, here, matey.

I tell him: That contract's not about the bloody *jobs*. It's about shared risk. I tell him it's about being able to work together so there's no *threats*, no unfair *liability*, no lopsided bullshit.

Mutually-assured-destruction, I tell him.

This is a borrowed-wisdom phrase that means: *You bomb me, comrade, I bomb you.* Who wins?

I tell him it's a gimmick to make sure I don't spend my life waiting to get fucked up the arse, because if he so much as *tries*, he's bending over next in line.

I tell him: 'It's about mutual *trust*, mate.'

Here's the trick. Pay attention: 'Mutual Trust,' he says, quiet. He's still staring.

Let me tell you, windows into the soul, right?

Sometimes – and we've all done it – you stare through a window and see something you wish you hadn't. Pensioners trying their hand at S&M. Newborns with explosive diarrhoea. Lonely housewives getting personal with Great

Danes. The vicious indescribable smoky golden-glowing impermanence bubbling from the pits of a spooky shithead's heart.

For example.

As the CEO of an ambitious young fashion design studio, I have to borrow a lot of money in order to stay afloat.

This is what I will tell Them, if they ever ask. 'Them' is the Tax Man. The Auditors. The Bank Managers. *Them*.

Listen, me and money: it's an open relationship.

As the CEO of an ambitious young fashion design studio, I have high costs. At present my company is trying to court some of the larger high-street outlets to retail my amusing yet surreal T-shirts, and that's an expensive business. That's executive lunches, smart suits, company cars, departmental gifts, blah, blah, blah.

All this cash, my fledgling company (which will fold by the end of the year, to be replaced by Some Other Business) needs to borrow from somewhere. The banks won't touch me with a barge pole, on account of my business plan being basically bullshit.

Lucky for me there's a wealthy lending corporation in Panama, the Bahamas, Guatemala, the Cayman Islands, et cetera et cetera.

This is me borrowing money from myself. This is me making unclean digital funds into shiny dry-cleaned steampressed Wonga. This is how I cover my expenses.

The thing with this job is, it's easy when you know how.

In my flat are boxes and boxes of T-shirts.

One batch says: DO NOT READ THIS.

This is sarcastic surreal semi-comedy. Ahahaha, etc. etc.

Mr Call-Me-Boss, he turns the contract round so it faces me.

The T-shirts in my flat, they're not for sale. They're for samples on the off-chance They – the same *Them* from before – show up to pay attention.

This is called a J.I.C.

Just In Case.

Stop. Listen.

Whoa.

On the contract, in the pudgy hand of this sub-zero arsehole, seriously, the text has changed. I can't read it at this distance, but the paragraphs have moved.

The contract which I made, which I designed little-by-little, this isn't it.

But.

My signature is at the bottom.

This is a symbol meaning: ME.

That sinking feeling.

Let me tell you, my signature is there, as plain as day, and his, ohoyes, his is not.

That bubbling flaming cold-sweating feeling.

'But—' I say. This is what's called a false start. This is not cool.

This is smirk-fodder.

Let's try that again.

'I saw you sign,' I say. 'That's . . . That's crap. That's just fake. That's just Tippex and a photocopier.'

Still with the smirk.

I say, 'I've got my own one, remember?'

Still with the smirk.

I say, 'I've got your fucking *photo*, remember?'

Still.

With.

The.

Smirk.

I say: 'This is *bollocks*.'

'Let's roleplay,' says Mr Call-Me-Boss, still – guess what – *smirking*. 'Let's pretend you get home, after this, all . . . all trying not to look shaken. Heh. Let's pretend you open your mail, and there's a brown envelope with your own handwriting on the address. Classy idea, that. Very smart. Let's pretend you crack it open and get a nasty shock. Let's pretend there's just the one signature on *that*, 'n' all. Let's pretend the photo ain't *me*. Let's pretend, right, Mikey – you followin'? – that what this "contract" 'ere basically is now' – waving it left to right, eyes digging holes in my face, trap doors to the soul – 'is the signed confession of a nutter with a diseased mind. Can't even rely on his own senses, this twisted fuck. Can't tell real from not. Thinks his victims are coming back to life. Goes all Norman Bates on dead bodies, splatters 'n' squirts . . . Not *rational* any more, is the point. Not making clean kills. Starting to look like an amateur, ain't he?'

'*Kkkhh*.'

His eyes. Shit. *Shit*.

That sinking feeling.

'Now, Mikey, I've gotta tell you, son . . . If I was in that position, that one I just said, and some old geezer was dangling that shit over *my* head, I think I might just consider doing exactly what he says. What do you think?'

Behind me: '*Kkkhh*.'

*

Long story short: I take the folder for the Other Job.

Long story short: I roll over and stick my arse in the air, and take it, and he's beaten me, and it's exactly what I deserve. I'm not clever. I'm not quick.

Long story short: as I leave my eyes are flicker-flash-flicker-flashing, and Mr Call-Me-Boss is wearing white and silver, and his face is just *light*, and somewhere behind the glow there's a disc and a pair of golden eyeballs. And the Red-Tie-Guy nearby, saying: '*Kkkhh.*'

Long story short: I punch the wall outside the office building so hard my knuckles bleed on the stones, and there are tourists staring at me and now there's sleet falling and . . .

And *shit*.

Interview Room 2

Four minutes.

There has been a brief break. There has been a Stretching of Legs and a Cooling Off.

This is back in the Same Old Same Old. This is back with Jase and Anna, except *not*, because the rude bastards just got up and left without even a word. Without even a glance at each other.

Four minutes, I have counted the seconds and looked for cameras. There didn't seem much else to do. For the record, I haven't found any.

Sooner or later, these two goons, these clockwork soldiers, these smartly suited smugfucks, in they come once more. Sooner or later here's the Lovely Anna, now smoking a cigarette. Sooner or later here's Jason Durant, ohomymymy, this curtain-haired placental violation, this explosive human fannyfart, with a cup of coffee for me. There is no froth on the top.

It tastes like piss.

Jason Durant sips at his own foam cup and seems perfectly content with the flavour. I am, just so you know, not surprised.

Golden Showers. *Scheisse* specials. American Bukkake. No doubt about it.

'Tell us about this,' he says, and he lifts a manila envelope out of his jacket pocket, folded carefully in half. 'Tell us about this "Boss".'

The package has my address written on the front, in my handwriting. It has a postal stamp dated to a couple of days after I first met the Boss.

This is my copy of the Contract. They must've taken it when they tossed my flat.

I never opened it.

Right now, I'm wondering where the evidence baggie is. The latex gloves. I'm wondering: shouldn't this moment of mystery be a little more impressive than Jason four-in-a-bed no-KY sado-masochistic leather-goods Durant plucking it, folded, out of his papercut-sharp jacket?

'For example,' he says, 'what was his name?'

I shrug.

I say: the thing is, just right now, I don't remember.

'What did he look like?' says Anna, with smoke oozing upwards.

I say, 'I told you. His eyes were—'

'Not the eyes,' she says, and the clouds from her lungs shift and turn over. 'The rest. Could you pick him out in a picture? Could you describe him?'

Photofit. IdentiKit. E-Fit.

And I'm thinking, and I'm scowling, because I'm not sure I like the way my brain is working, and it's like there's a blockage, and eventually – just like giving up – I'm shrugging again.

'He . . . he was kind of old,' I try. 'And a bit fat . . .'

It sounds as lame as it is.

Jason sighs. Anna smokes.

I tell them, quietly, that people remember features, not faces.

Anna, she leans forwards and opens the envelope. For the record, this is a surprise. This is contamination of evidence.

For the record, even so, even after all the shit that's happened, still with the flicker of *hope* down inside me. Still with the *maybe, what if, perhaps*. Still with the beating little chance the contract will say what I *told* them it'd say, that the photo will show that fat freak-eyed motherfucker smirking out at us, that his fingerprints will be all over it like maggots in a morgue.

Note: if any of that happens, it won't change much. It won't change that they've caught me, that they know what I've done.

But they'll *understand*. They'll *see*.

They'll see I'm not crazy. They'll see I'm not making it up. That I'm not diseased inside my skull. They'll believe me. *I'll* believe me.

Inside the envelope, the Polaroid photo is of a man. This is a good start. He looks ill. He looks green and white, and maybe any moment he's going to puke.

Did you know: Crazy Horse, who led the Lakota and Cheyenne at the Battle of the Little Bighorn, who was there when General George Armstrong Custer was caught between Sitting Bull and Gall of the Hunkpapa, who watched the floppy-haired twat with his floppy moustache make his last floppy stand, who saw American History in the making, there in the blood and mud, who was stabbed through his heart by a bayonet when he left the Lakota reservation to take his sick wife to her parents, who was killed at the age of twenty-eight by a modern world he didn't

Get, this guy, up until the end, he wouldn't let photographers come anywhere near him.

They stole pieces of his soul, he said. Borrowed Wisdom. I saw a documentary.

The face in the photograph, it has its eyes rolled upwards. It has sweat and a clammy sheen on both cheeks, and where it's breathing out there's a little twist of condensing breath in the air.

The face, the flash from the camera has caught in its eyes, and they're *glowing*.

Jason and Anna, as I stare at the photo, they watch my face.

Did you know: up to this day there are tribes of Australian Aborigines, whose name is derived from the Latin *ab origine* and means 'from the start', whose culture went the way of discoeing dodos about the same time drink, disease and despair washed up on their coasts with a bunch of funny-looking white fellers, whose bewildered sons and daughters were for years spirited away to be raised in Civilised Families, whose physiologies *proved*, ohoyes, if you asked the Right People, that they weren't as 'evolved' as those same funny-looking white fellers, whose Way of Life was quietly and firmly bent over a cultural table and fucked, there are tribes even now, some of them, who believe that a photograph or video or voice recording sucks away a little piece of the subject's spirit.

The face in the photo, it's not Mr Call-Me-Boss.

It's me.

In Interview Room 2, I nod. This is all sort of inevitable.

You ever spoken to someone who gets photographed a lot? Models, maybe. Fashion people. Celebrities. You seen a

TV star being interviewed? You delved at length into the personality of someone whose face and voice and thighs and arse and tits are a National Treasure?

Because here's the thing: these people, more often than not, they have a kind of *thinness*.

Like maybe they've been stripped down. Like maybe they've had little pieces, little slivers, whisked away. Cemented in celluloid and drowned in digits. Reprinted, dragged thinner and thinner, dispersed, scattered to the wind and – and maybe, seriously, those little chunks that've been ripped off and stored away, those little soul-slices, maybe . . . maybe they have a life of their own.

Bear with me here.

In Interview Room 2, Anna flicks her eyes across the sheet of paper inside the envelope. Her eyebrow does not twitch. Her lips don't part. She's stopped smoking, and the fag eats away at itself in a long black ashy slug in an ashtray that – *for fuck's sake* – wasn't there before.

She passes me the paper. The Contract. The contract *I* wrote.

At the top is a letterhead, with a logo. It says: MAKE YOUR POINT, INC. The logo is of a pointing finger.

My little joke.

This contract is supposed to set out in black and white the relationship between me, the killer, and the Boss, the employer. It's supposed to make it totally clear that we share culpability. That I'm being paid for a service. That we both understand the mutual risk being taken, and – by signing – agree to share any punishment, penalty or legal snooping that occurs as a result of one of us slipping up. It's supposed to say: *Don't fuck up*.

CONTRACT

This thing in my hand, it is not the contract I wrote. I do not know how this has happened. I do not know how come I can't remember what he looks like, except his eyes. I do not know how come I've forgotten the bastard's real name.

Memory loss is the first sign of dementia. This could be Huntingdon's Disease. This could be Parkinson's, Creutzfeldt-Jakob's, liver dysfunction, kidney inflation, hypothyroidism, vitamin deficiency, syphilis, AIDS, encephalitis, meningitis, overdose of lead, mercury, anti-anxiety drugs or anti-seizure drugs. This could be my reality dissolving in a monsoon of psychotic divergence. This could be I just wasn't paying attention.

The photograph and the contract, these little slivers of myself, these little cutaway pieces that have captured parts of *me*, it's like they have a life of their own. It's like they've changed just to spite me.

Here and now, with Jason and Anna staring, in this dank, echoing, migraine-noisy shithole of an interview room, what this sheet of paper says, is:

1.

1.1 I, the undersigned, hereby declare that all actions undertaken by me or on my behalf – particularly as relating to the termination of persons within (and affiliated to) the so-called 'DisRing' – are under-taken freely and without external instruction, motive or financial incentive. All pieces of equip-ment and all monetary funds are to be provided by me alone, all surveillance to be undertaken single-handedly, and all research gathered without aid.

1.2 Those motherfuckers have it coming. I will not apologise.

1.3 These ones are for free.

Signed,

Michael Point

Michael Point

I tell them: look, *listen*, that's not what it said before. I tell them: this isn't fair. Somebody's . . . somebody's playing a . . . or . . . but . . .

I tell them: I can't explain it, but . . . that's not how it . . . that's . . .

Sooner or later, I run out of steam.

Anna blows smoke into the air above us, where it shivers and twists and spreads out too fast. Jason Durant just smirks.

I mutter, just loud enough so that they can hear, defeated and dead and I don't-give-a-damn: *That's not how it was.*

Anna looks me in the eye and says: 'So tell us how it was.'

Chapter Twelve

Today is Thursday. Today what I'm doing is: Sweet Fuck All.

Yesterday . . . Yesterday I was primarily occupied with: Sweet Fuck All.

On Tuesday . . . let's see. On Tuesday I was busy. On Tuesday I sat in a car and did Sweet Fuck All. Also, I sat on the kerb for a while, doing Sweet Fuck All. On Tuesday night, just for a change, I sat on a bench near the car and tried my hand at a little Sweet Fuck All. Tuesday was hardcore.

This is sarcasm. I'm bored. Bear with me here.

Already I've spent three days doing Sweet Fuck All. I only got here Monday.

This could be anywhere. This could be Bristol or Birmingham or Brighton. It could be Edinburgh. Maybe Norwich, maybe Guildford, maybe Exeter. Maybe this is Cardiff or Southampton or Bradford or Swindon or Liverpool. Nottingham, even.

But it's not. It's none of those places. It's South West fucking London, on a fucking high street, covered in fucking shops, covered in fucking people; covered in litter and pigeons and beer and fag ends and leaflets and gum and newspapers and receipts and lottery tickets and you get the idea. And here's me, sat in a rental car, doing – Well, you know.

Let me tell you: Just. Walk. Away.

These three days, these were supposed to be surveillance. These were supposed to be watching a doorway across the street, which corresponds to the address inside the manila file given me by Mr Call-Me-Boss.

These were supposed to be identifying the routine of someone called Alex, who lives here, who I'm supposed to torture then kill. In the process of killing this person, I'm supposed to come away with a bunch of information, and I won't know if it's the right information till it's too late. In the process of killing this person, I won't know what he looks like, whether he's armed, whether he's edgy and nervy and expecting trouble, whether he's a prize bare-knuckle fighter who'll beat me to paste then chew off my nose, whether he's an ex-Nazi sympathiser with a secret Thule Society ectoblaster instead of a cock, whether he's a green-skinned mutant human/skink hybrid with laserbeam eyes and acidic nipples – et cetera et cetera. I'm exaggerating for effect. I'm Making a Point.

I'm bored. Bear with me.

For the record, the point I'm making is: I'm going in Blind. The point I'm making, in case you missed it, is: Just. Walk. Away.

The reason that doing this job inside London is a really *bad* plan is, there's a saying: You don't get high on your own supply. There's a saying: even animals don't shit in their own beds. You don't light fires in your own house, you don't piss on your own plate, you don't sprinkle broken glass in your own sandpit.

Listen: if this was Bristol or Birmingham or Brighton, or et cetera et cetera – then there's at least a *chance* you can get away with screwing up.

CONTRACT

This has to do with the fine men and women of the nipple-headed constabularies of the United Kingdom. Specifically, what it has to do with is: they don't share.

Today I'm wearing blue overalls, a blue baseball cap, a fruity beard and an Unsightly Hairy Mole on my left eyebrow. Today I am a plumber, perhaps, or a carpenter. Electrician, dishwasher repair man, mechanic, whoever. Maybe even a locksmith.

The blue overall is the same as the orange reflective jacket. This is the same as the pizza-delivery outfit. These are symbols that mean: I'm here on a job. These are symbols that mean: Leave Me To It.

Today I'm wearing a badge, which I made myself. It says my name is Malcolm.

My name is not Malcolm.

Today, to go with my overalls, I have a dusty holdall bag which looks heavy. Inside the bag is:

one hammer
one pair pliers
one stainless-steel rule, 50 cm
one kitchen knife with sharpening steel
one pot table salt
one fisherman's bait box
one pack fishing hooks
one junkie kit, containing syringe, needle, teaspoon
one set miniature flat files, with tapered tips
one pot KY jelly
one RIBDONG™ vibrating dildo, with battery case removed and six small holes punctured in outer shell
one Ruger Mk II .22 with a clip containing ten hollowpoint

bullets filled with optimum-grade rendered diamorphine
spare bullets inside empty matchboxes
one canister WD-40
one set homemade lock picks
one double-edged seven-inch hunting knife with a rubber sheath
one cheap novelty pornographic lighter
one packet cigarettes

For the record: I don't smoke.

This bag, the reason it looks heavy, is: it is.

Today, the reason I'm doing Sweet Fuck All is: this surveillance is *bollocks*.

The address, which is a tiny flat above a fried chicken shop, has only two windows. These windows, both are boarded up. This means, over the past three days, no walking back and forth. No blending in. No cover story. Just a guy, on a high street, sitting in a car. Feeding a hundred quid bit by bit into a meter.

Maybe this is the preservation of energy.

Maybe I'm losing my edge.

Maybe I'm just losing interest.

I am bored, and, seriously, sorry, you're just going to have to bear with me.

On either side of the chicken shop are newsagent/grocery shops, and above them are offices. Here and now it is the evening, and both offices are empty.

Over the past three days, the door has opened only three times. Each time the door has opened, it's been 11 a.m. This is when a pretty Muslim girl from the corner shop on the left walks, hijab fluttering, out into the street. Every morning, two carrier bags. Drinks and groceries and supplies. Every morning, two knocks on the door, then fumbling for a key, then inside.

Inside, in those thirty-second peeks, there are stairs leading up.

She comes out, she closes the door, she goes back into the shop, the world spins on.

Today, sitting here doing Sweet Fuck All, there comes a *point*, you know? There comes a time. There comes a J.W.A. feeling you can't ignore, and any other day or any other job, you'd do it. You'd walk away. You'd think: *This is stupid.*

I do not have this option.

Today, at No Particular Time, without waiting for the street to quieten down, without preparing or planning, bored so stiff I could play cricket with my face, what happens is:

I shrug.

I think: *Go*.

I think: Get it over with.

The thing with police not sharing, let's pretend: let's pretend the cops pull a print off a bloodstained lump of ex-person meat. Let's say this is in, ohoidunno, Devon. Let's say this is someone you have recently introduced to their own mortality. Let's say you were dumb enough not to wear gloves, or you dropped a hair, or ripped your jeans, or some other stupid cock-up that should've made you Just Walk Away. Let's say it's too late to worry. Let's say you head back to London. Let's say you're picked up drunk. This is months later. This is nothing to do with being a sociopathic mercenary terminator of human life. This is nothing to do with anything, except for you being an alcoholic tit. Let's say they take your prints – standard procedure – and whack them into the System, and lock you up for the night to Sleep It Off. What you're thinking is: *Uh-oh.*

Today, outside the door of the flat, I open the windows of the car and switch on the stereo. I crank the volume up to full. This is directly outside the door. This is *noisy*. This is in my overalls and cap.

This is me, waiting, grinding my teeth.

Oom-chkka-oom-chkka-oom-chkka

It had to be, didn't it?

Oom-chkka-oom-chkka-oom-chkka

With the System, the Cop Computer, the Filthmatron, the crazy thing is this: those splodgy inky little fingers here in London, unless someone *specifically* runs a cross-reference, those blackstained little piggies and those bloody prints in Gloucester aren't checked against each other.

Checks are internal. Checks are geographical. Checks are executed personally, not automatically, and unless you fucked up in the same place twice, unless they catch you out of character, unless that innocent little mistake happened *right here* in the same place you live, unless you've been arrested AS YOURSELF, unless someone decides to run a cross-reference check just on a jolly, you're OK. Probably.

I have never been arrested. To the best of my knowledge, my good friends in the London constabulary do not have my fingerprints, photograph or DNA profile on record.

But I could be wrong.

I could screw up today.

I don't drink. I always wear flesh-coloured latex gloves. I

don't take risks. And the thing with this job is, nobody ever got caught being *too* cautious.

Killing people in your own town, listen, honestly, seriously, trust me on this:

Not. A. Good. Idea.

For what it's worth, the cops aren't dumb. The System is changing. The technology is improving. This is just one more vote towards Getting Out Now.

Behold my flaming little Plan.

Behold my magic number, folded up tight in my pocket, with a bunch of zeroes and a pound sign.

Oom-chkka-oom-chkka-oom-chkka

After five minutes, nobody has come. Nobody is rapping on the window of my car to shout blue murder about *shut that fucking racket off*. Nobody is throwing open the door of the flat to yell. After five minutes I'm out on the kerb and squirting WD-40 into the lock, and whoever's inside; they can't hear shit over the racket.

I told you already, a simple and effective lock-picking set can be cheaply constructed from a pair of hacksaw blades. One filed away, one bent into shape.

Here and now the torsion bar's in; applying pressure so light you can barely feel it. This is not like on TV. This is slow, and gentle, and annoying.

Here and now the insert bar's in; spinning in its slot, finding gaps, tumbling pins, pulled through oh-so-gently by its bent-up partner.

Five minutes is what it takes, and this is a simple lock. Five minutes with me smiling and nodding at people walking by; just a locksmith; just a tradesman, and in their heads they smile and grin back, because *no one would be so brazen if they were doing anything illegal.*

The human race. You've just got to love it.

Five minutes is what it takes, and then the music is switched off and the car is locked, and the gun's in my hand, and I'm inside like a ghost.

And the cocking latch, the cocking *door*, clicks closed like an empty gun behind me.

Bugger.

And someone knows I'm here.

Which is annoying.

There is a voice, squawking from upstairs: 'Ilham? *Ilham!* What you doing back? You brung me fuckin' *milk*?'

Which is annoying.

Pop goes the element of surprise.

Maybe I'm losing my edge.

Maybe I'm just losing interest.

Upstairs there are two rooms. One, which is a toilet, is empty. The other is not.

Listen. Stop. Pay attention. Shut up. This is a *just-absorb-it* moment.

Inside the other room are flies and rotting food and pizza boxes and drink cans and fried chicken bones and three cold-air fans and one portable ice machine and six computers with six monitors and three Anglepoise lamps and cables everywhere and a plastic porta-potty and fifteen empty tubes of bedsore cream and at least four cats and more cat shit than you could scrape off the walls with a trowel.

Inside the room is a stink unlike any stink you have smelt before. This smell, it's apocalyptic. It's the stink of dead dragons. It's faecal matter mixed with burnt plastic mixed with dried vomit mixed with garlic and meat. It's gravy-and-spunk. It's graveyard ooze. It's just . . . *Nasty*.

The majority of this stink is not coming from the rubbish on the floor or the cat shit up the walls. The majority of this stink is because also in the room is a woman.

I think.

This is the largest human creature I have ever seen.

'I'll scream,' she says, staring at me.

'I'll shoot you,' I say, staring at her. 'Four times.'

She *hangs*. What I mean is, somewhere underneath it all there must be a chair. What I mean is, somewhere underneath it all is a base upon which some part of her rests.

This base is invisible. It is obscured by curtains made out of meat. It is covered over by waterfalls of stomach-roll, tit-wave, thigh-splash. This is not healthy meat. This is blotched and veined and too-pale, and sore all over. This is covered in food and flies and shit. This is perched between the six computers with the six monitors, and on top of it all, like a cherry on a cake, is a head.

The funny thing is, she'd be quite a looker – *if*.

The funny thing is, I think she might be naked. I can't really tell.

'You'd be Alex, then,' I say. It seems sort of inevitable. 'I was expecting a bloke.'

'Not . . . not fuckin' *jokin'*,' she says, and again I'm in *EastEnders*. 'I'll fuckin' scream so loud! You get the fuck out! There's nothin' here worth nothin' anyway!'

She points and waves her fingers. The funny thing is, her hands are sort of slender.

On the monitors in front of her are list after list after list.

Scrolling. Things bleeping and moving. Spreadsheets, databases. It's all very Hollywood.

I tell her I'm not a burglar. I say it softly, because already she's worked up. I look her in the eye and don't look down at the rest, and I tell her I'm not here to nick her money. I tell her: 'Mate, you *know* what I'm here for.'

Which is a good bluff.

I say, 'You hand it over nice and easy, everyone's happy, there's no trouble.'

She asks me what happens if she doesn't.

I wobble the gun around. This is me holding my nose with my spare hand.

The funny thing is, she might be obese. She might be a whale beached in a living room. She might be stinky like a demon's arsehole and she might get out less than Al Capone, but you can tell when you look in her eyes: she's not an idiot.

'Then there's no fuckin' *incen'ive*, is there?' she says. This is breathing heavy; being brave. 'Why the fuck . . . why tell you *shit* when you're only gonna . . . when . . .'

She can't finish the sentence. She trembles at the gun.

I say, 'Play along, nobody dies.'

This is a lie.

She spits on the floor. A couple of cats get out the way. This is me still standing on the other side of the room.

We stare at each other a while. There's a very tiny tear rolling down one of her very not-tiny cheeks. I was sort of hoping it wouldn't come to this.

The funny thing is this: this human woman here, this shuffling, unmoving invitation-to-vomit, this Jerry Springer reject, this cholesterol poster-girl, this living, breathing example of that which is disgusting, it turns out she'd be harder to hurt than a moist-eyed puppy.

I have never tortured anyone before. Seriously, honest injun, I'm just not *like* that.

Don't look at me like that.

This is a bad point to start learning.

I lift up the holdall and thump it down on a sideboard. 'Drastic measures, then,' I say. This is with a quaver in my voice.

This is with her composure, suddenly, all out of nowhere, going the way of the Dodo. This is with tears and howls and holding her hair. This is with snot. This is with more grief than you've ever seen in your life, all in one place at one time. This is shaking and thrashing and moving so hard the outlying bits *ripple*. This is where she's crying so hard she can't even cry. This is where she's got so little breath, the only noise she makes is: 'Uuuh ... Uuuh ... Uuuh ...'

This is pathetic. This is like treading on a kitten. This is Michael Point, aged twenty-eight, professional killer, finding his eyes filling up with salty water and having to *force* himself not to apologise.

Sooner or later she shuts up.

I begin. I tell her the simplest form of torture is beating. This is fists, feet, elbows. Concentrate on the victim's face, guts, genitals. Normally it's the aggression of the act rather than the pain that gets results.

This is without 'um's and 'ah's. This is autocue perfect.

I take the steel rule out of the bag and I wave it about. I tell her one form of beating is the Bastinado. This is where you strike the soles of the victim's bare feet over and over

211

and over with a cane, stick, rod or rule. This is across the toes, balls, insteps and heels. This is across more nerve-endings than you can shake a steel 50 cm-rule at.

This is a lot more painful than it sounds.

This giantess, this meteorite woman, seriously, despite the smell and the look and the swearing and the horror and the cats – no, seriously – you've just got to feel sorry for her.

Right now she's crying again, only quieter. Only less dramatic. Right now she's sobbing and trying to breathe, and saying *please, please, please, please* over and over.

She says, 'Please. I can't . . . I can't *move*. I'm fuckin' *helpless* here. Don't. *Don't.*'

This is my cold-shivering guilt-trip.

This is something behind my eyes flashing like a camera-bulb, pins and needles in my sinuses, the smell of sulphur, and –

Yep. Here it comes.

Today I'm ready. Today I'm prepared, and I sit down on a worktop and I breathe deep, and I don't let her see. I don't shiver.

I'm hallucinating again. Bear with me.

Today the rubbish all over the floor stands up on tiny, tiny baby legs and waddles around and around my feet, in time to music nobody can hear. Today the boards on the windows peel open like manky Elastoplasts, and the light coming in from outside isn't white daylight or yellow streetlight or green London skylight, but red. Just red. And it *moves*.

I tell her one good way to torture someone is penetration. This is because it doesn't leave much permanent damage.

I take the junkie kit out of the bag and open it up. I waggle the syringe in front of her.

CONTRACT

I tell her in Hindu mythology the earthly body is host to seven discrete focuses of energy, known as chakra. Each one represents a bunch of spiritual features and elemental qualities. Like earth, water, fire, air, life, time, heaven . . . I tell her each one corresponds to a region of biological importance: sexual, emotional, or just big fuck-off nerve-endings. I tell her the chakras can be stimulated to create the most intense sexual experience imaginable.

I tell her you can also jab needles into them and fuck someone up so badly their souls will fall out of their arseholes.

This is a little metaphysical.

I tell her, or, instead, I could just stick a needle under your kneecaps and pump them full of air.

I tell her, this will hurt like nothing has ever hurt you before.

In my eyes, this vast creature Alex is melting like wax. In my eyes she roasts and the air shimmers with heat, and when her hair's gone and her skin's peeling off you can see the black leathery thing inside, which squeals and laughs and moans as ice drips out of its nose.

I'm hallucinating.

That doesn't make it easy.

In my eyes, the rubbish on the floor becomes livestock, except only *bits*. In my eyes, I'm sitting on a cow's head, I'm wading in sheep's legs, I'm blowing pig's balls like bubbles.

In my eyes there's fire licking in through the window, and everything this colossal woman says, everything that spills out of her mouth, it goes to *fog*: words hanging, breaking apart, making new sentences.

Non sequitur poetry.

Beneath it all, back in the real world, she's a mess. She's sobbing and begging and her voice means nothing. I sit here and I'm big, and I'm filling the room, and she weighs maybe three times more than me but here and now she's small. Here and now I'm the poacher standing over a bunny with its leg in a trap. I'm the fisherman watching a trout flapping, drowning in air.

I hate this. I hate this superior bullshit. I hate this *impunity*.

Now I'm taking the kitchen knife out of the bag, and putting the gun down. I'm taking the sharpener out and slowly, *rasp-rasp-rasp*, I'm sharpening the knife.

I tell her cutting is an effective type of torture.

I tell her, it's worse than just stabbing, anyway. It's slow. It's dry, to start with. It's the *grinding* edge, unzipping cells. It's the papercuts on your tongue, and the scalpel-slices between the flaps of your toes. It's watching yourself bleed out, hot cells dying inside, grey-out behind your eyes.

I take the pot of kitchen salt out of the bag and tell her that it causes little scarring or genuine damage. I tell her, even so, in a freshly sliced wound, this will hurt like you've been set on fire. Inside.

She howls and screams and I tell her to shut the fuck up.

I take the fisherman's bait box out of the bag and pop it open. I'm wearing flesh-coloured latex gloves, and that's a good thing, because when I dip my hand inside and throw a handful of the contents at the blubbering, snotting, poor, poor – *I'm so sorry, this isn't me* – woman, it's maggots that rattle all over her and get caught in her hair.

I tell her that you drop a handful of these little beauties into a fresh wound, who knows where they'll end up?

For the record, this is a lie. For the record, maggots eat

only dead flesh, and are bloody useful for cleaning out wounds. The point is, she doesn't know this. The point is, spend enough time on the Internet, you can research *anything*. The point is, I came *prepared*.

And I still feel sick.

This isn't *me*. This isn't *clean*. This isn't *professional*.

This is like *gloating*.

In my eyes she's trying to stand, and her body flexes and twists and rises up like toffee. She's a black-skulled devil, with eyes like pearls, and her body bobbles and farts like a jellyfish skirt. In my eyes she's wreathed in flames, full of ants and flies, shitting and pissing herself, and *still and still and still* it's not fair to terrorise her like this.

Still and still and still with my sympathy. With my hating myself. With my guilt and horror and *look at you, Mike, look at what you've become*.

And then the Epiphany. Why am I doing this?

Let me tell you: because I've been told to. Because if I don't, I'm dead. Because They have me by the short-and-curlies. 'They' is just the Choir.

Why am I doing this?

Because this isn't *really* impunity. This isn't *really* me choosing to be cruel. This isn't *really* me at all.

This is me being *used*.

The fat woman Alex knows none of this. She thinks it's me. Just me. The threats, the fear, the horror. All my choice. But it doesn't matter, not really.

I am not my own boss any longer. I am a tool. I am being manipulated. And . . . and this is the most liberating thing that has ever happened.

I explain to her that I could burn her or scald her or flay

her. I take out the metal files with their tapered tips, and I tell her about insertion-under-fingernails. I take out the pliers and tell her about tooth extraction, about finger-joint destruction, about clitoral crushing.

All in books. All on the Internet. My library of Borrowed Horror. None of it my fault. None of it my idea.

I take out the hammer and tell her about heels, kneecaps, ligaments and tendons and elbows. I tell her about putting the steel rule between her teeth then thumping her on her chin.

She is, by now, barely human. She is a fear-ghost. She is a hollow terror-shape. She's not real.

It's easier this way.

In my eyes, she burns and moans and writhes, and she's horrific, and she's scary as fuck, but it doesn't matter. She's too scared to be frightening. Too *beaten*.

Listen, just because you've been forced to do something hideous, doesn't make it easy.

I take the dildo out of the bag. Through the tiny holes in its sides I thread the fishing hooks, so the barbs protrude downwards towards the base. I hold up the bottle of KY jelly and tell her: sorry. I was expecting a bloke.

I tell her this pink rubbery dick with its shiny secrets, it'll go *in* easy. It's the coming out that'll be tricky. (It's not my *fault*. It's not my *idea*.)

She watches it with eyes like lamps, and by now she's stopped crying. There's nothing left. She's peaked.

It's *time*.

I take the cigarettes out of the bag. I don't smoke.

I take the cheap novelty pornographic lighter out of the bag, and light up a smelly little cancer stick.

I tell her, with torture, you've got all these options. All these creative ideas. I tell her, but still: it's best to start with the classics.

I suck on the cigarette till the end glows bright, and always you can hear the paper burning down – *kkkhh*, like an annoying wanker with his weird laughter right over your shoulder – and I take two steps forward so she knows the lecture's over and it's *time*, and *this is it*, and *ohsweetJesus, please, please, please* make her give in, make her crumble, make her see sense. And I hold out the cigarette and I tell her: 'Open your eyes. And don't blink.'

She crumbles. She hits keys on the keyboards. She says nothing, cries nothing, stares at nothing. She's beaten.

You did this, Mike. YOU. (Not my fault. Not my idea. They *made* me do it.) I tell myself: at least you didn't have to hurt her. I can almost believe it.

The room swirls, and wounds in the walls trickle and bleed, and it's almost laughable, it's almost stupid, it's almost *pretty*, compared to what I just did.

This fat woman Alex, she prints out a sheet of paper. She hands it to me, and doesn't make eye contact.

It's an address. And a time. And a list of names.

At the top, it says: DISRING.

Slowly, her eyes creep up from the floor. Slowly, they meet mine. She's asking, though there're no words: is that it?

She's saying: You *promised*. Nobody dies.

I tell her to put the file on to a CD for me, and she nods and turns around and *that*, right there, right when she's full of hope and not fear, when she's reaching for a blank CD, *that* is when I lift the Ruger Mk II .22 to the base of her skull and blow her brains over the six monitors.

Small mercies, I tell myself.
The cats yowl.
It's not my fault.
They made me do it.

Listen, when she comes back to life, Alex barely has time to look up to snarl, to see her own juices on the monitors, before I cut her throat with a seven-inch double-edged hunting knife.

Using my hands. Routine, now. Expected, now.

Being liberated from responsibility would be a lot easier if the world was less red.

I believe that I may be going insane.

Contact 23

DAY: Today – Friday. Contact was Thurs.

TIME: 9.37 a.m. Contact @ approx 10 p.m. yesterday. Too exhausted to write entry immediately after. Have just woken.

LOCATION: @ home. Location of Contact = <u>Michael's Flat</u>.

Doesn't feel real this morning, but <u>is</u>: been inside dragon's lair.

CONTACT REASON: Normal situation. Called by M after job. Again, ready. His voice more desperate than before: nr-hysterical. Maybe afraid I wouldn't come – after 'I'm leaving London' (c.f. Contact 22), perhaps thought he'd never see me again? Begged down phone, 'Please? You've <u>got</u> to!' Desperate.

Deliberately sounded hesitant (complained again, re. his job – 'makes me uncomfortable, Mike . . .'). Eventually agreed, said: 'I'll come to your place.' M awkward @ suggestion but need for me = greater than need for secrecy. (Or perhaps thinks secrets exposed anyway – nothing to lose now?) Gave me address, told me to hurry.

Aim of Contact: simple. <u>Enter M's Flat</u>.

OBSERVATIONS: This morning: awful. Can't decide if rain during night or just wet air. Half-open window, whole room damp. Still in bed. Bedsit smells: haven't been taking care. Envelopes from Job Centre beside bed – used as drinks mats, bookmarks, etc. Couple upstairs arguing; am certain their place = crackhouse. Considered complaint to Housing Assoc., but – why? As every day, first thought on waking is: <u>me</u> – <u>here</u>, <u>why</u>? Then remember.

Won't go into it now. Last night more important.

Last night, M's flat: like cheap city hotel. Nothing personal (no pictures on walls, ornaments, plants, etc.). Floorboards & worn scrap carpet. Old pub sofa (not charming: dirty, faded), wooden chairs. Boxes in hallway full w/ printed T-shirts – not funny. Why here? TV, computer (on), kitchen (no washing, everything dried & away). Meticulous, neat – still shabby. Whole place: sad. Felt like old person died; all their shit taken out to jumble sale, only bare walls & furniture left. Smelled: stale bread.

His bedroom: same. Mattress w/ sleeping bag, no pillow. Wigs on stands by table, false glasses, make-up etc. Pitiful.

Him: spent most of meeting on sofa. Sitting → lying. Never seen him in state like this. Sweating. From outset on another planet, eyes rolling, trying to focus. Wearing blue overalls; spots of red. 'Work' clothes? Hasn't disposed yet. Getting sloppy. (If so, blood = from 'client'. Strange to see with own eyes.)

Either way, M is falling apart: looked like a wreck.

CONTRACT

*

NOTES: Met @ door of flat shivering, peering round door frame – Gollum moment. Pale, etc. Mumbled bout 'job' (told him didn't want to know details, but M not listening: already out of it). Slurred voice – I couldn't understand 100 per cent – but clear day's 'hit' (sounds so fucking macho) not routine at all (ie. usually talks about work like 'just another job' – not last night). Whatever happened = freaked him out, almost in tears. Kept saying 'didn't have any choice'.

Horrible to watch.

Complained again: <u>seeing</u> things. Made him lie down, got him water. Put up with SLURP SLURP SLURP, but worked: calmed. Stroked his head (can still smell sweat on fingers – haven't showered yet) till he dropped off. Talked to him all through – mostly nonsense. Slight smile, think my voice = comforting, poor fucker. Went into deep sleep – wouldn't wake, snored – pain in the arse. Reminder of Daniel again: used to breathe like a pig. Washed M's glass, put it away – down to business, not too loud to disturb him.

Found stash beneath bookshelf: hole in floor – he's mentioned it before. Guns, drugs, etc. Not subtle hiding place – floorboards badly sawed, botched DIY. Imagine him proud, making it (not often in business of creating).

Went to computer w/ disc from handbag. Hate computers, don't get them, but for days been memorising commands: all went perfectly. Codes on screen, encryptions, etc. Nosed in 'recently opened documents' while program ran – mostly porn. Whole thing only took 10 mins. M snored all way through.

Poked round bedroom. Biggest shock: bible, dresser-drawer. Gideon's edition – from hotel? Unopened – spine uncracked. What made him bring it back?

Under his skin, in his brain, but still has ability to surprise.

In next room, started crying in his sleep. Spoke re. family, 'the shower' incident, etc. Fucked up.

Me: stupid. Shaken by his state of mind, emotional enough already. Flicked through bible, chose passage @ random, testing knowledge. 1ˢᵗ one: 'For the invisible things of him from the creation of the world are clearly seen,' etc. etc. Sitting there, said aloud: 'Romans 1, Verse 20' – didn't even need to look.

Fucking hell.

Thought I'd got it all out of system. Left all that shit behind – convent school, early Sunday routine, good little girl, blah blah. Thought all been knocked out of me.

Started crying, there. Don't know why. M in next room, moaning in sleep. Felt responsible for everything – so fucking filthy. Forgot mission, task in hand. Stupid stupid stupid. Fucked up.

Went off-script. Thought about stuff, the deal, etc. etc. So many things not sure about myself, but still. Have to trust Daniel's guidance – HATE it. Thought if I could help – make it easier for everyone.

Sounds daft now! Morning after, don't know if done the right thing. Have to keep telling myself: Felt right at the time. He needed to be told . . .

Basically, decided Michael needed help. Couldn't shoulder it all himself, all in dark. Needed justification, etc. So . . . went back to him, woke him up, asked him:

CONTRACT

'Your hallucinations . . .'
  M said: 'What about them?'
  Asked him if he'd ever wondered.
  'Wondered what?'
  Told him:
  'Whether . . . Whether they really _are_ hallucinations.'
  Etc. etc. etc.
  Such an idiot.

THOUGHTS/CONCLUSIONS/OTHER: Task a success, suppose. Did everything was supposed to do. Just furious @ myself: let it all get to me. Scheme = so fragile, shouldn't be _anything_ left to chance now. Closing stages.

So awful, watching him. State of mind. Doesn't understand why he's like this. No frame of reference, no explanation. Obvious from outside: M spent so long becoming deliberately _amoral_ (not _immoral_! Never!), he can't understand source of own guilt/joy. I _had_ to give him something new, new _idea_, help ease it.

His soul = sick, but doesn't _get_ it. Can't be told. Can't be helped now. Too late.

Keep telling myself: All for the best. _All for the best_.
Don't think I'll see him again. Wonder if he knows.
God.

S

An Interlude of
No Importance Whatsoever

Listen. You might as well know now, so I'm just going to tell you.

But first.

First, *here's the thing*: what I'm going to tell you, it doesn't actually *mean* anything. It just *is*, it just *happened*, and that's all. This is my caveat.

The point is, this thing: it's not an excuse.

It would mean so, so much to me if you would bear that in mind. It's not an explanation for who I am or what I do. It's not a significant piece of my mental landscape. It's not grounds for any of your bullshit DIY psychoanalysis wank, it's not a Get-Out-of-Jail-Free card for my conscience, and it's not fair game for *judging* me.

Don't you *ever* do that.

OK. Here goes.

My father is in prison for murder. This has already been established, right?

Let me elaborate.

I found the body.

This is Michael Point, aged twelve, getting home from school, going for a piss, stopping in the doorway.

This is Michael Point, aged twelve, seeing red smears on white tiles, seeing shower-water gurgle away down the plughole, seeing that white/grey shape, all crumpled at not-normal angles. Seeing loops of guts like bubblegum spill over, seeing knife-wounds like tiny tidy fannies, washed clean so the edges are as clear as lipless mouths.

This is Michael Point, aged twelve, embarrassed at seeing his own mother naked.

Chapter Thirteen

London just doesn't stop surprising. London is the opposite of Pathetic Fallacy.

Pathetic Fallacy is a borrowed-wisdom phrase that means, in – say – films, *look*: how come it's always raining during the sad scenes? Pathetic Fallacy is the sun coming out when the lovers kiss. Pathetic Fallacy is the environment setting the tone.

In London, the tone sets the environment. Which is to say: *It is what you make it.*

I'm feeling a little airy-fairy. Bear with me. I'm feeling a little mystical, and any minute I'll be wading through happy bunnies and singing birdies. With a chainsaw.

Today is Monday. Today I'm walking through a cemetery. This is the most relaxing and peaceful thing I have ever done inside London.

Don't get me wrong. I don't wear black. I don't write shitty poetry. The thing is, this city, with the sun Mostly Out and leaves on trees and grass and sky and squirrels and NO CARS WITHIN EARSHOT and no wankers chucking frisbees and no kids smoking weed and no fumes on the air and no icecream stalls tinkling, with everything Just Pleasant, the only place you can be, seriously, is surrounded by corpses.

Anti-Pathetic Fallacy.

This is Kensal Green. This is 250,000 dead people inside 65,000 graves. This is Victorian sculpture and grand mausoleums, this is crypts and monuments and ivy-choked cherubs. This is something built to be awesome, something the ground and the green have simply . . . *swallowed.*

Here, the trees couldn't give a shit for preserving the ageless beauty of this angel or that crucifix. Here the squirrels wouldn't piss on this memorial bench or that drooping chrysanthemum if either were on fire. Here the crows and magpies and sparrows and starlings don't care how much this monument cost, or how hard it was to get rose limestone for that crenulated crypt. Here the grandeur is just . . . *beaten.* Here the birds just dig worms. The worms, *well . . .* Let's not go there.

I like this place very much.

Today is Monday, and today I am meeting Mister Call-Me-Boss. This is neutral territory.

Today we walk together along a gravel pathway that crunches like a breakfast bowl, and in my fists are two manila packages.

Mr Call-Me-Boss and manila packages seem to go hand in hand.

Today I have a headache, and if Pathetic Fallacy really worked, really reflected the tone, then right now the weather would best be described as: tempestuous.

In fact, it's a lovely day. I'm trying not to let it get to me.

In the first manila package is six thousand quid in cash. This is with one hundred £50-notes, thirty £20-notes and forty £10-notes. I know it's all there because a moment ago, propped up on a gravestone, I counted it. This is cash money I specifically requested in the letter I sent to Mr Call-Me-Boss, which accompanied a printout of extracted information I took from an obese, terrified female four days ago.

This business – killing people until they're dead – the sort of stuff you need to buy needs cash. This is from dodgy arms collectors who don't like credit cards and PIN numbers. This is from don't-leave-a-paper-trail ex-military guys. This is from skag-dealers, pawnbrokers, identity-thieves. This is why £6,000 in cash is as valuable to me now as the £194,000 in electric dreams this weird-eyed pinstriped piece of chronic rectal ejecta owes me. He says it's on its way.

My offshore account, getting fat. My Plan, getting nearer.

My balls, still inside this weird-eyed bastard's vice.

Inside the first manila package, that £6,000, Mr Call-Me-Boss swears blind it's clean. What I'm thinking is: is it worth the risk?

Mobster bullshit. Gangster bollocks.

These people, you don't accept their money and expect it to be whiter-than-white.

Today we stop beneath a copse of trees – I'm not sure what kind; they're brown and green, work it out for yourself – and the boss says:

'Doin' well so far, Mikey.' His mouth goes lopsided. 'You're a fuckin' credit.'

I stay quiet. Right now what's occupying me is the second manila package, which is just about chock-full of photographs and names and lists. He nods at it.

This is the Last Job. You recall. The one worth £600,000.

This is the one that lets me get out. The plan, the magic number, a bunch of zeroes and a pound sign, sunsets and snorkelling and sangria and blah, blah, blah.

This is after two jobs he said would be *standard*. This is after two jobs he said would be *easy*, which ended up being – well, you know.

This third job, when he first brought it up, he said: *third's trickier*.

Excuse my burning, sinking, sweating, fear. Excuse my drowning-in-faeces sinking feeling. Excuse the desire to Just Walk Away.

Today he smiles at the file in my hand and says: 'Plenty of stuff, right? Nice 'n' prepared. We knew there'd be a big meeting, all that stuff. We just wasn't sure when 'n' where. Wouldn't've got nearly so much if not for . . . well . . .' He locks eye contact and makes 'torture' gestures. These are inventive. '. . . *You* know.'

What I do, not to put too fine a point on it, is this: I throw the file at his head.

(For the record, this is all right beside the grave of Joseph Richardson [1790–1855], who, if you want to know, invented the rock harmonicon and several other unusual musical instruments. This person is dead, and already he's the most interesting guy I've met today.)

On Thursday, which was four days ago, after I had blown out the brains of a morbidly obese woman, what I did was: not go to a club. Not fuck. Not follow my routine. My routine, if you want to know, is buggered. This feels a lot like falling, only upwards. Like gravity just *changed its mind*.

On Thursday, Sally came round to my flat and said some Stuff. I forget some of it. Some I remember. On Thursday,

Sally suggested some Suggestions. Stir-fried some concepts in my think-wok.

Listen, these suggestions, these concepts: They. Are. *Stupid*.

Four days later, which is today, which is Monday, it just so happens I can't stop thinking about them.

Listen: the thing with cash laundering is, you need someone who can take a lot of cash off your hands, add it to a lot *more* cash, casually bank it or use it in the normal course of business, then give you a whole different set of cash back. Minus 10 per cent. Or 20. Or 90.

Depends who you ask.

And here's the thing: there aren't that many legitimate businesses out there that deal exclusively with notes.

Today the Boss stands not outraged or indignant or weird. He just smiles. Today he stands with paper and photos flapping and spinning around him, slapping to the ground. The sound they make is like spit hitting concrete.

Spwk-spwk-spwk-spwk

Today I'm shouting and screaming, I'm telling him this is *fucking idiotic*, I'm laughing at his use of the phrase 'nice and prepared' and above all I'm saying: 'This stuff is bullshit! It's all *guesses*!'

I have read the file carefully. It is, let me tell you, worthless.

He says: 'Now hang on a m—'

I tell him *no*.

I tell him he can't even tell me if these fuckers, these *multiple targets*, will be *armed*. I tell him I *kill* people. I don't *fight* them. I scream that he can't tell me how many of them there'll even fucking *be*. I tell him this is in *London*, for *fuck's sake*, and it's messy and unprofessional and *just not smart.*

I tell him he can KISS my GAPING CREVICE if he thinks I'm going to have ANYTHING to do with this festering pile of shit. I tell him: Fuck you, man, I'm out of here.

And then I'm walking away. Ohoyes. I'm the human JWA. I'm cool like the Fonz.

For maybe four steps.

He stands and watches, and – yes, yes, *all right* – when the tantrum's finished I'm turning round and bending down and picking up the photos, and glowering, and he doesn't even have to say a word. This is Michael Point, twenty-eight, sulking like a six year old.

I've got no choice.

'All that stuff,' he says, nodding at the file, 'what it is, it comes from the inside. One of the . . . what? . . . "*mark*"? "*target*"? . . . Hah. One of his own men, anyway. We tracked him down – thanks to your little chat with the Organiser. Made him some offers. Made him realise who he was workin' for.'

His eyes glitter.

'This geezer,' he says, 'he's sold out his people. Wants to help us. Reckons it's his last chance. Wants to swap sides.'

Sides. Like it's a war. Like it's *us* or *them*. Families and companies and Dons and lifelong loyalties and tommy-guns and blah blah blah blah blah blah blah fucking *blah*.

Too many Scorsese films.

What I'm doing is, rolling my eyes.

On Thursday, one of the things Sally said was: Joel 2, 28–31.

Prepare yourself. This whole thing is about to get

uncanny. This whole thing is about to get airy-fairy.

This is with Sally stroking my hair. This is with me not in a club, not having filthy high-octane sex with a random girl, not trying to forget the Fat Woman gasping and gagging and gulping back her tears.

On Thursday, one of the things Sally said was:

And it shall come to pass afterwards, that I will pour out my spirit upon all flesh; and your sons and your daughters shall prophesy, your old men shall dream dreams, your young men shall see visions.

And on my servants and on my handmaidens I will pour out in those days of my Spirit; and they shall prophesy.

And I will shew wonders in heaven above, and signs in the earth beneath; blood, and fire, and vapour of smoke:

The sun shall be turned into darkness, and the moon into blood, before the great and notable day of the Lord come.

For the record, Sally's never mentioned being a God-botherer before. Funny thing. I remember being sort of disappointed. For the record, this was just after I'd been telling her about my hallucinations.

For the record, I told her I could see what she was getting at. Then I told her to fuck off.

Politely.

Today in Kensal Green graveyard, with magpies saying *rakkakkakkakkakkak*, with dull-eyed mourners wandering by with fake flowers and bags of green pebbles, Mr Call-Me-

Boss flounces off along a path, hands in pockets.

He says, 'I know it don't sit easy, Mikey. I get that. But you know the score.'

I follow him, trying not to drop the photographs a second time.

'Question of trust,' he says, and he turns back to look at me. 'Ain't important what information you get. Where it comes from, any of that. What's important is, it's *right*. You got to believe that, or you won't get nowhere. What's important is, you do what you're told, and you do it right, and you'll get what's due.' He smiles.

'You can trust me,' he says.

Ahahaha.

The Reflected Risk Principle. You remember that? The Mutual Risk compromise. The Me-Getting-Shafted-by-Rewritten-Contracts-Reality.

Trust.

Ahahaha.

Next to him is the burial slab of Isambard Kingdom Brunel (1806–59), who designed bridges and tunnels and ships and railways. Who kept building bigger and bigger and better and better. Who just never knew when to quit. Who knew the value of everything, and didn't care much about the cost of anything. He built wonders, and spent far too much.

This probably means something.

Money. Let's talk about money.

Let's talk about *cash*.

Let's say you've come into possession of a respectable Wad. Let's say you think it's been nicked. Maybe it's drug money. Maybe it's forged or untaxed. Maybe, for whatever reason, the fine men and women of the anti-fraud department have a list of numbers just the same as the codes next to each gurning print of Her Majesty, and they're keen to bring the two together.

Maybe you were given it by someone just a little on the untrustworthy side.

What do you do?

Let me tell you, what *I* do is: I hit the arcade.

On Thursday, one of the things Sally told me was that St Paul, who was also Saul, whose eyes were seared to blindness by the Loving God on the road to Damascus, even after he got his sight back, he had *issues*.

She told me he wrote:

To keep me from becoming conceited because of these surpassingly great revelations, there was given me a thorn in my flesh, a messenger of Satan, to torment me.

On Thursday Sally looked at me, sweating and shivering on my sofa, and said: 'The point is, being chosen *hurts*.'

Right then, just like now today in the cemetery, my headache got worse. I told her to leave me alone. I told her to fuck off and stop talking religion.

Politely.

Today Mr Call-Me-Boss perches against a crumbling urn and sighs. His eyes glow. His cheeks hang.

He says he knows there's not much information for me to go on, but his tame little informer'll be there on the night. He says this untrustworthy sell-out turncoat piece of shit'll be waiting at the door to let me in, give me a rundown on who's inside and what's-what. He says, hey, don't worry.

He says, 'Sonny, you'll be *prepared*.'

I tell him, 'Yeah. Like a joint of meat.' (I'm sort of proud of that one. He doesn't laugh.)

Trust, for the record, is a funny thing. When you've got no choice except to do what you're told, maybe it looks kind of the same as doing it because you trust it's *right*.

In an arcade, everything is cash. Fruit machines, video games, cuddly toy crane grabbers, rocking-shelf coin slots, vending stands, pool tables, multiplayer driving units, flight simulators, kill-everything-that-moves marksmanship challenges, punchbag machismo tests, airhockey tables, sweet dispensers and grotesque hamburger pits. To experience this myriad of cultural delight you will need:

a dearth of anything better to do
an addictive personality
a fuckload of pound coins

For this, an arcade visitor must meet the humble change machine.

Paper goes in, coins come out. Bear with me here.

Robert McCormick (1800–90), it turns out, was a ship's surgeon on all sorts of Arctic and Antarctic adventures. Robert McCormick was onboard the *Beagle* with Darwin. Robert McCormick led a search expedition in a ship named *The Forlorn Hope*.

Right now I'm standing next to Robert McCormick's grave, and Mr Call-Me-Boss, he's like a little slice of the Arctic all on his own. His breath steams.

Mr Call-Me-Boss asks about torturing the fat woman. He doesn't know I managed to do without. He asks about how I handled it. He wonders out loud what methods I used, what techniques, what tools, and then he says: 'I had to guess, I'd say . . . I'd say you *cut* her.'

He says, 'Runs in the family, eh?'

He mentions slow cutting and slicing and Sabatier kitchen knives, and showers and red blood on white tiles, and little boys coming home from school, and I forget his exact words but ohoyeah, he's doing this on purpose, he's winding me up, and already my eyes are clouding.

Already the sky looks brown. Already the ground bubbles.

Already he wears white and shines.

I'm hallucinating. He can make this happen whenever he wants.

In my hand, listen, the file, the papers – they *burn*. They stink. Flies and dead meat hover around them. The people inside, on the photos, the way their faces look is: evil. Mr Call-Me-Boss grins and light pours out of his mouth.

On Thursday, four days ago, one of the things Sally told me about was St John the Divine. She told me about angels with trumpets and things falling from space. She told me about phials full of horror, and flaming swords, and cherubs with four heads, and *things* chained in the pit, and plagues and marks and numbers and cubic heavens and horsemen. She told me about shaggy monsters with horns and crowns and breasts, and the whore of Babylon, and armies of unkillable warriors sent to cleanse the earth, and blah, blah, blah, blah, blah.

She told me: *Mad Prophets*, Mike.

I told her, hey: I know all this stuff already.

She asked me what I see when the visions begin – *visions*,

she says, not *hallucinations*, not *delusions* – and before I even notice, I'm telling her about devils and flames and smoke and *things that will not die*.

Sally just gave me A Look, like: *See?*

I panic and sweat and shiver and tell her: seriously, please, *fuck off*.

Politely, mind.

Let me tell you: in an arcade, once a night, a man comes to empty the change machines. He carries his stacks of notes – hundreds and hundreds of worthless papery portraits of Her Scowling Majesty – in a bomb-proof box, to a van or car or whatever.

This money, it all adds up in the long run. Notes traded for coins, then back again at the bank. Fresh silver to top up the hungry slots for the next game.

This is sophisticated barter. This is modern alchemy.

This is turning woodpulp to metal.

Today Mr Call-Me-Boss, blazing with whiteness, flowers and gold in his hair, a million silver eyes winking from the patterns on his tie, he pats me on the shoulder and says, 'No need to worry, mate. You'll have help.' His voice sounds like a massage feels. 'Best men I've got.'

'Pigshit!' I say, and I'm fighting to hold it together, and I'm angry and I can't help it. 'I'll find my own fucking *muscle*, ta, and—'

'If that's what you w—'

'*Look.*'

And now I'm talking slow. This is how reptiles would talk. This is lizard conversation. This is serpent-speak.

I tell him, 'There's no discussion.'

I take a breath. I tell him, 'I'll do it. Probably . . .

probably I'll die. Or get done – whatever.' I shrug. For the record, here, 'done' means 'caught'.

He starts to talk.

I tell him, 'I haven't finished.'

I tell him: 'If I do it, if I survive, I'm out. Paid, receipt in my hand. If I survive, I come to your office, right? I come and see you. And you burn the contract in front of me.'

His body is white fire. His eyes are rivers of wine and honey and gold. There are wings made of music on his back. Somewhere there are trumpets honking and gravestones shifting.

I'm hallucinating. Maybe. Bear with me.

'Agreed,' he says.

Next to us is the grave of Stephen Ross Porter, who called himself Peregrine Took, who founded *T-Rex* and choked to death on a cherry pip in 1980. There's music coming from the ground.

Above me crumbled statues turn to look. Angels move, and feathers made of rock rasp together. Above me a headless Seraph plucks a harp made of granite, and its strings shatter like ice, then reform, then shatter again, each time a new note; a symphony of dust and shards.

I keep walking. The ground is moving. White and brown lumps break the grass. Fingers and eyeholes and polished, hairless domes. Which is odd.

I keep walking. Mr Call-Me-Boss winks.

He is light.

He is glory.

He is an agent of a divine power.

He's a fucking cunt.

He chuckles and waves an arm, and the dead go back to

sleep, and he says, 'You can trust me, my old china. See? I'm on the *right* side.'

He says, 'I made myself a deal too, Mikey.'

Money. Think of the money.

(Self-distraction. Self-distraction is the new self-destruction, which was yesterday's new self-improvement. Someone told me that recently. I wish I could remember who.)

In an arcade, at the weekend, the change machines need more coins than they need during the week.

Monday nights: the guy in his blue overalls and helmet visor takes the notes and pays them in. He doesn't need to swap them *all* for coins – weekdays are quieter – so a chunk of the cash is sucked, magically, into the arcade's account. Converted to digital nothing. Rendered-down as ones and zeroes.

And yeah, maybe some gets whipped off before all that. Jammed into tills in the arcade, crammed into envelopes for the minimum-wage ghosts that mop up the burger sick and scrape dirt from under the machines. But mostly it's temporary profit. It's temporary because next weekend it'll all be needed all over again, but here and now and in the present, the guy in the helmet is paying in more than he's taking out.

Let us say, for the sake of argument, you know this person. This is what we call: an opportunity.

On Thursday, which was four days ago, one of the things Sally said to me was: 'You shouldn't *have* to worry, Mike. You shouldn't be afraid that you're *sick*.'

On Thursday, one of the things Sally said was: 'What if you're doing something good? Huh? What if you're doing holy work?' And: 'What if you're working for . . . for the right people? What if you've been *chosen*?' And: 'What if the people you go after . . . what if they're not people at all? What if they *need* to be put down?'

I told her this is ridiculous, stupid, disgusting. I told her I had no idea she was mental like this, and I liked her better when she was just an unemployed fuck-up. I told her religion doesn't suit her, and I told her to shut up, to shut *the fuck up*, to stop going on.

She said she was only trying to help, but *no, no, no*, stupid, stupid, stupid. I told her to get out and shut up, and I puked all down the hallway and all across the cheap T-shirts, and she left without looking back, and *that*, my friends, is that.

Sally is gone from my life, and what's left is just smog.

Only . . . annoyingly, all this shit, going on here and now, all the stuff I've seen . . . maybe she was right.

Inside the second manila file – currently smouldering and devilish and stinking, with the photos inside showing not people but *horrors* with sloped muzzles and spiked chins – inside this file is an address and a date and a time.

This is when I will get out. This is when I will finish it.

Mr Call-Me-Boss asks if I trust him.

I don't answer.

'All you need to remember,' he says, and the light round his face is fading and the delusion sputters-out and the music dies away, 'is that you got no choice.'

And he's right.

I clutch the £6000 just a little tighter.

Listen, the guy who takes the arcade change to the bank. Let's say over the course of six weeks, all those crumpled notes are a spot heavier than normal. Let's say there's an extra grand each time, to be sucked-off into the belly of the computer.

'Busy weekend,' if anyone asks. Which they don't.

Let's say the owner of the arcade pisses your six grand in dirty notes into 1s and 0s, little by little. And if someone raises a flag: so?

Not his fault, is it, what the punters are feeding into his machines? He's insured up the sphincter.

Let's say he makes a one-off payment, right at the start, to a 'Gaming Consultant' of his acquaintance. All tax deductible. All above board.

Let's say he makes a payment of £4,500, give or take.

Let's say he makes it to me. Or at least, someone who looks like me, only with a different name. Different hair. Maybe a facial mole.

Let's say, as a result, I'm down 25 per cent on my original payment, but I'm clean; the money's rosy.

Worth every penny.

This whole thing looks simple and tacky and too obvious, and it is. The point is, it works.

Today I leave the cemetery when there's nothing left to say, and my head is a storm, and – ha – the sun really *has* gone in. Today I'm planning on visiting the arcade to put all this sneaky procedural bullshit into action, when someone says: '*Kkkhh.*'

For the record, he's lounging against the big old gates into the cemetery. For the record, he's wearing black with a red tie, and smiling like he's enjoying the sun even though it's gone.

'Afternoon,' he says.

I walk past him, not looking.

'That cash you got there,' he says, voice following me. 'You want to watch that.'

I keep walking.

'The old man's big on Trust,' he says. 'You got that, right?'

I keep walking.

'Don't disrespect him,' he says.

I keep walking.

'He'll *know*.'

I keep walking.

'Remember who you're working for.'

I keep walking.

'And don't shoot the messenger!'

He laughs his little laugh.

Long story short: I do not visit the arcade.

Long story short: I do not touch or spend this cash.

Long story short: I go home and place it beneath the floorboards of my flat, and then curl up in a ball on the floor and try hard not to cry.

This is trickier than it sounds.

Listen. This is important.

Whatever you do, whatever evil shit you pull, whatever reprehensible vile nastiness you're responsible for, *it's not your fault if you didn't have a choice*.

Call this my latest short-term motto. Call this my philosophy *du jour*.

Call this my crumbling unsustainable untrue lifeline.

Call this my sinking, ugly, guilty little feeling.

There is a bible in the drawer in my bedroom. I've never opened it. I'm not going to now.

CONTRACT

This isn't that sort of story.

But still, but still. This is Michael Point, twenty-eight, feeling stupid and addled and insane and diseased, wondering if just maybe he's doing something worthwhile for the first time ever. Wondering if he's wrapped-up in something spooky.

Wondering if he's making the world a better place.

Wishing someone'd asked him first.

Chapter Fourteen

It suddenly occurs to me, right out of nowhere, how *old* he looks. Probably it's the first time I've paid enough attention to notice.

Today is a day for Changes.

'You didn't come Friday,' he says.

He has a gift for stating the obvious. This runs in families.

He's not quick. He's not smart.

I nod and tell him, 'You're right. I didn't.'

Welcome back to Belmarsh. Welcome back to the Redbrick pit. Lives on hold. Pauseville. My old man.

'Usually come Fridays,' he mutters, like he's picking a scab, and he's trying to look away, trying to be nonchalant, but it's there in his voice: I scared him. I wasn't here when he expected. Didn't show at the Allotted Hour.

I nod and tell him: Yep. Yep, usually. Usually I come Fridays. Yep.

The thing is: If *I* didn't come, nobody would.

One day, maybe, that postcard. Airmail. Stamped from the Maldives, the Seychelles, the Canaries, the Wherevers. The Plan, made all real on a five-by-six-inch rectangle with a bland photo on the front. Maybe a beach. Maybe a sunset. Topless local. Whatever.

And a message . . . *not coming back, Pa* . . .

My one sliver of control. My one slice of malice, my one petty oh-so-cherished Sword of Damocles, available for the price of a piece of card and a foreign stamp.

He giveth, and he taketh away.

That postcard, if by some miracle things work out with the Choir, maybe it'll be arriving here sooner rather than later. Like next week, say.

Me, getting a tan.

I wonder if he suspects.

'So what happened?' my dad says. 'Why today? Eh? Why not Friday?'

Listen to me: This is delving below the surface. This is beyond the normal course of our bland, safe, disengaged conversation.

This is *personal*.

Today is Tuesday. Last Thursday, sitting in my flat, sweating and sleeping, et cetera et cetera, you remember, Sally did the exact same thing.

Went deeper. Pried.

All these safe little chats: it turns out they're not safe at all. It turns out, all at once, they're *sharp*. This comes as a shock.

All these safe little getting-to-know-yous: it turns out they're changing. They're becoming getting-under-your-skins, everywhere I go.

Shiver, shudder, that sinking feeling.

'Something came up,' I lie.

(The truth is: on Friday, which is normally when I come here, to this clanking magnolia breeze-block on-hold life, I was sitting on my arse in my flat, fidgeting and shivering and drumming my fingers.)

My dad, he rubs his temples and winces. He says, sometimes, he Just Gets These Headaches. He says, sometimes, Nothing To Worry About.

This runs in families too.

(The truth is: Friday was one day after I exploded the skull of a chronically wide-loaded demon-woman, then sliced open her carotid artery to prevent her from coming back to life. Friday was one day after Sally suggested I might be inadvertently doing holy work. Friday was one day after I told Sally to shut the fuck up, to get the fuck out of my flat, to get her sick fucking religious fucking bullshit out of my fucking ears, and to *fuck* the *fuck* off. Which she did.)

(Sally, I think I love her.)

(Friday, if I was in an American Soap Opera, I'd say I was *working through some issues*.)

My dad, he rubs his temples and sighs, and 85 per cent of male prisoners over the age of sixty, if you want to know, have at least one chronic medical condition.

(Friday, it turned out, was just a little too soon for me to be leaving the flat and wandering about. Like everything was normal, when it wasn't. Like the world was obeying the rules, when it wasn't. Like let's all SMILE and PRETEND and just get ON WITH IT, what a GOOD idea, when we *can't* and *won't* and *shouldn't*, and nothing is *fair*.)

You'll have to excuse me. I'm a little shaken.

(The truth is: on Friday, I was sending off the document I got from the Fat Dead Woman, the document with a time place list of names, the document I added to a request for £6000 in cash and a Monday Morning Meeting. The document I sent to Mr Call-Me-Boss. That meeting I arranged, for the record, was in Kensal Green Cemetery. This only just happened. *Remember?*)

Try to keep up.

(The truth is: on that Friday, when I should have been here visiting my only remaining biological relation, what I was doing instead was: staring at a blank piece of badly plastered wall in my flat, taking sleeping pills that Did Not Make Me Sleep, that Did Not Freak Me Out, that Did Not Sound Like Aztec Gods, and rocking back and forth. In the evening, I watched *EastEnders*.)

I digress.

Dad, sitting opposite me, he sighs again.

At the table next to us, a gargantuan man with more tattoos than braincells laughs like a drain at something his tiny, tiny wife tells him. Bless.

My dad, he looks around at the noise and suddenly he seems even smaller than usual. The big bear-man, the tattoo-giant, the inked-up colossus, he catches my dad's eye and what he does is: he scowls.

My dad looks away quickly.

The big surprise is, deep down in me, I feel sort of protective.

Today is Tuesday.

'How are you keeping?' I say to my father. Staying on track. Staying bland. Today, with him looking old, with him being hunched over, with him looking smaller and smaller every time I see him, this could be arthritis. This could be the first signs of kyphosis. This could be spinal trauma or drunkenness or narcolepsy or just bad posture.

He shrugs. He glances sideways at the big man, unconsciously, and double-double shrugs.

In prisons, if you want to know, for men over the age of sixty, the Number One Reason for them being banged-up is: sexual offences.

In prisons, if you want to know, for men over the age of sixty, the odds are sort of stacked against them.

Listen: in two days, which is Thursday, I will do the Big Job for Mr Call-Me-Boss. This has come slightly out of nowhere.

I will storm into an unknown place, facing an unknown number of people, armed with an unknown number of guns. This is very Hollywood. This is High Action. This is gung-ho glory.

This, *admit it*, you sick little bastards, is what you've been waiting for all along.

This, just let me make sure you understand, is almost certainly going to get me killed.

It's not elegant. It's not professional. It's not *how it works*.

One way or another, today is the last time I shall come here to this place.

The 'One' way is: on Friday I'll be a millionaire. Sipping the future. *En route* to the sun. Coral and coconuts and crabmeat and colonial stagnation.

The 'Another' way is: on Thursday night I'll be dead.

'Still finding new stuff in the library?' I say, oh-so-bland. 'Keeping you busy?'

He looks at me with eyes on pause. He looks at me, and it's like he's working out if he can be bothered. Like he's weighing the banality of the question against the energy it'll take him to answer it. This is modern intercourse. This is cultural exchange. This is Borrowed Social Wisdom, and sometimes, listen: it's just not worth the bother.

He sighs.

The Big Job, which I will do tomorrow, just so you know, which will almost certainly get me killed – I have no choice. If I don't do this job I'm in trouble, ohoyes. If I don't do this job, what happens is: Mr Call-Me-Boss shows the contract to the police.

The contract I signed.

The contract which was – you've got to laugh – my idea.

The contract which, it turns out, bears nobody's name but mine. The contract which is basically just a confession.

Ahahaha.

And if that happens, sooner or later, I'll wind up here. With Dad. Redbrick, magnolia walls, blue cell doors, fags for currency. On Pause. Waiting for visitors.

Listen: *Fuck. That.*

So, one way or another, yep. It's my last visit.

'Yeah,' says Dad, and for a second I have to try to remember what question he's answering. I get abstract when I'm bored. My mind wanders. 'All good,' he says. 'Mostly it's non-fiction.'

The prison library.

'Couple of old Christies, though,' he says. '*Poirot*, mostly. Bloody Poirot. Always preferred Marple.'

This is the last time I'll see the Human Being who gave me twenty-six of my chromosomes. This is the last time I'll ever meet the Human Being whose little Y-shaped bundle of genetic Borrowed Wisdom kick-started the chemical process that converted my cellular clitoris into a vestigial piece of gristle beneath my foreskin. This is the last time I'll chat, if you can call it that, to the Human Being whose biological contribution made me a Mike instead of a Mandy or

Melissa or Mary or Miriam or Mairi or you get the idea.

This is the last time I'll ever be in the same smelly prison room as my father, and guess what?

We're discussing detective fiction.

All these little getting-to-know-yous.

'It's the gardens,' he says. 'Marple always gets better gardens. We don't have gardens in here, see?' He gestures, vaguely. He means: This Place.

In prisons, if you want to know, suicide rates amongst men are five times higher than they are in the outside community.

My dad, he has my eyes. He has my mouth and my nose. If I wasn't covering it up beneath this grotesque crime-against-facial-topiary goatee, he'd have my chin. He has my voice, my stature, my shoe size, my callused knuckles and my uneven eyebrows. Thirty years' extra gravel, maybe. Extra lines. Extra withering. But still, but still.

'Gardens,' I say. 'Right.'

Is it just me, or: Crime Fiction in a prison library? Who's idea was *that*?

The thing with my dad having my eyes and my mouth, et cetera et cetera, you could reverse the trend. You could say: all those things, all those features, all those traits; they were *his* first. You could say *I* have *his* eyes. Dominant and recessive genes, unzipped DNA, a biological robot programmed by two people.

It's not my fault, you could say, It's my Body Chemistry.

You could say all that I have, I inherited from him, only he's on Pause, and he's in *here*, and so *he's* the echo.

Like looking at myself, *sans* the Plan.

Like looking at myself, except gone wrong.

Like looking at myself, except hurt and tired and old and *what a waste*.

Suddenly, I don't want to send him that postcard. Suddenly, the thought of it, of him reading it, of the fear, of the sickness, of the *cruelty* of him knowing, right then, that *no one else will ever come*, suddenly it makes me want to puke blood.

This is Michael Point, aged twenty-eight, discovering he's maybe not that petty deep down after all.

'New kid sharing my cell,' Dad says, matter-of-factly. Bored of Agatha Christie, maybe. Just moving on. Keeping it going. 'Cried all last night. His first time inside. I didn't get a wink.'

'Mmm,' I say.

In prisons, if you want to know, two thirds of self-inflicted deaths occur within the first week of arrival. This is early release for good behaviour, except cutting out the middleman.

Across the table, already there's an embarrassed silence brewing.

The thing is, my dad, he's the same height as me; only he looks shorter.

The thing is, my dad . . .

He's my *dad*.

And there it is.

Suddenly.

Suddenly, I have to tell him. Suddenly, I have to soften the blow, make it less painful, cushion the impact.

Lie, even.

Michael Point, aged twenty-eight, finding out maybe he's not who he thought.

'Dad,' I say, swallowing. My voice sounds weird. 'Dad, listen.'

I tell him, Dad, I might not be back to see you for a while.

I tell him, I've got this new job.

(This is not entirely true. I am, yes yes yes, a coward.)

I tell him this new job, this is something more like *real* work. I say this is with paperwork and weekends off and everything. I say this is a big deal for me, and it's screwing with my routine.

My dad, he just stares.

It was too good an opportunity to miss, I'm saying.

Bit of a shock to the system, I'm saying.

Dad just sits, still staring. Eyes empty. Hope gone. Like he knows.

In prisons, if you want to know, they resuscitate around two hundred men every year. Belt-strap, bed-sheet, coat-hanger, shirt-sleeve nooses. Smack overdose. Shaving-razor to the wrist. Damp beds and voided bowels.

This is in my dad's eyes right now.

He knows I'm lying.

He knows I hate him.

He knows this is it.

'I went to the prison chapel,' he says, right out of the blue.

Paint me unprepared.

I say, 'You . . . Hang on, you what?'

'Haven't been in . . . somewhere like that. Not since the wedding.'

I'm thinking: *Hold on. Whoa. Wait.*

He says, 'She used to go every week. Sunday mornings. Took you along, once in a blue. Thought I didn't know.

Doubt you'd even remember, heh. Not my cuppa.'

Here, 'she' is just . . . just . . .

'Dad,' I say, and this is with *colour* in my voice, this is with passion, this is just a bit desperate, 'Dad, w—'

'I didn't kill her,' he says.

BLAM.

No silencer.

Stop the clocks.

Shock the world. Heroin volcano. Krakatoa moment.

This is with him on 'unstoppable' mode. This is him with something to say, determined to say it.

This is not *fair*.

We DO. NOT. TALK. ABOUT. THIS.

'Hey,' I'm saying. Stupid-slow. Reacting like a slug catching its breath. 'Hey, just—'

He shakes his head. Bulldozes on. 'Please,' he says, 'shut up. Listen to me. You don't *have* to come back here. I understand why you wouldn't—'

'But that's not—'

'But you have to listen. *I didn't kill her.*'

Silence like blood. Roaring. All through my ears and in my arse and up my throat. Making me shiver.

'For fuck's sake,' I say, the wolf-thing slinking out to snarl, not happy, not listening, not putting up with this shit, 'this is—'

'We never talk about it. You can . . . you can sod off. You can sod off and never come back. If that's what you want, OK, OK, fine. But we *never talk about it*. You want to go and not know?'

His voice is loud. He's spitting as he talks, and everyone's looking.

253

'I *loved* her,' he hisses. Angry, now. 'You hear me, you little shit?'

Defensive. Dog-at-bay. *Desperate.*

All these little getting-to-know-yous.

'I loved her *so much*. You think . . . you think I could *hurt* her?'

All these under-your-skins.

Right here and now, I'm trying to stand. Bolshy, violated, furious. Right here and now, I'm trying to get out, away, up from this uncomfortable chair and across to the bolted door, past the security-troll, out, out, out.

Right here and now, the thing is, my legs aren't keeping up.

This is with the room turning to fire.

This is with everyone in the room being dead. Empty eyes. Grey skin.

Even Dad.

Especially Dad.

'Jesus . . .' he looks away, shakes his head. All the anger's gone out of him. All the fire and brimstone's cooled off.

This is my own father, bleeding out like a pig from a hole right through his wrist. Clotted vein juice spattering on the floor. One eye ruptured, blood-vessels engorged and leaking.

'Jesus,' he mutters again.

At the next table along, a scrawny black guy is talking to a mate. The way I would describe his face, if someone asked, is: maggoty.

His mate, for the record, his skin is blue and his eyes are bulging, and his tongue's down his own throat, and he's choking and writhing right there in front of me, pissing himself and filling his pants, eyes watering, lungs rasping, but here's the thing, stop press, listen: *at the same time*, he's chatting away about his new motor.

'Alloys,' he says, proud as punch, 'fuckin' *spinners*.' And he slaps together two knuckles to make a cracking sound, even though his knuckles are shattered and crumbling on the floor. 'Rrrespec' twenny-four.'

This is a hallucination.

Keep saying it. Over and over and over. It's not real.

This is happening with depressing regularity now.

My dad, he takes a deep breath. Probably he's wondering why I haven't got up and stormed off. Probably he thinks I'm here by *choice*.

My dad, with his shirt pink from the wrist-slash-splurt, with little spots of froth clinging to the corners of his mouth, he says, 'I saw her. D'you know that? Earlier, same day. Met me for lunch. Came all the way to the office.' He smiles. 'Brought me a cheese and cucumber sandwich, you believe that? I mean . . . 'sort of combination is *that*?'

This is false laughter. This is gallows humour.

What I'm telling him is: *shut up, shut up, shut up, shut up, shut up*.

What I'm telling him is: *don't want to know, don't want to know*.

What comes out is: nothing.

Right here and now, I can't move. Can't speak. Can't look away. Can't stop listening.

At the table behind Dad, some woman with curly hair, her back's broken. She's sitting at a weird angle. There's blood under her clothes. Right nearby there's a guard who has no eyeballs, and for the record his sockets: it's like Rapids Gone Red.

My dad, he's looking off into *nowhere*. If he's talking to me or the magnolia wall or the CCTV or the pig-like guard or the empty air, who knows?

He says, 'We sat in the car outside the office. She didn't like inside, that's all. The striplights gave her a headache. And it was too cold to go to the park. It was weird. She was in a –'

He stops.

He says, 'Some sort of mood, I don't know. All about . . . church. About her taking you. Getting you christened, head-dunked. She was being . . . *urgent* about it. No time to waste, wah wah wah. I *told* her. Not yet, I said. Let him make up his . . . his own . . . *Hhh*. Same as anyone, half a brain.' His jaw clenches. His head twitches. 'We had a row.'

This is how he talks. Snapped-off sentences, like a stapler punching through paper. This runs in families.

What I'm telling him is: *You had a row and you drove her home, didn't you? You had a row, and you waited till she was in the shower, you old shit, you old bastard. You waited till she was naked and warm and calming down, and then you went Norman Bates on her. Didn't you? You stabbed her first between the ribs on her right side, the forensics said, with the Sabatier carving knife from the high-up kitchen drawer that you – only ever you, Dad, nobody else – used every Sunday to dissect pork, beef, turkey, lamb, chicken.*

What comes out of my mouth is: Nothing.

At the next table along from us, the big man, the Walking Tattoo, his tiny, tiny wife is bleeding from between her legs. She's dead already. Her stomach is lolling and bright red, like it's hot, and there are things moving inside, through the skin.

I'm hallucinating. So far, so B-movie.

My dad, he waves a hand.

'She . . . she went storming off, anyway. Said she'd make her own way home. Left me there in the car.'

He blinks. Three times. Wants me to believe he's clearing his eyes.

'That was the last time I saw her alive, Mike.'

You are a liar, liar, liar, liar, liar, liar, liar.

He says, 'Mike, I *swear* it.'

Listen: self-distraction is the new self-destruction, which was yesterday's new self-improvement. Me coming to see Dad like this, it only works because we Don't Actually Talk.

He says, 'Jesus Christ, I thought . . . you know . . . it's just a row. A . . . a fucking *squabble*. I didn't want them fucking with your head. The vicars and that. Filling it up before . . .' He coughs. Eyes red. Nose pink. 'Before you were old enough t'see fact and fiction.'

This is Michael Point, aged twenty-eight, still waiting for *that*. This is Michael Point, dying a little bit on the inside, wondering who decided every conversation in the fucking world had to end in *religion*. This is Michael Point, me, now, here, keeping his thoughts on the subject to himself.

Me coming to see Dad like this, it only works because I get to Ignore The Truth. It only works because we stick to the bland.

He says, 'I thought it'd be . . . I'd . . . I'd get home that evening and everything would be OK.'

He says, in a marriage, stuff like that just happens.

He says, 'Chrissakes, Mike. Please. I didn't *hurt* her. I *swear*.'

You drove her home. You had a row and you sliced her – slowly, the forensics said – across her belly and her tits and her back. You waited till her insides spilled out like balloon animals, like uncooked sausages, like used condoms. Then you cut her in the cheeks, and in the legs, and in the eyes. Didn't you? You old shit. You old bastard.

Off to the other side, the blue-jumper guard standing at the door: his leg has been ripped clean off. Somewhere in all that mess, there's an artery blasting like a hose.

This is a hallucination. My legs, for the record, still do not work.

Bear with me here.

The first blow, the forensics said, it glanced off the bone. Not enough to kill. Broke two of her ribs. Maybe punctured her lung, or maybe that happened later.

This is squirting and moaning and colour dissolving in water and Michael Point, aged twelve, soon to be on his way home from school.

'In the evening,' Dad's saying, and he can't read my eyes, can't hear what I'm shouting and screaming, can't do anything but keep LYING, keep TWISTING THE KNIFE, keep TALKING and TALKING and TALKING, 'the . . . the time I got home from work . . . Jesus. It was all over with. Police there. You there. H-her. There.'

Skin pale, like a fish. Vaginal knife wounds. Shower water evaporating. Bloodless scratches and wormflesh slashmarks.

Michael Point, aged twelve, embarrassed at seeing his dead mum naked.

Dad's fingerprints on the weapon. Dad's skin under her

nails. No sign of forced entry. Nothing stolen. No sexual assault.
Him getting back to the office, late, after lunch.

At the next table, the enormous man with the tattoos,
you remember him, he's glancing towards us.

This man, he is not dead. Out of everyone. Out of the
whole room.

This man, it's like he's in a bubble. There's like an
outline. Like a shadow round him. It's like he's wearing a
comedy sumo suit, only it's made out of smoke.

I'm hallucinating. Bear with me here.

This man, he is *green*. He is scaled and furred and
feathered. He has a hawk's beak above each eye, and his
tattoos . . . his tattoos are *alive*.

My dad, he's run out of steam. There are maybe tears in
his eyes.

The man next to him, he looks over at me and his eyes
are just Bees, swarming. He looks over and he lifts a hand,
and what pokes from the palm aren't fingers. They're too
thin. Too long. Too *many*.

My dad, he seems so small, so pathetic, so broken. He
seems so *nothing*.

The man next to him, who blazes and smiles and
dribbles, he points at my father, and he grins wider, and he
puts the tip of a finger against his own neck, and he draws
it across.

My dad, it's hard to hate something so pitiful.

'Say something. Mike? Please.'

And this time, I do not choke. This time, I do not wear
my own vomit. This time, what I do is: I take a deep breath.
I calm the fuck down. I tell myself: *Stop it.*

I stand up.

In this room, nobody is dead any more.

In this room, my dad stays sitting, and this murderer, this shitty lump of meat, this old withered, walking heap of scum, this *liar*, he's saying, 'Mike . . . Mike, please . . .'

And I'm walking away.

Interview Room 2

This place, I mentioned already: everything is migraine-noisy. Down here the walls are dry, rough, dull, ugly, but still the sense of damp, moss-and-rot-stink, still the grotty nocturnal shiver.

Down here Anna, she of the Face to Launch a Thousand Shitty Poems, she of the skin so pale she could be albino, she could be a vampire, she could be a corpse (if not for dark eyes, twitched-up-brow, wet lips, not calling me a cunt), she's stopped smoking her cigarette and gone back to her notebook.

Her pen goes: *skritchaskritchaskritch.*

It's annoying.

Listen: where the fag went to, I just don't know.

In the US, where everything is Bigger and Better, a 'fag' is a faggot, which is not a cigarette, which is not a bundle of twigs or a spicy meatball or an ugly old woman. In the US, a faggot is a homosexual man.

This is ironic, because at some point, while I sat here in this uncomfortable plastic chair telling an uncomfortable plastic story to two uncomfortable plastic people, Jason Durant – the mullet-headed kinky fetishist streak of diarrhoeic splatter – got up and left the room without me noticing. He's no longer here.

Listen: this means two fags have just vanished into thin air, As If By Magic.

See also: the ashtray. See also: the cloud of smoke.

In the US, smoking a fag has a whole different meaning.

The exit from this room keeps swapping sides. If I watch hard enough, I will catch it in mid-air.

Listen: where Anna got the notepad and pen from, I still don't know.

In this pause, she glances up and says, 'Did your parents argue much?'

I stare.

I tell her, *ohono*.

I tell her, don't try *that*.

I say: what's next? *Did your daddy touch you? Did you have secrets? Did Mummy ever work from home?*

I say: Freud can kiss my arse.

I say, 'Don't try and explain me with that shit.'

Anna smiles, warm. This is a first.

She says, 'We're not trying to, Michael.'

This is the first time she's used my name.

She says, 'This isn't about your . . . *motivation*. Anyway – we already *know* that. It's all about the money. Right?'

I say, 'Right.' I say this with too much caution.

With Anna, ohsweetfuckedup*god*she'sgorgeous, you sort of always suspect she's taking the piss.

There's a pause.

In the pause I scowl and I tell her, for fuck's sake, look, I was only twelve. I can't give you a detailed report.

I say, 'They argued a *bit*. Same as anyone. Couples *do* that.'

Skrichtaskritchaskritch

I imagine her writing. I imagine: *repressed memory – specific trauma?*, and get all worked up. Here's me on the edge of shouting, on the verge of losing my temper, on the verge of doing something silly, when I remember: I'm just guessing. I'm being paranoid, I'm *protesting too much*. It's possible she's just drawing a smiley face, or a duck, or a fish.

She says, 'Can you remember what they argued about? You mentioned church . . .'

I tell her, *yeah*, but . . . That doesn't mean anything either.

This is Michael Point, aged twenty-eight, noticing he doesn't like the idea that *something* might explain *anything* about him.

This is the painting raging against the paint. This is the car denying the existence of a factory. This is a cake getting uncomfortable with the idea of ingredients.

I tell her, look, you've got two different people, OK? That's just *marriage*.

I tell her, Mum was this . . . this Catholic. Polish family. Never forced it down your throat, you know?

I tell her, 'It meant a lot to her, though. She took it seriously.'

'And your dad?'

'Too stupid to care. Lived in the present.'

I say this too fast.

Anna scowls. 'Too *stupid*?' Her eyes go narrow. 'But . . . you said he wanted you to be able to make your own mind u—'

'So?'

'So . . . That sounds like something he gave a lot of thought to.'

I huff. There's a coat of sweat on my head and I can't work out why. It's pissing me off, and the fact I'm getting pissed off so easily pisses me off *more*, and now I'm a freight-train building up speed with a junkie at the controls and—

'It just got to him,' I snarl. 'Wanted to play football in the park every Sunday with his boy. Thought that made him a dad, made up for the rest of it.'

I'm being unfair. I know this.

The truth is, he was Just My Dad.

The truth is, we played football and it was Just OK.

There is no 'rest of it' to make up for.

The truth is, once in a while, I quite liked to go to church with Mum. The truth is, I liked the pictures of guys killing dragons in the windows.

The truth is, we're making far too much of *all* this.

'*Seriously*,' I say, 'listen.' This is me, telling Anna. I'm breathless. I'm red in the face. 'Seriously, you go looking for . . . for reasons behind all this. Behind why *he* did what he did. Behind why *I'm* me . . . you're just going to come up disappointed. Or see stuff that's not there.'

She just stares.

I say, 'Look, the point *is*. The point *is*, it doesn't *matter* why they disagreed. OK? Or argued, whatever. It *especially* doesn't matter who was right and who was wrong.'

Jason Durant says – *Where the fuck did he come from?* – 'OK, Michael . . . No big argument bubbling away, then, nothing serious to undermine the marriage.' He smiles. 'Religion didn't matter. So . . . he killed her over a game of football in the park? That *is* what you're telling us?'

This is the SURGE of adrenaline in my guts.

This is me KILLING him in my head. A lot.

This is me burning in silence and dry heat.

This is the room pulsing and trying to go *wrong* in my head, and me breathing, breathing, breathing. Focusing.

Brooding.

'The point is,' says Anna, fussy, a wife embarrassed by her husband, 'you were . . . exposed to religion from an early age. You're familiar with the iconography. The imagery?'

I croak: 'So?'

She smiles, warm – disingenuous – and says, 'Nothing.'

Skritchaskritchaskritch

I get myself together and turn to look at Jason. He looks, against the odds, what a surprise, *smug*.

'I don't know why he killed her,' I say. 'He never said.'

Anna says, 'So you've given up on him? Guilty as charged?'

I chew my own jaw.

She says, 'Why? Didn't you ever wonder? Didn't you *want* him to be innocent?'

I tell them it doesn't matter. I tell them they know all this. I tell them he's dead, and that time in the prison was the last time I saw him, and the twisted old shit was as guilty as hell, and he sat that day while I hallucinated and spun through reality, and lied and lied and lied to me.

I tell them: he did it. That's all there is to it.

Maybe he . . . maybe he blacked out. Maybe he went nuts. Maybe that runs in families too.

But he did it. Oh yeah. And he *knew* he did it.

I tell them: Some stories . . . you expect too much from them. You expect neatness and drama and a killer twist, to make everything OK.

Hollywood ending. Angry Son Faces Undeniable Proof of His Father's Innocence.

I blow a raspberry.

I tell them: some stories just . . .

Stop.

Chapter Fifteen

Today is Wednesday.

Yesterday I visited my father in prison for the Very Last Time. You remember, don't you?

Tomorrow, which is Thursday, I'll become a walking, talking murder machine. That sounds Hollywood. It isn't.

Tomorrow, just so you know, just so you're anticipating, just so you get to share my crumpled-gut nervosity, is when the Last Job occurs. Try not to smile, you fucks.

The *'trickier'* job. The *multiple targets* job. You remember?

I'm feeling a little bitter. Bear with me.

Today . . . let's see. Today I've been busy. Today I've been a recruitment officer, locating personnel with a natural aptitude for the HR skills central to my project specifications. This is the business-bullshit way of saying: headhunting.

Today, also, I've been a hardware specialist. This was locating outsourced supply-providers to execute Equipment Satisfaction protocols. This is the office-junkie middle-management yuppietwat way of saying: Tooling Up.

(Ruger Mk II .22, un-deactivated, spare ammunition, ex-Met flak-jacket, hockey mask, blah, blah, blah.)

Today I do not have time to go to Bristol, so I stopped at

This Place I Just Know by King's Cross station.

(Skag-smack-brown, bullet-filler, overdose fodder, intravascular evil mixed with lemon juice to keep it liquid)

Today, also, I liaised with my data collection operative as he sat, paper folded on his lap, travelling up and down the East London Line. Shoreditch, Whitechapel, Shadwell, Wapping, Rotherhithe, Canada Water, Surrey Quays, New Cross, back and forth, back and forth. This is the polite way of saying: I met Wilson.

Catching up. Little pieces of paper, names and numbers, passed back and forth.

Today I stood for an hour, watching every train that went by, feeling sick at the blurred motion, crick in my neck, bored of the *Metro*, looking for his little nut-brown head.

Today he gave me a couple of names, and did not mention the whole 'accusations of betrayal' thing, and did not sulk, and did not ask me who I'm working for.

Today, as I got off the train, Wilson looked up from his paper and said, 'Tek*care*, Michael.'

Today has been hardcore, ohoyes, and it's not over yet.

Today and here and now, and ready to do this last thing, and fighting the jitters, where I am is inside a rental car. This car, I hired it this morning from an office in Twickenham.

False I.D., ginger wig, birthmark.

Today and here and now, and letting the knot in my intestines untangle just an inch, someone leans forward from the back seat and, over the music, shouts, 'You *ah* mate, hey. You *ah* mind turning that off?'

This is the first indication that All Things Are Not Normal.

I am not alone. I am not cool. I am not the *Fonz*.

J.W.A.

Today in the car, the music, what are the chances, goes: *oom-chkka-oom-chkka-oom-chkka*

There's a bag on the passenger seat next to me which sloshes when I brake. This bag, it's full of budget-price cans of extra-strength supermarket's-own beer, and every five minutes a hand reaches forwards to take one, then *pssht*, then *unk-unk-unk*.

Today I am not alone. Today I am running reconnaissance on the place where tomorrow night I will break several laws, kill several people, wade in blood, Hollywood bullshit, and *I am not alone*.

This cuts against the grain. This is not normal. This is unexplored territory.

J.W.A.

That beer, sometimes the hand that takes it is black, sometimes the hand is white.

Today and here and now, there are buildings clustered up both sides of the car – derelict, worn down, crones and OAPs slumping on priority seating – and somewhere near here tomorrow I will inflict large-scale slaughter upon a group of individuals I've never met.

Mikey, listen, seriously: *Just. Walk. Away.*

The car stereo says: *oom-chkka-oom-chkka-oom-chkka*

This is self-distraction, which is the new self-destruction, which etc. etc. Whatever.

This is sonic-leprosy, resonant-frequency, to abuse my brain, to kill the jitters, to fade out the nerves. This is a shrill tone to cure tinnitus. This is aversion therapy. Submerge yourself in ugliness, maybe you can filter it out.

Behind me another voice, deep and slow and cold, a

glacier voice, an ice-age voice, purrs: 'Nah, boss. Why not you chus' leave it?'

Somebody makes a sound like dentures being sucked.

Oom-chkka-oom-chkka-oom-chkka

First voice: 'You're *ah* you're kidding. Seriously? Christ . . . Shit'll do my head. Doing my *ah* head!'

Too high. Too quick. Sweaty little voice, that voice, like maybe a ferret would have if it could talk. Like a magpie, twitchy and sped up, half-a-beat removed for every pause. 'Doing my head, doing my head, that's all. Listen. Driving me *ah* fucking insane. That's all.'

Oom-chkka-oom-chkka-oom-chkka

Second voice: 'Chus' need chill.' And then a pause. And then an aftershock, a Richter-scale smile: 'Innit.'

Honey and dreadlocks and yellow eyes, that voice. Clouds of smoke and thoughtful laughter, that voice. Dark alleyways and dubshack records, that voice.

Oom-chkka-oom-chkka-oom-chkka

This is me not looking in the Rear View Mirror (which Gobbles All Things). This is me avoiding eye-contact with my passengers.

'You saying you *like* this? You *like* this shit, man, how can you even *listen* to this, this is completely fucking dreadful, how's it *ah* possible, this is the *worst*, listen, Jesus. You *ah* you *like* this?'

Oom-chkka-oom-chkka-oom-chkka

'Y'ah like this.'

Oom-chkka-oom-chkka-etc. etc.

'Completely fucking *awful*, shit, how can you *ah*, how, it's, it's, it's *Jesus*, someone hooked up a-a-a heart-monitor, OK, and stuck on a *buhm buhm buhm* drum and *ah* God, it's givin' me a headache, mate, I'm not *joking*, and –'

Oom-chkka-oom-chkka-etc. etc.

'Sguhd. You chus' flow.'

Oom-chkka-oom-chkka-etc. etc.

'Man, what the fuck is *wrong* with your *ah* your ears? It's like stereo-fucking-diarrhoea, OK, and –'

And so on. And so forth. *Ad. Nauseum.*

For the record, this doped-up little scenario is not fulfilling its purpose. It is not self-distracting. It is pissing me off. It is extending the jitters. It is dulling the *sharp.*

Oom-chkka-oo—

Long story short: I turn it off.

'Thank you! Thank *yooooou*!'

'Sheeeeeee. Was *on*dat.'

This is the modern nuclear urban family. This is Michael Point, in the driver's seat. This is Michael harassed-single-parent Point, trying to control his squabbling crackerspawn on the way to school.

This is sitcom fodder. This is laminated gold to pitch to your TV chums.

Like: Listen, right, the dad's this sociopathic serial killer who keeps, aha, *hallucinating*. Is that a *hoot* or what? Huh? Huh? He has no solid perspective on reality! He's consciously *a*moral! He's on a mission from God! A-*haaaa.*

Like: And the *kids*, OK, wow, hoooo-*eee!* The first one, listen, a-*haaaa*, he's this buttoned-down neurotic white-collar *psycho*, always on speed, with these *serious* violence issues! Yeah, man!

Like: And the *other* one, wow, you're gonna love this, yeah, yeah, he's a fucking spaced-out *crackhead* with a *machine gun!* A-*haaaa*! And, ohmigod, he's *black*!

Like: And they're all having to, y'know, co-operate!

Like: With hilarious consequences!

Like: Is this a *hit* in the making or *what*? Somebody PISS ON ME, I'm on FIRE!

And so on.

And so forth.

Right here and now, on Wednesday, on the outskirts of an industrial estate in the East of London, the thing is, nobody's laughing.

Let me tell you: on sitcoms, the laughter-track in the background, seriously, they have a machine. Digital mirth, as quick or slow as you want. More titters, fewer guffaws? No problemo. Bassier side-splitting, like there are more men than women? Not an issue. The drawn-out death-rattle of some fat fuck in the make-believe audience choking on their own diseased lungs from laughing too much? Fine. Leave it with me, man.

On sitcoms, c'mon. You've just gotta laugh.

Sooner or later, I stop the car. Sooner or later, I get out. I point.

I say, 'There.'

My flaming, shivering, jittering goosebumps.

'There', if you want to know, is a deserted grey-brick warehouse with a corrugated roof and broken-glass windows. Weeds grow through cracks in the walls. This is set right back from anywhere. Car wrecks for gateposts, graffiti for signs.

This is the urban desert. This is the encroachment of wilderness on fertile land. This is beer-can sand dunes. Gorse-bush mescaline. Parched-earth concrete.

This warehouse, the door, if you want to know, it's a sheet-steel tombstone built into an out-jutting section of wall. This door, you can tell straight off, it doesn't lead inside the building.

Heavy-arsed hinges, hardcore locks. Everything migraine-noisy.

This is three guys preparing for a massacre.

A-*haaaa*.

My two companions look around. They look at each other. They look at me.

The first one, who is tall and white and sweating, says, 'OK, OK. Yeah. That's no *ah* no problem. Nother door in the back you said, wasn't it? Easy. Not a problem in *ah* in the world and –'

Et cetera, et cetera.

Ladies and Gentlemen, meet Tom.

Tom twitches and shivers and nods and grins, and this is Just the Way He Is. Tom mutters to himself. Tom's veins poke out from his temples and his neck like tree roots. In Tom's arteries, amphetamines do not dissolve in blood. In Tom's arteries, blood dissolves in amphetamine.

For the record, Tom has an enormous fucking shotgun. I tell him to leave it in the car.

I'm still pointing at the warehouse. The industrial estate is deserted. Mostly, it's unused. Mostly, lights don't work. Mostly, it's dark, and the sky is yellow/green, and *ah*.

Ah, London.

Never shit in your own bed.

'Kaythen,' says the other guy, not even looking where I'm pointing. He is black and wide and is not fat, and has his hair braided like a ploughed field across his head. The parts that aren't covered look polished. He starts walking towards the warehouse.

Ladies and Gentlemen, meet Ty.

Ty walks in a way that doesn't seem to make much use of his knees or hips. Ty walks from his shoulders, like tilting back and forth. Ty's way of walking, it's more like slouching indefinitely postponed.

For the record, Ty has an enormous fucking machine pistol. I tell him to leave it in the car.

Tom and Ty, Ty and Tom. These are my Strategised Goal-Attainment Managers. These are my Project-Fruition Imagineers, as provided following today's resources-liaison operation. These are my Target-Actualisation Liability-Coordination Personnel Assistants.

These are a pair of junkie fuck up shithead scumbag filth-merchant FUCKS, as suggested to me by my broker Wilson.

Let me tell you, in this trade, if these men had business cards, if they were even a little bit on speaking terms with reality, their job title would be: *Disposables.*

This name tells you everything you need to know.

Listen:

Ty is short for Tyrone.

Tyrone T. Levy was born in Lewisham in the South East of London, on 15 October 1967. He is forty years old.

He told me this stuff in a pool hall in Walthamstow at 12.43 p.m. today. I didn't ask.

This was with him slurring and upping and downing. This was with him vanishing to the John once an hour, coming back ten minutes later chilled like a penguin's prick.

All these little getting-to-know-yous.

The gun that Tyrone T. Levy brought with him today –

a day early, premature, dangerous, reckless, stupid, leave it in the car, *what am I doing in public with these bloody amateurs?* – is a MAC-10 .45 machine pistol with an enormous silencer. The MAC-10 .45 machine pistol is a Hollywood screaming-blasting-cut-you-in-half rapid-fire monstrosity which fires fourteen rounds a second, and I do not know where he got from it. Gun porn.

Listen: Tyrone T. Levy's grandparents arrived in the UK aboard the *SS. Windrush* on 22 June 1948. These days, we call the Jamaican Londoners of the fifties and sixties the Windrush Generation.

Tyrone T. Levy likes motors, playing pool, revive reggae and fucking. His interests include smoking crack, smoking crack while fucking, and smoking crack to music. While fucking. Tyrone T. Levy has two kids that he knows of.

Tyrone T. Levy, when he laughs, it's like the same honey note, detached, repeated maybe ten, maybe twenty times.

'Eh eh eh eh eh. Eh eh eh eh eh.'

His laugh, if you want to know, it isn't funny.

All these little getting-to-know-yous.

At the age of fifteen, Tyrone was expelled from his shitty little school by his shitty little teacher. At the age of seventeen, Tyrone was arrested for the fifth time. These arrests were for car crime, pushing chemicals, burglary, mugging, assault, blah, blah, blah.

His mamma said: he fell in with the wrong crowd. His mamma said: *Damned white kids.*

Tyrone T. Levy, here's the thing. This life story, all these getting-to-know-yous, *ignore* it.

Really. Pay no attention. Skip this section. It's for your own good.

Tyrone T. Levy, you do not want to grow attached to this guy. You do not want to sympathise with him, or pity him, or respect him.

Tomorrow this person will be dead.

Tyrone T. Levy's gun, his MAC-10 .45 machine pistol, the silencer on its muzzle is so big and fat and long it looks like an elephant's prick. I imagine.

A big, black, elephant's cock of doom.

At the age of eighteen, his mamma scraped up as much cash as she could find and sent him to the Caribbean to meet the family, stay out of trouble, get clean.

In 1991, Tyrone T. Levy was deported from Kingston Town for gun-crime drug offences, extortion, smuggling, blah blah blah.

His mamma wouldn't even see him.

For the record, the first person to die from smoking crack in the UK was Anthony 'Crumpet' Lemard. This was 1986. This was a guy face-down, drowning in puke in a police cell. This was two years before the fine men and women of Her Majesty's constabulary even knew what crack *was*.

Tyrone T. Levy, he has three spare clips for the MAC-10 in the pockets of his jacket. His jacket is mock-leather and elasticated at the hem. Tyrone T. Levy, he wears a real Rolex, air-cushioned trainers and a gold signet ring. He does not wear latex gloves. He does not wear a wig or a mole.

Tyrone T. Levy, as we walk together round the warehouse, the three of us, he's staring at nothing.

Crack cocaine, which is coke dissolved in ammonia, water and bicarbonate of soda, then heated until solid, is cheaper and crazier and easier to find than powder.

Crack cocaine, which is also freebase, pasta, crackers,

gravel, hail, rox, rooster, applejacks B.J.s, Baby-T and Bazooka, when smoked, it creates a high that lasts maybe forty, maybe fifty, maybe sixty seconds.

Earlier today, talking about his life, Tyrone T. Levy was paid £500 in cash by a man in a red wig, with a birthmark on his neck. Earlier today, Tyrone T. Levy was informed his unique talents were required, some people needed killing, and afterwards he'd be paid a further £1000.

This money, he was told, he could accept in the form of cash or rocks.

It's. All. About. The. Next. High.

Tyrone T. Levy, he does not talk about his father. I do not know why.

Crack cocaine, which is also boulders, egg, caviar, bobo, cloud, and bele, that forty-fifty-sixty second high is the Best Thing That Will Ever Happen To You.

I do not smoke crack.

Tyrone T. Levy's gun, his MAC-10 .45 automatic machine pistol: a single clip will last him just two seconds. This is very Hollywood. This is noisy and spectacular and as frightening as fuck. This is going to get him killed.

This means the man in the red wig with the red birthmark wasn't being entirely honest when he offered Tyrone T. Levy payment in cash or crack.

Sue me.

Listen: when the man in the red wig with the red birthmark, the man who drove him in a rental car tonight, the man who didn't bring a gun with him, the man who is now halfway round his first circuit of the dead, dull, derelict, decrepit building, when that man offered Tyrone T. Levy £1500 to walk into a roomful of strangers and kill them all dead, when that man barely even bothered to embellish the 'no-risk' nature of this task, Tyrone T. Levy didn't even stop to think.

'Yeh,' was all he said.

He's just that sort of guy.

This place, there are two doors.

The plan is: Tomorrow we will burst into the basement of this empty warehouse, this tumbledown brick mountain right here, from both directions. Guns-a-blazing. Very Hollywood. Very mythic.

Very stupid.

From one direction, the *main* direction, Ty and Tom. From the other direction, the back door, me.

The plan is: anyone down there gets sliced to ribbons in the crossfire.

Let me tell you: today and here and now we stand looking at the front door. It's locked.

Tom is pretending like he's still got his shotgun in his hands, whisper-hustling, '*kroom kroom*' under his breath. He's Judge Dredd, blowing away the lock on a sealed door. He Is The Law.

He's a scrawny wanker out of his tree.

Listen, Tom and Tyrone, if they *really* believe I'm going to come rushing in through the opposite door at the allotted moment, if they *really* believe my best course of action is to stare directly down the barrels of their big dumb guns, if they *really* believe we're sharing the jeopardy in that moment of slaughter, they've got another think coming.

I'd feel bad, except: I'm working for the Good Guys now. *It's not my fault. They made me do it.*

These poor motherfuckers, they don't call them 'disposables' for nothing.

Listen: Tom is short for Thomas.

Thomas Hilton Devizes was born in Christchurch, New Zealand, on 12 June 1973. He is thirty-three years old.

I met him for the first time earlier today. This was him jittering and twitching and giggling at odd moments.

This was in a sports bar in Shepherd's Bush. This was watching the All Blacks steamroller an under-funded Polynesian no-team. This was cheap carbonated beer spraying hickledy-pickledy.

All these little getting-to-know-yous.

Today Thomas Hilton Devizes is carrying a Winchester 1300 12-gauge shotgun. It was a present, he says, from his flatmate. This is difficult to believe.

Thomas Hilton Devizes went travelling at the age of eighteen. This is Commonwealth Normality. This is seeing the world first-hand, no borrowed wisdom, no middleman permitted. This is Indonesia, Thailand, Vietnam, China, backpacks and elephant rides and hitching along unmarked roads. This is Europe, wall-to-wall. Amsterdam weed, Parisian sex, Roman violence. This is Yankee Burgers and the Inca Trail and blah blah blah.

Thomas Hilton Devizes settled in the UK at the age of twenty-two.

He says, 'I like it *ah*, I like it here. Mostly.'

Listen: this cheeky Antipodean chappie, don't don't *don't* get attached.

Don't think about all those photos he took, round the world. Posing with alpacas in the Andes. Dancing at Thai full-moon parties. New diary-page every day. Voyage of self-discovery. Don't think about all those people he met, all those dreams he had, all those experiences he should be passing on.

Listen: tomorrow, here, Thomas Hilton Devizes will burst through a steel-plate door next to Tyrone T. Levy. They will charge down a staircase and fly out into a basement, where they will open fire on a group of unsuspecting nobodies.

At this point, Thomas Hilton Devizes will stop being Thomas Hilton Devizes.

What he will be then is: dead.

Thomas Hilton Devizes' Winchester 1300 12-gauge shotgun, let me tell you: this will be difficult for him to conceal. This is a black US monstrosity with an 8-shell load, 18-inch cylinder bore-barrel combi-version with pistol grip and full stock.

Those Americans. Always bigger, always better.

This is a gun that will blow a fist-sized hole in your head. This is firearms triple-X. Hardcore shooty-death-kill pornography.

Thomas Hilton Devizes, in the UK, he got a job in a call centre. His job is cold-calling random customers to sell them utilities schemes: electricity, gas, water, Internet deals, mobile telephone contracts. This job, it's depressing. It's the sort of job you do to earn money because you couldn't find a vocation. In this job, he told me earlier, without me asking, you get told to Fuck Off a lot. You get told to Stop Pestering Me a lot. You get told You Just Got Me Out Of The Shower For *This*, You Fucking Dribble Of Spunk, If I Ever Find You, I'll Rip Off Your Eyelids, et cetera et cetera.

A Lot.

Thomas Hilton Devizes, one of the ways he coped was, he went out more.

Stayed out late. Came to work tired.

Needed energy.

Coffee wouldn't cut it.

Thomas Hilton Devizes, one day he discovered speed.

That Winchester 1300 shotgun, before he left it in the car, Thomas Hilton Devizes loaded eight little cartridges into the bay beneath the muzzle. He wears a pocketless denim jacket and jeans that make him look too skinny. He has a professional clay-pigeon-shooter's suede belt to hold his spare ammo.

Speed is amphetamine sulphate, phet, billy or base. The way Thomas Hilton Devizes takes it, is wrapped up in a cigarette paper like a tadpole with a tail, which he swallows with his coffee when he gets into work. This is called a speedbomb.

Cold-calling and speedbombing, he says, is a lot of fun. He says it's like calling strangers to listen to them sing. Their voices, he says, go too slow. He says on a heavy day, he feels like he can pour his words into the gaps, like honey down ravines, like gas-water-electricity deals injected intra-venously into conversational silence. He says, on those days, he gets a headache just thinking about it.

Thomas Hilton Devizes, he wears a blue baseball cap marked with the legend DPL, hard-worn shoes with mismatching laces, and no watch. He likes sport, social drinking and casual ultraviolence. His interests include hurting people, breaking fingerbones and fine food.

He does not wear latex gloves. He does not wear a

birthmark or a moustache or glasses. Tonight, today, here and now and preparing ourselves for tomorrow night, what he won't stop doing is: moving. Twitching. Jerking. What he won't stop doing is: smiling.

Speed, which is usually 10 per cent phet and a mixed-up gutful of caffeine, vitamin C or powdered milk, produces a sensation of euphoria, a surge of energy, and the curious conviction that you're Travelling Too Fast.

I don't do speed.

Thomas Hilton Devizes, let me tell you, the thing that defines his paltry soon-to-end existence is: His Boss. Tom's boss is a twenty-one-year-old. He has a degree and a chiselled jaw and a perfect wife and a young son and a fast car. He does not take speed three times a day. He is a manager, a supervisor. He does not do the cold-calling. It's his job to make sure that Tom and Tom's colleagues *do*.

Listen, this man, this post-uni *fuck*, he does not *have* to deal with Mr Irate, who resents his bath being interrupted. He does not *have* to handle Mrs Screaming Abuse, who just got little Jenny off to sleep when the scummy advertising arsehole rang. He does not *have* these issues to prey on his mind, and yet this man, this clean-shaven Nazi bastard, he makes Thomas Hilton Devizes' life a living hell.

This man Tom, this fun-time-guy, it turns out if you ask him once about his boss, he *won't shut up*.

Thomas Hilton Devizes, hating his boss is sort of his life, now. This is called amphetamine psychosis. This is when all his ambitions and dreams and urges, what happens is, they swirl around that core. All his little frustrations, what happens is, they grow and get big, and his boss's face is all over them.

CONTRACT

On his back, Tom says, he has a tattoo. This is a quote from a Hunter S. Thompson book. The quote says: *'Faster, faster, until the thrill of speed overcomes the fear of death.'*

Hunter S. Thompson, Tom says, was a renegade US journalist, writer and gen-yoo-ine genius who blew out his own brains in 2005. Tom's eyes go sort of misty while he says this.

Thomas Hilton Devizes, the way he deals with the cold, clammy hate tucked up inside of him is: he hurts things. He does night-jobs. Doorman. Bouncer. Thug. Protection enforcer. Whatever. More and more every night. Harder and harder every time. *Faster, faster, until the thrill of speed overcomes the fear of death.*

With Thomas Hilton Devizes, don't, don't, don't pity him. Don't feel bad for his flaming chemical life.

Seriously. Don't get attached.

With Thomas Hilton Devizes, when he was paid £500 this afternoon in a sports bar in Hammersmith, when he was promised a hefty follow-up by a man in a ginger wig with a birthmark, when he was offered a tasty deal for bursting into a basement full of strangers and blowing the living shit out of them, let me tell you: he didn't even ask how much money he'd get. It's. All. About. The. Hate.

All these little getting-to-know-yous.

We leave after half an hour. I'm not sure what we've accomplished.

Bonding, maybe.

Ahahaha.

My head hurts. It hurts like I think it's never hurt before, and I want to cycle through diseases, tumours, conditions, congenital defects, cranial traumas, I want to frighten myself, I want to filter the rushing in my ears, I want to list the vile, ulcerous afflictions that may or may not be sludging and twitching through my brain, but all I can think is: *To keep me from becoming conceited because of these surpassingly great revelations, there was given me a thorn in my flesh, a messenger of Satan, to torment me . . .*

No. No, that is wrong. That is not what I'm thinking.

What I'm thinking is this: *Tomorrow.* Tomorrow I will die.

I drop Ty and Tom outside Paddington station. They never said where they wanted to go, I never asked. Paddington is central enough.

I drive. And I fall, in ways I can't work out, and it's pissing me off. It feels like maybe I've been falling all along. Like maybe it's all been one, big, tumbling, stupid plummet, only without air, without the wind rushing past me, so I didn't even *know* I was falling until I was close enough to see the ground. Maybe.

I'm bitter and tired and hurting, and I get surreal. Bear with me.

I drive home. The rental car is mine for two more days. Tomorrow I will change the plates, for one day only. I don't suppose I'll need to change them back, but the thing is, this job, nobody ever got caught being *too* cautious.

Today I have not hallucinated. I am proud, like a kid with a blobby drawing. Like a killer standing over a clean kill, I'm proud.

I want coffee with froth on top, and cheap burgers, and Ariadne prattling, and maybe to see Dad again, and *oh fuck, Mike, what are you doing*, and the magic number burns through my jacket pocket and sets fire to me, and this is dream-logic, and I'm burning up as I drive, calm, relaxed, giving in.

It turns out, don't laugh, there's a strange sort of freedom in being a slave.

Outside my flat, Sally is waiting.

We don't talk.

We drive.

Contact 24

DAY: Wednesday Night (actually Thurs. morning).

TIME: 1.32 a.m.

LOCATION: Park, bench, Shepherd's Bush Green. Just walked from B&B, Goldhawk Road. Feet hurting. Junkies & weirdos also in park, so far ignored me. Must look like baglady anyway: giant coat, wild hair, writing in tattered book w/ Biro. Soon: taxi or, bus home – first want to write this down, not wait till morning, not get comfy. Cold and sore, need to get this out <u>now</u>. Unburden.

CONTACT REASON: <u>My</u> instigation. Stupid. No call from Michael, no café bullshit. Not part of plan, not part of anything. Been thinking all week. Know what's coming. Time running out for M. Tomorrow (today now) = all be over. Had to <u>do</u> something (help him?). Couldn't stay away, couldn't live w/ myself if I didn't try before the end – make things better, make him smile. Sympathy 4 condemned man.

Waited @ his flat for him to come home – no idea what to say or do. Just try to make it better, easier, whatever. Ultimately just easing my guilt – know that. Doesn't matter: selfish. Don't care.

CONTRACT

OBSERVATIONS: Mike pulled up approx 9.36 p.m. Rental car. Looked calm: 1st shock. Wild eyes gone away, no sweat, no shivers. Just resigned: tired. Dead man walking? No reaction @ seeing me (2nd shock), stood next to car, waiting, silent. Like shellshock – nothing gets through. Wonder whether stuff I told him last time (re. 'hallucinations' = not hallucinations) had effect. Wonder if helped or made worse? Wonder 1,000,001 things! Not what I'm here for. Concentrate on now. Observations.

Wore: red wig, hair hangs over ears & brows like hippy. Ridiculous. Make-up birthmark, brown jacket, jeans, black T-shirt, black trainers. Eventually walked over to him, got into car. Drove. Silent.

B&B: random cheap hotel. Small room, boring, no frills, damp walls. Like being @ home, or M's flat. Functional. Occupied but empty. Bed creaked, didn't care. Uncomfortable. No en suite: toilet in hallway. People talking, rooms either side – foreign voices? Speaking in tongues – ha!

M looks smaller without clothes, fragile, vulnerable. Child. Uncomfortable.

NOTES: Before B&B, outside his flat: shared understanding. Spooky. No words. Very 'movie': unspoken agreement, got into car, drove off to fuck. Knew what we were doing; tacky maybe, kids playing moviestars – still. Needed to happen. Couldn't inside his flat: wrong. Wrong for me (return to scene of crime) & him (impossible inside his nest: his place, not shared).

In B&B (name in register: Mr & Mrs Jones) kissed,

stripped, fucked. No talking. Felt mad all through, ½ revolted, ½ pity, ½ lust (too many halves), just sex. Can't work it out. Attracted? Not really. Pity him, yes, feel guilty, yes, but enough to do this? Why then?

(Reward 4 him? Payment? Shit, just don't know!)

Doesn't matter. Diary not about me. About <u>contacts</u>. 1st fuck: too hard. M zoned out, eyes closed, staring off into space, arms right-angles (lizard). Just fucking random girl – had to say 'hey' – reminder, bring him back: recognition in eyes. Saw me as me. Changed after that. Pulled out, started over, kissing touching, etc. new johnny. Slow to start with. (Better than Daniel.)

Varied speed, force, etc. <u>His</u> game, not mine. (Funny. Only 'control' left.) Still came too soon; no announcement, no build-up, just 'oh, I've . . .' Looked aghast, genuine horror, told him didn't matter, all OK; stroked his hair, etc.

Tried to run his fingers along my shoulders, spine, but = too clumsy. Heavy handed. So uncomfortable inside own skin. Had to stop myself laughing @ him, hating him. Affection for ugly, crippled puppy. So fucking worthless. So fucking <u>nothing</u>. Take it to vet, put it down, out of misery, all FOR THE BEST, but don't expect to feel good about it.

Think I fell asleep. Dreamed about M turning into Jesus, Daniel walking in, reminding me re. 'the deal'. Voices: all for the best all for the best, etc. etc., hospital machine beeping. Surreal melodramatic b.s. Hate dreams. Hate fantasy – but seems whole life has become one. Woke up (one hour? two?), Michael going down on me. Thought I'd pissed myself to start with, laughed w/ relief.

CONTRACT

2nd fuck better. Confidence, more moving, less fakey tenderness. Odd: M looking down at me with squint, like a light too bright (but only street light through window, no lights on). 'Hallucinating'?

2 peaks for me – one after next, like two merged: orgasm in stereo. Afterwards, no sign he'd stop, just kept pumping away. Carried on long time on his own, seemed happier – no need to think about me, like wanking in company. Very alone, suppose, but = where he's most comfortable.

Finally came (me: starting to get bored). Looked down w/ wince, shielded own eyes, then collapsed down & gurgled in ear: 'Angel.' Slept.

Let myself out. Feel better? Good to see him sleep, slight smile, relaxed, calm. Given him something good. Sure of it. Positive.

Probably patronising there, false charity. Who gives shit: tonight everyone wins.

Tomorrow he loses.

THOUGHTS/CONCLUSIONS/OTHER: All this = for the best. Done everything I can. Made it easier. Gave him something.

Must remind myself, if pangs of guilt in future, who he is, <u>what</u> he is. Gave him more than deserved. (What Daniel would say if he knew – <u>mustn't</u> tho!)

Made it easier for me, too. Conscience lighter.

God help him. Ha!

S

Chapter Sixteen

And then, sooner or later, yeah.

It's time.

Round here, at night, everything looks the same. Round here we're maybe a half-mile from anything residential, with factories warehouses chimneys barbed fences all over. We're maybe a half-mile from where the light-pollution makes the sky yellow-green on a Good Night, and tonight, listen, you can even see stars. Round here, there are no cars and no witnesses. Round here there's nobody staggering home from the pub, singing songs about curry. Round here, the only thing on the skyline which isn't a warehouse is –

Ahahaha.

It would be.

– is a church steeple.

Round here are three guys struggling to conceal weapons, getting out of a rental car with false plates.

Tonight is Thursday evening.

Tonight is *too late to change your mind, boyo.*

If you *have* to lower yourself, if you *have* to get mixed up in this farcical unprofessional bullshit, if you *have* to get tangled up in something this messy, if you *have* to charge into a room full of people, if you *have* to shoot and shoot and shoot until every last thing is dead, if you *have* to go bloody

Hollywood and it's probably going to kill you, here's the thing: doing it in a place like *this* is the best you can hope.

The whole area is dead. I park a long way from the warehouse.

Tonight I'm wearing a pair of flesh-coloured latex gloves. Tonight, I have two matchboxes containing bullets and two spare clips of .22 hollowpoint rounds, each containing a liquid gram of uncut heroin. Tonight I wear an ex-Met Kevlar vest over my nondescript clothing and hold a hockey mask in my hand. Tonight there is something big and heavy and long taped to the inside of my left leg, and this is not a dick joke. Tonight the piece of paper with the magic number, which has a bunch of zeroes and a pound sign, is folded and resealed in the back pocket of my jeans. Tonight I'm maybe, possibly, might be, you never know, executing the holy will of God Almighty.

Ahahaha.

The piece of paper in my pocket, stop the clocks: I opened it this morning.

I opened it for the first time in a long time. I opened it in a B & B in Shepherd's Bush where I woke up confused and aching, and wondered-wondered-wondered.

Last night I fucked Sally. I hallucinated her with a halo. Ahaha, etc.

Last night she left while I slept.

This morning I woke up and ached inside in places I don't know, and I thought about the Plan, about getting *away*, getting out, and I thought of Sally gasping into the pillow beneath me. This morning, that magic number, the money I'll get from this job *right here today now* more than covers it.

More than enough money for two.

Providing I survive this. Ahaha etc.

Providing she says 'yes'.

Listen: Tonight, there is no borrowed wisdom. There is no clever-clever bullshit. There is no attitude, no philosophy, no wit. No stories.

Tonight there is Get It Done.

Tonight there is Try Not To Die.

I lock the car behind me.

Tonight Tyrone T. Levy stands, silent as a grave, with his Doom-Cock gun hanging in his hand. He looks like someone switched him to 'standby'.

Tonight Thomas Hilton Devizes is muttering about how far we've got to walk to get to the target. He's jittering. He's wobbling his shotgun about like it's a toy, and he's *ready*.

I envy him.

'Short walk,' I say. 'Best not leave the car right outside.'

To myself, I say, *You're not coming back, boys.*

The Man, if you want to know, he stands outside the main door and watches us come over.

He holds a gun. In a non-threatening sort of way.

Ahaha, etc.

'You're late,' he says.

'No we're not,' I say. I show him my watch.

The man, if you had to describe him, the first word you'd choose would be: Edgy. It's dark so I can't be sure, but by the starlight sky I'm guessing he's Latino, Spanish, Middle European. Either tanned or dark. The thing to remember is: people don't see faces, they see details.

CONTRACT

The man, when I was little, my dad would have called him: Not Quite White.

'How many in?' I say, and I nod at the door behind him.

The man, he is the Turncoat. He is the backstabbing traitorous piece of shit bought wholesale by Mr Call-Me-Boss. He is the treacherous little arse-scraping who will aid me tonight in slaughtering his pals downstairs, by telling me all about them.

The man, he has black hair, cropped-close. He has an earring in the top flap of his right ear.

'Ten,' he says. His eyes flick left, right, up and over Ty, Tom, me, down to the ground. His voice: he's trying to whisper, but forgetting to keep it quiet. He's sweating. 'One more out the back.' He swallows. Something on his mind.

Greener than a diseased frog.

I pull the man away, just me and him, thicker than thieves.

'Armed?' I say. 'How many? What kit?'

The man at the door, he wears a bleeding-edge suit with a dark-red shirt. On his cuffs, he wears silver links in the shape of bullets. This not-white man, he has the look of someone trying to look cool. This wide-eyed in-over-his-head man, he has a gold tooth: second-in from the right on the top.

People don't see faces, they see features.

Just so you know, I'd bet the contents of my scrotum that gold tooth, it's as genuine as the name I used to rent the car. It's as genuine as this red wig and the birthmark on my neck. It's a clip, is what I'd guess. It's a cheapo fake.

Remember: PhotoFit, IdentiKit, E-Fit.

'All packing but one,' he says, twitchy. 'Chubby geezer. He's the . . . he's your guy, right? Doesn't carry.'

'The client.'

'Yeah.'

'And the rest?'

He shrugs. This is trying-to-be-macho talk. This is using words like 'packing' with casual cool, while sweating. This is gangster bullshit Just The Way We Like It, which is sleazy and hard-talking and completely ludicrous.

This guy, he's greener than apple snot.

'Handguns,' he says. 'Nines. Couple of foreign kits, didn't recognise.'

Gun porn.

I ask him: 'Autos?'

Military gratuitousness. Artillery centrefolds. Reader's Wives with Cannons.

He shakes his head *no*. 'Small-time. Nobody's expecting *shit*. They're . . .'

He looks away. His forehead drips.

'They're *busy* down there.'

I purse my lips.

The man at the door, his eyes are small and afraid. He makes me think of a fox, maybe. He makes me think of damp things eating from bins, prowling in the night and screaming like babies.

'Layout,' I say, louder now so the Disposables can hear.

'Basement. Door at either end. One here, one round the back. No direct access to the warehouse either way. Only down.'

'Straight stairways?'

He stops. Scowls. And he was doing so well. 'W-what?'

I ask him: straight stairways, mate, or corners?

I ask him: are we going to go down the first step and get shot in the ankle?

I tell him: your fucking description, mateyboy, leaves a lot to be desired.

'Corners,' he says, cold and sweating and out of his depth, and it turns out, *shit*, it turns out I'm enjoying this. It turns out it's a good feeling, Being the Pro, making the rookie look daft.

'Both sets,' he says, bristling now. 'Corners.'

He says the basement is basically one long room. He says there are places to duck and cover, but no doors. No other rooms. He says everyone's clustered in in one place, and if we go in fast we'll get 'em all at once.

He sweats and swallows and looks at me and says, 'So you're the guy, huh?'

That sinking feeling.

Ty and Tom are looking at me.

I let my eyes go narrow.

'What guy?'

This man, his lip sort of half tilts like I'm bullshitting him. He looks from face to face, hunting the trick. He looks at me and smirks, like I must be stupid, like I must be mentally diseased, like I must be a *fool* to not know what he's talking about.

He says, 'The *guy*.'

This is all quiet. This is all whisper-wet. In scripts, this is called *sotto voce*.

And he flicks a finger straight up, pointing at the sky, and his eyebrows jink upwards. Like we're trading code.

Behind me, Tyrone T. Levy says: 'Thafuck?'

There are no clouds in the sky.

The guy shrugs.

'G'luck.' And then he starts away, slinking into shadow.

The man at the door, listen: I sort of admire him. He's sweaty and sleazy and probably he's going to die sometime this week, or whenever the Boss is done with him, but he's doing his best. He's too young too deep too soon, bailing while the bailing's good. So far, if you want to know, he's made just one cock-up I can see, and I'm feeling generous.

'Your new employer,' I say to his back, so quiet the others can't hear.

He stops. Doesn't turn. 'Yeah?'

'Be careful, there.'

And then he's running, dwindling away, and Then There Were Three.

'Stopwatches,' I say.

My puppets rummage in their pockets.

Right here and now, there are thirty seconds to go.

If you want to know, anxiety is your amygdaloid and hippocampus palpitating, your blood pressure and pulse skyrocketing, your palms sweating, your immune and digestive systems shutting down, your muscles receiving additional blood, your skin turning pale, your breaths becoming laboured. This is fight or flight. This is *beware the sabre-toothed-tiger*.

Right here and now, I'm wearing the hockey mask.

Right here and now I've come right round the other side of the building. This is over shrubs and cracked bricks and concrete. This is part of the circuit I made with Tyrone T. Levy and Thomas Hilton Devizes yesterday. Here, I'm as far from the road as it's possible to get. Here, it's quiet. The city is asleep, maybe, or just too distant to hear. Here, in grey-concrete smog-stained green-sky-lit nowhere, I could even feel a little calm.

This is living in fear, and it has its own serenity.

Being afraid of something that hasn't happened yet, the thing is: this is just a reminder we're cavemen, only *worse*. We're cavemen, only with better imaginations.

I step carefully around the corner.

There's another door.

There's another man.

Listen: I shoot this man twice through the face and twice in the chest with heroin-filled .22 hollowpoint rounds before he can react, while he's still noticing me, while he's saying, 'Buh.'

The noise my gun makes is: *spwk-spwk-spwk-spwk*.

It seems sort of pointless, describing him to you now.

Listen: just so you know, just in case you were wondering, just in case maybe you've come to *expect* it, this man, he does not come back to life.

He is only human.

Listen. Pay attention.

It's time.

The stopwatch beeps.

A world away, there's a bang like a door slamming, and I'm counting in my head: one, two, three . . .

My guys, my minions, my stringless little puppets, they're expecting me from the opposite direction.

Four, five, six. Et cetera et cetera.

Somewhere under my feet there's a thunderstorm. A couple of pigeons flutter up in the dark of the warehouse roof. I wonder if I should be feeling bad about this.

I give them a minute or two.

These men, I told you already. They're not called Disposables for nothing.

Underground, what this reminds me of most of all, is walking into a room where They've All Been Talking About You. You know the kind.

A room like that, you don't have long to absorb the feel of a place. It's about impressions. It's about assessing the situation without going too deep.

Skimming the surface.

Borrowed sensations.

Adrenal fly-fishing.

Listen: you step into a room where They've All Been Talking About You, you just *know* it. Half a second of greasy not-quite-sure silence. Glances, maybe. Burning, invisible *you just missed it*-ness.

Pay attention now: *spwk-spwk*

This is the sound made by a Ruger Mk II .22 with a disposable homemade silencer, firing twice from close up into the head of a Japanese man in a suit, crouching and moaning, slumped with half his leg missing.

His brains. His brains slap out the side of his face like a waterbomb. Like snot hitting a hankie.

Somewhere else, somewhere else in this room, there are people dying. There are voices, saying: 'Uuuuuuuuuh.'

I'm watching the Japanese guy go still and *not come back to life*, and I'm squatting somewhere, half aware. Somewhere safe, I hope. Not sure where or how or why. Not sure if it's safe in here, yet.

This is a hi-tension situation. Un-fucking-reliable. Sensation overload.

There's a lot of smoke in the air. There are things scattered across the floor. My brain can't absorb it all at once.

At a time like this, distractions are important.

Under my feet, listen. Every footstep is sticky.

At a time like this, everything is a blur. Everything is watercolour-weak.

At a time like this, imagine the adrenal medulla squirting like Billy-O. Like a fire-hose. Like a watering-can. Imagine epinephrine hormone dousing my bloodstream, binding to receptors, altering the chemistry of Me.

Borrowed wisdom. Self-diagnosis. Pain-in-the-arse.

This is my heart rate, tripling in an instant.

Oom-chkka-oom-chkka-oom-chkka

This is my pupils dilating like the nether regions of a birthing whale.

Oom-chkka-oom-chkka-oom-chkka

At a time like this, this is the arterioles in my muscular tissue expanding like balloons, venting blood, pumping me up, rapid oxygenation and invigoration and stimulation and animation and you-get-the-idea-ation. This is glycogen in my liver being processed, churned, mashed, mixed, made anew into glucose.

I am a walking chocolate bar.

Ahaha, etc.

I am an isotonic drink in human form.

This is my body screaming and burning on re-entry, flight-or-fight, instincts hotwired, nothing real.

This is me walking through a basement, stepping over

ex-people, feet sticking, killing anyone not already dead.

This is the blood pumping in my ears.

Oom-chkka-oom-chkka-oom-chkka

Right here and now, in the instant, there's a man standing against the wall, snotting and breathing blood, eyes half closed. The thing is, he's fighting to stay alive. You can see it. The thing is, he's bleeding out from a hole in his collar like a harpooned seal. Bleeding out like a kosher cow, head braced, arteries opened with a knife so sharp it

cuts

the

air.

This man, he's bleeding out in a hot spout, frothing and baking and you can *see* in his eyes he knows it: the grey-thing coming over him, the sounds getting distant. And still he's gasping away and moaning and choking and trying to lift the gun in his hand.

Spwk-spwk

The way his knees fold, when he's dead it's like he's sitting up against the wall. Meditating.

Twenty-first-century urban Buddhism.

At times like this, first impressions are important. At times like this, distractions are important. How do you reconcile the two? I tell you: it's like walking into a room where they've Just Been Talking About You.

In here, somewhere, there is a man talking. This is not in English.

In here, somewhere, he talks fast and without breathing, and in amongst the splatter it takes me some time to find him. Nudging people out the way. Dragging at *bits*.

So far, so B-Movie.

CONTRACT

This man, he's naked. He's fat and naked and too short, and where his flesh folds over it dimples like orange-peel, like snow before an avalanche. This man, this fat, naked lump of meat, his legs are full of holes.

I can image Tyrone T. Levy doing this. There he is, in my head, shouting and roaring and spraying bullets from his stupid toy gun, from his Big Cock of Doom. There he is, barely bothering to aim. Honey-voice raised. Yellow eyes blinking.

This man on the floor, trying to lift himself, grunting and groaning and talk, talk, talk, talking endless talk, his left hand is just Not There.

I can imagine Thomas Hilton Devizes doing this. See him? See him in my head, jittering and twitching and blasting with his gargantuan US cannon, racking and rearming like Arnie.

My Disposables, for the record: somewhere in this room, they're *disposed* of.

Don't look. Don't look.

Only, listen, here's the thing. This fat man. This fat, bleeding, dying, naked shit, with his still-in-shock face and his still-in-shock voice and his still-in-shock body, I don't mean to be crude but, but, but – he has an erection like the Eiffel Tower.

This – and let me make this perfectly clear – is not normal.

Spwk-spwk

He goes limp.

Ahaha, etc.

You'll have to excuse me. I'm feeling a little crazed.

Hormone overload. Adrenal O.D.

It's not my fault, it's my body chemistry.

You've got to wonder: what sort of meeting was this anyway?

On the stairs opposite the ones I came down, Tyrone T. Levy sits on the bottom step. His head is sagging forwards almost on to his knees, but I can see the hole. I can see the exit wound out the back, and the little white-grey-red edges where a solid pound of his crackaddled cerebral matter slapped like cowshit on to the ground. I can see the damp on his legs. There are more shell casings round his feet than I can count and the MACH-10, the Big Cock of Doom, just sits where he dropped it, oily with something that isn't oil.

If I had to guess, I'd say Tyrone T. Levy killed the fuck out of this room before someone took a lucky shot.

Everything is silent.

Everything is dead.

Everything is bleeding out and going hard and seizing up. Everything is losing oxygen. All round me, I can feel it. Lungs crinkling. Skin cells starving and bleating and turning blue, white, grey. Blood clots, just because.

Eyes go dry.

On the floor off to the side, Thomas Hilton Devizes looks like he stayed alive longer than most. He looks like he was sitting against the wall until gravity nudged him over. He looks like he took a stray in his chest, maybe from the guy with the hole in his collar, and there's a graceful arc on the brickwork behind him where he slid down, down, down. Like an unimaginative rainbow.

On the floor round his legs are more shotgun cartridges than I can count. This means Thomas Hilton Devizes was alive long enough to reload. All around him are people with holes. These holes, just so you know, they're not *neat* holes. Not cute Hollywood vaginal-bullet-bullshit holes, ohono, but *craters*. Hands, feet, legs missing. Clods of *stuff* ripped out.

If I had to guess, I'd say Thomas Hilton Devizes blew the living shit out of this room before someone took a lucky shot.

Let's hear it for the Disposables.

I've got to say, I'm sort of proud.

I've got to say, I'm sort of sad.

(Is this how farmers feel when they eat their prize-winning cattle?)

Somewhere, someone moves. Somewhere, among dead things piled up, among unrecognisable shapes, among business suits and dropped weapons and peeled-back lips and matted hair and puckered squirting B-movie *just-don't-look* nastiness, something moves.

(Is this how funeral directors feel when they bury their own parents?)

Somewhere, something dead clambers to its feet.

Admit it. You were waiting for this.

The room goes wrong. Ohoyeah. You've been expecting it.

Me too.

Someone moves towards me. This is like something clawing its way out of hell. This is like something that was once a person. It's short and it's fat and it's naked and its face is missing, and its legs are just gristle, and its hand is gone, and its whole fucking body is just blood, blood, blood.

Also, it has an erection.

Also, didn't I just kill this guy?

Ahaha, etc.

I'm hallucinating. Probably. Maybe.

Possibly.

Bear with me.

This thing with the room going wrong, the bodies are filled with worms.

The thing with the room going wrong, the smoke keeps forming faces. Moaning and agonised and screaming, ohoyes, faces that hiss and slide past.

The thing with the room going wrong, under my feet the blood turns to sticky jellybaby fingers and tries to touch my ankles.

My head is full of fire and swords. My ears ring.

There's blood coming from my nose. Down my top lip. Over my chin. Sweaty and sticky inside the hockey mask, gumming it to my face.

My blood.

DNA crime-scene contamination. Just walk away just walk away just walk away – fuck, my *head* –

The little man smiles, though his mouth hangs off at the jaw. The smoke moves round him like there are parts I can't see. There are teeth growing in patches from his chest.

He has an accent I can't place.

Oh, and his eyes . . . his eyes run like liquid gold.

That sinking feeling.

The little man says, 'Nice try, fuckwit.'

The little man says, 'You send in the goons, hah? Smooth.'

The little man says, 'Want to shoot me some more, mister killer man?'

The little man says, 'I doubledoubledoubledareyou.'

He starts stroking his cock. He pushes his shoulders back

and slouches in mid-air, and there are extra arms, like insect-antennae, slipping down from the crooks of each elbow.

For the record, by this stage, his eyes have regrown, gone black, gone yellow, and then stared at me with a twinkle.

He laughs, and I lower the gun because *fuck yeah*, this is *funny*, and I laugh too.

I'm a little crazed. Bear with me.

I am doing God's work. I am a demon killer. I am doing something *good*.

'Guns,' I say, 'don't seem to cut it.'

Ahaha, etc. Aaaahahahahah. Etc.

Yesterday, I told you already, one of the jobs I did was Tooling Up.

The little man is heading towards me, and his laughing, it's stopped.

This thing with the room going wrong, there are puddles of sulphur oozing up out of the floor. The place is getting hot and tight, and the smoke, shit, fuck, piss, the smoke is a great hand stroking my head.

Listen. Pay attention.

At times like this, distractions are important. Adrenaline burning. Eyes rolling.

Zombie midget-arsehole lurching and not laughing, tossing himself off as he walks.

This is a bad time to take a proper look around the room.

This is a bad time to notice the bare-brick walls.

The cameras and tripods, all facing in one direction.

The bed.

This is a bad time to notice ropes and cuffs and tubes of lube and toys, toys, toys.

Today, I told you already, there is something big and

heavy and long taped to the inside of my left leg. This, for the record, is not a dick joke.

This is a bad time to notice the shadow under the bed.

The face. Muddy, small, scared.

The eyes, wide like dinner plates, watching.

And right on the edge of hearing, lost behind His Undead Nibs dripping and slopping and putting himself back together, just like the Vicar, just like the Fat Man in Bracknell, lost behind the *fap-fap-fap-fap-fap* of his hand on his cock, lost behind the giggles and laughs and *what the fuck is happening*, there's a whimper.

Let me tell you, back in the real world, back in the tunnel-vision-focus-on-incoming-death reality, the man is reaching out his hands and his antennae and the dream logic makes it all normal, and I'm yanking the shape from inside my leg away from the tape holding it there, and in my hand it's heavier than I remember.

This thing, you can buy ones just like it from pretty much anywhere you want.

This thing, all you need is a decent carving-steel and a lot of time.

The leather sheath, I drop it in a puddle of something that isn't water.

Under the bed, stop the clocks. Hold the front page. Everyone just *listen*: under the bed, scared to death, there is a child watching me.

The little fat, naked tumescent man who-is-dead-who-is-not-dead, he's almost on top of me now, nails all outstretched and he's snarling and his eyes, *shit*, they're not normal and this is how it feels to be mauled by a tiger and the smoke has become great unfurled bat wings pouring from his shoulders and, oh, *I'm hallucinating again* and I'm not quick and I'm not clever but I'm not *stupid*, and there's a meeting underground and a fat webmaster woman in a bedsit organising attendance, and there's a bed with ropes and chains, and there are cameras set and waiting, and there's a naked man with an erection, and there's a Scared Naked *Child*.

– and I may not be quick, and I may not be clever, and I may not have many scruples, but I *get* it, you know? I see what's going on here.

Michael Point, aged twenty-eight, signing up for Disapproval Duties.

Long story short: I swing the completely 100 per cent legal machete I bought for £29.99 yesterday in an Outdoor Pursuits Shop like a match-winning Ace at Wimbledon.

Using my hands. The fourth time. It seems to've worked so far.

The kid, I recognise him from the photos in the church. His eyes, I can't decide what colour they are.

Long story short, I hack the little man's head clean off his shoulders. It makes a noise like: *spwk*.

Long story short, there's blood like a water-fountain and tiredness in my arms and legs, and *oh look I've survived*, and my brain, which is diseased and twisted right round in its skull and rotting and stinking up my head, my brain, which is *unreliable* and *stupid* and *temporary*, it performs a manoeuvre as a result of adrenal over-saturation and over stimulation which I can only describe as: a backflip. Which is to say: I faint.

Everything changes.

I believe I hear angels singing my praises as I go.

For the Record:

For the record, in the year 2000, in a little village in South Wales, a licensed, qualified paediatrician had her home attacked – covered in graffiti, windows broken, the whole caboodle – by a mob of locals.

The police later suggested there'd been confusion over her professional title.

The police later said locals had thought she was a sicko who abused kids.

The police later said 'paediatrician' and 'paedophile', *hey*, they sound sort of similar.

If anyone ever wanted to ask me why I kill people for money, this would be a good story to tell.

Chapter Seventeen

In this dream, there's an angel riding my cock like Seabiscuit. She keeps shouting about Seven Seals and Seven Trumpets, and every time I try to grind against her she slaps me in the face.

I'm in charge, she says. *Not you.*

In this dream, there's a shooting star tearing down out of the sky, only it's not a star, it's a boy, a little boy, and he lands on the white tiles of a bathroom sixteen years ago to stare, stare, stare. There's a thing made out of red and white in the shower, and it has dozens of smiley little faces.

It makes me laugh.

The angel slaps me again.

Pay attention, she says.

In this dream, a man with three (maybe four?) faces stands watching me as I try my best to drill the angel. He has a black crow on his shoulder with a red stripe down its belly, and it keeps making a noise like paper tearing.

Kkkhh

He's shouting something, though his mouth doesn't move.

In this dream, the angel slaps me again, harder, and says, *Hey.*

*

You never hear the noise that wakes you.

I'm back and I'm up and I'm gasping, and I *hate* waking up like this.

I'm back and I'm in a basement full of gunsmoke and blood and bodies, and there is a light in my face, and my head hangs against the wooden frame of a small palette bed, and there is a child slapping my cheek.

I'm back, and still the room is *wrong*.

The kid hits me again.

'M'awake!' I half lie. 'Look, I'm . . . Stop it! M'awake!'

He pulls his hand back and moves away, scared, then just stands and stares like he's been switched off. He's shaking.

There are sores on both his wrists, and he holds the hockey mask from my face in one of his little hands. The inside is sticky with blood from my nose.

His eyes keep changing colour.

I have no idea what to say to him.

The light in my face is part of the filming set-up. I'm sort of glad it's there, on account of how it's too bright for me to see the rest of the room. The way my head is – or maybe just the way the *world* is – out there in the dark outside the beam you've got bodies twitching, devil-faces grinning, whistling teeth dislodging, fingertips exploring, jaws popping, fires flickering, et cetera et cetera.

I ignore it.

In any standard lighting set-up there are three basic components. This is regardless of what you're shooting. (The *other* kind of shooting.)

This is whether it's a scene with a running man, a passionate clinch, or a child being –

Anyway.

CONTRACT

In lighting, the softest source is mostly the backlight. This goes behind the subject, hidden away, aimed from behind. This provides a sense of depth. This is intangible, photo-luminous, three-dimensional air-drawing. This is a quiet corona, killing the flatness.

Here and now today, this is a flickering thing hidden behind the bed. Malfunctioning, cracked, broken, shot up. It makes shadows dance up walls, and to me they're *not* shadows but ant-things with faces and fingers, which laugh and sing.

To me it's not a broken light, but miniature lightning. A diminutive storm.

It picks out the edges of the little boy's legs, shows me bruises.

Cuts.

Blood.

There are voices coming nearer. The boy twitches every time he hears them, but his eyes are hollow. They keep changing colour.

The backlight is on, but nobody's home.

Here's me trying to get up. Here's me staggering and holding my head, feeling my brain rattle inside, and treading on somebody dead. The boy backs off as I get up.

'It's OK,' I say.

This is possibly the stupidest thing ever to leave my mouth.

The little boy, if he can see the shuffling, scampering weirdness all around the room, if he's aware of it like me, he's not saying so.

In lighting, the next important source is usually the fill-light. The fill-light is from in front, catching the subject

311

from one side, only softer and dimmer than you'd expect.

This is to stop faces being white-and-black mosaics. This is to stop features being lost, hard shadows sticking like glue, jagged shade-lines slicing in half every nose, every lip, every brow. This is to stop you and me and Little-miss-filmstar from having a *dark side*.

You've got to laugh.

Here and now today, the fill-light has been comprehensively fuckerised by a desperate large-scale exchange of shooty-death-kill gunfire. It's dead.

Here and now today, one half of everything is just: black.

Here and now today, the little boy next to me: his face is just *terror*.

The way things are – ohoyes, with my brain, with my world, with my perception, *whatever* – the way things are, the shadows are oil-sludge that slip around when I'm not watching. The world is falling apart. My senses are borrowed wisdom, fact/opinion/culture/bullshit, and who knows which is which?

The way things are, the boy glows. The boy is the sun. The boy is radiation glory.

Seriously. I'm not making this up.

Let me tell you, this boy, it's like he's got a backlight of his own. It's like he's more real than anything here. He's small and shivering and terrified, and covered in mud and blood, and when he moves it's like . . . like singing, in three-D.

And it hurts to look at him.

I'm tired. I'm half asleep. I have a head like a fireball. I'm freaked out. I'm maybe, possibly, could be, you just can't say for sure, hallucinating. I'm on a mission from God. Ahahaha.

CONTRACT

The point is: I'm getting abstract.

The point is: bear with me.

There are voices up the stairs. The front set: the main door, up to the outside world. Voices crooking around behind the back of Tyrone T. Levy, who sits on the bottom step staring at his knees and the brains all over them.

The little boy twitches again, and holds my leg.

'It's . . . It's OK,' I say again. 'Just stay there.'

I hate kids.

Let me tell you: I have my gun in one hand. I have a machete in the other. Strictly speaking, my job was to kill all the people I found down here.

Don't look at me like that.

The voice, getting closer, here's the thing: I recognise it.

The voice, getting closer, here's the thing: the voice belongs to Mr Call-Me-Boss.

That sinking feeling.

There are footsteps on the stairs. There are echo-words filtered and clattering like concrete bats, and I maybe half hear – *ld her to stay in the ca* – and – *viously wants to see for herself but even so* and – *uch of an idea what to expe* – and *kkkhh* and *bloody sure your lot uphold their end of thi* – and ohoyeah, yeah, yeah, that sinking, drooping, plunging-away-into-the-dark feeling.

Someone says, 'Kin' hell. Look at it down here . . .'

Someone calls out: 'Anyone alive?'

In lighting, the most important light – stop me if I'm being obvious – is the key-light.

This is the one that hits you from in front, ever-so-slightly to one side. This is the one that casts the shadow that the fill-light tries to fill. This is the one the backlight

313

tries to deepen. This is the pretend sun. This is the directional source. This is *important*.

Here, the key-light is still on. Here, the key-light stands next to a pulverised digital camera with a dead woman wrapped around the tripod.

Here, the key-light is right in my eyes, making me blink, making the room wobble, making weird colours blob in my vision.

Here, all I can see beyond the fill-light is *shapes*.

They see me. I don't see them.

That sinking feeling.

'Fuck,' a voice says.

Someone looking around the room.

'He's still ali . . . Look. Shit.'

Someone seeing me.

'And what's . . . oh. Oh, *Jesus*. Look. *Look.*'

Someone seeing the kid.

HINT: They didn't expect me to survive this.

HINT: They didn't expect the kid to be here.

HINT: This little boy, this hollow little life, whatever he's been through, down in the filth and blood and sweat and, oh for God's sake, don't *think* about it . . .

Whatever he's been through, he's clinging to my leg and hiding from the two man-shape-shadows beyond the light.

Mr Call-Me-Boss. The Red-Tie-Guy.

All these little getting-to-know-yous.

Let me tell you about dream logic.

In dreams, we don't *know* we're asleep. In dreams, our unconscious brain deals with incoming shit in the same way as it does when awake. In dreams that spaghetti-splat in your skull doesn't know it's being lied to. In dreams your brain is trusting like a dog, chasing after a ball you pretended to throw, running and running and running for joy.

Borrowed wisdom.

One day, all that is 'new' will be old-but-forgotten.

One day, every variable will be used up, every equation solved and exploded and deconstructed, every sentence rearranged, every colour fractured.

One day, dreams will be the only thing left worth anything.

In dreams, it's normal for snakes to fall out of taps, and people to email themselves back-and-forth, and teddy bears to start talking, and badgers to fly, and calculators to wear crowns, and fathers to be innocent and mothers to come back and – and you get the idea.

The point is, in dreams, you might be surprised when strange things happen, but you never stop to wonder if it's *impossible*.

'Michael?' says Mr Call-Me-Boss. I cannot see his face.

'What are you doing here?' I ask. The room bulges and I nearly fall over.

My eyes see only grey for a second. Maybe I'm dying.

'Let's . . . let's get the lad out of here, mate.' His voice is different.

The kid clings tighter.

In dreams, there is no preparation for What Comes Next. No staying-close-to-bolt-holes. In dreams, there is the exact opposite of assiduousness and anal retention.

Listen. Stop the clocks. Here is a Turning Point.

It's possible, Sally said so, that I've been *chosen*.

It's possible, Sally said so, I'm working for a higher power.

Maybe I'm just nuts. Bear with me here.

It's possible, the weird-eyed scumfuck Boss said so, that there are *sides*.

OK.

OK.

We're talking Good and Evil, aren't we? We're talking a simplistic, stupid, polarised idiotic view of morality, aren't we? We're talking gods and devils, and *wouldn't it be nice if life was that easy*, and we're talking endless, endless war, aren't we?

We're talking about me being sent out to make Evil People into Ex-People, aren't we?

We're talking about Heaven and motherfucking Hell, don't laugh, I know, I *know* it sounds stupid. We're talking about them squabbling over a little boy –

– who *glows*.

In dream logic, you just accept what happens and don't question it, and go with the flow. In dream logic, you don't get deep. You don't get metaphysical. You don't laugh at the stupidity of the situation. You don't wince with embarrassment just by considering something daft.

The kid stays behind me.

This is the kid who I first saw in a photo in a church, in the wallet of a man who dressed like a vicar but swore like a trooper. A vicar who came back to life with a second face in his belly and a fish on a chain round his neck, and slugs for lips and fiery clothes and teeth-too-big. A vicar with a big muddy hole in his graveyard.

Like something fell from the sky.

Tumbling, crashing down from above.

I'm not quick. I'm not smart. But I *can* put two and two together.

'You want him back,' I say.

Symbols, listen: symbols fill up with meaning. Symbols are only worth a damn if you know what they mean.

Symbols can be anything. Shapes. Words. Colours. People.

'You want to use him,' I say.

'What?' Mr Call-Me-Boss, voice tight, lost behind the light. 'What's that?'

'Your . . . your side. You want him back. *They* wanted him too . . .'

Sometimes you put two and two together and the answer is five.

And the fifth angel sounded, and I saw a star fall from heaven unto the earth: and to him was given the key of the bottomless pit. And he opened the bottomless pit; and there arose a smoke out of the pit, as the smoke of a great furnace; and the sun and the air were darkened by reason of the sm—

Oh, shut the fuck up.

In dream logic, the important thing is this: The Truth Doesn't Matter. You cling to your certainties, you decide what you believe, and you *stick to it.*

Whatever you perceive, that's what's real.

Let me tell you, I'm not letting anyone take this child.

This is Michael Point, aged twenty-eight, taking a moral stand for the first time in his life.

Moral stands would be easier if I had legs.

I can nearly see Mr Call-Me-Boss now. His eyes pour with gold. The key-light . . . The key-light just moved.

I'm not letting the kid go. He clings to my leg and *nobody is taking him anywhere*.

'Mikey,' the Boss says. 'Mikey, let him go. Send him over here. He needs help.'

The kid stares at the dead woman wrapped around the tripod. I wonder who she was.

'You know how he feels, Mikey. Right? Don't *do* this to him. Let's get him out of here. He's been through enough.'

No, no, no, no, silver tongue, snake, snake, *I'm cracking up* what's—

And then movement.

On the left. In the shadow. Sneaking round from the back. Keeping me dazzled by the light while the boss talked to me.

Creeping round to get the kid.

A voice.

'*Kkkhh.*'

Chaos.

Listen: the room moves. The light flares. Something jumps in my hand, something says *spwk*, shapes crumple . . . things readjust.

The Red-Tie-Guy is dead at my feet.

Smoke and silence, a hot Ruger Mk II .22 in my hand, and Mr Call-Me-Boss shouting, storming, snarling: 'No! For fuck's— NO! *No!*'

And I push the kid, hard, angry, towards the door, the *back* door, and I tell him, '*Run.*'

And I kick the key-light out the way and I hit the boss in the face, and this is all dream logic, this is all fake, and my knuckles hurt and the kid's sprinting away and *thank fuck, thank fuck, he's out, he's made it, he's free*, and the magic

number burns my side and I'm pounding this sinister fucker
on the floor in his face over and over and I'm saying:

What
Fucking
Side
Now
What
Fucking
Side
Now

And he looks up between blows, eyes puffy, face cracked,
lips opened up like tubes of toothpaste, and he's not looking
at me. He's looking at something standing behind me.

I have just the tiniest glimpse of a piece of wood.

It hits me, hard, behind my ear, and shatters. The
greyness comes down.

I have an even tinier glimpse of who just hit me.

'Sorry,' says Sally, as the shadows eat me up.

Interview Room 2

Some silences are anti-noise.

Some silences, if you could record and play them, people would have to raise their voices to be heard. These are silences that are *infectious*, that spread out and kill the little sounds still trying to be heard.

Anna's pen against paper. Jason sniffing because he's too bone-idle to go and blow his nose. My fingernails on the top of this table.

Silenced, silenced, silenced.

This place, everything is migraine-noisy. Normally.

These two pinstripe goons, these two interrogation-robots, they just stare. I have just this instant finished telling them about the Thing in the Basement, with the guns and the lights and the kid and the Red-Tie-Guy dead at my feet.

They just stare, and I just stare, and this is a good, solid, dramatic, respectable, British silence, to be appreciated for all it's worth.

It's ruined, of course.

'I'm confused,' says Jason Durant. Jason cockheaded, fuckknuckle, moronic, arsefaced Durant.

'No shit,' I say.

'Why was this "Sally" down there? You sure it was her?'

I tell him, no, *mate*, of course I'm not sure. She was

hitting me round the head with a plank. That was sort of a distraction.

I tell him, Anyway, I was in the middle of a reality-altering event at the time.

I tell him, Or maybe I was just going crazy. Either way.

I tell him, it looked like her, that's all.

I tell him, you don't see faces, you just see features.

I say this so it sounds like I'm convinced.

The silence comes back.

The truth is, Jason asked a sensible question. The truth is, every time I think about it I get a thing in the small places of my belly, a thing like sickness mixed with fear, and it's cold and sharp and makes me want to puke out my soul. The truth is, there's an awful lot I still don't know, and today is maybe days, maybe weeks, maybe months later.

I'll get back to you about that.

The truth is, there's a lot I don't get about the Boss and the kid, and . . . and that woman, whoever she was, and the Red-Tie-Guy, and . . .

And I'm not quick. I'm not smart. I get things wrong.

This is important.

'What happened?' says Anna. 'Afterwards, I mean.'

But no. No, I'm not in the mood for this; not any more. I've depressed myself, and I rattle it off quick.

I tell them I woke up outside the warehouse, on the floor. I tell them it was still the night and there was fire and smoke coming up through the door, and the smell of petrol, and nobody else for miles around. I tell them: hey, at least they dragged me out first, I guess.

Before they lit the fires. Before they ran.

I tell them I could hear sirens.

I tell them my head hurt. A *lot*.

I tell them I couldn't find the little boy.

I tell them I made it home and I don't know how, and I kept blacking out, and as I came round the corner towards my flat what I saw first were: flashing lights. Yellow tape. Badges. Reflective jackets.

I tell them my reaction was something along the lines of: *Fuck. Fuck fuck fuck fuck fuck. Fuck.*

I tell them I slept in a park.

I tell them, by the way, the morning after that, in the *Metro*, it said my dad was dead. It said he killed himself using a sharpened knife taken from the prison kitchens, by opening the radial arteries of each wrist.

I tell them, by the way, that was the bottom falling out of my world.

The silence again.

'Can I have some coffee?' I say.

Anna.

Anna is smoking again.

Anna pulls the cigarette from its packet in a way which, look, if she doesn't *mean* it to be sexual, she's just got No Idea.

This is with fingertips only. This is twisting the shaft, just a little, to free it from the other fags. This is gripping it between the Last Lady Lips I'll ever see.

This is with me drumming my fingers on the table, maybe just a *little* too fast.

The lighter, when she thumbs the flint, it makes a sound like: *spwk-spwk-spwk-spwk.* (Twice in the head, twice in the chest.)

CONTRACT

This woman Anna, this ice-statue, she breathes out and the smoke is a dissipating splat of carcinogenic fun, a blink-and-you'll-miss-it masterpiece, a half-hearted massage, dissolving in air.

Anna, watching her breathe out that first satisfying black-lung suck, it makes me wish I smoked. It makes me wish I *was* smoke.

It makes me shiver, is my point, and she's watching. She's doing that thing with her eyebrow.

'Someone walked on my grave,' I say.

She smiles. Only, listen, not in a good way.

This is with Anna and me, lovely Anna, just us two, all on our lonesome.

Jason Durant went for coffee. This room, it's suddenly not so bad.

Only, here's the thing: I depressed myself, before. I entertained some unpleasant ideas, about Exactly What's Been Going On.

Here's the thing: suddenly I'm getting dark.

For what I am about to do, may my conscience prick me often.

'Ask you something?' I say, and I'm trying to sound dangerous, and there's smoke coiling over her top lip like she's spilling grey water and gravity took a day off.

'Mm.'

I hold up my hands. 'Why no cuffs?'

Anna, lovely, lovely Anna, her eyes go narrow.

She sits back in her chair and crosses her legs, one over the knee of the other. She's wearing a skirt – not short, but flesh is flesh – and she gives me a stare. Head on one side. Fag coiling smoke from her fingers.

The way most people would describe this look is: Frank.

'I could run amok,' I say.

'Hypothetically,' I say.

And I give her a Look.

Listen to me: maybe, it's just possible, the reason I'm trying this shit is that I'm feeling threatened. I blame biology. I blame the male brain. *Me*? it says, *under* her *control*?

This is a modern excuse for Bad Behaviour. This is the cry of the murderer, paedophile, addict junkie, alcoholic, fattie. This is the twenty-first-century explanation for any motherfucking thing that happens to be undesirable, that you can't blame on anyone else:

It's Not My Fault, It's my Body Chemistry.

I say, 'I mean.' And I scowl, because it's not in my nature to sound sleazy or threatening, so I'm having to force it, and if that surprises you, maybe you haven't been paying attention. 'I mean, here we are. Just the two of us. No guard . . .'

She breathes out. Smoke coils. Eddies. Sucks back and twists around.

This is the mechanics of sighing.

'You on your own,' I say.

'A woman,' I say.

'With me.

'A dangerous criminal,' I say.

'A desperate man.

'Nothing to lose.'

Let me explain. Don't hate me. Please. Please. Listen.

I'm in custody. I'm being questioned. I'm being placed in a position socially and morally inferior to my captors. I'm feeling slighted. I'm feeling as though I lack control. Control is what makes me me. And no, I couldn't escape if I tried. I wouldn't get that far.

And no, I wouldn't hurt her. Honest injun. I wouldn't beat her with this chair. I wouldn't rape her over this table. Seriously, truly. I'm not *like* that.

I don't *think* criminal.

But just to see her go pale. Just to see her sweat. Just to see her nervous. That would be something. (It's not my fault. It's my body chemistry.)

'Just think about it,' I say. 'I mean, come on. It's not very clever, is it? Not the level of security you'd expect.'

Eye contact. Swallow. Clench jaw.

Go for it.

'It's not very *safe*,' I say.

'For you, I mean,' I say.

(It's not my fault. It's my body chemistry.)

This is clumsy. This is Veiled Threats 101. This is the wolf part of my head, playing at Power. This is the testosterone Brain.

Reacting. Trying to assert itself.

I can almost feel the activity. Testosterone androgenic steroids. Industriously synthesised from cholesterol bundles in my gonads. Binding to globulin, diffusing into cyto-plasmic oceans. Fucking with my brain. It's not my fault, etc. etc.

Right now, even deeper down, I'm getting that old clit-envy feeling.

I waggle my fingertips and move my hands apart.

'No cuffs,' I say.

She keeps staring.

She keeps smiling.

What I'm getting at, is: she doesn't look vulnerable.

She keeps smoking.

No sweat.

If this is a Poker Face, ohmychrist she's *good*.

And you know what happens, right then and there? With her staring, not being scared, not reacting at all?

What happens is this: the wolf part of my brain, he slinks off into the hills.

The veiled threat, it hides under its veil and refuses to come out.

My gonads, they stop producing androgenic steroids.

They stop doing much of anything, as far as I can tell, except for maybe withdrawing into my chest.

Anna, she keeps staring.

Smoke coils some more.

And then I'm muttering Sorry without thinking, and I'm back at school, and I can't meet her eye, and this time . . . this time it wasn't me who scored the point.

Every time she sucks on the cigarette, in the silence, you can hear the paper burn.

Kkkhh

Long story short: eventually Jason Durant comes back.

Let's never speak of this again.

An Interlude Of Negligible Value

It's time you and I had a talk about religion.

It's time we talked Faith. Don't panic. I'll be quick.

I'm not subtle. Try to remember that.

Well.

I mean.

Not on purpose.

Let me tell you: there was a time – when I was younger – I had *opinions*. Real actual opinions made up and thought through by myself. I *considered*.

Don't look at me like that.

There was a time, I was in a pub. This was between nothing-jobs. Bar work, admin, sales, number-crunching, van-driving. This was before guns and heroin and Wilson and killing and hallucinations and not drinking and all the things you people out there think of as *me*.

This was proto-Mike.

This was impassioned me, just a little drunk, holding forth. This was agnostic militancy. This was the stringent advocation of ignorance. This was the International Church of 'Who Knows'?

This was back when I had friends who listened.

This was back when I had friends at all.

'If we just . . . admitted it,' I said, 'just accepted we don't

327

know shit – no, no, no . . . that we *can't* know shit – then, then . . . *Just think* what we could fucking *do*! Think how *free* we'd be!'

This was me, thinking I was the only one who'd ever been so enlightened.

Bankrupt the churches, I figured. Irrigate Africa. Stop all wars. Spread the Word Of Uncertainty.

Listen.

I.

Was.

Stupid.

Someone overheard. Nearby table, sipping at orange juice. Someone debated. This happens. I forget their face. I forget their religion.

This poor bastard, I tore him down in front of everyone. This poor bastard, I undermined his beliefs like a mole under a castle. I accused him of preaching, of trying to inflict his dogma on the rest of us, of pursuing his dirty little Conversion Agenda in the seediest, most reprehensible way.

This poor bastard, ohoyes, you saw it coming, he shook his head and said, 'What the fuck are *you* doing, then?'

What I'm getting at is: what you believe belongs to nobody but you. And the only time it gets to be a problem, ohoyes, whether it's belief or denial, or uncertainty, or a burning conviction in the Spiritual Magnificence of Bethshamzakhal the Purple Alligator Deity, is when you decide Everyone's Entitled To Your Opinion.

And that's not the fault of the opinion in question, is it?

*

CONTRACT

In a particular kind of light, for the record, this story – this one you're reading right now – is sort of about religion. Ish. Kind of.

That doesn't mean we have to talk about it.

Let's change the subject.

Chapter Eighteen

Right now, which is maybe Monday, maybe Tuesday, some days have gone.

By this I mean: *gone*. Not just gone *by*, not just passed, not just proceeded-in-time as-per-normal, but *gone*.

Vanished.

Zzzip.

Which is odd.

Right now, which is maybe Tuesday, maybe Wednesday, maybe Thursday, maybe You Get The Idea, there's a *Simpsons* chess set in my motel room which probably wasn't there when I first arrived. That means I probably went out and bought it. I have no memory of this.

Right now, which could be any fucking day of the week for all I know, I've probably been sitting here playing against myself, all day every day.

I don't think I even know how to play chess.

Right now everything seems just a little grey.

Listen: post-traumatic stress disorder is a reactive mental state caused by exposure to or confrontation of stressful, traumatic experiences. Which is to say: it does exactly what it says on the tin.

Whatever it is that causes PTSD in a living, breathing human being, it mostly involves actual or threatened death, or actual or threatened violence, or actual or threatened terror.

The best thing about PTSD is, it's *normal.*

The best thing is, it doesn't mean you were already mental. Borrowed wisdom.

Right now is what you could ironically refer to as A Bit of a Low Patch.

Right now I've been lucid maybe four days. This is since Waking Up From the Grey. Before that, I have no idea. Before that, I don't know how long I've been in this motel, playing chess with myself.

Let me tell you: on the first day of Waking Up From the Grey, I went back to my flat, just like on the Night Of the Thing in the Basement. That day, the way my flat was, was: still surrounded.

Boxes and boxes being carted out: guns, fake I.Ds, books, my computer. Overpriced salon downstairs closed, the leopard-print owner being questioned.

Loving the attention.

On the first day of Life Take 2, I watched the clutter of Life Take 1 being bagged and tagged and prepared for forensic inspection, and all I could think was: they're going to find all the porn on my P.C. All I could think was: how embarrassing.

On the first day, there was yellow police tape and neighbours staring from windows, and me in a hoodie I got from a charity shop at the back with the crowd. On the first day there was a police sergeant on duty, and, *flash-flicker-flash*, he's the guy who came to my door, the guy who posted that photograph, the guy who's just one of the Choir's 'mates', and now . . .

331

. . . now he's here, at my flat, watching.

Mr Call-Me-Boss has done this. He has served me up. He has thrown me to the lions, which are tame only to him.

On the first day, that police sergeant, that guy who maybe two weeks ago, maybe three, he had a halo, you remember, he's pocketing a manila envelope holding £6000 in used notes, which I Did Not Launder At My Local Amusement Arcade.

On the first day, the cops bring out a crate of T-shirts, only the bottom of the box is too weak and it breaks, and the clothes come spilling out. Multicoloured rainbows.

The one on top reads: *SMILING GIVES YOU CANCER.*

They have my fingerprints. They have my DNA. They have skin cells and plug-hole pubes and shoe-prints and hair samples and reading materials, etc. etc.

I can't even remember which fake I.D. I was using before all of this. Which is awkward.

The police, you've got to love them, they own me.

With post-traumatic stress disorder, which is PTSD, which does not mean you're already a nutcase, symptoms include nightmares, flashbacks, emotional detachment, insomnia, irritability, memory loss, hypervigilance, anxiety, depression, excessive startle-responses, loss of appetite, and dissociation.

Dissociation is where you slice off chunks of yourself to avoid the world.

Dissociation might be multiple personalities or acting-out-of-character or whatnot. Dissociation might be oh so very Hollywood.

Dissociation, also, might just be where everything goes grey for a little while.

On the second day of Not Being a Memoryless Zombie, my head and heart and balls were filled up, all of a sudden, all out of nowhere, all *sharp* and unexpected with this: I Must Find Sally.

On the second day, I dialled her number from the motel desk, because my mobile, ahahaha, seriously: I'd have to be *stupid* to use that. On the second day of being vaguely human, vaguely lucid, it rang and rang and then –

Stopped.

On the second day, I went to Ariadne's Café. I went to the cinema. I lurked and wandered and poked in places, and She Was Not There.

On the second day, I went back to the motel and just sat. Just sat. Just sat.

Eventually, I went to a guy I know in Walthamstow. This guy, he's like an unofficial pharmacy. This guy, he's unofficial in that you don't need a prescription. I don't even remember his name. Or what he looks like. Or where he lives.

These things are unimportant. These things have been fed to the Rear View Mirror, which Gobbles All Things.

What's important is, what I remember is, I bought some stuff.

Post Traumatic Stress Disorder, which I have diagnosed myself, of myself, which is PTSD, which is nothing to do with being a delusional hallucinogenic frothing-at-the-mouth nutcase, which is nothing to do with being Touched By the Divine Will, is mostly treated with therapy.

But: Effexor (venlaflaxin), Remeron (mirtazapine),

Zoloft (sertraline), Prozac (fluoxetine). Pick 'n' mix.

On the second day, I slept well.

On the third day, which was yesterday, don't ask me what day of the week, I went to Belmarsh. I went to pick up my father's possessions, only I couldn't use my real name and they'd only release his shit to a member of the family.

On the third day, which was yesterday, I was an inch away from getting stroppy. While surrounded by prison guards.

While Very Wanted.

I'm not quick. I'm not smart. Sometimes, if you want the truth, I'm pretty fucking stupid.

On the third day, which was yesterday, the guards said Sorry Mate, Relatives Only. The guards said, But still, it was a shame, huh? They said they'd sort of liked the old goat. They said there was no warning, no foul play, nothing.

I remembered the big guy with the tattoos who turned into a devil, drawing one spindly not-finger across his throat.

Kkkhh

The guards said: 'Yeah, shame. Guilty as hell, though.'

The guards said: 'Always are, your suicidals.'

Bang goes the Hollywood ending.

Bang goes Angry Son Faces Undeniable Proof of His Father's Innocence.

Listen: post-traumatic stress disorder, which it's possible I've been suffering from over the past four, five, six, who-knows-how-long, days, which it's possible I've been suffering from over the past four, five, six, sixteen, who-knows-how-long years, may have a delayed onset. It may not hit you till something triggers a repeat episode.

Like, another stressful event. Like, the death of another family member. Like, seeing someone in a similar situation to yourself.

Whatever.

Did you know, traumatised kids who have PTSD are more likely to turn into criminal, disaffected, antisocial, mercenary-killer scumfucks than those who haven't? This can be proved by doctors with impressive graphs. Honest injun.

All in books. All on the Internet.

Today, which was the fourth day since waking up in the motel room with a chess set and no idea how long I'd been out, since hitting that special secret red-indigo *splatzone* at the core of my skull marked ROCK BOTTOM, since wigging-out and backflipping in time and just . . .

Falling

Apart . . .

I went to find Mr Call-Me-Boss.

This was not for revenge. This was not to get answers, though it would've been nice. This was not to take him and shake him by the throat for setting the cops on me, or for screwing with my head, or anything you care to name. This was because I have become *unstuck*. I have floated adrift of my defining principle. I have gone Amateur, Let Myself Down.

I have Forgotten the Cardinal Rule: It's. All. About. The. Money. I *want* mine.

There's no answer at the office buzzer. The buzzer that let me in on time, without mucking me about, a week or two or three ago. Here's me in a hoodie, as conspicuous as a diarrhetic dinosaur, buzzing and buzzing and buzzing.

Today, which was the first day since . . . since the thing in the Basement . . . that I felt like my brain was even Mostly switched on, I waited, waited, waited. At lunchtime, someone came down from the office on the top floor, and I waited, waited, waited, while they went out, got a sandwich, had a coffee, read some shit fiction in a shit park on a pigeon-shit-covered bench, then came back. When they came back, I waited, waited, waited, until the door was *almost* closed, and I inserted a foot.

I told you already: I am not subtle. Well. I mean. Not on purpose.

In the offices of Mr Call-Me-Boss there is Nothing. In the rooms on either side of the hall, no desks, no carpet, no blinds, no lights. In the rooms on either side of the hall are tiny, tiny tape players, dumped on the floor. On one of them, I press 'play'.

People typing. *Clittaclattaclittaclatta.*

The Boss's office is smaller than I remember.

The electric fire is gone. The desk is gone. The chair, the chair I sat on, you've got to laugh, that's still there.

'Bugger,' I say, ever-ever-ever-so-quietly.

On the way home, in the *Metro*, there is a photo of me.

For the record, I don't know for sure that I have post-traumatic stress disorder. I'm just saying, is all. I'm just making a point. I'm just suggesting, ohoyes, that it's *plausible*, it's sort of possible, that I'm fucked up in all kinds of interesting ways.

For the record, when you can't even trust your own brain, when you can't even trust what's real and what's not, when you have no sodding *clue* what's going on half the time, being a wanted criminal with nowhere to hide is sort of shitty.

I need Sally.

I need to wake up.

I need to get my head together and work this out.

I need another pill.

Contact 25 (no contact)

DAY: Saturday.

TIME: 10 p.m. approx.

LOCATION: On tube. Going home (suppose). Currently: Circle Line. Would go round & round all night – if could. (Hard to write here – shaky rails, pen slipping. Can't be bothered to hold tighter.)

CONTACT REASON: No reason. No contact. Just . . . saw him. Sheer chance. Saw him. Still alive, still free – but looks dead. Looks how I feel.
    (Self-pity now, Sally? Stupid. Get grip! All over with. Got what you wanted, all worked out. Why aren't you relieved?)

No point. All over now. This = footnote. Not worth reading. Not worth writing.

NOTES: 7.30ish, earlier, sitting @ home watching film. Trying to get lost in it – 'borrowed wisdom' (borrowed life) – not working. Too distracted. Still thinking bout last Thursday, down into warehouse basement, finding –

CONTRACT

Not here. Can't bring myself to remember it, not for here.

Anyway. Film pissed me off, went out, couldn't be inside, sit still, no. Fidgeting, scratching, stifled. Out into streets, already dark (winter?). Just walked, not looking. People = blur. Tramps, tourists, etc. etc. Feet still hurt, walked too far. On to tube (did I? – don't remember getting on, getting off. Must've used Oyster card, no ticket in purse). Sat thinking, like now.

Eventually – outside Ariadne's Café. Don't remember walking there. Feet on autopilot, standing outside door ready to go in, and BANG. Eye contact. Michael = inside, staring through glass door. Eyes dead. New haircut, AIDS victim: pale, scrawny, sunken eyes. Looking right @ me. Just froze there, trying not to sob, hand on handle. Must've been there 2 minutes.

Except something not right – realised eventually café well lit inside, total dark outside: M not staring at me at all, not even see me. Looking @ himself in reflection. Horrified by what he saw.

I ran. Broke both shoes, now barefoot on tube, round and round Circle Line, just thinking.

Wondering @ diary, mostly. Why bother? Something to do with keeping a record. History of crimes? Hard copy – like arsonist filming fire.

Somewhere (haven't visited her yet, don't dare, haven't courage), she's awake. Daniel called to tell me this morning. Whole world changed. She's AWAKE. Always been goal, aim, fucking deal we made. Realised now this diary = record for her, my little angel. Show her when she's older. Let her judge me. Ask her: for the best? Things I did, ways I did them. Price worth paying?

Ask her: do you hate me now?

One last secret, then. Final diary entry. Need to paint a full picture for her – no half-measures: got to expose everything. Lay it all down.

Been meeting M's father every second Friday. He's dead now – was in papers last week. Belmarsh prison. Went every fortnight, avoid overlaps w/ Michael (know he goes every <u>other</u> week, visitation order stops awkward meetings, clever system – never guessed his dad had another friend). Found out about him (about where he <u>is</u>) from M during Contact 1: stoned, gabbling away, surrendering secrets. Mentioned Dad, Mum, 'shower' incident. Never remembered what he told me that time.

Old man: visited him because I was told to – did <u>everything</u> because <u>told to</u>. All part of the plan. Made him keep it secret, lied & cheated & confused him. All Daniel's plan. All of it: once husband, now controller. Can't even think of him as human any more. Just shit. Helped me get what I wanted – wanted the same! – but a shit.

M's dad: told him I = psychiatrist, helping son beat childhood trauma. Told him M less & less stable: false identities, bipolarity, disassociation, bullshit phrases to get sympathy. Did it well. Playing w/ old man's fears. Last chance to help son he hardly knows. <u>Of course</u> took it.

Told him wanted to find out about M's past, childhood, etc. – stuff never tells me <u>himself</u>. Told him: give me an insight into Michael = able to <u>help</u> him. Old man described <u>everything</u>. Doing it for months.

CONTRACT

Know M better than he knows himself, maybe. Funny: felt closer to him chatting to his dad, than fucking him in B & B room. Pitiful.

Both of us.

THOUGHTS/CONCLUSIONS/OTHER: She's awake, my angel = all that matters. Saved the boy too, boy from basement; didn't even expect him to be there. All positive, everything better. Even M survived, never expected.

But feel dead anyway. Feel like haven't won anything.

M = destroyed. Daniel's fault, know that, but –

Anyway. Diary not for judging. Diary just for You, my angel, my sleeping beauty. Wait for you to grow up. Show you. Decide how much you hate me then, for the things I did. The price I paid to wake you.

S

Chapter Nineteen

This is freefall. This is plummeting out of control while sitting still.

It would be useful if I knew what I was about to land on.

If you want to know, my reflection looks like shit. He looks like shit covered in flies, left overnight to fester, then scraped at 9.30 a.m. down a pavement by the heel of a £100-pair of trainers. He looks at me from his windowpane with this whole 'accusation' thing in his eyes, and even maybe a sliver of contempt, and the tragedy is I can't say I blame him.

He looks rough. He looks stupid and rough and empty, like a hobo under a flyover waiting to be boozed to death. He looks like a guy who shouldn't start reading any long novels. He's had a haircut since last time I saw him.

If you can call it that.

Tonight Ariadne's Café is the perfect venue for my tumbling, flailing, screaming clothes flapping eyes watering lips peeled bladder-emptying fists clenching descent towards . . .

Whatever.

Tonight I don't know where I'm falling from or to, but that's not the point, is it? Tonight all the assiduousness and anal retention in the world is a joke, and I am, I believe, slowly now, crumbling apart.

CONTRACT

Tonight Ariadne's Café is a fine place for falling down.

This place, if it was anywhere else, the layer of saturated fats and syrupy discharges that smear every surface, like petrol on a puddle, would be a source of affectionate amusement amongst the customers.

All the customers in Ariadne's are falling down like me.

Anywhere else, there's a running joke about how many years the tea's been stewing, how the eggs are fried so long that you could use them as frisbees. Anywhere else, being rude is All Part of the Experience. Not here.

Here, all the customers are empty midnight grease-guzzlers. See here spotty goons, see guys with beards clogged with last week's food, see cheap leather jackets and crumpled *Racing Post* junkies hunched over two-hour teas. See here greasy stains and cholesterol crimes and cutlery like lard-dispensers and gammy ketchup bottle tops. See me with my coffee (breaking the surface-skin before slurping) half listening to fat obnoxious people talking fat obnoxious things, staring at my skinheaded self in the mosquito-eye window, squinting past condensing sweat and thinking only: *Why here?*

It reminds me of Sally, I guess.

See greasy smears on patchy glass like oil spills at sea, cluttering my view of the outside world.

For the record, the best material for stopping an oil spill from spreading – a real one, I mean – is human hair. Bags and bags and bags of it, dumped in a ring round the slick.

The reason that no one in Ariadne's complains or makes jokes or even scowls at those hair-in-burger, grease-fountain-from-egg, mashed-up-cow-lips-in-sausage moments, those awkward little instants when you realise, ohofuckyes, exactly what it is you're *eating*, is this: Ariadne gets *difficult*.

Hair salons, those drifts of blond-black-brown-ginger on the floor, those cast-off mountains being churned together and swept up by the speccy acne monster who maybe cut off someone's ear and isn't allowed near scissors, that stuff could be saving lives. My hair, freshly sliced off my head this evening, bobbing in the surf.

Tonight, for the record, I am feeling sorry for myself. I keep telling myself I'm *allowed* to. This is bollocks.

Tonight, for the record, I am on pills and pills and pills, and I have not had a religious experience in the last week, or even an hallucination, and reality has begun to look more real. When I can stay focused on it, I mean. When I'm not rambling about Random Shit, I mean. When I can even form words, I mean.

Experiencing reality in a real sort of way would be OK, ohoyes, if it didn't also look so fucking nasty.

I was sick. Now I'm better.

Ahahahaha.

Oil spills. This is a tangent. Bear with me.

Oil spills. Murderous wildlife-killers. See here the sweet, innocent, naïve, unsentient beneficiaries of my shorn-off hair. See black oystercatchers (*Haematopus bachmani*), pigeon guillemots (*Cepphus columba*), mussels (*Mytilus edulis*), harlequin ducks (*Histrionicus histrionicus*), common loons (*Gavia immer*), common murres (*Uria aalge*), cormorants (*Phalacrocorax*), marbled murrelets (*Brachyramphus marmoratus marmoratus*), cut-throat trout (*Oncorhynchus clarkii*), Dolly Varden trout (*Salvelinus malma*), harbour seals (*Phoca vitulina*), Kittlitz's murrelets (*Brachyramphus brevirostris*), killer whales (*Orcinus orca*),

CONTRACT

Pacific herring (*Clupea harengus*), river otters (*Lutra canadensis*), sea otters (*Enhydra lutris*), pink salmon (*Oncorhynchus gorbuscha*), rockfish (*Sebastes sp.*) and sockeye salmon (*Oncorhynchus nerka*).

All of them choking, retching, drowning, freezing, shivering, gagging, flapping, coated in oil, for want of the little guilty heap you made during your £7.50 grade-two-all-over.

Even oil started out as fossilised life.

Tonight, with reality coming back slowly-slowly, what I'm realising is: GAME OVER.

What I'm realising is: Time to go.

Tonight, I'm fiddling with the piece of paper in my pocket.

Listen. This place, the sign above the door says CAFÉ.

Ariadne behind the counter, she loses her temper whenever she hears the word 'Caff'. She says her husband was careful, meticulous, scrupulous, about getting that little accent above the 'E' from his cousin who made the sign. Then she goes and has a cry, and blows her nose like this: *Shkroooooooooom*, with a *Chfk-chfk* at the end, like an afterthought.

Then with the dabbing.

Ariadne behind the counter, she flies off the handle when people make jokes about hygiene. She sometimes throws a skillet-spatula. She sometimes shouts in Greek, then bursts into tears and leaves the guy who does the dishes to serve while she goes for a fag out the back.

The regulars learned to be nice about the place.

In Ariadne's café, a lot of guys talk to each other. This is top-volume, cigarette-smoke-spillages, forced laughter, comparing tips on the 10.20 turf. This is a background hubbub, a general crowd murmur, a *rhubarb rhubarb rhubarb* crumble.

The thing is, despite that, in Ariadne's Café, *everyone* is alone.

When I used to come here with Sally, we were the only ones listening to each other.

I noticed. I watch. I see stuff like that. Everyone else: talking without listening.

Sally.

Sally, please.

Where *are* you?

Ariadne behind the counter, she's maybe fifty, maybe sixty. She's a Cypriot with skin like an elephant, and she swears it's the Mediterranean Sun that gives her such a youthful complexion.

Also, skin cancer.

Also, poor circulation.

Also, tyrannical delusions of power.

The rumour goes, her husband died of a massive myocardial infarction. The rumour goes, he was laughing so hard at some punter, some twat complaining at having to wring out his fried-slice, that he suffered a fatal heart attack and croaked then and there, face-down on the griddle.

Tsssss

The rumour is, she keeps a sharpened sausage-pricker by the till for the next guy who makes a joke about arterio-sclerosis.

This is London, and every poky, shitty little place has a story.

The piece of paper in my pocket is folded six times and

sealed with sellotape. I know what's written on it like I know my own name and my own face.

When I'm using them, I mean.

My name: these days, it's sort of variable.

My face: these days, it comes with glasses, beards, moustaches, piercings, As Standard.

The thing with falling down, with spinning and stomach-lurching and wind roaring and you get the idea, the thing with being beyond control, beyond salvation, beyond any fucking thing except terminal velocity and the promise of a *splat*, the thing is, sooner or later, you just stop being . . . *you*.

You become just a tumbling object. Mannequin-soft. Boneless, futureless, unworthy of thought. A solidified shit frozen at 30,000 feet, jettisoned from a passing Boeing.

Today on the tube the caption under the picture in the *Metro* said *Michael Point*, twenty-eight, *sought by police*. Today on the tube I stared at myself from a monochrome page, and this thing with me sitting here now, staring at my own reflection: this is getting old, fast.

My name is not Michael Point. Not any more.

Pay attention: there comes a time, if you want to know, when you just give in. There comes a time when you've got to Make the Most, Cut Your Losses, Get Out. There comes a time when you say: Enough's enough.

What I'm getting at is: the Plan. The money, the flight, the fake passport. The magic number, with a bunch of zeroes and a pound sign. All of this, I've prepared for. White beaches, bikinis, topless sunbathing, sleeveless T-shirts, fishing in the surf, watching sunsets, being eaten alive by mosquitoes, drinking sweet things with strange names, living, living, living. What I'm getting at is: *rescue me from this tumbling nothing*.

What I'm getting at is: the Boss has gone. My life – ahahaha, call it what you want – is done. My routine's an O.D. victim in the corner, my sense of perspective has been garrotted, my nerves are marmalised and The Whole Thing is Fucked.

Sally's not coming back, is she?

So.

The thing is, this job, all you need is assiduousness and anal retention.

In Ariadne's Café, at the back, in the corner, is a computer you can use to access the Internet for £3 per hour. That's expensive. Ariadne knows me well enough to let me use it for free, and the other customers stare and mutter all the way through.

I tell her: 'Thank you.'

She smiles and touches my shoulder and says: 'Whensa nice girl come back, heh?' and she makes 'curly hair' signs next to her head, and she's saying: Sally.

I tell her Soon and I do not vomit.

The computer, there's so much grease on the monitor I have to rub it with a napkin to see anything. For a minute I forget why I'm doing this at all, and I wonder idly what websites I should visit. www.getmethefuckawayfromthis flamingcorpseofanexistence.com, maybe.

But no. I'm here to Bank. Here to move digital-pretend-shared-illusion money from place to place, to check there's enough, to stay On Top. I'm here to feed hungry offshore reservoirs, bolster tax-haven windfalls, make sure they're safe and stocked and robust. I have prepared for all this. I have been ready for the axe to fall.

This trade, the thing is, nobody ever got caught being *too* prepared.

The computer, I hit the numbers. I enter the memorable info, the password, the mother's maiden name, blah blah. I wait.

The statement arrives on-screen and there's too much grease to be sure but . . .

Oh. Oh, that sinking feeling.

Here's me scraping the monitor clean with the edge of a knife, just to be certain.

Here's me staring at the ACCOUNT TOTAL section.

Here's a 0.

And another.

And another.

Listen.

Someone has stolen from me.

Someone has broken into my digital vault and cleared it out.

Who?

How?

It's

All

About

The

Money.

Here's the thing: you can't Just Walk Away, ladies and gentlemen, when there's nowhere to walk to. Falling, falling, falling.

Chapter Twenty

In a car park, there's *drag*. Like inertia for the brain.

In a car park, which the Americans call a Parking Lot, which in movies are always bigger, are always better, are always more *exciting-looking* than the ones we get here, in a car park, stuff goes slow. Car parks are all about waiting. Car parks are concrete versions of life-put-on-pause. Car parks are prisons for machines.

Listen: this has gone on too long. This whole thing. This tumbling, crashing fall. This no-life. This post-climactic fog. This *Me*.

Something has to happen soon.

I've realised, y'see. I've realised that I am waiting, waiting, waiting – only I don't know what for. I'm a lobster in a restaurant aquarium. I'm adrift in a fucking spacesuit, only here's the thing: I can't see the oxygen dial. I can't tell how much longer I've got. I can't tell where I am or what time it is or, or, or –

You get the idea.

This is rock-bottom, and, despite what you may have heard,

It

Is

BORING.

CONTRACT

Today is Tuesday. *A* Tuesday, anyway. Today is my father's funeral, and today is when I sit wearing raggedy clothes in a rental car I got with the last of my cash, in the car park of a church, opposite a falafel place and a Pound Stretcher.

Today is when the solid bits of my old man that weren't taken by the donor-service, medical students, morticians, embalmers, etc. etc., will be placed in a hole and covered over with earth. Today is when a small group of people I don't know – prison mates, guards, *whoever* – are standing right now inside a poky chapel singing hymns he never knew and praying prayers he never believed, next to a box full of Him.

Today is when I can't go inside, and not just because there are cops in there too.

Today the lethargy has got me, and nothing is worth anything.

Today there are cops watching, waiting. Today they know this old man, this dead guy, this cold corpse, his son is a Known Criminal. Today they figure, hey, there's a good chance he'll show. Today I'm slinking low in the seat of my car, with hoodie, beard, glasses, mole, birthmark, and any other damn thing I can think of.

Listen: I once shot a woman so close to the back of her head her right eyeball left its socket. Her hair caught on fire.

Once, this guy in Scotland puked on me right before I blew his face open. I had to put down plastic bags in the car and burn my clothes.

I once cut a student's throat while he slept, slumped in his chair and surrounded by computer screens.

Today I sit in a car and everything is grey.

Let me tell you: I know the best places to shoot, stab,

punch, kick someone to disarm, disable, damage, destroy. I know that if you want to sever a jugular vein you don't slice across the front, but punch the knife through the side and saw your way forwards. I know the best places to buy unlicensed handguns and illegal bullets. I know the best places to get false I.D. at forty-eight, twenty-four, twelve hours' notice. I know how to dispose of a body, if I have to, so all the fingerprints, dental records, identifying features in the world won't do a dribbling prick's worth of good. I know how to cut and hide a body so it'll never be found, with bleach or lime or fish or seagulls. I know pigs will happily eat bones, muscles, flesh, eyeballs, joints, teeth and fingers, but won't guzzle long hair or clothing if their lives depend on it. I know how to kill someone as quickly, as quietly, as anonymously as possible.

But I do not know what to do today.

I'm not quick, I'm not smart. I don't have . . . I don't have *ideas*. I don't have *new* things in my head. I'm being dragged along by a rope, still hooked up to the wreck of my old life, and the knot's too complicated to pick. I'm whingeing endlessly inside my head. I'm feeling sorry for myself. I am Boned.

Borrowed wisdom won't help. Not any more. Assiduousness and anal retention won't help, not today, not now. See also: a certain moral lassitude.

Today I'm sitting watching the church entrance, waiting for them all to come filing out on to the grass for the committal, when the door of the car opens and there's Wilson, getting in, sitting down, sucking on a mint humbug.

Wilson, my once-upon-a-time-information-broker.

Wilson, with his little head polished black like a swimming cap, with his bright eyes and his white teeth, and his smart little clothes.

'Wilson,' I say.

'Huhm,' he says, and sucks his mint. He glances round in case anyone's watching.

The thing is, being seen here today, now, with me, here today, now, in this car, that wouldn't do him much good at all.

Wilson, being here today, he's taking a big risk.

We watch the church.

Eventually, they come out. 'They' is just people.

There are:

> *Four men in black, carrying a nondescript coffin. Professional mourners. Paid-to-be-sad*
> *Two men in cheap suits, staring at the sky. Inmate-pals. Day release. Freed by misery*
> *Four prison guards*
> *Two uniformed cops*
> *One man in a black jacket with small glasses and scruffy black hair. There is a large white patch down the left side. He looks lost*
> *One tall man with floppy blond hair*
> *One tall woman with pale skin and long dark hair. She looks like ice*
> *One chief mourner*
> *One vicar*

I recognise exactly none of them. I watch them head towards the graveyard. The cops standing out the front, their eyes follow the coffin past, like they're expecting a surprise, like they're tensed and ready.

'Wilson,' I say. I am empty. I am hollow. I am too tired to be interested in anything. I am drugged out of my skull. I have no money left. 'Why you here, Wilson?'

'Payin' respects,' he says, shrug-smile-shrug. He watches the mourners shuffle.

'But . . . You didn't know him.'

'Don' mean t'*him*.'

Oh.

'Oh.'

Far away, the mourners place the coffin on its straps and start lowering. I wonder if anyone ever dropped a corner halfway through. Flipped-over box, pedal-bin lid spilling, body tumbling, crack snap scrittle.

The grass of the graveyard wobbles in my head. I close my eyes and breathe.

Not now. I'm through with all that.

'You stayin' 'live?' says Wilson. He's looking at me. He has no paper in his hand, no scraps of notepad passing back and forth, no tension. He's here to see *me*.

This is nearly concern. Today, of all days, this is nearly paternal.

'Staying alive,' I say, just. For some reason I can't talk. For some reason there's a choke-thing in my throat and my eyes hurt. 'Thanks, Wilson,' I croak.

He nods.

'Boy,' he says, taking a packet of peppermints out of his pocket and passing me one. 'Who you bin workin' for, boy?'

I look away.

'Y'in all the pia-per,' he says.

He unwraps his peppermint and tucks it into his mouth, pocketing the cellophane with a crackle. Like a cigarette burning down. Like a stiff old body tumbling out of its coffin. Like a smarmy man laughing through his teeth.

The peppermint smells good. I stare at the black-white-black stripes on mine and try to hear the vicar's voice through the window.

. . . therefore, commit his body to . . .

'I don 'ear 'bout it, boy,' Wilson says. 'See, I' – he taps his chest, balling the mint into one cheek – 'I 'ear 'bout *everytin*.'

I nod. 'But not this?'

'Not this.'

He looks put out. I almost want to laugh.

. . . to ashes, dust to . . .

I tell Wilson I don't have any answers. I tell him, probably I was used. I tell him: maybe *he* was too. I tell him, that first job in Bracknell, remember that, that was when it started.

He says, 'The whun you was sayin' was . . . "messy"?'

The way he says this, it's music.

I smile and tell him, yeah. Yeah, that one.

I tell him, since then, think of it as *pro bono* work.

The grass wobbles again, out by the grave. The sky pulses red, then settles. The church bulges. Ugly things, unreal things, unnatural things, trying to come through. I breathe.

I cling to the one and only thing I have left.

'I was on the right side,' I say.

Wilson frowns.

I says, 'I'm pretty sure, anyway.'

. . . the sure and certain hope of the resurrection to Eternal Life . . .

Wilson says: 'Side?'

Wilson says: 'What side, boy? Huhm?'

Wilson says: 'No *sides*. Hah. No. All 'bout the money. I no' teachyuh that, boy?'

I tell him: 'Yeah. Yeah, you taught me that.'

We sit in silence.

Far away, people are paid money to throw mud into a hole.

Pay attention to me, you. You reading this now. You with your confusions. I am a ghost trapped in cogs of morality. I'm . . . I'm a wisp of gas trying to pull levers.

For the record, outside the car, the sky tears open. Fire dribbles out. It lasts just a second. Music, angels. Ha, a Choir.

Leave me alone.

I am a bloke, is all. I'm not quick, I'm not smart. I spent my life trying to get out of . . . of morals and rights and wrongs and those *stupid stupid* fucking simplicities all you empty zombies think really exist. I just *did* stuff, cos nobody else wanted to. Not because of . . . of having any guts, not because anything except *if they won't, I will.*

I got by and got paid and got laid and: it worked.

Guilt? I've lived with guilt. I've buried guilt. I've told myself, oh God, over and over: *it's just a chemical reaction.* Push it away. Swallow it down. It's artificial.

But it's not. I'm here to tell you. It's not, and when the hope comes along you've been doing something *right* all along, you've been working for a noble cause, then LISTEN: all that philosophising bullshit, all that self-righteous amorality, all that certainty, *bang*. Right out the window.

Everyone wants to feel they're doing the right thing.

Everyone wants to exorcise their guilt. That's if they know it or not. If they believe it or not. Welcome to Religion.

I'm exhausted. I'm on drugs. I'm rambling.

Bear with me here.

The mourners leave the grave. The man in the black jacket with the white streak in his hair stays longest. He's not important. He's just somebody Dad used to know, I guess, some random. I wait and wait – it's all I ever do, all I ever did.

The cops stand out the front of the church and stare at their watches.

The graveyard is quiet.

Far away, my dad lies in a box. This box, it's in a hole made of mud. My dad murdered my mum and swore he didn't. He cut her up with a Sabatier kitchen knife in the shower one day after a row over whether or not I should go to church. He said he didn't. He sobbed and begged, then went quiet, and just sulked with his life on pause.

Outside the car, the world shivers.

My dad, a week or two ago, I told him I wasn't coming back, wasn't going to visit any more, and he opened his veins. He might as well have just written a motherfucking confession.

In the car, I want to go over to the grave. I want to stand next to my father.

The cops stare and stare and stare, and wait for a Wanted Man.

In the car, I sigh, and maybe I've forgotten Wilson's here or maybe I haven't. Maybe it's important this is heard.

'There was a little boy,' I say, and this is the only eulogy I can think of. 'He was told . . . praying to God could make miracles happen. He was told God could do anything, and he loved people, and he'd give all sorts of . . . of happiness, and all that, to anyone who loved him back. To anyone who prays.'

The sky splits again above the car. Dead babies tug at my feet, where there should be pedals. I ignore them. I ignore Wilson, watching me. I ignore everything.

Now's not the time.

'So this boy, he's a good lad. He takes it on board and when his birthday comes round, seven – maybe eight – he prays to God *really fucking hard*, all night long, he'll get a radio-controlled car for a present the next morning.

'So the morning comes and he's knackered from not sleeping for all the praying, and he opens his presents and there's no car there.'

I cough. Above me angels wrestle demons amidst seas of flame and light, and their blood splatters the graves and awakes hissing corpses. Snakes with too many heads, lambs and lions and eagles and you get the idea. I ignore it all. Now's not the time.

'Come Christmas,' I say, 'this little boy tries again. Prays *so* hard to God for a toy car. Prays like he's never prayed before. See, he *really* believes. It's what he's been told by his mum, all these years; bedtime tales and whispers and that. God's good. God'll give him what he needs. God makes people feel *happy*.

'There's no radio-controlled car in his Christmas stash either.'

The earth quakes under my feet. Far away a guy is starting the engine of a miniature digger to come fill the hole. In my head it's a yellow-pistoned dragon, scales coiled about legions of archangels, roasting them with pilot-light fires.

So far, so B-movie.

I ignore it.

Now's not the time.

Wilson sucks his peppermint and says nothing.

'Anyway,' I say. 'This happens over and over. And every time this little boy's disappointed. God just won't give him the stuff he wants. So one night he complains to his mum. She listens, all seriously, and nods once or twice – Christ, she was beautiful, his mum – and then she tells him: "That's not how it works. God won't give you *things*. God won't give you *materials*." She says, "That's all just *stuff*. That's not important."

'So the little boy feels stupid, and he asks: "Well . . . what *does* God give you?" Cos this lad, he's not smart or quick, and he doesn't get it.

'His mum says: "*You know*. Love. Happiness, security, protection, forgiveness . . ." And he sleeps well, that night.'

I shift my feet.

'So the next day he goes out and nicks a toy car from the shops, and prays to be forgiven.'

Next to me, Wilson 'hems' under his breath. Funny story. Good joke. Har-de-fucking-har.

The grave, far away, it's turned into a fiery mouth, and a tongue made of mud is tasting the coffin. I breathe, *breathe*, and ignore it. Now is not the time.

'Anyway,' I say. 'That's how it starts. And maybe somewhere along the way the little boy realises he can get away with anything, like that. Maybe one day he forgets to even bother with the pray-for-forgiveness bit. Or maybe he just figures it's not worth worrying about.'

I close my eyes and make the visions go away. Let the drug-haze take over. I open them and stare out across the graves, across the grass, through the windscreen, past the bored cops and the cold driver of the digger.

It scoops mud and farts smoke.

'Sleep well, you old bastard,' I say.

The ground shifts beneath the car, and I ignore it all.

Sooner or later, in the car, Wilson sucks his sweet and says, 'Time ahwus aweh.'

Before he leaves, with me still flailing, with me trying to recoup, trying to *salvage*, what I say to him with my voice all cracked and stupid is: 'Hey, Wilson . . .'

He leans back into the car.

'Is there any . . . Is there work going?'

He just smiles.

I am falling, falling, falling. I am waiting.

Sooner or later, it gets dark.

Sooner or later the cops finish their shifts and wander off, muttering, and *that sick bastard; didn't even come to his old man's funeral* . . .

Sooner or later, in the cold air, between the car and the empty little church, the carpark splits and heaves, and sulphur spews out, and bats and clawed things and rats and blah blah blah. I ignore it. I make it stop.

I am on drugs. I am a stronger human being now. I walk past it all.

In the church, which is empty, which has no saints staring down and no little vicars waiting to die, I sit on a pew and think.

CONTRACT

And I am crying. And my lungs hurt. And my ribs ache. And the tears keep coming, until I'm making dry-paper noises, walrus-calls, snotting and helpless.

And still nothing happens.

I am waiting for a branch to break beneath me.

Interview Room 2

'It was you two,' I say.

They just stare.

'It was, wasn't it?'

Here, now, cold. Back in this echo-womb. Back in this no-camera, no-mirror magnolia pit. Back where pinstripe bastards watch and little ice-maiden Anna smokes, smokes, smokes. Clouds like veils, eyes like snowstorms.

Here, the door (which is an exit, which is also an entrance, which is the door I used to come in, which should *not* be moving) is currently on the left of the room. A moment or two ago I swear it was on the right.

Maybe it's switching sides. Maybe there are two doors, only one's always invisible.

Maybe my brain's rotten.

A door is a symbol meaning: Escape.

Also: Welcome.

Also: Trapped.

Show a door to a caveman, what does it mean?

Show a swastika to a Tudor, what does it mean?

Show a Holy Child to the masses, etc. etc. etc. . . . .

Here, I'm back with a table and three chairs and three people and breeze-blocks and a long, long, shifting, ugly, embarrassed silence.

'At the funeral,' I say, 'I thought I recognised you from somewhere.'

Jason nods. He sits with his fingers steepled and one curtain of his floppy hair hanging over his face. He sits with his chin on his chest. Like he's trying to look serious. Like he's trying to look professional.

Like he's a pompous idiot.

'Why?' I say.

Jason shrugs. 'We . . . dealt with your father's case.'

He flicks a glance at Anna. She's looking at me.

He says, 'And we thought you might show.'

Anna just stares and just smokes and just makes me think dirty thoughts. Her lips have a twinkle – not gloss, not spit, just . . . a *sheen* – and I'm seeing Deep Throat specials, gag-reflex inhibitors, ball-nibblers, glans-lickers, Cum On My Face fun for the whole family. I'm not proud.

'Should've looked harder,' I say. 'I was inside a long time.'

Jason says: 'Sitting in the church?'

'Yeah. Yeah, just sitting.'

The door switches sides. This is very annoying.

Jason says, 'And?'

I tell him, 'And nothing.'

I tell him, '*And* I was just thinking. Not like I was in a rush. Not like I had much else to do.'

'Thinking about what?' says Anna, and it hits me then, she's been leading me. It hits me she *knows* what she wants me to say and she's herding, poking.

'Life,' I say, and I look her in the eye.

And this time I don't look away, because this is *important*. This is down at the base of it all. She sucks on the fag and maybe smoke's in her eye, because she blinks too fast and looks away, and maybe – *maybe* – that's One Last Point to me. 3-1 on aggregate.

'Had to work it out,' I say. 'Nothing left to do, was there? You get . . . you get all this proactive shit out your system, eventually you got just yourself. Just your brain. Just a fuckload of stuff you don't understand and all the time in the world to work it out.'

'And?' Anna again, rallying. I don't care, now.

'And I had to see. About whether I'm . . . on some stupid mission. Or just diseased, mental, whatever. Or maybe cursed. Maybe I'm in a . . . a fucking Virtual Reality prison. Maybe it's all a big dream in the brain of a marmoset in London Zoo. Maybe I have an imagination parasite.'

Jason smirks. 'You *did* say you were taking pills?'

'Ha. Yeah.'

Anna, serious, not smiling, not playing. Anna, listening like this *matters*.

'And what conclusions did you draw, Michael?'

I sit back.

I work my tongue. I phrase it.

'I decided . . .'

They watch. Spellbound. Maybe. Sitting just a fraction forward.

'I decided whatever it is, whatever's been . . . causing all this . . .'

'Yes?'

'It doesn't matter.'

They blink.

Jason says: Uh.

I say: *Look*.

You see. You hear, you smell. You get all this shit

happening to you. It's all you can be *sure* of.

I say: How do I know we all see the same colour when I say 'blue'?

I say: How do I know we all taste strawberry the same?

I say: Your . . . your *perceptions*. That's all you've got. And you're on your own with them.

Jason says: 'I don't see h—'

I tell him to shut the bollocks up. I tell him, I'm not finished.

I tell him, at the end of the day, *mate*, it doesn't matter if I'm cerebrally diseased. Doesn't matter if I've been selected from on-high to persecute heretics and followers of the Great Beast. It doesn't matter *why* I see what I see.

I tell him: What's 'real' anyway?

The door switches sides again.

Anna says: 'Michael. Stop a mome—'

I tell her: So all you can do is the Best You Can.

I tell her: I worked out what I'd done. I looked hard, you know? I wanted to . . . point to places in my life and say, *look, see, here*.

Here I did something good. *Indisputably*.

Not because I was told to. Not because I wanted a reward.

Just *because*.

I tell them both: I raked up the debris left over from being me, and went through it looking for anything shiny.

Anna blinks more.

Jason sits back in his chair, frowning.

Anna says: 'And . . . and did you find any?'

I say: 'Just the one thing.'

Chapter Twenty-one

In the end, what it comes down to is just a kid. In the end, it's a freaked-out little boy who saw shit he shouldn't, whose eyes bulged and filled up with fear, and listen: there's something . . . I don't know . . . something *right* about that, maybe.

Sort of like it was inevitable.

Given where this mess started, I mean. With a boy, and a bathroom, and red tiles and et cetera et cetera.

Swings-and-roundabouts, full-circle, back-to-the-start. Get home before the sun comes up.

Snail life.

Maybe I'm just looking for patterns.

In the end, what it comes down to is a man hammering on the door of my motel room saying my fake credit card just chimed out and Sir, You're Going to Have to Leave. In the end, it's me on my last sertraline-fluoxetine fistful of pills, imagining Aztec gods dragging branches through my veins, lying wet and cold on the bed. In the end, it's me reading the copy of the *Metro*, soggy from drizzle, I picked up at the tube stop at first light, and wondering where to go next, and two stories side-by-side that look unconnected.

This is a mirror for newsworthy human beings. This is seeing yourself out of context. This is the *Metro* saying:

> *. . . ntinue to seek him. Point, twenty-eight, dubbed 'The Smack Killer' by the tabloid press for his alleged use of heroin as a poison, has been connected to approxima . . .*

This is a story all about me. This is my face, still staring, still expressionless, still hollow, hollow, hollow. This is time tick-tock-tick-tock-tick-tocking out. This is me still waiting, still falling, but confident now. Something is coming. An end.

One way or another.

The second story is more important.

> *. . . ose real name remains unknown, was found wandering in East London on the 24th of last month. He has since been transferred to a specialist trauma facility in North London, where a spokesman described his condition as 'stable'. The same spokesman speculated that the youth had experienced 'extreme psychological trauma', and repeated the clinic's plea for the child's parents to make themselves kno . . .*

A mystery, this. The sort of thing Joe Average could get his teeth into, could worry at and discuss round the water cooler, over papers and coffees and doughnuts. Something to mutter about.

This is a story all about a little boy I saved.

You hear me?

Are you *listening*?

I *saved* him. I got him out. I *rescued* him.

These two stories, you'd have to be insane to connect them together.

The man at the door hammers harder. I stare at the

photo in the paper below the article – redbrick and blue signs; a private clinic in North London – and I think, think, think.

It looks sort of familiar.

In the end I'm an artist in love with my own canvas. I'm an arsonist hungry to watch the fire flicker. I'm the man who gives to charity then wants a badge to show off. I'm the snail who lives at night, but always, always, always knows where salvation lies.

In case the sun comes. In case the booted foot falls. I'm dying. I can feel it.

My soul's sick and I don't know what's happening, but I know time's running out.

Let me tell you: in the end I need to see him. I need to see the boy I saved. It's all about the money, and I have none left. J.W.A., until there's nowhere left to walk. Assiduousness and anal retention, until there's *no point*. All my little getting-to-know-yous, all my little platitudes, all my little rules, all my little catchphrases: unravelling at my feet.

Today is . . . just some day.

Today is later than it was before, today is when I've left the motel, today is when it's still wet and cold, and today is when *this is the end*.

Today I'm a stop-you-in-the-street merchant with a clipboard, waiting to survey likely looking people. This means I get avoided like the plague. This works well, unless an Old Person wants to chat.

This hasn't happened yet.

Today I stand in a doorway just off a main road in

Islington, which is North London, which is N1, which is expensive and well-to-do and riddled with crackhouses and upper-middle-class-keep-your-perversions-in-the-cupboard Johnny Everyone.

Today I am wearing: whatever I was wearing yesterday. See also: the day before. Et cetera et cetera.

In Islington, a lot of the kerbs are much higher than usual. This is because Islington used to be a little village outside the city where cattle were kept overnight and the roads were always full of –

Wait. Borrowed Wisdom. Who gives a fuck? Seriously?

Today behind me is the TADC, which is the Trauma & Anxiety Disorder Clinic, which was in the picture in the *Metro*, which is a Private Healthcare facility only nominally affiliated with the NHS. This place, it's the primary centre of excellence for treating brain-strain amongst children and adults.

Today a middle-aged woman looks tired and irritable as she walks out the door, and I'm on her like a vampire before she's even blinked.

In Islington, round the corner, is a pub, The Old Red Lion. In this pub the regulars have included V.I. Lenin, Charles Dickens and . . . and who honestly *cares*?

In this pub a part of *Rights of Man* was written by Tom Paine, which forms the basis of the constitutions of France and America, where everything is bigger and . . . and blah, blah, blah.

Borrowed fucking boredom.

This woman, scowling, hurrying on her way, I tell her: Excuse me, luv, have you got a minute? I brandish the clipboard.

She starts to say, 'Actually, I'm in a bit a hu—' but this is OK, this is not a problem, because already I'm interrupting.

I say: It's about the level of care at the clinic. I say: I'm working for the Standards Bureau, that's all. We just like to make sure the customers are satisfied.

She looks at me. She blinks. Stops. Reassesses. She has Things to get off her chest.

There is no such thing as The Standards Bureau.

Private Health is a More Expensive Alternative to using the National Health Service. The National Health Service is a free Welfare State system designed to give everyone free and easy access to medicine, surgery and treatment. This is just in case you didn't know. This is just in case you've never needed it.

This is just in case you've never been in one of those out-of-the-way wards, up on the top floor of NHS hospitals. The ones with the easywipe wallpaper and the chrysanthemum-print curtains that never *quite* cover over the stuff you don't want to see.

Bedbaths. Colostomy bags. AIDS zombies. Stomach-injected meds.

The thing is, the NHS, depending on who you ask, it's not the quickest. It's not the best.

This woman, 'Well,' she says. 'Well, OK. But make it fast.'

I ask her if she's been visiting a relative today.

It's her husband, she says, and I say *of course, of course, of course*.

'Nervous breakdown,' she says, like it's a dirty admission, like he was caught wanking on rabbits in a petting zoo. I ask her for his name and room number – just for my records –

and she blurts, blurts, blurts, blurts, blurts without thinking.

Human beings. Seriously, sometimes, you've just got to laugh.

Let me tell you: some people, the idea of being fixed, the idea of being Put Back Together, by low-paid doctors in wards full of low-paid people surrounded by low-paid nurses and low-paid cleaners, it makes them check out Private Health.

I have no opinion on the subject.

Here and now and today, I'm finished. My double-clever plan has succeeded. I'm back to being in control. I'm smooth. I'm ice-cold. I've got what I wanted.

In Private Health clinics, a name and room number is all you need to saunter past the receptionist.

See also: hotels. See also: office blocks. See also: *who cares?*

This woman, she's still staring at me.

'So,' she says.

'Um,' I say.

'Don't you . . . don't you want to ask some questions?'

'Yes. Yes, of course. Um.' I'm not smart. I'm not quick. I'm on drugs and I'm falling apart and I'll be dead soon, and I forgot that in this job nobody ever got caught being *too* prepared.

'Um,' I say. 'Are you happy with the level of healthcare your husband's getting?'

She rants.

Some Private Health clinics, just so you know, they receive NHS patients too. This is because the NHS is overstretched. This is because it makes sense to farm out little dying Agnes, little heart-failure Johnny, little spinal-surgery motorcycle zombie victim number 23, to the Private Sector. Space. Spare beds. Et cetera et cetera.

This pisses off a lot of people. These lot of people, they're the ones who pay a lot of money. This lot of money, it's supposed to get Tip-Top service. This Tip-Top Service, it's supposed to be Exclusive.

This woman, with her fruity little handbag, her three-layers-thick foundation-cover, her pencil-thin lips, you can see every inch of resentment in her eyes.

Bad food, she says. Foreign nurses, strange smells, poor levels of care. My husband *hates* it, she says. No privacy for the poor man, she says. And the *hygiene*! Ugh!

She says the phrase, *and I mean we pay a lot of money for this, we've worked hard all our lives for this, but some of the people in there . . .*

She says this maybe four times.

She rants, rants, rants, rants. I like to think it makes her happy.

Eventually, I tell her: Thank you, that's very helpful. Eventually, I walk away, and she gapes at me all the way down the street.

This performance, ohoyes, has been smooth like sandpaper.

On the fifth floor of the TADC is a window just the same as all the others. From this window comes a glow. It surprises me for a moment that no one seems to be stopping to look, but then: why would they?

I'm coming, I say, quiet and under my breath, and then I go away and wait two hours.

*

CONTRACT

Sooner or later, the crocodile-woman on reception looks at me like I'm filth. Like I'm a human walking rectal discharge. Like I'm something she slipped on once in the street, evolved up and looking for revenge.

You can see her, ohoyeah, thinking: *NHS ward . . .*

She says: '*Yes?*' and she has eyebrows made of make-up, not hair.

I tell her I'm here to visit my neighbour, Alistair George-Brass, in room 322. I tell her: I hear he's been a bit . . . *under the weather*.

She looks down at the list and up at me. Twice. Then she does something with a plastic envelope, fiddles, looks, looks away, and passes me a badge saying 'visitor'.

This badge is a symbol meaning: Free Access.

'Third floor,' she says, pointing to the lift.

I am cracking and crumbling and splitting apart. This is the flaming spinning splintering wreckage of Me. I'm ruining myself, and it is *joy*.

I have no mole. I have no wig, no birthmark, no disguise. I have only stubble and bags beneath my eyes, only patchwork clothes and filthy shoes and, and . . .

And a Ruger Mk II .22 in my pocket.

And two matchboxes full of spare bullets. Each one hollow. Sealed with wax.

In the lift, which Americans call elevators, I press the button marked '5'. For the record, the label-plate next to the number says: *CHILD TREATMENT*.

I knew this before I got in the lift. I knew this because of the glow in the window, the roaring in my ears, the certainty: he's there. The boy. The boy *I* saved.

Lifts, which are also elevators, if you want to know, are

fascinating inventions. I saw a documentary once. For instance, did you know: blah blah blah.

Something above me says '*ding*'. The door slides opens. Before even I step out, before I move my feet, there's a smell.

This smell, it's from every school hallway you were ever in, every doctor's waiting room, every public toilet. This smell, it's something to do with magnolia paint and breeze-blocks and linoleum floors. It's something to do with cheap detergent and plastic chairs and forgotten urine and confused old people, et cetera et cetera. That smell, seriously, what it's mostly to do with, just so you know, is this: a complete, 100 per cent lack of hope.

Stop me if I'm repeating myself.

See here: cream/magnolia walls. Breeze-block corridors. Linoleum flooring. Strip lights that flicker from the corner of your eye. Same as every surgery, dentist, school, town hall, prison, library, office, you get the idea.

I put my head down and walk, walk, walk. Nurses go by. Men in suits look at their watches. The walls are full of symbols.

Doors, doors, doors, doors. Labels with names and ages – 6, 12, 5, 10, 6, 16, 14 – and parents holding hands with dead eyes and seats outside rooms and the sounds of crying and people drinking tea and coffee and talking like this: 'murmurmurmurmurmurmurmurmur.'

This is womb-life. This is whisper-and-bear-it life.

This is the place where they bring broken children. This is the place they try to fix them. It looks sort of familiar.

Round a corner: *them*. Police. Uniformed, one standing, one sitting. Drinking tea, talking. Round a corner, a door marked with no name, with no age. *UNKNOWN*.

Let me tell you, from this room, from the gaps round the door, from the broken edges of hinges and the bulb-shape key hole: *light*.

Not normal light. Ahahaha, ohono. Not sun or tungsten or halogen, but liquid: like honey and acid, like slow-light that puddles into shadows, like a timeless wave, like melting wax.

I'm almost at the end. I'm getting weird. Bear with me.

It gloops past the cops like a horizontal stream, breaking and globulating around nipplehats and *Village People* moustaches, and it bobs in air and shatters across the opposite wall.

There is music.

Listen: this room contains the little boy. The child I saved.

The cops look up at me as I walk towards them.

This little boy, I *know now*, he fell down. He crashed and tumbled and tore a hole in the ground, and the wrong people found him – the wrong *side* – and they wanted to hurt him, to do unspeakable stuff to him, ohoyes, and the other side wanted him too, and they squabbled and sniped and bitched, and ohoyes, ohoyes, *I saved him*.

ME.

From what? Doesn't matter. From the shit going on in the basement, yeah, fine, fine. But more than that. Don't you *understand*? Don't you *get it*?

I saved him from being *important*.

Symbols, full up to the brim with resonance. Given meaning. Claimed by this or that side, this or that nutter, this or that belief. And . . . and symbols can be people.

Symbols can be children as well as shapes and words and signs.

I feel this in my broken brain. I feel the certainty.

This child is a would-be. To the wrong people, to the Choir or the fat, naked fuck in the basement, this child matters.

This child is a symbol which means: everything.

This little boy, this little boy, *please*, just listen: he has the right to mean Nothing. He has the right To Not Matter.

Reader, I have tried to tell you everything I believe, faithfully and truthfully, up till now. I've tried to work through the fact I'm ill. I've tried to steer round metaphysics and gods and devils and blah, blah, blah. I've made sure you know, don't you: I'm not reliable. I've tried to be *honest*.

I'm not subtle. Remember that. Well. I mean. Not on *purpose*.

Let me tell you, then, what I believe in this instant, in this hospital, in this bleach-stinking place. Let me tell you what I have learned.

Ssshh, now.

Some things are right because they're *right*. Beyond money and . . . and amorality and selfishness and all that, they just *are*. In your bones, I mean. In your cells. You just know.

I have spent my life trying not to believe this. But no. No, no, no.

Some things are right just *because*. This does not make them 'virtues'.

Some things are wrong because they're *wrong*. You tell

yourself guilt means nothing, you push it away, you question it. You convince yourself 'wrong' is just a viewpoint. But in your flesh, in your decaying little brain, no. Some things are Just Plain Wrong.

This does not make them 'sins'.

We don't need symbols to tell us what works.

There is a Ruger Mk II .22 in my pocket. I need to see the child.

The cops watch. I walk by, legs dragging on where my brain shouts *he's here he's here*!

I walk by, walk by, hand in pocket, face down, stubble itching, sweat prickling, and – and then they're behind me, and that was attempt number 1.

The cops watch my back until I turn the corner. Burning blood in my ear. I need to think about this.

How do I get in there?

Around the corner there's a recess with a vending machine against the wall. It has no coffee, so I press 'tea' and scowl. I'm not thirsty. It takes four 20ps, but spits out the last one. I have to swap it with a nurse. It makes a sound like a fairground ride.

Around the next corner, listen, the *other* one, not the one I just came round, there are voices.

'—ust . . . thought it'd change things.' This is a man talking. This is me listening to him, aural distraction, displacement, not paying full attention, thinking about the room and the boy and the gun in my pocket. This man, his voice is tight, desperate, whiny. 'She's awake!' he hisses. ''S'what we been waiting for, ain't it? Just . . . one more chance, eh? Fer *us*. Like a family again. That's all I—'

And a woman's voice, now. Low. Calm. Cats and hyenas in every vowel, not moving an inch.

'Nothing's changed,' she says. 'Not with us.'

This is me suddenly paying attention. Listen, forget the boy for just one second. This is the corridor bulging around me.

'Nothing's changed?' the man shouts. 'Nothing's fu—! How can you even *think* that? After everything!' He huffs. Deep breaths, then quiet. He says, 'We could . . . look, look, it'd be like, like a new start. 'Olidays. Get a nice place, outta town. Think about it. We can do *anythin'* now. We got *futures*. Us and our girl. We got our lives back, all of us.'

'We've got *money*,' the woman says. 'That's all. And it's not even *ours*.'

Indignant, arctic silence. Round the corner. Metres from me.

Listen. This is the tea slipping out of my hand. Spilling down my leg, into my shoe. Across the floor. This is my arm shaking.

This is fire and smoke and pestilence choking the air around me.

'You,' the woman says. 'You fed him to the fucking sharks. You didn't need to do that. You *shit*, y—'

'Nonono, *you* did that. That was *you. You* found him. Don't forget that. You started this, I just made it *work*.'

'Served him up, you bastard! Might's well've just *killed* h—'

'No more'n he deserved! Coulda left him *down* there, you know that. Down in that basement. Set them fires, easy, no one the wiser. He killed the messenger, you forget *that*? Coulda left him to burn, no problem.'

CONTRACT

The woman grunts, and there's tea in my shoes and the world goes away and I'm stepping closer, towards the corner, feet heavy.

'Might've been kinder,' the woman says.

Both voices.

I recognise *both* voices.

That sinking feeling.

This is the Ruger Mk II .22 in my hand.

This is me stepping around the corner, and the little boy is Forgotten.

Interview Room 2

'Wait,' says Anna. Beautiful, cold, perfectly pert nipples-like-razors Anna. 'You're getting ahead, hang on . . . Go back. The "symbols" stuff.'

The way she says this, it's like a rocket scientist talking horoscopes.

I glare at her. I give her a look you normally save up for people breaking the flow, taking the piss.

Then I sigh and repress the urge to apologise.

'Doesn't *matter* now,' I say, sort of embarrassed, sort of angry, sort of confused. 'Story's moved on. Was just trying to explain, anyway. Makes no difference to the fucking end.'

'I'm interested,' she says. 'Seriously.'

Jason Durant, for the record, stares off into space like he's bored, like he's sick of the airy-fairy stuff, like he's listening to a football game on a tiny earpiece.

Scratch that, a rugby game. Maybe golf.

No, no, *polo*. Yes. *Yes*. Jason Durant is a Polo-wanker. There is no doubt.

'Michael,' says Anna, pulling my eyes back towards her. 'Do you *really* believe . . . really . . . this boy was a . . . that he had some sort of special significance?'

Fallen Angel.

Messianic Child.

Grail of Hope.

Pile of Shit.

I tell her: I told you already. Doesn't *matter*. That's what made the most sense, based on what I'd seen. That's all.

I tell her: You got to respond to your senses, right?

She sits back. Tweaks a piece of hair. Frowns.

'And you wanted to stop the kid from being a . . . like, an icon?'

Yes.

'Because you think people can do without?'

Yes.

'And you took a gun with you?'

Yes. What? Hang o—

'You wanted to visit the little boy, who you didn't want becoming a . . . a pawn, right? To be squabbled over by these two . . . *sides*, whatever –'

Next to her, Jason sneers. Now that Anna comes to say it out loud, OK, I guess, *fine*, it *does* sound sort of stupid.

'– and you took a gun.' She blinks. Her voice is the voice of psychiatrists, therapists, hypnotists, evangelists, *people who fuck with your mind*. 'That is what you're telling us?'

Anna. Frosty, cold, icicle Anna. Anna who I thought was *interested*. Anna with her D.I.Y psychoanalysis bullshit. Anna who seemed *insightful*.

Anna who was leading me all along.

Bitch.

'No,' I say. 'The gun wasn't for the kid.'

'Then why did you want to see him?'

'I *told* you.' I'm getting angry. Need to be cool. Need to be the Fonz. Nothing to lose, now. 'I told you, it was just to be sure. Just one last time. Proof, if you want.

Something . . . real. Something I saved. Something I *did right*. I just wanted to see him, before . . .'

I tail off.

Anna says: 'Then the gun was for . . . ?'

I just stare.

Time goes elastic. Anna lights another cigarette. I look at my feet.

Jason *hems* under his breath.

'Look,' he says, eventually. Anna glares at him sideways, smoke spilling, like it's not his turn yet. He doesn't care.

He says, 'You're not stupid, Mike.'

I tell him, *thanks*.

'You just sat there and told us you killed . . . we're up to . . . how many?'

'Eight specifics,' Anna says, not looking. 'Three more alluded to.'

'Right. A lot of dead folks.'

'Why lie?' I say.

'Exactly. We can pin it anyway.'

I shrug.

'So that's bad.' Jason twinkles. He's enjoying himself.

Listen: I can't see because the table's in the way, I can't see for sure, but he's got an erection. Ohyeah. You just know it.

A small one.

'That's major punishment stuff,' he says.

I sigh. 'You think I want . . . What. Diminished responsibility?' I say this like I'm bored. 'Insanity Plea?'

I say this like I'm bored because, listen: I am.

Jason shrugs. '*Do* you?'

I tell him, look.

CONTRACT

I tell him, I'm telling you what happened to me. I'm not saying it's real or fake. I'm saying to me, it seemed real. Either way: I did stuff. I'm being honest.

I lean forwards.

I tell him, And the least you can do –

I tell him, Motherfucker.

I tell him, – is not to fucking *patronise* me.

Anna coughs.

She asks if I've ever had any major illnesses.

Or, she says, brain conditions?

She says: Astrocytoma? Glioblastoma multiforme? Ependymoma?

She says: Oligodendroglioma, Mixed glioma, Meningioma, Haemangioblastoma or Acoustic neuroma?

She's not even reading from notes. This is borrowed wisdom, seen from the outside. God, she's gorgeous.

I tell her, talk English, mate.

She says, have you used hallucinogenic, psychotropic, psychotomimetic or psychedelic drugs for extended periods of time, either recently or in the past?

She says, Mescaline, psilocin, psilocybin?

She says, LSD, PCP, MDMA?

She says, Salvinorin A, Ibogaine, Scopolamine, Atrapine, Sodium Pentothal?

All off the top of her head. All without moving her eyes.

I slump back into my chair and wonder if I want to play any more. My stomach hurts. The back of my head hurts, and the door, that bloody door, keeps hopping left-right-left. The room's full of smoke, though Anna only just sparked up.

Black smoke.

'No,' I say. The way I say this is: sulky.

Anna says: 'Did you consider there might be . . . *intermediary* possibilities?'

I say: Intermediary?

She smiles at me. Smoke comes out of her nose. 'Between extremes,' she says.

Jason snaps: 'Between "Holy War" and "frothing nutcase", mate.'

I look at Anna. My eyelids droop. I'm post-exhausted, I'm post-give-a-shit, I'm post-alive. Give me my cell. Give me my Dettol-stinking breeze-block magnolia hole. Give me my Belmarsh. Give me some bloody *peace*.

'No,' I say. 'I didn't.'

She says: 'Michael.'

She says: 'How do you suppose . . . *Sally* fits in to all this?'

Jason flicks her a glance. His cheeks, that fucker, that podgy genetic disaster, that floppy-haired McFucknugget with his suit and his shoes, his cheeks jink upwards, like a smile.

Here is me, sitting silently for a minute. Here is me contemplating without showing it. Here is me struggling with the hardest part of this whole thing, the biggest question, the worst mystery.

'I don't know,' I say, eventually. I say this and it hurts.

I say: 'But she helped me.' And this sounds like a lie in my mouth.

Sally trained as a psychiatric nurse. Sally said I didn't need a doctor.

Sally said I'd be OK.

I say: 'You know? She *helped* me.'

CONTRACT

For the record, on Anna's face is a mixture of pity and disgust, and she stands up without saying a word and heads for the door.

For the record, right now, the door is on the left.

'I'll be right back,' she says, as she opens it.

Heavy-arsed hinges, hardcore locks. This place, everything is migraine-noisy.

The door makes a sound like a wad of spit a mile across, made of steel, hitting a pavement made of numbers. *Spwk* – only more so.

Somewhere outside, just, I can hear another door groaning open. The next room along, maybe.

Given why I'm here, you've got to wonder what sort of sick bastard ends up in Interview Room *1*.

Jason says: 'Finish the story, Mike.'

Chapter Twenty-two

Listen. This is hard to describe.

This is hard to explain. Cut me some slack.

This is sort of like if I was a conspiracy theorist, like a paranoid nut, say, stepping into a room and finding proof – real, actual, incontrovertible motherfucking evidence – that aliens abducted the Loch Ness Monster, brainwashed him using CIA mind chemicals, and made him shoot JFK. Inside a crop circle.

This is making light of bad mojo. I'm displacing. Bear with me. This is sensory overload. This is too much to take. This is *serious*.

I am almost on my knees. I'm almost down, and all that matters here, all that has any substance, all that holds me up, is the gun. The Ruger Mk II .22, with ten bullets in a clip, with each bullet hollow and sloshing with runny smack skag China White aunt Hazel chiva brite, with my arm tense and not shaking, with my finger ready, ready, ready to *twitch*.

The gun is my legs, now. My law, my foundation, my hold-me-up scaffold. The gun is my sanctuary. The gun is my bolt hole; my retreat from the sun.

Sally drops to her knees. Sally looks ready to die. Sally smiles.

Behind her, listen.

CONTRACT

Pay attention.

Behind her: Mr Call-Me-Boss.

Ohoyeah.

And I am shouting. And I don't know what I'm saying, what words these are, what sounds are shitting from my mouth, but it's about *him*, about *why is he here*, and Sally looks up and sees the gun aimed at him, not her, and frowns, and protests, and stands, and shouts.

Behind her: Mr Call-Me-Boss is backing away.

Sally snarls. Sally pushes into a door next to her. A little room, just like the one with the boy and the cops round the corner. Two little rooms, on the same floor, in the same building, in the North of London, and me shuttling between with a gun.

Coincidence, right?

This little room, this little room with a little plastic chair outside, Sally points through the door and shouts *Let me show you! Let me show you!* and from inside come the bleeps of machines and the *gaaahkt-gaaahkt-gaaahkt* of keeping-someone-alive respirators.

Behind her: Mr Call-Me-Boss, making a break for it.

The corridor pulses. My brain goes arse-over-tit and I am staggering, and there's pain, oh *fuck* what pain, right here between and behind and under my eyes, and there's too much light and pillars of smoke down both sides of my vision, and I'm chasing that fat bastard, ohoyes, chasing him now until I'm dead.

Sally tries to stop me.

'Just look!' she shouts. 'Just see! Come and see her!'

But all I see is a devil-thing, and even *she* is lost, even *she* is scaled and blackened and bleeding, and her teeth are needles and her eyes are just holes – empty, *sucking* – and I push her aside and run, run, run.

I think she hurts herself, maybe, as she stumbles. The world pulses black.

Things getting weird again. One last hurrah.

Bad timing.

Nurses stagger out the way. Somewhere behind me, the cops in the next corridor shout out. Fire doors swing-clunk-swing, stairwells gape.

Leaving a world of broken children behind.

Running is fine. Running is nothing new.

Running is just falling, only sideways.

Outside, at last: London plays the game.

Outside, at last: my pathetic fallacy.

Outside is rain sleeting, slanting, sloughing and pricking at my face, and around everything is a halo; around everything is a backsplash aura. The world sounds like Niagara.

Outside I slip and skid in puddles and pools, and above Islington is thunder and dark and the end of Time, and lightning flash-flicker-flash in the faces of drabbards.

It makes me grin. There is joy in reaching the End.

Just so you know, this is all bullshit. Just so you know, between blinks, the sky is just a smog-duvet, the lightning is just birdsong, the rain is just London Damp. Just so you know, outside of my eyes and ears and wet, wet skin, is just a dull normal day. Just so you know.

Mr Call-Me-Boss is ahead, somewhere. I see him not like a person but like a disruption: a blur-obstacle that barges through tourists buskers beggars, upsetting baby-prams and shouting.

'Help!'

Hoarse. Uncool. Panicky.

'Help! For . . . for fuck's sake! He's got a gun! Somebody *help*!'

Running is good. Opening-up is good. Letting it all pour away like the rain, reduced-down, simplified. Forget the boy upstairs. Forget Sally. Forget the no money and no where and no hope. Forget the dead-in-the-water Plan.

Forget the paper in my pocket with its magic number, forget the bunch of zeroes and the pound sign, forget Escaping.

Forget running *from*. Forget running *to*.

Across main roads where motion is car-horn, brake-screeching, chassis-slapping horror. Where vans lorries bicycles steaming in rain and filth go strange and shift, become flame-eyed horses, skeletal scrap-heap horrors, scuttling lobstertrucks with blazing eyes and JCB claws. Bat-winged mopeds. Skodas From Hades.

And above? Ha! Above, the storm is a flaming sword beating against a dragon's scales. Above is all archangels with spears and bows; chariots on gauss-lightning wheels. The Host playing trumpets.

War in Heaven, all around. Fun for the whole family.

I have a nose bleed.

On the corner of Upper Street I see him ahead and I shoot. No silencer, not now, but still no noise, not over the rain. It misses – a mile off – but still there's a reaction; still there are people dropping down and silent-screaming, like tubeworm polyps, retracted too fast to see.

There are devils wrestling cherubs in the sky.

I run on.

Ahead is a tube sign. The Fat Man waddles beneath it, pauses and pants, slings a glance over his shoulder. Sees me. His eyes are liquid gold. His spine is a maggot made of light, shimmering through the thin flesh of his back, and I *see* his wings now; furled beneath his jacket. Made of ice. Steaming.

He no longer looks impressive. He no longer looks unflappable.

Above his head, seriously, you won't believe it, the tube sign says:

ANGEL.

You've got to laugh.

Did you know: Angel station was opened in 1901. Angel station sits on the Bank Branch of the Northern Line, which is thirty-six miles of tunnels, trains, stairs, otis-drum elevators escalators security-staff barriers, machines, announcements, rats, mice, *culex molestus* mosquitoes, and you get the idea. Angel station, the whole area, was named for a pub which used to be right opposite. Now, there's a Co-op bank there.

Listen to me: *Who gives a fuck?*

In the station he's away and over the barriers. In the station are guards shouting after him, trying to stop him, but here's me with a gun in my hand and there are screams and people dropping down and, ohyeah, this is the end.

I vault the barriers like a young man. This is very Hollywood. My lungs hurt. I laugh.

The drugs are gone, maybe. My body is exhausted and crippled and crying out, maybe. My brain is rotten. My brain is toxic sludge, is shrivelling up to die, maybe.

I'm hallucinating. *Maybe*. But probably not.

Probably all it is, is me experiencing reality on a

profound metaphysical level redolent with case-relevant Catholic Semiotics.

Probably.

Did you know: the escalator in Angel station is the longest continuous escalator in Western Europe. It is 60m long, and ascends 27.5m vertically.

Today it is a gullet.

Today it is a slippery oesophagus, clogged with souls, delivering themselves down, down, down into smoke and fire and sulphur. Today it swarms with midget devils, and each one has my father's face, and they wink at me and giggle as they drag people off their steps and into the maw.

Today, this is all sort of tacky.

I ignore it.

Today at the bottom of the escalator, which is a long way below me, a figure pushes and shoves, and people grunt and bark 'oi!' and 'cunt!' and 'wanker!'. At the bottom he's not a man but a red thing made of light and fire, and his face is just blank as he turns to stare, and he scampers like a fat spider off the last step. He leaves a trail of red gossamer.

Am I creating this?

You've got to wonder.

Listen, stop, look. Before, before he was an angel. He was a callous manipulative shit, but it *helped*, you see? It helped me to know I was on the *right side*.

Now I know nothing.

Now he's just a bastard who lied. Who stole my money. Who *used* me.

And now my brain, here it is, all coincidental, telling me he's a devil. A thing made of shadows and angles and broken reflections.

Am I *creating* this?

You've got to wonder.

Listen: the best thing about chasing someone, the best thing about having *prey*, the best thing about focus, about wanting *nothing* except to KILL some SICK FUCK in front of you, the best thing about it is this: *No*. You *don't* have to wonder at all. You just chase, and ignore everything else.

I lift the gun and aim.

The world is one long scream. People duck and dodge and shout.

My brain says: *look, Mikey. Ahahaha. You're going down into hell.* The walls ripple with saliva. Fires and braziers burn on iron spikes.

My brain says: *Do you even believe in Hell, Mikey? Do you even believe in an afterlife? Do you care?*

My brain says: *Did you save up your good behaviour Brownie points for a rainy day? For a rainy death?*

Mr Call-Me-Boss, this sub-temperate fuck, this chubby mystery, this improbable baddie, he starts to sprint off into the connecting tunnel.

For the record, there are people in the way.

For the record, collateral damage is a no-no.

For the record, he has no gun. He's running away. He has his back to me.

As climax-moments go, this one doesn't exactly stink of nobility.

Fuck it.

I shoot him.

His shoulder froths with red. He runs and screams and is gone.

All happening to someone else. Of course, of course. All

happening in slow motion. Underwater, on the moon, no perspective. Filtered through smoke and light and sound. Everyone screams. Everyone goes silent.

Gunsmoke and blood on metal escalator slats, and station-alarms screaming.

Ooom-chkka-ooom-chkka-ooom

Is *this* a hallucination?

For the record, there's something sort of funny about people trying to duck and cover their heads at the bottom of an escalator. A lot of them have fallen over one another, piled up.

I run past and don't smile. I'm empty.

I'm revenge.

I'm a cipher. What I am is: a terrier chasing a rat, not knowing why.

I want answers, I guess, but it's too late to rationalise now. Too late to wonder *why*. Too late to ask why I *hate* him.

Too late to ask him anything, anyway. Inside each bullet is a liquid gram of high-grade heroin.

Mr Call-Me-Boss will soon be dead.

In the tunnel to the Northbound platform, blood on yellow-stained tiles. It ripples on the floor, crystallising in numbers and words. I kick it, shattering it across my foot and my leg. I'm not running now.

The platforms in Angel station are amongst the widest in the London Underground system.

Why? Who knows? Who cares? Borrowed bollocks.

Today the North-bound platform is a road made of interlocking vertebrae. Just so you know, parts of it are still alive; scraps of flesh clinging to interwoven spines, heads locked upside-down, eyes peering out through dislocated ribs. Fingers wriggling through bony gaps. It crunches underfoot. Demons gibber underneath and poke at the soles of my feet.

I am *sick* of it all.

Today the tracks next to the plateau are covered with water; black like oil, and in glossy hints I can see faces – drowned, ghostly, grasping – peering from below. The water is so still I imagine I can walk on it.

I hate it all. I'm exhausted by it all. I'm a dream in my own brain, or a brain in my own dream.

I'm a man with a gun.

Cling to that.

Mr Call-Me-Boss is on the ground. People fuss over him until they see me – until they see the gun – and then they gabble and scuttle away, becoming great red bats as they pass the NEXT TRAIN board, flittering away into the tunnels.

He lies in his own blood. He shivers. His wings are tattered around him. There's no fight. There's no dramatic last stand. There's no Hollywood. Sometimes stories just . . .

Stop.

And *oh God*, I'm so tired. *Oh God*, I'm so *ready*, now.

I sit down next to him. Just cross-legged there, on cold tarmac. I think I sit in someone's chewing gum. You've got to laugh.

He coughs blood and shivers.

He asks for an ambulance, just quietly, and his eyes roll.

People are screaming behind me. There's so much blood coming from my nose now, I must look like my face has fallen off. It patters off the backs of my hands and down the grip of the gun.

He jerks. His arm flexes twice. The drug is in him.

He comes and goes.

Somewhere people are shouting.

Listen.

Pay attention.

This is the end.

I lean down so slowly. I touch him on his forehead, and his eyes open and he looks, then fades, then looks again. His eyes are holes into nowhere, and gold glitters out of his tear ducts.

I put my lips against his ear.

And what I say is: *Please. Please, would you tell me? You have to tell me. Did I do anything good?*

He stirs. He stares. Sticky things move in his mouth.

And his hand – his good hand, the one at the end of an arm which isn't bloody and limp – his hand creeps into his jacket.

Into his pocket.

I wonder, dully, if he has a gun.

From his pocket he takes a piece of paper folded six times, small and tight, and he places it in my hand with a spastic release, whole body trembling, vomit puddling out of his lips. And he says something that might be: 'ysss.'

And then he gasps out loud, and the drips clear from his eyes, and the red crackling shape fades, and his wings smoulder away, and something dry rustles out of him. Something dry rustles out of *me*.

Today is a Thursday.

Today I am in a tube station.

I am on a platform with a dead man, surrounded by horrified commuters, tourists, jobseekers, students, OAPs, shoppers, daytrippers, nobodies. I am not on a ledge in hell.

At the end of the platform, over my shoulder, there are six men in blue bulletproof jackets holding rifles. They are shouting.

I can't hear what.

These men, their caps say: POLICE.

I unfold the piece of paper in my hand. It's glossy, stiff like card, and as I open it up, I see *oh, oh*, it's a photograph.

A little girl. Smiling. Happy.

I say: *What?*

But it's too late. It's too late, and I stand up, and I'm tired, and that's that.

I stand up and there's blood down my face, chest, arms, legs, crotch, and there's a gun in my hand.

And someone shoots me in my gut.

And someone shoots me in my head.

And, for just a little while, in white, then grey, things go away.

Interview Room 2

There's something . . . enduring . . . about this silence.

It's solid, I mean. It's not awkward or comfortable, or anything rational like that, it's not anti-noise, it's not embarassing, it's more like . . . more like winter falling.

Things get cold. People shiver. Stuff withers and dies. But nobody ever stops to feel uncomfortable about it. Nobody ever panics over what to say, what insipid, boring, bloody platitude to trot out, to kick start the seasonal cycle.

This silence, listen: it just *is*.

Jason Durant stares too long. Sort of quizzical, maybe. Sort of surprised, sort of sad. Anna's still out of the room – next door, next world, wherever – and maybe he figures he's got to pick up the slack in the paying-attention stakes, maybe he's fallen asleep with his eyes open, maybe – *ha*, you never know – he's genuinely interested.

Eventually, I let the quiet get to me. Eventually, with enough time, the way I feel is: stupid.

'That's it,' I say.

Jason Durant nods and goes on staring. Like he's still listening to a monologue I can't hear, like there's evidence still to consider. Church bells toll, tumbleweeds tumble, my story refuses to die. A thought swims up from nowhere.

'How long was I in hospital?' I say. This is just out of

interest. My memories on the subject are what you might describe as confused.

Jason Durant looks down at notes that aren't there and sighs. Jason Durant, this puppy-fat goon, this pinstriped bookend-to-my-life, this human lizard, for just a moment he looks . . . what? Sympathetic?

'About an hour,' he says. His eyes shimmer.

I'm on the *buh* of 'but' when the door shrieks open. This is Hammer Horror Effects CD number 1. This is heavy-arsed hinges, hardcore locks. Anna stepping back inside.

Winter falling. For real.

She holds a small file in her hand, tied with string. Its colour, look, listen – what are the odds? – is manila.

She looks at us, me, then him, then me again, then comes in and sits down.

I sigh.

'You want me to go over what you missed again?' I say.

She shakes her head *no* and rifles through papers in the file, not even looking up.

'That's OK,' she says. 'I was listening.'

Yeah.

Yeah, of course she was. Through the sound system I can't see. Through the microphones that aren't there. Via all those invisible cameras.

'What's that?' I say, nodding at the file.

Jason looks away.

Anna doesn't.

She says: 'It's something you should know about.'

Hold on to your hat, Mike.

She says: 'Little over two years ago, this. Was in all the papers at the time, you might remember.'

She fusses through the file as she goes, not exactly reading out loud, not exactly from memory. A piece of this report, a shred of that article, and she builds as she goes.

'So. Small town, nice area. Commuter belt. Suburbs, easy access to London. Private schools, well-to-do, white as you like. Worried mother calls the police one evening.' Anna flicks a strand of hair out of her face. 'She tells them her husband's out looking already. Their daughter – eleven year old – never made it home from school. She's panicking. I mean, you would, wouldn't you?'

Anna looks at me as if I'm expected to answer this. I don't.

This all seems a little random.

'Next morning, still no sign. Police are doing their best, you know? Journos show up; national campaign. The girl's a cute little thing too – that always helps. Home videos, birthdays, Christmas. Emotional appeals from relatives, all that stuff. Come the end of the first week, it's looking bad.'

Anna, when she gets going, she talks like she's reading from a list of bullet points.

'They started dredging local ponds, rivers. Looking for bodies, now. More and more, it stops being *help us find this kid* and starts being *help us find whichever sick fuck did this*.'

Jason Durant chews his own cheeks.

I listen. I don't remember this. Even from papers, even from TV, even from Anna's bullet-point details. The thing is, this stuff, it just . . . happens.

This is once, maybe twice a year. This is journalistic feeding-frenzies, Little Girl Missing, Little Boy Abducted, Two Friends Sought By Family, Toddler Led Away, dot dot dot. This is so regular it gets so it's all just a blur.

It gets so you can't even remember names.

More than anything, what I am, right here and now, is confused.

Little Arctic Anna, why is she telling me this? Why the ceremony?

What's this got to do with *me*?

'Now the girl's dad,' says she-of-the-icy-white-skin, she-of-the-immaculate-tit, she-of-the-iceberg-stare, 'he's a cop himself. Not just your local plod though; he's T.S.G. You know what that is, Michael?'

'The Spice Girls,' I say. This is police humour.

Jason gives me a look.

'Territorial Support Group.' I shrug. 'White Van Cops, right? London fast-response.'

'Right,' says Anna. 'But our man's likeable enough, got a lot of mates. Easy enough for him to pull some strings in admin, get a look at the local register.'

Sex offenders. White pins in a map. *Huhm.*

'Where's this going?' I ask, quiet. This is one tangent too far.

I'm not quick, remember? I'm not smart.

Anna wets her lips.

'Turns out our devastated parents were good little churchgoers.'

Here, listen: Jason butts in. Here, listen: a significant look stretched over floppy features. '*Both* of them,' he says.

Anna barely pauses. 'Every week,' she says, 'regular as clockwork. They take the daughter with them. Flower arranging, cake sales, you name it. Both on the church choir.'

She sighs.

'Aaaand . . . well, it turns out there've been one or two complaints against the local vicar.'

Ah.

She rifles through the file.

'Nothing that stuck. No charges, even a caution. But still. When you're an angry dad looking for someone to blame, especially when you're used to clotting people over the head, well . . .'

I sit back and cross my arms. My brain hurts.

'Still don't see what this has got to do with—'

'The father beat the vicar to paste. Put him in hospital, fucked him up good. And two days later, as if by magic, the little girl shows up.'

Anna looks at me.

'Naked. Comatose. Dumped outside a G.P.'s in Wrexham.'

She turns over a few photos in the file. Mostly, they're purple. Mostly, they're bruise-colour. Mostly, she turns them over too quick for them to even look like a real person. Mostly, I don't look too hard.

'No arrests ever made,' she says. 'The father blamed the detective in charge. Conspiracy, he said. All sorts of mad theories. Insisted there was some . . . some nefarious little ring of sickos all tied in, high-up, odd stuff going on. Said it'd keep happening, again and again. Didn't make much difference, in the long run. He was too busy being dishonourably discharged. Abuse of his position, all of that.'

She looks up again.

'A lot of cops were very unhappy about it, at the time. Even now. Prepared to help him with a favour or two, you'd think.'

She's trying to tell me something.

I'm not quick.

I'm not smart.

I say, 'What's—'

'The mother,' she says, '*well*. Doing well for herself, up till all this. Psychiatric nurse, training at the local ward. Book groups, film appreciation society, neighbourhood watch, dinner parties . . .' Anna leafs through pages. 'All *that* went down the chute. At first you got just little spats at home – social disturbances. Then bobbies called in, breaking up arguments. Drugs found. Things being thrown, complaints about noise. Counsellors, all that. Eventually the marriage broke up, they sold the house. She just . . . dropped off the radar.' Anna coughs. 'They *both* did.'

She fiddles with a creased corner poking from the file.

'No records of *him*, either. Where he went afterwards, what he did for money, who he worked for. Maybe changed his name.'

She rocks back into her chair, winding up. 'Bad business,' she says. 'Nobody came out clean.'

Jason slides in, like a greased turd, eyes narrowed.

'The detective in charge, he took early retirement.' *Making a point.* 'Moved to a town called Bracknell.'

Oh.

'The vicar came out of hospital, moved north. Some poky village, arse end of nowhere. Forest of Dean, I think.' His eyes twinkle. His eyes *glow*. His eyes don't look naural.

Oh, wait—

'And no sign whatever of this . . . this sick little ring. No members, no organisers. Nothing.'

Hang on, what's—

'Case closed. Nothing changed.'

They stare at me.

Like they're expecting something.

Like I should *get* it. Like my brain isn't festering, and my skin crawling, and my face itching, and oh, oh Jesus, ohoyeah, all I can think to say is: 'A-and . . . and the little girl?'

Anna says: 'Spent two years sleeping in a clinic in Islington. Best place there is, I understand, for this sort of thing. Profound mental trauma.'

Jason Durant leans forwards. Smiles. Enjoys the moment.

'She woke up three days ago.'

Anna says, 'Her doctors say it's a miracle.'

I say: 'But –'

Anna closes the file and sits back. 'I just thought you might like to know.'

They get up.

They leave.

There are no shadows in this room.

How long have I been sitting here?

You've got to wonder.

My head hurts. My guts hurt. I'm tired and my brain aches from thinking too much, and *oh God*, I wish. Not for anything in particular, I just *wish*.

Eventually, they come back. Eventually, they close the door behind them, and sit down, and Anna takes a piece of paper from a pocket or a briefcase or a file or, or, or *something*, and lays it down so it faces me.

This piece of paper, the text begins:

1.

1.1. I the undersigned hereby declare that all actions undertaken by me or on my behalf – particularly as relating to the termination of persons within (and affiliated to) the so-called 'Disring' – are undertaken freely and . . .

This piece of paper, the text ends:

Those motherfuckers have it coming. I will not apologise. These ones are for free.

This piece of paper, at the top, is a logo next to a letterhead. The letterhead reads: *MAKE YOUR POINT, Inc.*

The logo is a pointing finger. This is a symbol, meaning: Well. You know.

My little joke.

Anna and Jason look from the piece of paper to me. Jason says: 'So.'

I sound calmer than I feel. I say: 'How did they make me sign this? How did they . . . how did they change it?'

But Jason and Anna don't answer. Jason and Anna just stare, and that's OK, because already I know the 'maybe' answer. Already I know this man, this Mr Call-Me-Boss, maybe he knew just what to say. Maybe he knew what subjects to raise, what situations to refer to. Pretending he knew my father, bringing up the . . . the thing in the bathroom, the . . . anyway.

Maybe he knew *just* how to make me lose it. To make me wig out long enough to . . . to do *anything*. To forget names

404

and numbers. To addle me. To *use* me. Swaps. Changes. Twists. Maybe.

For a moment I wonder *how* he knew so much, but then, but then – *she* told him. Didn't she? *Didn't* she?

I sit back and let the roof cave in. I sit back and let gravity suck me into a meaty puddle on the floor. I sit back and let my bones collapse under their own weight, my heart detonate, my blood squeeze between the pores on my skin.

I sit back and am Defeated.

'I want a test,' I say.

Anna frowns. 'A test?'

'CAT scan. Brain function, whatever. I want to know.'

'Know what?'

'If I'm . . . if there's a fucking bubble in my brain. If I'm sick.'

They trade a look. Jason scratches his ear.

'That's . . . that's not possible,' he says. 'They shot you. Far too much damage for anything like that.'

I stare at him. This seems to make sense, except, except . . .

I put a hand to my head and poke around. It feels solid. There is no damage to my head.

'Blood tests,' I say.

'What?'

'Blood tests. Check for . . . chemicals. Psychotropics. *Something*.'

This is me clutching at straws. This is me wanting to know, one way or another.

He shakes his head, waves his hands like a chopping motion. 'Too late,' he says. 'Too late, sorry. Sorry.'

He sounds nearly sincere.

We sit and we stare. Anna's blouse has crept open again, and I can't even bring myself to ogle. The badge pinned there, beside the lacy edge of her bra, like a fortress on a disputed border, it has a crest of arms I don't recognise.

A crest of arms is a symbol meaning blah, blah, blah.

I wonder which constabulary it was they said they were with. I don't remember.

My brain hurts.

The contract sits there in front of me. My signature, my symbol, my shape. A contract with myself, and nobody else.

Jason and Anna appear to be waiting for something.

I want to know. Oh God, please, I need to know. One way or the other.

'Did I do any good?' I ask.

This is the second time I have asked this question under circumstances I don't understand. I'm not quick. I'm not smart.

They look at each other.

Anna says: 'That's something you have to decide for yourself, Michael.'

She points a thumb over her shoulder, towards the back wall, and her eyes . . . listen, I'm serious: Her eyes glow.

Somewhere, there's music. Somewhere, there are screams. There are two doors. There is one door on each side of the room. The two doors are alike in every single respect.

'You're free to go,' she says.

I'm not quick. I'm not smart. I'm missing something.

I get things wrong. I'm not reliable. I warned you.

I stand up. I look at the two doors. They do not move.

'Hey,' says Jason. 'Hey, listen.'

Anna glowers at him.

He says, 'Hey, while you're deciding . . . I just wondered . . .'

I know what he's about to ask. I was waiting for it.

Our man Jason, I told you already: he's the curious type.

'The piece of paper,' he says.

'The Plan,' I say.

'Right. The Plan, yeah. You said you gave it a price, right? Getting out.'

'Yes.'

'So?'

My head hurts. My guts hurt. For the record, there is: *no hole in my skull. No bleeding wound in my stomach. No scarred keloid lump of healed tissue.*

This doesn't make any sense. I'm missing something.

I reach into the back pocket of my jeans and find the piece of paper. I flick it across the table to Jason, not looking. He catches it.

I go and stand with my back to both of them, facing the doors.

Behind me, the sounds of Sellotape unpeeling. Paper unfolding. A pause.

Jason says: 'Hey.'

Jason says: 'Hang on, you—'

I say: 'I told you.'

A bunch of zeroes and a pound sign.

This number, listen. You *know* what it is, don't you?

Listen, I'm not reliable like you might expect. I warned you. I'm not quick. I'm not smart. But I'm not stupid. The thing I am most of all, if you absolutely want to know, is this: a realist.

This is just for the record.

*

I choose a door. Opening, it groans like a whale. I step through.